When Cultures Collide

Managing successfully across cultures

A major new edition of the global guide

Richard D Lewis

NICHOLAS BREALEY
PUBLISHING
LONDON

To
Jane, Caroline, Richard and David, multicultural all...

This revised edition first published by
Nicholas Brealey Publishing in 1999
Reprinted with corrections 2000 (twice), 2001, 2002 (twice)

Nicholas Brealey Publishing
3-5 Spafield Street
Clerkenwell London
EC1R 4QB, UK
Tel: +44 (0)20 7239 0360
Fax: +44 (0)20 7239 0370

Intercultural Press Inc.
PO Box 700
Yarmouth
Maine, 04096, USA
Tel: (207) 846 5168
Fax: (207) 846 5181

http://www.nbrealey-books.com
http://www.interculturalpress.com

First published in hardback by
Nicholas Brealey Publishing Limited in 1996

© Richard D Lewis 1996, 1999
The rights of Richard D Lewis to be identified as the author of this work have
been asserted in accordance with the Copyright, Designs and Patents Act 1988.

ISBN 1-85788-087-0

British Library Cataloguing in Publication Data
A catalogue record for this book is available from the British Library.

Library of Congress Cataloguing-in-Publication Data
Lewis, Richard D.
  When cultures collide: managing successfully across cultures / Richard D. Lewis. –
Rev. ed.
    p. cm.
  Includes index.
  ISBN 1-85788-087-0
    1. International business enterprises--Management--Social aspects. 2.
Management--Social aspects. 3. Intercultural communication. I. Title.

HD62.4.L49 1999
658´.049--dc21

99-051394

Printed in Finland by WS Bookwell.

Contents

Preface to the New Edition

US AND THEM

I WAS ONCE IN CHARGE OF AN ENGLISH LANGUAGE SUMMER COURSE IN North Wales for adult students from three countries – Italy, Japan and Finland. Intensive instruction was relieved by entertainment in the evenings and by day excursions to places of scenic or historical interest.

We had scheduled a trip up Mount Snowdon on a particular Wednesday, but on the Tuesday evening it rained heavily. Around 10 o'clock that night, during the after-dinner dancing, a dozen or so Finns approached me and suggested that we cancel the excursion, as it would be no fun climbing the muddy slopes of Snowdon in heavy rain. I, of course, agreed and announced the cancellation. Immediately I was surrounded by protesting Italians disputing the decision. Why cancel the trip – they had been looking forward to it (escape from lessons), they had paid for it in their all-inclusive fee, a little rain would not hurt anyone and what was the matter with the Finns anyway – weren't they supposed to be tough people?

A little embarrassed, I consulted the Japanese contingent. They were very, very nice. If the Italians wanted to go, they would go, too. If, on the other hand, we cancelled the trip they would be quite happy to stay in and take more lessons. The Italians jeered at the Finns, the Finns mumbled and scowled, and eventually, in order not to lose face, agreed they would go. The excursion was declared on.

It rained torrentially all night and also while I took a quick breakfast. The bus was scheduled to leave at half past eight, and at twenty-five past, taking my umbrella in the downpour, I ran to the vehicle. Inside were 18 scowling Finns, 12 smiling Japanese, and no Italians. We left on time and had a terrible day. The rain never let up, we lunched in cloud at the summit and returned covered in mud at 5 o'clock, in time to see the Italians taking tea and chocolate biscuits. They had sensibly stayed in bed. When the Finns asked them why, they said because it was raining...

Getting to grips with cultural diversity

Cultural diversity is not something that is going to go away tomorrow, enabling us to plan our strategies on the assumption of mutual understanding. It is in itself a phenomenon with its own riches, the exploration of which could yield incalculable benefits for us, both in terms of wider vision and more profitable policies and activity. People of different cultures share basic concepts but view them from different angles and perspectives, leading them to behave in a manner which we may consider irrational or even in direct contradiction of what we hold sacred. We should nevertheless be optimistic about cultural diversity. The behaviour of people of different cultures is not something willy-nilly. There exist clear trends, sequences and traditions. Reactions of Americans, Europeans and Asians alike can be forecasted, usually justified and in the majority of cases managed. Even in countries where political and economic change is currently rapid or sweeping (Russia, China, Hungary, Poland, Korea, Malaysia, etc.) deeply rooted attitudes and beliefs will resist a sudden transformation of values when pressured by reformists, governments or multinational conglomerates. Post-*perestroika* Russians exhibit individual and group behavioural traits strikingly similar to those recorded in Tsarist times – these had certainly persisted, in subdued form, in the Soviet era.

By focusing on the cultural roots of national behaviour, both in society and business, we can foresee and calculate with a surprising degree of accuracy how others will react to our plans for them, and we can make certain assumptions as to how they will approach us. A working knowledge of the basic traits of other cultures (as well as our own) will minimise unpleasant surprises (culture shock), give us insights in advance, and enable us to interact successfully with nationalities with whom we previously had difficulty. This book aims to facilitate the acquisition of such insights.

Cultural differences in international business

International business, especially where joint ventures or prolonged negotiations are involved, is fraught with difficulties. Apart from practical and
technical problems (to which solutions are often readily found), national
psychology and characteristics frequently interfere at the executive level,
where decisions tend to be more complex than the practical accords
reached between accountants, engineers and other technicians. Corporate
cultures vary widely inside one country (compare Apple and IBM in the
US, or Sony and Mitsubishi in Japan); national business styles are mark-
edly more diverse. In a Japanese–US joint venture, where the Americans
are interested mainly in profit and the Japanese in market share, which
direction is to be taken? When a capitalistic company from the west sets up
business in a socialist country, the areas for conflict are even more obvious.
But how similar will be the business ethics or cultural background of
Sweden and Greece, both European?

National characteristics

Determining **national** characteristics is treading a minefield of inaccurate
assessment and surprising exception. There exist excitable Finns, wooden
Italians, cautious Americans and charismatic Japanese. There is, however,
such a thing as a national norm. For instance, Italians are in general more
loquacious than Finns. Yet talkative Finns and silent Italians will overlap.
The individuals who overlap are actually *deviates* in terms of that
particular characteristic.

In this book, with the object of making meaningful comparisons
between different cultures, I have made certain generalisations regarding
the national characteristics of one people or another. Such generalisations
carry with them the risk of stereotyping as one talks about the typical
Italian, German, American, etc. It is evident that Americans differ greatly
from each other and that no two Italians are alike. However, my experience
during 30 years of living abroad and rubbing shoulders with individuals of
many nationalities has led me to the conviction that the inhabitants of any
country possess certain core beliefs and assumptions of reality which will
manifest themselves in their behaviour.

Culture, in the sense that it represents one's outlook and world view, is not, however, a strictly national phenomenon. In some countries **regional** characteristics can prevail to the extent that they relegate the 'national type' to second position. Basques and Andalucians have little in common apart from a Spanish passport; Milanese businesspeople often feel more at home with French and Austrians than with Sicilians. In the USA – nation of many subcultures – differences in race and language have led to the creation of three major divisions: Black, Hispanic, English-speaking whites.

In certain cases **cities** have developed such a strong cultural identity that it transcends the traits of the region. Thus Londoners are not just southern English, Parisians not simply northern French, Berliners are more than just eastern Germans. The inhabitants of Marseille have created their own city culture, the citizens of Liverpool have an accent and lifestyle completely different from the northerners surrounding them. Hong Kong, even after integration, is likely to be a special enclave in southern China.

Cultural groups can cross or span frontiers of nations or regions; they may also align themselves in ways other than geographical. Muslims and Christians are cultural groups; so are engineers and accountants. Graduates of the universities of Oxford, Cambridge, Harvard and Yale would claim separate cultural identities. **Corporate** culture affects the lives of many of us to a greater or lesser degree. It is particularly strong in Japan. In other countries, such as Italy, Spain and China, **family** culture is considered more important. The smallest cultural unit is the personal one – the **individual**. Individualistic views are shown great respect in countries such as Britain, France, Australia and the USA.

Perhaps the greatest cultural divide is not national, religious, corporate or professional, but that based on **gender**. It is quite possible that an Italian woman has a world outlook more similar to that of a German woman than to that of a male Italian.

What the book is about

In Part One we explore the vital question of how the mind is **conditioned**, culturally, at an early age. Once one realises the almost irreversible nature of this childhood training, creating in each of us a set of values so different from those extolled in other parts of the world, the possibilities for complex or hampered interaction in later life become clear. This book attempts to show that there is no good or bad, logical or illogical, in cultural values, just as one cannot argue about taste. The British, American, Chinese each see themselves as rational and normal. Cross-cultural training makes one see others as normal too, when viewed from a different perspective. We also discuss the fascinating subject of the inter-relationship between **language and thought**.

In Part Two we classify the world's cultures in three rough categories:

+ **Linear-actives** – those who plan, schedule, organise, pursue action chains, do one thing at a time. Germans and Swiss are in this group.
+ **Multi-actives** – those lively, loquacious peoples who do many things at once, planning their priorities not according to a time schedule, but according to the relative thrill or importance that each appointment brings with it. Italians, Latin Americans and Arabs are members of this group.
+ **Reactives** – those cultures that prioritise courtesy and respect, listening quietly and calmly to their interlocutors and reacting carefully to the other side's proposals. Chinese, Japanese and Finns are in this group.

We go on to demonstrate how each group **gathers information** in a different way – the linear-actives relying mostly on data, the multi-actives on face-to-face encounters and dialogues, the reactives on a combination of both styles.

Further chapters in Part Two show how the values taught to us in early life give us an entrenched approach to the use of **space and time** and how we accord **status**, respond to different types of **leadership**, and organise our society and business to fit in with these attitudes.

Language is an important part of our functional activity and we indicate, often in diagrammatic form, the varying **communication patterns** used in meetings and during negotiations. **Listening habits** are also important to communication, and a discussion of these leads us on to aspects of sales, marketing and advertising.

Body language is said to convey anything up to 80 per cent of our message, and a chapter on this is followed by a comprehensive survey of **manners** in business and society around the world.

There are then separate chapters devoted to a particular country or area, explaining why people's behaviour there follows certain paths and giving practical advice on how to minimise friction with each group.

In the new edition

Part Three has been expanded to include some 30 additional countries that, for a variety of reasons, play significant roles on the world stage. The inclusion of Denmark, the Netherlands, Belgium, Greece, Austria and Ireland completed coverage of the EU member states. Hungary, Poland, the Czech Republic and the three Baltic states will join soon. Switzerland and Norway, with the second and fourth highest living standards in the world, merit dedicated chapters. Turkey and Iran are pivotal and powerfully influential nations in the Middle East that should be clearly distinguished from their Arab neighbours. Close to them are the resource-rich Central Asian republics, which have emerged as individual nation states after the demise of the Soviet Union.

Further east, the Indian subcontinent – soon to replace China as the world's most populous area – deserves more detailed examination, as does Indonesia, with its 200 million inhabitants. Export powerhouse Korea, the world's eleventh biggest economy, will acquire added clout with reunification, while Vietnam, Thailand, Malaysia and the Philippines make diverse and important contributions in Asia and worldwide. Finally, the giant Latin American area is destined to shake off its numerous twentieth-century political and economic problems. Argentina, Brazil, Chile and Mexico have been chosen to exemplify the cultural values of this region.

Acknowledgements

No new work on cross culture escapes the influence of Edward and Mildred Hall and Geert Hofstede, and I would like to acknowledge their pioneering of certain concepts which figure prominently in this book. I am equally indebted to the perceptive writings of Desmond Morris on body language, to Glen Fisher for his comprehensive analysis of the international negotiation scene, and to David Rearwin and John Paul Fieg for their authoritative views on Asian countries. Yale Richmond, Margaret Nydell and Joy Hendry have written impeccably penetrating insights into the cultures of Russia, the Arab world and Japan respectively, and I have leant leavily on their experience in the relevant chapters of *When Cultures Collide*.

Part One

Getting to grips with cultural diversity

1

DIFFERENT LANGUAGES, DIFFERENT WORLDS

For a German and a Finn, the truth is the truth. In Japan and Britain it is all right if it doesn't rock the boat. In China there is no absolute truth. In Italy it is negotiable.

COMPARISONS OF NATIONAL CULTURES OFTEN BEGIN BY HIGHLIGHTING differences in social behaviour. Japanese do not like shaking hands, bow when greeting each other and do not blow their nose in public. Brazilians form unruly bus queues, prefer brown shoes to black and arrive two hours late at cocktail parties. Greeks stare you in the eye, nod their head when they mean 'no', and occasionally smash plates against walls in restaurants. French people wipe their plate clean with a piece of bread, throw pastry into their coffee and offer handshakes to strangers in bistros. Brits tip their soup plate away from them, eat peas with their fork upside down and play golf in the rain.

Appearance and reality

These various manners and mannerisms cause us great amusement. We smile at foreign eccentricity, congratulating ourselves on our normality. And yet we are aware that these idiosyncrasies are largely superficial. If we stay in France a while we are sooner or later happy to dunk our croissant and make a mess; we discover the unhurried delight of turning up outrageously late in Brazil; we throw vodka glasses over our shoulder with abandon in St Petersburg. Such adaptation of our behaviour leaves no scar on our psyche. We join strangers in their little ways partly to conform and partly for fun. Our appearance is not our reality. We can become French or Greek for an evening, a party or a dinner, we can sit on *tatami* with Japanese and eat legs of lamb with one hand among Arabs. But what goes on in our head remains a private, well-protected constant. We may put on a show for others, but all the while we follow our own silent programme.

Concepts and notions

Part of the superficial public behaviour we have cited above is cultural in origin, and yet we can adopt these manners without prejudice to our own core beliefs. Actions are not difficult to emulate, even different varieties of speech can be imitated to some extent. Thought is a different matter. We cannot see it, we cannot hear it, it may be revealed to us with reluctance, simulation or cunning. Cross-cultural problems arise not so much on account of our unfamiliarity with a bow, a Gallic shrug or chopsticks. Our society has trained us to adopt certain concepts and values. We know that many of these **concepts** are shared by other cultures. We can teach a Spaniard nothing about honour, the Japanese are masters of courtesy, Swedes, English and Germans are all convinced of their own honesty. It is remarkable, given the size of the world, its long history and immeasurable variety, how many common concepts are rooted so firmly in a similar man-ner in wildly different societies. Honour, duty, love, justice, gratitude and revenge are basic tenets of the German, Chinese, Arab and Polynesian alike. A Tasmanian knows his or her duty as clearly as a Greenlander does. What we often overlook is the fact that everyone has different **notions** of these concepts which appeal to so many cultures. Chinese duty is not American duty. Romantic love is seen differently in France and Finland. The English notion of revenge bears little similarity to the Sicilian.

Extreme differences

We readily accept that cultural diversity is vast and formidable. If we take an extreme example, the barriers against communication or mutual comprehension between an Eskimo and an African Bushman might prove insurmountable. Given their different backgrounds, what could they talk about? They would be completely unaware of the structure or politics of each other's society; it is hardly likely that they could imagine the opposite extremity of climate; their religion, taboos, values, aspirations, disappointments and life style would be in stark contrast. Subjects of conversation (if they had some mode of communication) would be minimal, approaching zero. Weather, sex and food, you say? Those are certainly basic issues. Yet if they met in a temperate climate (say England in spring) the Eskimo would find it hot, the Bushman cold. Their notions of sexual attractiveness would differ so strikingly that it is hardly likely that they would want to indulge in wife swapping. A tasty snack? Here, try this bit of blubber – ugh! Give me snake *flambé* any time.

The wildly differing notions of time, space, life after death, nature and reality held by isolated societies will have little impact on international business (although they may contribute usefully to our morals or philosophy). The Navahos with their nuclear concept of speech, the Zulus with their 39 greens, the Eskimos with their 42 types of snow, the Aborigines with their dreamtime, the Lapps with their eight seasons, all provide us with cultural gems, striking insights, unique thought and speech processes which intrigue and fascinate those of us who have time to study them. We are thrilled by these phenomena, take joy in their appreciation. We see, learn and sometimes understand. Deceived we are not. They are differences which we perceive, acknowledge and accept. We know, more or less, where we stand with these people. They live in another world and we know we live in ours.

Closer to home

In our world, there are others who are more like us. They have modern civilisations, political parties, factories, cars and stocks and shares. We meet them regularly and their clothes resemble ours. We appear to have similar concepts and values. They seem to talk 'our language'. Yet for some reason, French and Germans don't always get on. In Belgium half of society dislikes the other. Chinese and Japanese are wary of each other, to say the least; neighbourly Swedes and Norwegians snipe at each other, and the mutual exasperation that British and American cousins experience is only too well documented.

Truth

The concepts are shining and clear: our notions of them are different. Both Germans and British people conducting a business meeting wish for a successful outcome. The German notion is that truth, absolute honest truth, even if somewhat unpalatable, will achieve this. The British, by contrast, give priority to not rocking the boat. But *die Wahrheit ist die Wahrheit* say the Germans. Not so, the Chinese would add – these is no absolute truth. Two conflicting views may both be correct. Most Orientals and many Italians would agree with the Chinese.

In Germany, Sweden and Finland, where people are generally concerned about what the neighbours think, the drive towards conformity imposes checks and constraints on a person's ability to refashion veracity. Brits and Americans, with that wonderfully idiomatic, nuance-rich tool of expression (the English language) at their disposal, are economical with the truth. The French, Italians and other Latins are not famous for their candour, which might interfere with the smooth social intercourse they are so fond of. In Japan, where no one must face exposure, be confronted or lose face, truth is a dangerous concept. In Asia, Africa and South America, strict adherence to the truth would destroy the harmony of relationship between individuals, companies and entire segments of society. Only in Australia is a spade called a spade continent wide, and even there truth often occasions dismay and leads to fist-fights.

Contracts and ethics

As the globalisation of business brings executives more frequently together, there is a growing realisation that if we examine concepts and values, we can take almost nothing for granted. The word 'contract' translates easily from language to language, but notionally it has many interpretations. To a Swiss, German, Scandinavian, American or British person it is something that has been signed in order to be adhered to. Signatures give it a sense of finality. But a Japanese regards a contract as a starting document to be rewritten and modified as circumstances require. A South American sees it as an ideal which is unlikely to be achieved, but which is signed to avoid argument.

Members of most cultures see themselves as ethical, but ethics can be turned upside down. The American calls the Japanese unethical if the latter breaks the contract. The Japanese says it is unethical for the American to apply the terms of the contract if things have changed. Italians have very flexible views on what is ethical and what is not, which sometimes causes Northern Europeans to question their honesty. When Italians bend rules or 'get round' some laws or regulations, they consider they are less ideal bound than, say, the Swiss, and actually closer to reality. They do not consider themselves corrupt, or immoral, nor do they admit to illegality. There are many grey areas where 'short cuts' are, in Italian eyes, the only intelligent course of action. In a country where excessive bureaucracy can hold up 'business' for months, currying favour with an official is a matter of common sense.

Common sense

The very term 'common sense' has to be watched carefully, for it is not as common as it seems. The English dictionary defines it as judgement gained from experience rather than study; the American lexicon gives it as judgement which is sound but unsophisticated. Academics are uncomfortable with common sense, which tends to preempt their research by coming to the same conclusion months earlier. But we must not think that this rough-and-ready wisdom will unite our mix of nationalities. Common sense, although basic and unsophisticated, cannot be neutral. It is derived from experience, but experience is culture bound. It is common sense in Germany or Sweden to form an orderly bus queue. In Naples or Rio it is common sense to get on the bus before anyone else. It would seem common sense for the Japanese to have discarded the Chinese writing system which does not suit their language and which takes ten years for Japanese children to learn. But they have not done so. Japan is a rather regimented society, yet the police let a man urinate against a public wall if he really has to and will drive him home in his car if he is too drunk to drive himself. When asked why they are so lenient in such matters, they reply it is common sense.

Gossip

Gossip has negative connotations in the Nordic countries and hardly a good name in the Anglo-Saxon world. Yet gossip proves far more important to us than we would at first admit. It is a vital source of information in business circles in many countries. In cultures like Spain, Italy, Brazil and Japan, gossip quickly updates and bypasses facts and statistics, provides political background to commercial decisions, and facilitates invaluable debate between people who do not meet officially. The Italian *chiacchiera* or Spanish *paseo* may be largely limited to women and youngsters, but the cafés of Madrid and Lisbon overflow with businessmen, Japanese executives make momentous decisions every evening from 6–10pm in the bars of the Ginza, and the whole of Central and South America 'networks' merrily until one or two in the morning.

The corridors of power in Brussels, where European business and political legislation are inevitably intertwined, reverberate with gossip. European countries which do not have access to this hot-house exchange of information will be severely disadvantaged.

Another positive aspect of gossip is that it appears to be good for us – that is to say, in line with our natural evolution. Professor Robin Dunbar of University College London points out that humans live in much larger groups than other primates and that language may have evolved as a form of social glue holding us together. While some animals obviously communicate well in small groups, it is hardly likely that they can gossip about third parties. This ability enables us to form social or working groups of approximately 150 members. This number holds true for ancient 'clans', military fighting units (a company) and even modern firms. Once a commercial enterprise swells well beyond that it has to be organised into divisions or it becomes less manageable. Intense interest in what other people are doing, finding out from our 'group' the latest news about third parties, enables us to network on a large scale and calculate our positions and reactions accordingly. So the Latins, Greeks and Arabs have got it right after all!

Silence

Silence can be interpreted in different ways. A silent reaction to a business proposal would seem negative to American, German, French, Southern European and Arab executives. In countries as dissimilar as the USA, Peru and Kuwait, conversation is a two-way process, where one partner takes up when the other one leaves off. The intervening silence is two or three seconds in Britain or Germany, less than that in Greece or Kuwait and hardly noticeable in France, Italy and America. However, the 'listening cultures' of East Asia find nothing wrong with silence as a response. 'Those who know do not speak; those who speak do not know', says an old Chinese proverb. Japanese and one European nation (Finland) do not quarrel with this assertion. In both these countries silence is not equated with failure to communicate, but is an integral part of social interaction. What is **not** said is regarded as important and lulls in conversation are considered restful, friendly and appropriate. Silence means that you listen and learn; talking a lot merely expresses your cleverness, perhaps egoism and arrogance. Silence protects your individualism and privacy; it also shows respect for the individualism of others. In Finland and Japan it is considered impolite or inappropriate to force one's opinions on others – it is more appropriate to nod in agreement, smile quietly, avoid opinionated argument or discord.

Powerful mental blocks

As international trade and scientific and political exchange intensify, there is a growing effort on the part of academics, multinational organisations and even nations and governments to improve communication and dia-logue. It is becoming increasingly apparent that in pursuit of this goal it is desirable not only to learn foreign languages on a much wider scale, but to show a sympathetic understanding of other peoples' customs, societies and culture. Many binational and international bodies have been created to fur-ther this aim, and the personnel and training departments of many large companies have invested substantial sums of money in cross-cultural and internationalisation programmes and briefings for those staff members who will represent them abroad.

The question I would like to raise is whether or not cross-cultural train-ing and a willingness to adapt will achieve anything at the end of the day, in view of the interlocking nature of our own language and thought. I am not necessarily suggesting that cross-cultural training might eventually be seen to be in vain – I believe the contrary to be true – but I would like to play devil's advocate for a while and consider how powerful mental blocks may hinder our ability to change our attitudes or adopt new approaches.

In infancy we are conditioned by various factors and influences – not least by the behaviour and guidance of our parents, teachers and society. But they and we are subjected at every turn to that dominating and pervasive 'conditioner' – our common language.

Many linguists adhere to the Benjamin Whorf theory or hypothesis, which states that the language we speak largely determines our way of thinking, as distinct from merely expressing it. In other words, Germans or Japanese behave in a certain manner because the way they think is governed by the language they think in. A Spaniard and a Briton see the world in different ways because one is thinking in Spanish and the other in English. People in the British Isles act and live in a certain way because their thoughts are channelled along Anglo-Saxon grooves which are different from neo-Latin, Japanese or Chinese grooves.

The Briton, the German and the Eskimo may share a common experience, but it appears to each as a kaleidoscopic flux of impressions which has to be organised by the mind. The mind does this largely by means of language. Thus the three individuals end up seeing three different things. What is 'fair play' to the Briton may be something else to the German, who needs to translate the concept into different words, and it may mean nothing at all in a society where there are no organised games.

English and Zulu

If you think 'fair play' is rather abstract, let us go to another instance where a very basic concept is seen in a completely different way by two people of diverse origins. My example involves an Englishman and a Zulu. While the cultural chasm is clear, it is the linguistic factor which dominates this instance.

As you may know, Zulu tongues have 39 words for 'green', while English has only one. (If we wish to modify the shade we have to bring in another word, e.g. bottle green, leaf green). I was interested in how the Zulus could build up 39 one-word concepts for green, and discussed this at length with a former Zulu Chief who had taken a doctorate in philology at Oxford. He began by explaining why Zulus needed 39 words for green. In the days before automotive transport and national highways, the Zulu people would often make long treks across their savannah grasslands. There were no signposts or maps and lengthy journeys had to be described by those who had travelled the route before. The language adapted itself to the requirements of its speakers. English copes with concepts such as contract deadlines and stock futures (Zulu doesn't), but our tongue is seen as poverty stricken and inadequately descriptive by Africans and Amerindians whose languages abound in finely wrought, beautifully logical descriptions of nature, causation, repetition, duration and result.

'But give me some examples of different green-words,' I persisted.

My friend picked up a leaf. 'What colour is this?' he asked.

'Green,' I replied.

The sun was shining. He waited until a cloud intervened. 'What colour is the leaf now?' he asked.

'Green,' I answered, already sensing my inadequacy.

'It isn't the same green, is it?'

'No, it isn't.'

'We have a different word in Zulu.' He dipped the leaf in water and held it out again. 'Has the colour changed?'

'Yes.'

'In Zulu we have a word for "green shining wet".'

The sun came out again and I needed another word (leaf-green-wet-but-with-sunshine-on-it!)

My friend retreated 20 metres and showed me the leaf. 'Has the colour changed again?'

'Yes,' I screamed.

'We have another word,' he said with a smile.

He went on to indicate how different Zulu greens would deal with tree leaves, bush leaves, leaves vibrating in the wind, river greens, pool greens, tree trunk greens, crocodile greens... he got to 39 without even raising a sweat.

Language strait-jacket

It was evident that my Zulu friend and I saw the world through different eyes. And yet it was not a question of eyes. However 'international', multicultural or all-embracing I wished to be, there was no way I could perceive or feel about nature the way he did, **because I didn't have the language to do it with**. It was not just a matter of familiarising myself with the cultural habits, preferences and taboos of his tribe or even adopting his religion and philosophies. I could only experience reality as fully as he did by learning his language and escaping (in terms of descriptive ability) from the strait-jacket of my own.

Just as seeing with two eyes gives us stereoscopic vision, and a sense of depth, thinking in two different languages gives us added dimensions of reality. Finn–Swedes are a case in point. A striking thought is that while French (a language very similar to English) would give a Briton maybe an extra 10 per cent of the observable universe, a 'primitive' language wildly different from our own, with its other logic and set of assumptions, might show us things we have never dreamed of!

It is not difficult for us to comprehend (once we are awake to the language strait-jacket phenomenon) that the Japanese, for example, with their reverse word order will organise their thoughts and priorities in a different manner from that of Europeans. But if we think more closely about the European scene, we discover that English, French and Spanish speakers use language and think in quite different ways, and may seem at times to be on a common wavelength when in fact they didn't really know what the other has said or what they actually meant when they said it.

Translation inadequate

The Greeks, who were the first people to enquire in depth into logic and reason, assumed that language was a universal, untampered-with element of reason. They believed it was a phenomenon shared by all mankind and, in the case of educated people, would provide a standard yardstick for comparison of ideas, experience and reality. They also assumed that ideas could be translated freely into any language. This is only true up to a point. Swedish translates readily into English and vice versa, but with Finnish and English the task is far more complicated.

Even those of us who have learned languages at school have noticed the difficulty our teachers have in translating such words as *panache*, *esprit de corps*, *Gemütlichkeit* and *Zeitgeist* into English. Interpreters at the United Nations are faced daily with similar problems, even with languages which are closely related. In one recorded case, the English speaker said 'I assume', the French interpreter translated as 'I deduce', and this was rendered by the Russian as 'I consider' – by which time the idea of assumption had been lost!

Different worlds

If this can happen working with three close relatives of the Indo-European group, we see that two languages as different as English and Navaho literally operate in two different worlds. I think it is important for businesspeople to consider carefully the implication of the words 'in two different worlds'. All observers are not led by the same physical evidence to the same picture of the universe, unless their linguistic backgrounds are similar, or can in some way be calibrated. English, French, German, Russian and other Indo-European languages can be roughly calibrated (although not always satisfactorily), but where does this leave us with Chinese, Indonesian, Finnish or Japanese? If the structure of a person's language influences the manner in which they understand reality and behave with respect to it, then we could have four individuals who will see the universe through Sino-Tibetan, Polynesian, Altaic and Japanese eyes respectively and then comport themselves accordingly.

Internalised thought

There is a good deal of scientific support for the hypothesis that higher levels of thinking depend on language. Language can be regarded as internalised thought. Most of us conduct an interior monologue, often accompanied by visual imagery. The more educated and literate the individual, the more complex and sophisticated this monologue becomes. It was not until the Middle Ages that people learned to read without reading aloud. Today, talking to or reasoning with oneself is accepted as quite common and there is no doubt that most of this goes on 'in words', whether expressed aloud or not.

We can assume that German, Italian and Malaysian businesspeople do the same thing in their own language. When each speaks, we merely glimpse the tip of a huge iceberg of verbal activity which never breaks the surface of audibility. If you make this reasonable assumption, then you can presume that whatever is said to you will be a brief projection of that inner world of the other person's thoughts. What is said may be grammatically accurate or erroneous in the extreme, but it will be coloured by the foreigner's view of reality, this itself influenced by the rigidity of his or her own language structure.

This line of reasoning tends to become somewhat involved – and clearly thought may also influence one's choice of expression – but to clarify the point, one can take a few practical examples.

The German language is a tightly disciplined, no-nonsense entity with long, compound words often expressing complex concepts. We might therefore expect the internal monologue of a German person to be serious rather than casual, concentrating on weighty issues, and resulting in verbalisation which will be anything but flippant.

Mobile American

Contrast this with the interior monologue of an American counterpart. The nature of American English is interwoven with the character and history of the youthful United States. American speech or thought is mobile and opportunistic; it shifts quickly for advantage or compromise and excels in casual and humorous shafts. The German will take Americans seriously when they do not intend to be taken as such. A further complication is the deep slide that American English has taken into clichés and 'tough' talk. Such expressions as 'gotta deal', 'gotta be jokin', 'no way', 'full of shit', 'over the top', 'you can't do this to me' and 'give away the store' fail to indicate properly what the American is really thinking, but are verbal escape routes to simplified analyses or solutions not necessarily in their favour.

Britons are guilty of other clichés indicative of near-stultifying vagueness of thought, well designed to convey very little or nothing at all to their foreign interlocutors. Such expressions, occasionally derived from sport, include 'fair play', 'sticky wicket', 'a good innings', 'good show', 'bad news', 'not on' and 'a bit thick'.

Clinical French

The French thought monologue is quite different. They have dissected their universe better than most of us and they try to think about it clearly. They know where they are going and what it is that they want. Their clinical vocabulary is conducive to quick thinking, its lack of vagueness leads to a cutting directness, and their ruthless pursuit of logic will often irritate Anglo-Saxons or Japanese, who tend to 'feel their way' towards a solution.

The Spanish speaker's monologue is earthy, emotional and generous. The wealth of Spanish vocabulary and the wide range of endearments and diminutives (shared with Italian and Portuguese and often untranslatable into English or Finnish) enable the Spaniard to communicate in a warm, human manner indicative of an expansive character and lack of cunning. Exporters should not, however, read this as a sign that the Spanish speaker can necessarily be taken advantage of.

Foggy Japanese

The Japanese have the most difficult task of all in making the transition from their internal monologue to actual verbal utterance. In their thoughts they agonise over striking a balance between gaining advantage and correctness of behaviour. Their thought (we can also regard this as internalised speech) has to be polite in the extreme in view of the fact that they are to address others. But the speech mechanisms involved in such politeness often lead to incredible vagueness of expression, so that whatever message they seek to convey may well get lost in a fog of impeccable behaviour. On top of that, their formidable battery of honorific expressions – so useful in communication between Japanese – are rendered useless in the face of impossibility of translation, so that their conversation with their foreign counterpart emerges as terribly platitudinous, even if grammatically correct.

Humour across frontiers

It has been said that humour crosses national boundaries with difficulty, especially when heading east. If we analyse this assertion for a moment, several implications emerge. First, it is self-evident that the victim of a humorous attack is hardly likely to see the funny side of it. French anecdotes depicting the Belgians as a collection of slow-witted yokels fail to gain appreciation in Brussels. Dutch people resent similar treatment at the hands of the Belgians.

Secondly, failure to appreciate the funny side of a 'foreign' anecdote does not necessarily depend on one's being the victim. Serious-minded, factual Germans do not split their sides on hearing American jokes about Texas, which usually depend on gross exaggeration. The story about the Mexican driving just as fast as he could for 24 hours to get out of Texas, but finding he had not managed it, thrills the American imagination but sounds far fetched to the German, who would usually reply, 'He should have used a German car.' This response would be considered very funny in Germany and fairly good in England and Scandinavia.

Apart from the Koreans (who seem to like everybody's jokes), few Orientals are amused by American or (most) European jokes. The Confucian and Buddhist preoccupation with truth, sincerity, kindliness and politeness automatically eliminates humour techniques such as sarcasm, satire, exaggeration and parody, and finds little merit in crazy humour or jokes about religion, sex and underprivileged minorities. Sick or black humour is definitely out.

So what is left, you might ask? Eastern humour, such as we understand it, is couched in subtlety, gentle, indirect reproach or reprimand, occasionally victimising listeners in a sly but non-aggressive manner which yet leaves them room for response and stops short of depriving them of their dignity. Even the rougher, occasionally bawdy Koreans take great care to protect the listener's 'wholeness' or standing. Chinese are noted for their aphorisms and proverbs, and they and Indians find great sources of humour in parables, which we in the west find only moderately funny, although they do combine wisdom, moralising and a sense of perspective. We can understand the point of most Confucian aphorisms and Indian or Malaysian tales, while we rarely understand Japanese jokes. But then, neither do the Chinese.

Is there such a thing as a 'national style' of humour? Before answering this question directly, one must accept the fact that there **is** such a thing as international humour – that is to say, some types of humour and some jokes gain international acceptance. In particular, this is true of slapstick, age-old in its use and laughed at by Europeans, Americans, Africans and Orientals alike. It is very much in evidence, for instance, on Japanese television. There seems to be a general love of witnessing violence, which may compensate, in the international arena, for not always being allowed to practise it. There are also 'international' jokes repeated across many borders, such as the one about who must jump first out of the aeroplane, elephant jokes, restaurant jokes and hilarious stories about golfers.

Even in the area of international jokes, however, the national 'rinse' begins to show. Take, for example, the old joke about the journalists who organised a competition to write an article about elephants. The titles were as follows:

English	Hunting elephants in British East Africa
French	The love life of elephants in French Equatorial Africa
German	The origin and development of the Indian elephant in the years 1200–1950 (600 pages)
American	How to breed bigger and better elephants
Russian	How we sent an elephant to the moon

Swede	Elephants and the welfare state
Dane	Elephant-meat smørrebrød
Spaniard	Techniques of elephant fighting
Indian	The elephant as a means of transportation before the railway era
Finn	What the elephants think about Finland

This joke, which probably originated at a conference of journalists, pokes fun at various national *faiblesses* – French lust, German seriousness, American bragging, British colonialism, etc. The punchline is the laugh about Finns' preoccupation with what others think about them. In Helsinki, however, they developed an alternative punchline where a Norwegian was added, the title being: 'Norway and Norway's mountains'.

Finns, Swedes and Danes find this alternative absolutely side-splitting. The Norwegians (who consider themselves a humorous people) do not find this ending funny at all. In fact, **they do not understand it**. Do you?

Humour in business

As world trade becomes increasingly globalised, businesspeople meet their foreign partners more frequently and consequently feel that they know them better. It is only natural that when one develops a closer relationship with a stranger there is a tendency to avoid overseriousness and to begin to converse in a more relaxed manner. Swapping anecdotes is a good way of melting the ice in many situations and gaining the confidence of one's listener. A funny incident involving some personal discomfort or embarrassment is a good start; a sly attack on a 'common enemy' may soon follow.

Humour during business meetings is not infrequent in most European countries, although it is less common among Latins than with Northern peoples, where it is a valuable tool for breaking the ice. Perhaps among the Spaniards, Portuguese and Italians, there is little ice to break. Their own racy, gossipy, confiding, conversation style constitutes in itself, however, a valid humorous element.

It is in the Anglo-Saxon countries that humour is used systematically. Relaxed in Canada and New Zealand, it can be barbed and provocative in Australia. In the USA particularly, sarcasm, kidding and feigned indignation are regarded as factors which move the meeting along and get more done in less time. Time is, after all, money. It is perhaps in the UK that humour is most intertwined in business talks. The British hate heavy or drawn-out meetings and will resort to various forms of humour and distracting tactics to keep it all nice and lively.

However, two nationalities in particular avoid jokes and other forms of humour during the actual business sessions. Germans find it out of place during negotiations. Business is serious and should be treated as such, without irrelevant stories or distractions. If you do not concentrate on the issue, you are not showing respect to your interlocutor. Kidding is, in their eyes, not honest and creates confusion in business discussion. They want to know about price, quality and delivery dates, with some precision, please.

After the meetings are over, Germans are quite willing to relax and joke with their partners in bars, restaurants and at home. Humour and anecdotes are more than welcome in these circumstances. Relaxation, like business discussion and many other activities in Germany, is fairly strictly compartmentalised.

Japanese also fail to see any benefit in introducing humour into business meetings. They will laugh if they are aware that you have told a joke (it is unlikely they will have understood it) but that is out of sheer politeness. They are normally nervous about understanding your straight talk in the first place, so that any clever nuances or tongue-in-cheek utterances will leave them floundering. They take anything you say quite literally. Americans using expressions like 'You are killing me' or 'Say that once again and I'll walk away from this deal' cause great consternation among their Japanese partners. One US executive who said a certain clause would blow the deal out of the water was asked, 'What water?' An Englishman was asked by the waiter at the end of a business dinner if the ten men present required ice-cream for dessert. As the table was laden with beer, the Englishman replied humorously that everyone was having beer for dessert. Two minutes later the waiter appeared with ten beers.

While the introduction of humour in international business talks may bring considerable gain in terms of breaking the ice, speeding up the issues, escaping from deadlock, putting your partners at ease and winning their confidence in you as a human being, the downside risks are often just as great. What is funny for the French may be anathema to an Arab; your very best story may be utterly incomprehensible to a Chinese; your most innocent anecdote may seriously offend a Turk. Cultural and religious differences may make it impossible for some people to laugh at the same thing. Who can say with certainty that anything is funny? If all values are relative and culture based, then these include humour, tolerance, even truth itself. And remember that laughter, more often than not, symbolises embarrassment, nervousness or possibly scorn.

Making allowances

International businesspeople cannot escape the bottom line – a good American expression – of the considerations made above. The picture of the universe shifts from tongue to tongue, and the way of doing business shifts accordingly. There is no one metaphysical pool of human thought – or of behaviour. Different languages provide different 'segments of experience' and there is little we can do about it, except to learn more languages. We cannot learn all of them, but at least the awareness of the problem and any allowances we can make for a foreign friend's *Weltanschauung* will help us to establish whatever degree of communication our different mentalities permit.

2

CULTURAL CONDITIONING

We think our minds are free, but, like captured American pilots in Vietnam and North Korea, we have been thoroughly brainwashed. Collective programming in our culture, begun in the cradle and reinforced in kindergarten, school and workplace, convinces us that we are normal, others eccentric.

What is culture?

HOFSTEDE DEFINED CULTURE AS 'THE COLLECTIVE PROGRAMMING OF THE mind which distinguishes the members of one category of people from another'. The key expression in this definition is **collective programming**. Although not as sinister as 'brainwashing' – with connotations of political coercion – it nevertheless describes a process to which each one of us has been subjected immediately after birth (some people would say even before birth, but that is a little deep for me!) Certainly when parents, returning from hospital, carry a baby over the threshold, the first decision has to be made – where to sleep. A Japanese child is invariably put in the same room as the parents, near the mother, for the first couple of years. British and American children are often put in a separate room – right away or after a few weeks or months. The inferences for the child's dependence/interdependence and problem-solving abilities are obvious. To follow up one theory, Japanese children – used to doing everything jointly with their parents 24 hours a day for the first year, then acting thereafter in strict unison with 50 clones in kindergarten – develop an addiction to group activity and 'group think' which leads to (and is reinforced by) close cooperation and joint pursuits in school, university, clubs and ultimately their company.

Parents and teachers obviously give children the best advice they can. It fits them out for successful interaction in their own culture and society, where good and bad, right and wrong, normal and abnormal are clearly defined. Unfortunately (at least in one sense) American and European children are being given a completely different set of instructions, although equally valid in their own environment.

As we grow up, these taught-and-learned 'national' concepts become our core beliefs, which we find almost impossible to discard. We regard others' beliefs and habits (Russian, Chinese, Hungarian...) as strange or eccentric, mainly because they are unlike our own. There is no doubt about it, Japanese are not like Americans!

On the other hand, we have a sneaking feeling (and we frequently hear it expressed) that 'deep down all people are alike'. There is also truth in this, for there are such things as universal human characteristics. They are not too numerous, for our national collective programming 'distorts' some of our basic instincts (Scots thrift v American free spending). Figure 1 shows how national collective programming is 'grafted onto' inherited traits. In the top section we add individual characteristics. Some people, by dint of personal originality, extra powers of perception, stubbornness or even genius, stand apart from their colleagues and deviate sharply from the national track. Such people often become famous for their 'idiosyncrasies' and a few have actually changed the course of their nation's destiny (King Henry VIII, Kemal Atatürk, Emperor Meiji of Japan).

In general, however, our national or regional culture imposes itself on our behaviour rather than the other way round, and we become a solid German, a good Swede, a real American or a true Brit, as the case may be. Interacting with our compatriots, we generally find that the closer we stick to the rules of our society, the more popular we become.

Culture shock

Our precious values and unshakeable core beliefs take a battering when we venture abroad. 'Support the underdog!' cry Guy Fawkes-loving English.

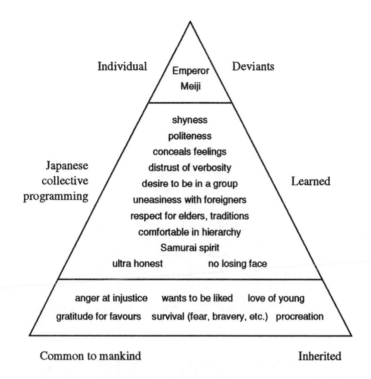

Figure 1   Human mental programming – Japan

The Australians – famous historical underdogs themselves – echo this to the full. Germans and Japanese, although temporary underdogs themselves after the Second World War, tend to support the **more powerful** of two adversaries, seeing the underdog as necessarily the less efficient. The Japanese government, through MITI (Ministry of Trade and Industry), issues directives to the larger banks to lend money to those industries which are currently thriving and have the potential for further growth, while discouraging loans to enterprises which have become old-fashioned or have little hope for future success. This attitude is in marked contrast to that so long prevalent in Britain, where ancient factories were kept alive and industrial underdogs such as textiles and coal-mining were supported long after they were economically viable.

Figure 2 shows the different paths which our core beliefs take according to the culture we try to impose them on. Others are not aware of our values simply by looking at us. They may draw certain conclusions from the manner in which we dress, but these days most businesspeople dress in a similar way. It is only when we **say** or **do** something that they can gain

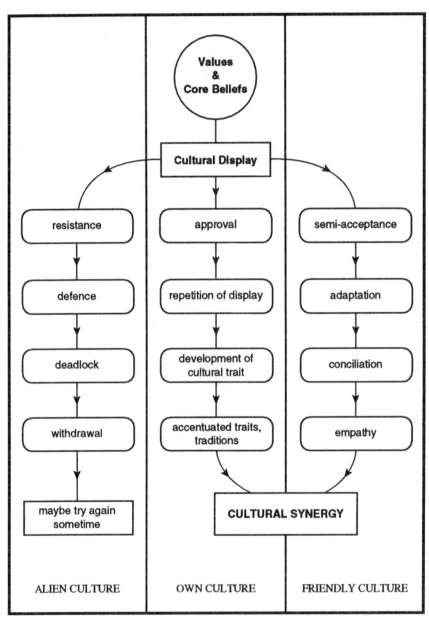

Figure 2   Paths for core beliefs

deeper insight into what makes us tick. This utterance or action may be described as a **cultural display** or **event**, since, by its execution, we reveal our cultural attitudes. In Figure 2, the cultural display might be that an Italian (probably Roman) turns up half an hour late for a scheduled meeting. In her own cultural environment this will make no waves, for most of the others will be late too. Her behaviour is approved and eventually it becomes a cultural tradition. Were she to turn up 30 minutes late in an alien culture (say Germany) she would deliver a culture shock of no mean proportions. Germans do not like to be kept waiting for three minutes, let alone thirty. Immediate resistance and protest leads to Italian defence (traffic jam, daughter was ill) and eventually a defence of the Italian way of life ('Why are you Germans so time dominated – you are like clocks!') Such confrontation leads to deadlock and probable withdrawal from a project.

In a friendly culture (shall we say the French), the criticism will be couched in cynicism, but will be less final or damning. (*'Mon vieux, tu m'as volé une demie heure, tu sais!'*) The Italian, sensitive to Latin objections, next time comes only 20 minutes late. The Frenchman, no great believer in punctuality himself, eventually settles for 15 minutes. The Italian concurs. This is Latin understanding.

Who is normal, anyway?

Most English people think they are normal and that all others (whom they call 'foreigners') are abnormal – that is to say, they might be all right, but they really cannot act and think like the English, because, after all, they are foreign. You only have to look at them, you'll know what that means...

Chauvinism

Americans think America is the biggest and the best, the newest and the richest, and all others are a bit slow, old fashioned, rather poor and somewhat on the small side. They can't call the British foreigners, so they call them 'limeys'.

Spaniards think they are the bravest because they kill bulls, the French think they are intellectually superior to everybody else, the Japanese are quite **sure** they are superior to others, including the French. The Germans admit that they are not as big as the Americans, as agile as the Japanese, as historical as the French, as smooth as the British, but what really counts in life? Efficiency, punctuality, *Gründlichkeit*, method, consistency and organisation. Who can match Germans on these counts?

There are few countries in Europe or the world where people do not believe, at the bottom of their heart, that they are the best, or the most intelligent, or at least normal. Perhaps in Europe the Italians and the Finns are the most innocent in this regard, often being willing to criticise themselves before others, yet both still consider themselves normal.

I am reminded of the old story of the 80-year old couple sitting by the fireside looking back on their lives. The wife says to the husband: 'John, everybody is strange except you and me. And even you are strange sometimes.'

Normal and abnormal

If each culture considers itself normal, then the corollary is that it considers everybody else abnormal. By this token Finns consider Italians over-emotional because they wave their arms while talking. The individualistic Spaniards consider the Swiss stuffy and excessively law-abiding. Lively Italians find Norwegians gloomy. French-influenced Vietnamese find Japanese impassive. Argentinians are considered conceited by all other South Americans. Germans think Australians are undisciplined. Japanese see straight-talking Americans as rude.

We can achieve a good understanding of our foreign counterparts only if we realise that our 'cultural spectacles' are colouring our view of them. In fact, both calm and excitable Italians use many gestures during conversation. Finns see them as overdemonstrative, Spaniards see them as normal. Conversely, Finns would not agree with Italians about Norwegians being excessively gloomy. Germans view the law-abiding Swiss as correct. The stereotypes described above derive largely from the 'abnormality' of the viewer, e.g. the ultra-politeness of the Japanese, the social shyness of the Finn, the Spanish tendency towards lawlessness.

What is the route to better understanding? To begin with, we need to examine the special features of our own culture. Finnish taciturnity scores good points in Britain and Japan, but will forever be considered very odd indeed in Portugal, Greece, the Middle East and Latin America. The

Japanese will have to learn one day that when they say 'yes' the rest of world does not know that they mean 'no'.

Our second task, once we realise that we too are a trifle strange, is to understand the subjective nature of our ethnic values. While Scots see stubbornness largely as a positive trait, flexible Italians may see mainly intransigence, the diplomatic English possibly lack of artfulness or dexterity. We also make assumptions on the basis of our subjective view and, even worse, assumptions of other people's assumptions. The Italian who assumes that French people feel intellectually superior also judges that French assume Italians are suitable mainly for manual labour when emigrating to France. The Finn who judges Swedes are snobs also assumes that Swedes assume Finns are rough and rustic. There may be a grain of truth in many of these judgements and assumptions of assumptions, but the danger involved in making them is only too obvious!

Legal and illegal

Our perception of reality (what a word!) may be assisted if we can wear someone else's shoes for a moment – if we can see how they view some matter in a way very different from our own. Figure 3 illustrates differing viewpoints of Finns and Spaniards on legality and illegality.

Both nationalities agree that trafficking in drugs is bad and that laws against drunken driving are socially beneficial and justified. When it comes to restrictive immigration laws, the Finns' subjective view is that the fragile, delicately balanced national economy must be protected, while semiconsciously their instinct is to protect the purity of their race. Spaniards, born in a country where no one dares trace their ancestry further back than 1500, have a reflex distaste for prohibitive immigration policies which hinder the free movement of Spaniards seeking better wages abroad. Such policies or laws they see as negative, or simply bad. A Finn consistently making expensive telephone calls for which she need not pay will ultimately fall victim to her own inherent sense of independence, not least because she is building up a debt to her friend in Finnish Telecom. The Spaniard, on the other hand, would phone Easter Island nightly (if he could get away with it) with great relish and unashamed glee.

It is by considering such matters that we realise that all that is legal is not necessarily good and everything illegal not necessarily bad. Finns,

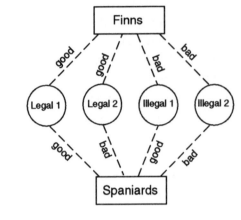

Legal 1 = restrictive drink-driving laws

Legal 2 = restrictive immigration laws

Illegal 1 = consistently making use of
a friend at the telephone exchange to
make free international calls

Illegal 2 = drug traffic

Figure 3

Swedes, Swiss and Germans do not make this discovery very easily. Americans, Belgians, Danes, Hungarians, Slovenes, Croats, Chinese, Koreans and Australians can accept it without losing too much sleep. Latins, Arabs, Polynesians, Africans and Russians see it clearly from the beginning. A Sicilian friend of mine has not paid for a telephone call since 1948. His father owns a vineyard.

Recently I tested mature Finnish executives on cross-cultural seminars with the following exercise:

NATIONAL CHARACTERISTICS

heavy   humorous   excitable   honest   risk taking   snobbish
serious   diplomatic   talkative   slow   opportunistic   weak willed
humourless   laid back   sly   emotional   reliable   true
money minded   collective   wise   take things literally   open   shy
good manners   unreliable   direct   joking   sociable   hard working
conservative   individualistic   loud   no manners   caring   extrovert
efficient   punctual   flexible   reserved   quick   polite
time dominated   vague   boring   polished   strong willed
old fashioned

*Study the characteristics above and select eight for each of the following
nationalities: German, British, Italian, Finnish, Swedish, American*

Attributing 8 of the 48 available characteristics to 6 different nationalities, Finns invariably select the following qualities to describe themselves:

honest, slow, reliable, true, shy, direct, reserved, punctual

Six of these characteristics are clearly positive; even 'shy' and 'slow' do do not have negative connotations in Finnish ears.

Germans could be considered punctual, Swedes honest, Britons true and reliable, Americans direct, but the seminarists had a natural tendency to paint a positive picture of the Finnish character. Swedes, Germans and Britons, when tested in a similar manner, do the same, selecting euphemistic adjectives to describe their own culture.

In another exercise, Finnish seminarists were asked to perform role plays in which Finnish, Russian, American and Polynesian characters were involved. The executives played the Finnish and Russian roles well, but invariably exaggerated the traits of Americans and Polynesians, magnifying and distorting the brashness and blustering nature of the former and the innocence, clamour and chatter of the latter. This illustrated the Finnish tendency to resort to stereotype categorising when actual familiarity is lacking. (Russian characteristics, on the other hand, are well observed by Finns).

Stereotyping is dangerous, but it is also a fair guide at the national level. A particular Dane may resemble a certain Portuguese, but a Danish choir or football team is easily distinguishable from its Portuguese equivalent. Generalising on national traits breaks down with individuals but stands firm with large numbers.

Cultural spectacles continue to blur the vision of any nationals when they look at their foreign interlocutors. Figure 4 illustrates the barriers to communication which Japanese reticence erects when faced with Latin exuberance, and Figure 5 shows the relative ease with which two Latin peoples can communicate with each other by virtue of wearing similar spectacles.

It is worth pointing out that French and Italian people do not like each other particularly, but they are both good communicators and there are no substantial barriers in the way of rapid and mutually intelligible discourse.

If a Japanese or anyone else takes off their national spectacles, the world is initially blurred and out of focus. Many other pairs of spectacles will have to be tried on before 20/20 vision is achieved. This is the process of **developing intercultural sensitivity**.

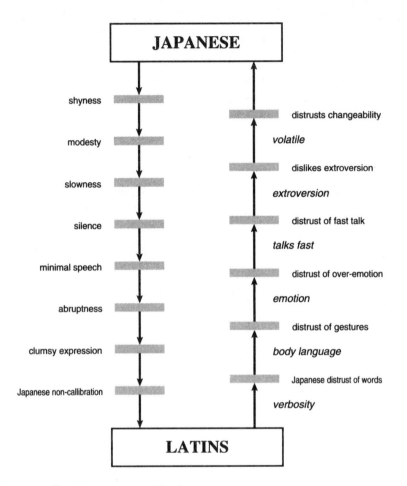

Figure 4   Barriers to communication

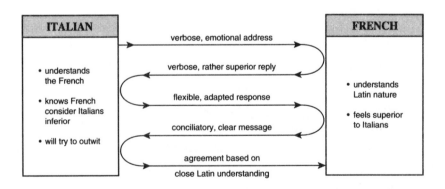

Figure 5   Interaction among Latins

Part Two

Managing Across Cultures

3

CATEGORISING CULTURES

The several hundred national and regional cultures of the world can be roughly classified into three groups: task-oriented, highly organised planners (linear-active); people-oriented, loquacious interrelators (multi-active); introvert, respect-oriented listeners (reactive). Italians see Germans as stiff and time-dominated; Germans see Italians gesticulating in chaos; the Japanese observes and quietly learns from both.

Linear-active and multi-active cultures

SVEN SVENSSON IS A SWEDISH BUSINESSMAN, LIVING IN LISBON. A FEW weeks ago he was invited by a Portuguese acquaintance, Antonio, to play tennis at 10am. Sven turned up at the tennis court on time, already in tennis gear and ready to play.

Antonio arrived half an hour late, in the company of a friend, Carlos, from whom he was buying some land. They had been discussing the purchase that morning and had prolonged the discussion, so Antonio had brought Carlos along in order to finalise the details during the journey. They continued the business while Antonio changed into his tennis clothes, with Sven listening to all they said. At 10.45 they went on court and Antonio continued the discussion with Carlos, while hitting practice balls with Sven.

At this point another acquaintance of Antonio's, Pedro, arrived in order to confirm a sailing date with Antonio for the weekend. Antonio asked

Sven to excuse him for a moment and walked off court to talk to Pedro. After chatting to Pedro for five minutes, Antonio resumed his conversation with the waiting Carlos and eventually turned back to the waiting Sven to begin playing tennis at 11. When Sven remarked that the court had only been booked from 10 to 11am, Antonio reassured him that he had phoned in advance to rebook it until 12 noon. No problem.

It will come as no surprise to you to hear that Sven was very unhappy about the course of events. Why? He and Antonio live in two different worlds or, to put it more exactly, use two different time systems. Sven, as a good Swede, belongs to a culture which uses linear-active time – that is to say, he does one thing at a time in the sequence he has written down in his diary. His diary that day said 8am get up, 9am breakfast, 9.15 change into tennis clothes, 9.30 drive to tennis court, 10–11am play tennis, 11–11.30 beer and shower, 12.15 lunch, 2pm go to the office, and so on.

Antonio, who had seemed to synchronise with him for tennis from 10 to 11, had disorganised Sven's day. Portuguese like Antonio follow a multi-active time system, that is, they do many things at once, often in an unplanned order.

Multi-active cultures are very flexible. If Pedro interrupted Carlos's conversation which was already in the process of interrupting Sven's tennis, this was quite normal and acceptable in Portugal. It is not acceptable in Sweden, neither is it in Germany or Britain.

Linear-active people, like Swedes, Swiss, Dutch and Germans, do one thing at a time, concentrate hard on that thing and do it within a scheduled timescale. These people think that in this way they are more efficient and get more done.

Multi-active people **think they get more done their way**. Let us look again at Sven and Antonio. If Sven had not been disorganised by Antonio, he would undoubtedly have played tennis, eaten at the right time and done some business. But Antonio had had breakfast, bought some land, played tennis and fixed up his sailing, all by lunchtime. He had even managed to rearrange the tennis booking. Sven could never live like this, but Antonio does, all the time.

Multi-active people are not very interested in schedules or punctuality. They pretend to observe them, especially if a linear-active partner insists. They consider reality to be more important than manmade appointments. Reality for Antonio that morning was that his talk with Carlos about land was unfinished. Multi-active people do not like to leave conversations unfinished. For them completing a human transaction is the best way they can invest their time. So he took Carlos to the tennis and finished buying the land while hitting balls. Pedro further delayed the tennis, but Antonio would not abandon the match with Sven. That was another human transaction he wished to complete. So they played till 12 or 12.30 if necessary. But what about Sven's lunch at 12.15? Not important, says Antonio. It's only 12.15 because that's what Sven wrote in his diary.

A friend of mine, a BBC producer, often used to visit Europe to visit BBC agents. He never failed to get through his appointments in Denmark and Germany, but always had trouble in Greece. The Greek agent was a popular man in Athens and had to see so many people each day that he invariably ran over time. So my friend usually missed his appointment or waited three or four hours for the agent to turn up. Finally, after several trips, the producer adapted to the multi-active culture. He simply went to the Greek's secretary in late morning and asked for the agent's schedule for the day. As the Greek conducted most of his meetings in hotel rooms or bars, the BBC producer would wait in the hotel lobby and catch him rushing from one appointment to the next. The multi-active Greek, happy to see him, would not hesitate to spend half an hour with him and thus make himself late for his next appointment.

When people from a linear-active culture work together with people from a multi-active culture, irritation results on both sides. Unless one party adapts to the other – and they rarely do – constant crises will occur. Why don't the Mexicans arrive on time? ask the Germans. Why don't they work to deadlines? Why don't they follow a plan? The Mexicans on the other hand ask: Why keep to the plan when circumstances have changed? Why keep to a deadline if we rush production and lose quality? Why try to sell this amount to that customer if we know they aren't ready to buy yet?

Recently I visited a wonderful aviary in South Africa where exotic birds of all kinds were kept in a series of 100 large cages, to which the visiting public had direct access. There was plenty of room for the birds to fly around and it was quite exciting for us to be in the cage with them. One proceeded, at one's leisure, from cage to cage, making sure one closed doors carefully.

Two small groups of tourists – one consisting of four Germans and the other of three French people – were visiting the aviary at the same time as us. The Germans had made their calculations, obviously having decided to devote 100 minutes to the visit; consequently they spent one minute in each cage. One German read the captions, one took photographs, one videoed and one opened and closed doors. I followed happily in their wake.

The three French people began their tour a few minutes later than the Germans, but soon caught them up as they galloped through the cages containing smaller birds. As the French were also filming, they rather spoilt cage 10 for the Germans, as they made a lot of noise and generally got in the way. The Germans were relieved when the French rushed on ahead towards more exciting cages.

The steady German progress continued through cages 11–15. Cage 16 contained the owls (most interesting). There we found our French friends again, who had occupied the cage for five minutes. They filmed the owls from every angle while the Germans waited their turn. When the French eventually rushed out, the Germans were five minutes behind schedule.

Later on, the French stayed so long with the eagles in cage 62 that the Germans had to bypass them and come back to do the eagles later. They were furious at this forced departure from their linear progression, and eventually finished their visit half an hour 'late'. By then the French had departed, having seen all they were interested in.

A study of attitudes to time in a Swiss–Italian venture showed that each side learned something from the other. After initial quarrelling, both parties cooperated for a few months. The Italians finally admitted that adherence at least in theory to schedules, production deadlines and budgets enabled them to clarify their goals and check on performances and efficiency. The Swiss, on the other hand, found that the more flexible Italian attitude allowed them to modify the timetable in reaction to unexpected developments in the market, to spot deficiencies in the planning which had not been evident earlier, and to make vital last-minute improvements in 'extra time'.

Germans, like Swiss, are very high on the linear-active scale, since they attach great importance to analysing a project, compartmentalising it, tackling each problem one at a time in a linear fashion, concentrating on each segment and thereby achieving a near perfect result. They are uneasy with people who do not work in this manner, such as Arabs and those from many Mediterranean cultures.

Americans are also very linear-active, but there are some differences in attitude. As Americans live very much in the present and the future, they sometimes push Germans into action before the latter want to act. Germans are very conscious of their history and their past and will often wish to explain a lot of background to American partners to put present actions in context. This often irritates Americans who want 'to get on with it'.

Figure 6 gives a suggested ranking on the linear/multi-active scale, showing not unsurprising regional variations. German and other European influences in Chile have caused Chileans to be less multi-active than, for instance, Brazilians or Argentinians. The differences in behaviour between northern and southern Italians are well documented. Australians, with a large number of southern European immigrants, are becoming less linear-active and more extrovert than most northern peoples.

Figure 7 lists the most common traits of linear-active, multi-active and reactive cultures.

LINEAR-ACTIVE–MULTI-ACTIVE SCALE

1.   Germans, Swiss
2.   Americans (WASP)*
3.   Scandinavians, Austrians
4.   British, Canadians, New Zealanders
5.   Australians, South Africans
6.   Japanese
7.   Dutch, Belgians
8.   American subcultures (e.g. Jewish, Italian, Polish)
9.   French, Belgians (Walloons)
10.   Czechs, Slovenians, Croats, Hungarians
11.   Northern Italians (Milan, Turin, Genoa)
12.   Chileans
13.   Russians, other Slavs
14.   Portuguese
15.   Polynesians
16.   Spanish, Southern Italians, Mediterranean peoples
17.   Indians, Pakistanis etc.
18.   Latin Americans, Arabs, Africans

* White Anglo-Saxon Protestant

Figure 6

LINEAR-ACTIVE	MULTI-ACTIVE	REACTIVE
introvert	extrovert	introvert
patient	impatient	patient
quiet	talkative	silent
minds own business	inquisitive	respectful
likes privacy	gregarious	good listener
plans ahead methodically	plans grand outline only	looks at general principles
does one thing at a time	does several things at once	reacts
works fixed hours	works any hours	flexible hours
punctual	unpunctual	punctual
dominated by timetables and schedules	timetable unpredictable	reacts to partner's timetable
compartmentalises projects	lets one project influence another	sees whole picture
sticks to plans	changes plans	makes slight changes
sticks to facts	juggles facts	statements are promises
gets information from statistics, reference books, database	gets first-hand (oral) information	uses both
job-oriented	people-oriented	people-oriented
unemotional	emotional	quietly caring
works within department	gets round all departments	all departments
follows correct procedures	pulls strings	inscrutable, calm
accepts favours reluctantly	seeks favours	protects face of other
delegates to competent collegues	delegates to relations	delegates to reliable people
completes action chains	completes human transactions	reacts to partner
likes fixed agendas	interrelates everything	thoughtful
brief on telephone	talks for hours	summarises well
uses memoranda	rarely writes memos	plans slowly
respects officialdom	seeks out (top) key person	ultra honest
dislikes losing face	has ready excuses	must not lose face
confronts with logic	confronts emotionally	avoids confrontation
limited body language	unrestricted body language	subtle body language
rarely interrupts	interrupts frequently	doesn't interrupt
separates social/ professional	interweaves social/ professional	connects social and professional

Figure 7

Reactive cultures (listeners)

Japan belongs to the group of reactive or listening cultures, the members of which rarely initiate action or discussion, preferring first to listen to and establish the other's position, then react to it and formulate their own.

Reactive cultures are to be found in Japan, China, Taiwan, Singapore, Korea, Turkey and Finland. Several other East Asian countries, although occasionally multi-active and excitable, have certain reactive characteristics. In Europe, only Finns are strongly reactive, but Britons, Turks and Swedes fall easily into 'listening mode' on occasion.

Reactive cultures listen before they leap. They are the world's best listeners in as much as they concentrate on what the speaker is saying, do not let their minds wander (difficult for Latins) and rarely, if ever, interrupt a speaker while the discourse/speech/presentation is going on. When it is finished, they do not reply immediately. A decent period of silence after the speaker has stopped shows respect for the weight of the remarks, which must be considered unhurriedly and with due deference.

Even when representatives of a reactive culture begin their reply, they are unlikely to voice any strong opinion immediately. A more probable tactic is to ask further questions on what has been said in order to clarify the speaker's intent and aspirations. Japanese, particularly, go over each point many times in detail to make sure there are no misunderstandings. Finns, although blunt and direct in the end, shy away from confrontation as long as they can, trying to formulate an approach which suits the other party. Chinese take their time to assemble a variety of strategies which would avoid discord with the initial proposal.

Reactive cultures are introvert, distrust a surfeit of words, and consequently are adept at non-verbal communication. This is achieved by subtle body language, worlds apart from the excitable gestures of Latins and Africans. Linear-active people find reactive tactics hard to fathom, since they do not slot into the linear system (question/reply, cause/effect). Multi-active people, used to extrovert behaviour, find them inscrutable – giving little or no feedback. The Finns are the best example of this, reacting even less than the Japanese, who at least pretend to be pleased.

In reactive cultures the preferred mode of communication is mono-logue — pause — reflection — monologue. If possible, one lets the other side deliver their monologue first. In linear-active or multi-active cultures, the communication mode is a **dialogue**. One interrupts the other's 'monologue' by frequent comments, even questions, which signify polite interest in what is being said. As soon as the opponent stops speaking, one takes up one's turn immediately, since the westerner has an extremely weak tolerance of silence.

People belonging to reactive cultures not only tolerate silences well, but regard them as a very meaningful, almost refined, part of discourse. The opinions of the other party are not to be taken lightly, or dismissed with a snappy or flippant retort. Clever, well-formulated arguments require – deserve – lengthy silent consideration. The American, having delivered a sales pitch in Helsinki, leans forward and says, 'Well, Pekka, what do you think?' If you ask Finns what they think, they begin to **think**. Finns, like Orientals, think in silence. Another American, asked the same question, might well jump to his feet and exclaim, 'I'll tell you what I think!', allowing no pause to punctuate the proceedings or interfere with western 'momentum'. Oriental momentum takes much longer to achieve. One can compare reactions to handling the gears of a car, where multi-active people go immediately into first gear, enabling them to put their foot down to accelerate (the discussion) and to pass quickly through second and third gears as the argument intensifies. Reactive cultures prefer to avoid crashing through the gear box. Too many revs might cause damage to the engine (discussion). The big wheel turns more slowly at first and the foot is put down gently. But when momentum is finally achieved it is likely to be maintained and, moreover, tends to be in the right direction.

The reactive 'reply-monologue' will accordingly be context centred and will presume a considerable amount of knowledge on the part of the listener (who, after all, probably spoke first). Because the listener is presumed to be knowledgeable, Japanese, Chinese or Finns will often be satisfied with expressing their thoughts in **half-utterances**, indicating that the listener can fill in the rest. It is a kind of compliment one pays one's interlocutor. At such times multi-active, dialogue-oriented people are more receptive than linear-oriented people, who thrive on clearly-expressed linear argument.

Reactive cultures not only rely on utterances and semi-statements to further the conversation, but they indulge in other oriental habits which confuse the westerner. They are, for instance, 'roundabout', using impersonal verbs ('one is leaving') or the passive voice ('one of the machines seems to have been tampered with'), either to deflect blame or with the general aim of politeness.

As reactive cultures tend to use names less frequently than westerners, the impersonal, vague nature of the discussion is further accentuated. Lack of eye contact, so typical of the east, does not help the situation. The Japanese, evading the Spaniard's earnest stare, makes the latter feel that they are being boring or saying something distasteful. Oriental inscrutability (often appearing on a Finn's face as a sullen expression) adds to the feeling that the discussion is leading nowhere. A Finn or a Japanese, embarrassed by another's stare, seeks eye contact only at the beginning of the discussion or when they wish their opponent to take up their 'turn' in the conversation.

Japanese 'opposing' delegations are often quite happy to sit in a line on one side of the table and contemplate a neutral spot on the wall facing them as they converse sporadically or muse in joint silence. The occasional sidelong glance will be used to seek confirmation of a point made. Then it's back to studying the wall again.

Small talk does not come easily to reactive cultures. While Japanese and Chinese trot out well-tried formalisms to indicate courtesy, they tend to regard questions such as 'Well, how goes it?' as direct questions and may take the opportunity to voice a complaint. On other occasions their over-long pauses or slow reactions cause westerners to think they are slow witted or have nothing to say. Turks, in discussion with Germans in Berlin, complained that they never got chance to present their views fully, while the Germans, for their part, thought the Turks had nothing to say. A high-ranking delegation from the Bank of Finland told me recently that, for the same reason, they found it hard to get a word in at international meetings. 'How can we make an impact?' they asked. Japanese suffer more than any other people in this type of gathering.

The westerner should always bear in mind that the actual content of the response delivered by a person from a reactive culture represents only a small part of the significance surrounding the event. Context-centred utterances inevitably attach more importance not to **what** is said, but **how** it is said, **who** said it and what is **behind** what is said. Also, what is **not** said may be the main thrust of the reply.

Self-disparagement is another favourite tactic of reactive cultures. It eliminates the possibility of offending through self-esteem; it may draw the opponent into praising the oriental's conduct or decisions. The westerner must beware of presuming that self-disparagement is connected with a weak position.

Finally, reactive cultures excel in subtle, non-verbal communication which compensates for the absence of frequent interjections. Finns, Japanese and Chinese alike are noted for their sighs, almost inaudible groans and agreeable grunts. A sudden intake of breath in Finland indicates agreement, not shock, as it would in the case of a Latin. The 'oh', 'ha' or 'e' of the Japanese is a far surer indication of concurrence than the fixed smile they often assume.

To summarise, the programme for reactive cultures is sequential in the following manner:

+ listen carefully
+ establish understanding of the other's intent
+ allow a period of silence in order to evaluate
+ query further
+ react in a constructive manner
+ maintain a certain amount of inscrutability
+ imitate the other's strengths or products
+ improve on them
+ refine
+ perfect if possible

Reactive people have large reserves of energy. They are economical in movement and effort and do not waste time reinventing the wheel. Although they always give the impression of having power in reserve, they are seldom aggressive and rarely aspire to leadership (in the case of Japan, this is somewhat surprising in view of her economic might). France, Britain and the USA, on the other hand, have not hesitated to seize world leadership in periods of economic or military dominance.

Data-oriented, dialogue-oriented and listening cultures

Interaction between different peoples involves not only methods of communication, but also the process of gathering information. This brings us to the question of dialogue-oriented and data-oriented cultures. A data-oriented culture is one where one does research to produce lots of information which is then acted on. Swedes, Germans, Americans, Swiss and

1.	Japan	**Strongly**
2.	China	**reactive**
3.	Taiwan	
4.	Singapore, Hong Kong*	
5.	Finland*	
6.	Korea	
7.	Turkey+	
8.	Vietnam, Cambodia, Laos+	
9.	Malaysia, Indonesia+	
10.	Pacific Islands (Fiji, Tonga, etc.)+	

11.	Sweden*	
12.	Britain*	**Occasionally**

----

* Linear-active tendencies when reacting
+ Multi-active tendencies when reacting

Figure 8   Reactive cultures (listeners)

Northern Europeans in general love to gather solid information and move steadily forward from this database. The communications and information revolution is a dream come true for data-oriented cultures. It provides them quickly and efficiently with what dialogue-oriented cultures already know.

Which are the dialogue-oriented cultures? Examples are the Italians and other Latins, Arabs and Indians. These people see events and business possibilities 'in context' because they already possess an enormous amount of information through their own personal information network. Arabs or Portuguese will be well informed about the facts surrounding a deal since they will already have queried, discussed and gossiped in their circle of friends, business acquaintances and extensive family connections. The Japanese (basically a listener) may be even better informed, since the very nature of Japan's web society involves them in an incredibly intricate information network operational during schooldays, college, university, Judo and Karate clubs, student societies, developed intelligence systems and family and political connections.

People from dialogue-oriented cultures like the French or Spanish tend to get impatient when Americans or Swiss feed them with facts and figures which are accurate but, in their opinion, only a part of the big human picture. A Frenchman would consider that an American sales forecast in France is of little meaning if he (the Frenchman) does not have time to develop the correct relationship with the customer on whom the success of the business depends.

It is quite normal in dialogue-oriented cultures for managers to take customers and colleagues with them when they leave a job. They have developed their relationships.

There is a strong correlation between dialogue-oriented and multi-active people. Antonio does ten things at once and is therefore in continuous contact with humans. He obtains from these people an enormous amount of information – far more than Americans or Germans will gather by spending a large part of their day in a private office, door closed, looking at the screen of their personal computer.

Multi-active people are knee deep in information. They know so much that the very brevity of an agenda makes it useless to them. At meetings they tend to ignore agendas or speak out of turn. How can you forecast a conversation? Discussion of one item could make another meaningless. How can you deal with feedback in advance? How can an agenda solve deadlock? Dialogue-oriented people wish to use their personal relations to solve the problem from the human angle. Once this is mentally achieved, then appointments, schedules, agendas, even meetings become superfluous.

If these remarks seem to indicate that dialogue-oriented people, relying on only word of mouth, suffer from serious disadvantages and drawbacks, it should be emphasised that it is very difficult to pass over from one system to the other. It is hard to imagine a Neapolitan company organising its business along American lines with five-year rolling forecasts, quarterly reporting, six-monthly audits and twice-yearly performance appraisals. It is equally hard to imagine Germans introducing a new product in a strange country without first doing a market survey.

It is noticeable that most of the successful economies, with the striking exception of Japan, are in data-oriented cultures using processed information. Japan, although dialogue-oriented, also uses a large amount of printed information. Moreover, productivity also depends on other significant factors, particularly climate, so that information systems, while important, are not the whole story of efficiency and its logic.

One might summarise by saying that a compromise between data-oriented and dialogue-oriented systems would probably lead to good results, but that there are no **clear** examples of this having happened consistently in modern international business communities.

Figure 9 gives a suggested ranking for dialogue-oriented and data-oriented cultures. Figures 10–12 illustrate the relatively few sources of information that data-oriented cultures draw on. The more developed the society, the more we tend to turn to print and database to obtain our facts. The information revolution has accentuated this trend and Germany, along with the USA, Britain and Scandinavia, is well to the fore. Yet printed information and databases are almost necessarily out of date (as anyone who has purchased mailing lists has found out to their cost). Last night's whispers in a Madrid bar or café are hot off the press – Pedro was in Oslo last week and talked Olav off his feet till two in the morning. Few data-oriented people will dig for information and then spread it in this way, although Germans do not fare badly once they get out of their cloistered offices. Northerners' lack of gregariousness again proves a hindrance. By upbringing they are taught **not to pry** – inquisitiveness gains no points in their society – gossip is even worse. What their database cannot tell them they try to find out through official channels – embassies, chambers of commerce, circulated information sheets, perhaps hints provided by friendly companies with experience in the country in question. In business, especially when negotiating, information is power. Sweden, Norway, Australia, New Zealand and several other data-oriented cultures will have to expand and intensify their intelligence-gathering networks in the future if they are to compete with information-hot France, Japan, Italy, Korea, Taiwan and Singapore. It may well be that the EU itself will develop into a **hot-house exchange** of business information to compete with the Japanese network.

Listening cultures

Listening cultures, reactive in nature, combine deference to database and print information (Japan, Finland, Singapore and Taiwan are high tech) with a natural tendency to listen well and enter into sympathetic dialogue. Japanese and Chinese will entertain the prospect of very lengthy discourse

Dialogue

1.   Latin Americans
2.   Italians, Spanish, Portuguese, French
      Mediterranean peoples
3.   Arabs. Africans
4.   Indians, Pakistanis
5.   Chileans
6.   Hungarians, Romanians
7.   Slavs
8.   American subcultures
9.   Benelux
10.   British, Australians
11.   Scandinavians
12.   North Americans (US WASPS* and Canadians),
      New Zealanders, South Africans
13.   Germans, Swiss

Data

* White Anglo-Saxon Protestant

Figure 9   Dialogue-oriented, data-oriented cultures

in order to attain ultimate harmony. In this respect, they are as people ori-
ented as the Latins. The Finns, inevitably more brief, nevertheless base
their dialogue on careful consideration of the wishes of the other party.
They rarely employ 'steamrollering' tactics frequently observable in
American, German and French debate. Monologues are unknown in
Finland, unless practised by the other party.

Listening cultures believe they have the right attitude to information
gathering. They do not precipitate improvident action, they allow ideas to
mature, they are ultimately accommodating in their decisions. The success
of Japan and the four Asian tigers – South Korea, Taiwan, Hong Kong and
Singapore – as well as Finland's prosperity despite few economic strengths,
all bear witness to the resilience of the listening cultures.

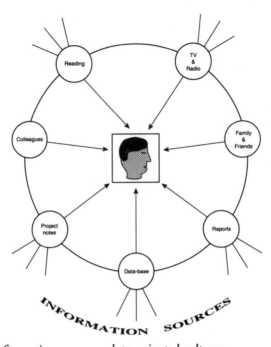

Figure 10   Information sources – data-oriented cultures

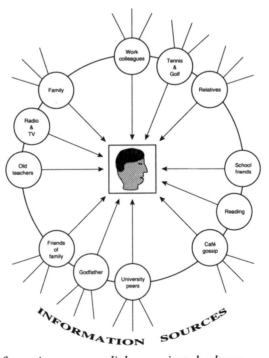

Figure 11   Information sources – dialogue-oriented cultures

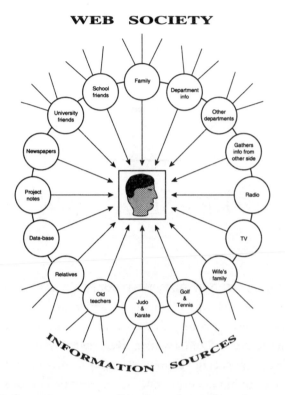

Figure 12   Information sources – listening culture (Japan)

4

THE USE OF TIME

THE WORLD VIEWS HELD BY DIFFERENT CULTURES VARY WIDELY, AS DO A multiplicity of concepts which constitute and represent a kaleidoscopic outlook on the nature of reality. Some of these concepts – fatalism, work ethic, reincarnation, *sisu*, Confucianism, *Weltschmerz*, *dusha*, etc. – are readily identifiable within specific groups, societies or nations. Other concepts – central and vital to human experience – are essentially universal, but subject to strikingly different notions of their nature and essence. Such concepts are those of space and time.

Time, particularly, is seen in a different light by eastern and western cultures and even within these groupings assumes quite dissimilar aspects from country to country. In the western hemisphere, the USA and Mexico employ time in such a diametrically opposing manner that it causes intense friction between the two peoples. In western Europe the Swiss attitude to time bears little relation to that of neighbouring Italy. Thais do not evaluate the passing of time in the same way that the Japanese do. In Britain the future stretches out in front of you. In Madagascar it flows into the back of your head from behind.

Linear time

Let us begin with the American concept of time, for theirs is the most expensive, as anyone who has had to do with American doctors, dentists or lawyers will tell you.

For an American, time is truly money. In a profit-oriented society, time is a precious, even scarce, commodity. It flows fast, like a mountain river in spring, and if you want to benefit from its passing, you have to move fast with it. Americans are people of action; they cannot bear to be idle. Past time is over, but the present you can seize, parcel and package and make it work for you in the immediate future.

Time looks like this:

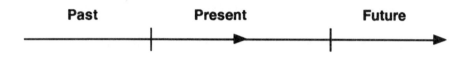

Figure 13

This is what you have to do with it:

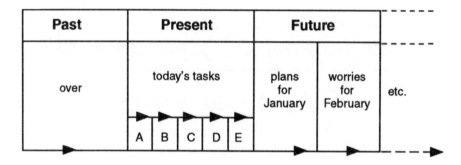

Figure 14

In America you have to make money, otherwise you are nobody. If you have 40 years of earning capacity and you want to make $4 million, that means $100,000 per annum. If you can achieve this in 250 working days that comes to $400 a day or $50 an hour.

Figure 15 suggests that you can make $400 a day if you work 8 hours, performing one task per hour in a planned, time-efficient sequence. In this orientation Americans can say that their time costs $50 an hour. The concept of time **costing** money is one thing. Another idea is that of **wasting** time. If, as in Figure 16, appointments D and E fail to show up, Americans might say that they have wasted 2 hours – or lost $100. Thus:

'Time is money!'

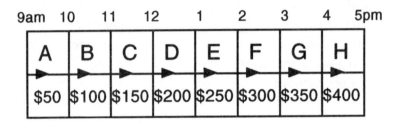

9am	10	11	12	1	2	3	4	5pm
A	B	C	D	E	F	G	H
►	►	►	►	►	►	►	►
$50	$100	$150	$200	$250	$300	$350	$400

8 hours of his time <u>cost</u> $400

Figure 15

9am	10	11	12	1	2	3	4	5pm
A	B	C	D	E	F	G	H
►	►	►	►	►	►	►	►
$50	$100	$150	did not show	did not show	$200	$250	$300

he wasted 2 hours or lost $100!

Figure 16

This seems logical enough, until one begins to apply the idea to other cultures. Has the Portuguese fisherman, who failed to hook a fish for two hours, wasted his time? Has the Sicilian priest, failing to make a convert on Thursday, lost ground? Have the German composer, the French poet, the Spanish painter, devoid of ideas last week, skipped opportunities which can be qualified in monetary terms?

The Americans are not the only ones who sanctify timekeeping, for it is a religion in Switzerland and Germany, too. These countries, along with Britain, the Anglo-Saxon world in general, the Netherlands, Austria and Scandinavia, have a linear vision of time and action which the above figures have illustrated. They suspect, like the Americans, that time passing without decisions being made or actions being performed is streaking away unutilized in a linear present and future.

Anglo-Saxon, Germanic and Scandinavian peoples are essentially linear-active, time-dominated and monochronic. They prefer to do one thing at a time, concentrate on it and do it within a scheduled timescale. They think that in this way they get more things done – and efficiently. Furthermore, being imbued with the Protestant work ethic, they equate working time with success. (The harder you work – more hours, that is – the more successful you will be, the more money you will make). This idea might sound reasonable in American ears, would carry less weight in class-conscious Britain, and would be viewed as entirely unrealistic in southern European countries where authority, privilege and birthright negate the theory at every turn. In a society such as existed in the Soviet Union one could postulate that those who achieved substantial remuneration by working little (or not at all) were the most successful of all.

Multi-actives

Southern Europeans are multi-active, rather than linear-active. The more things they can do or handle at the same time, the happier and the more fulfilled they feel. They organize their time (and lives) in an entirely different way from Americans, Germans and Swiss. Multi-active peoples are not very interested in schedules or punctuality. They pretend to observe them, especially if a linear-active partner insists, but they consider reality to be more important than appointments. In their ordering of things, priority is given to the relative thrill or significance of each meeting. Spaniards, Italians, Arabs ignore the passing of time if it means that conversations would be left unfinished. For them, completing a **human transaction** is the best way they can invest their time. Germans and Swiss love clock-regulated time, for it appears to them as a remarkably efficient, impartial and very precise way of organising life – especially in business. For an Italian, on the other hand, time considerations will usually be subjected to human feelings. 'Why are you so angry because I came at 9.30?', he asks his German colleague. 'Because it says 9am in my diary', says the German. 'Then why don't you write 9.30 and then we'll both be happy?' is a logical Italian response. The business we have to do and our close relations are so important that it is irrelevant at what time we meet. The **meeting** is what counts. Germans and Swiss cannot swallow this, as it offends their sense of order, of tidiness, of pre-arrangement.

A Spaniard would take the side of the Italian. There is a reason for the Spaniard's lax adherence to punctuality. The German believes in a simple truth – scientific truth. The Spaniard, in contrast, is always conscious of the double truth – that of immediate reality as well as that of the poetic whole.

The German thinks they see eye to eye, as in Figure 17:

Figure 17

In fact the Spaniard, with the consciousness of double truth, sees it as in Figure 18:

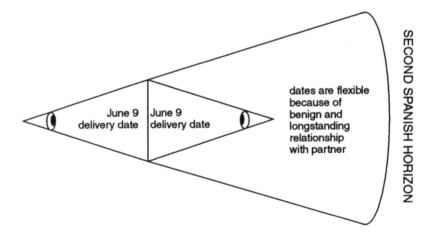

Figure 18

As far as meetings are concerned, it is better not to turn up strictly on time for Spanish appointments. **In Spain, punctuality messes up schedules**, as in Figure 19.

Few northern Europeans or North Americans can reconcile themselves to the multi-active use of time. Germans and Swiss, unless they reach an understanding of the underlying psychology, will be driven to distraction. Germans see compartmentalisation of programmes, schedules, procedures

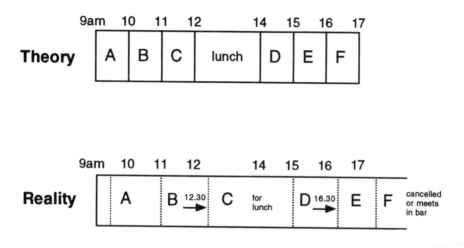

Figure 19

and production as the surest route to efficiency. The Swiss, even more time and regulation dominated, have made **precision** a national symbol. This applies to their watch industry, their optical instruments, their pharmaceutical products, their banking. Planes, buses and trains leave on the dot. Accordingly, everything can be exactly calculated and predicted.

In countries inhabited by linear-active people, time is clock and calendar related, segmented in an abstract manner for our convenience, measurement and disposal. In multi-active cultures like the Arab and Latin spheres, time is event or personality related, a subjective commodity which can be manipulated, moulded, stretched or dispensed with, irrespective of what the clock says. 'I have to rush.' says the American, 'my time is up'. The Spaniard or Arab, scornful of this submissive attitude to schedules, would only use this expression if death were imminent.

Cyclic time

Both the linear-active Northerner and the multi-active Latin think that they **manage** time in the best way possible. In some Eastern cultures, however, the **adaptation** of humans to time is seen as a viable alternative. In these cultures time is viewed neither as linear nor event–personality related, but as **cyclic**. Each day the sun rises and sets, the seasons follow one another, the heavenly bodies revolve around us, people grow old and die, but their children reconstitute the process. We know this cycle has gone on for one hundred thousand years and more. Cyclical time is not a scarce commodity. There would seem to be an unlimited supply of it just around the next bend. As they say in the East, when God made time, he made plenty of it.

As many Asians are keenly aware of the cyclical nature of time, business decisions are arrived at in a different way from in the West. Westerners often expect an Asian to make a quick decision or treat a current deal on its present merits, irrespective of what has happened in the past. Asians cannot do this. The past formulates the contextual background to the present decision, about which in any case, as Asians, they must think long term – their hands are tied in many ways. Americans see time passing without decisions being made or actions performed as 'wasted'. Asians do not see time as racing away unutilised in a linear future, but coming round again in a circle, where the same opportunities, risks, dangers will re-present themselves when people are so many days, weeks or months wiser. How often do we (in the West) say 'If I had known then what I know now, I would never have done what I did'?

Figure 20 compares the speed of Western **action chains** with Asian reflection. The American goes home satisfied with all tasks completed. The German and the Swiss probably do the same; the French or Italian might leave some 'mopping up' for the following day. John Paul Fieg, describing the Thai attitude to time, saw it as a pool which they could gradually walk around. This metaphor applies to most Asians, who, instead of tackling problems immediately in sequential fashion, circle round them for a few days (weeks etc.) before committing themselves. After a suitable period of reflection, A,D and F may indeed seem worthy of pursuing. B,C and E may be quietly dropped. Contemplation of the whole scene has indicated, however, that task G (not envisaged at all earlier on) might be the most significant of all.

In a Buddhist culture – Thailand is a good example, although Buddhist influence pervades large areas of Asia – not only time but life itself goes round in a circle. Whatever we plan in our diary, however we organise our particular world, generation follows generation, governments and rulers will succeed each other, crops will be harvested, monsoons, earthquakes and other catastrophes will recur, taxes will be paid, the sun and moon will rise and set, stocks and shares will rise and fall. Even the Americans will not change such events, certainly not by rushing things.

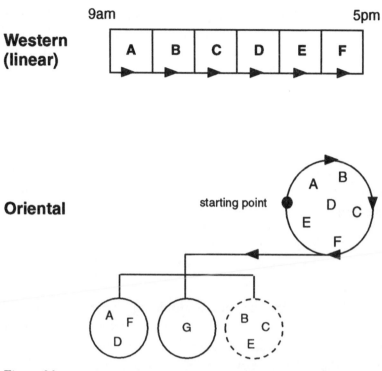

Figure 20

Chinese

Chinese, like most Asians, 'walk round the pool' in order to make well-considered decisions, but they also have a keen sense of the value of time. This can be noticed especially in their attitude towards taking up other people's time, for which they frequently apologize. It is customary, at the end of a meeting in China, to thank the participants for contributing their valuable time. Punctuality on arrival is also considered important – more so than in many Asian countries. Indeed, when meetings are scheduled between two people, it is not unusual for a Chinese to arrive 15–30 minutes early 'in order to finish the business before the time appointed for its discussion', so not stealing any of the other person's time! It is also considered polite in China to announce, 10 or 15 minutes after a meeting has begun, that one will soon have to be going. Again, the worthy aim involved is to economise on their use of your time. The Chinese will not go, of course, until the transaction has been completed, but the point has been made.

This is indeed a double standard. The Chinese penchant for humility demands that the interlocutor's time be seen as precious, but on the other hand Chinese expect a liberal amount of time to be allocated to repeated consideration of the details of a transaction and to the careful nurturing of personal relationships surrounding the deal. They frequently complain that Americans, in China to do business, often have to catch their plane back to the US 'in the middle of the discussion'. The American sees the facts as having been adequately discussed; the Chinese feels that he has not yet attained that degree of closeness – that satisfying sense of common trust and intent – that is for him the bedrock of the deal and of other transactions in the future.

Japanese

The Japanese have a keen sense of the **unfolding** of time – this is well described by Joy Hendry in her book *Wrapping Culture*. People familiar with Japan are well aware of the contrast between the breakneck pace maintained by the Japanese factory worker on the one hand, and the unhurried contemplation to be observed in Japanese gardens or the agonisingly slow tempo of a Noh play on the other. What Hendry emphasises, however, is the meticulous, resolute manner in which the Japanese **segment** time. This segmentation does not follow the American or German pattern, where tasks are assigned in a logical sequence aiming at maximum efficiency and speed in implementation. The Japanese are more concerned, not with how long something takes to happen, but with how time is divided up in the interests of properness, courtesy and tradition.

There are various phases and layers, for instance, in most Japanese social gatherings, e.g. retirement parties, weddings, parent–teacher association meetings. On such occasions in Sicily or Andalucia, people would arrive at different times, the event would gradually attain momentum and most satisfaction would be derived from spontaneous, often exuberant behaviour or speech-making which would follow no strict pattern or ritual. There would be no distinct phases for passing from one activity to the next, whether eating, drinking, toasting, playing music, dancing or gossiping.

In Japan, by contrast, there would be quite **marked beginnings and endings**. At Japanese weddings, for example, guests are often required to proceed from room to room, as the ceremony and celebrations unfold, usually according to a strict schedule. The total time involved is not so important; it is the significance of passing from one phase of activity to another which puts a particular Japanese stamp on the event.

In a conformist and carefully regulated society, Japanese like to know at all times where they stand and where they are at: this applies both to social and business situations. The mandatory, two-minute exchange of business cards between executives meeting each other for the first time is one of the clearest examples of a time activity segment being used to mark the beginning of a relationship. Hendry points out that this 'marking' applies to a wide variety of events in Japanese society, in many cases where 'phases' would have little significance in the West. An example she gives is the start and finish of all types of classes in Japan, where activity cannot take place without being preceded by a formal request on the part of the students for the teacher to begin and a ritualistic expression of appreciation at the end.

Other events which require not only clearly defined beginnings and endings, but also unambiguous phase-switching signals, are the tea ceremony, New Year routines, annual cleaning of the house, cherry blossom viewing, spring 'offensives' (strikes), wrapping up of agricultural cycles, midsummer festivities, gift-giving routines, get-togethers of school and university colleagues, company picnics, *sake*-drinking sessions, approaching Shinto shrines or Buddhist temples, even the peripheral rituals surrounding judo, karate and kendo sessions. None of the above activities can be entered into by a Japanese in the casual, direct manner which a westerner might adopt. The American or northern European has a natural tendency to make a quick approach to the heart of things. The Japanese, in direct contrast, must experience an 'unfolding' or 'unwrapping' of the significant phases of the event. It has to do with Asian indirectness, but in Japan it also involves love of compartmentalisation of procedure, of tradition, of the beauty of ritual. Hendry suggests that this 'unwrapping' is a consequence of the Japanese having wrapped things up in the first place – social wrapping, the wrapping of the body, of space, of people. The fact that the Japanese imposed both the Chinese and Gregorian calendars on their earlier system means that the Japanese year itself is a veritable series of layers of openings and closings.

To summarize, when dealing with Japanese, one can assume that they will be generous in their allocation of time to you or your particular transaction. In return, you are advised to try to do the 'right thing at the right time'. In Japan, form and symbols are more important than content.

Back to the future

In the linear-active, industrialised western cultures time is seen as a road along which we proceed. Life is sometimes referred to as a 'journey' – one also talks about the 'end of the road'. We imagine ourselves as having travelled along that part of the road which is behind us (the past) and we see the untrodden path of the future stretching out in front of us.

Linear-oriented people do not regard the future as entirely unknowable, for they have already nudged it along certain channels by meticulous planning. American executives, with their quarterly forecast, will tell you how much money they are going to make in the next three months. The Swiss stationmaster will assure you, without any hesitation, that the train from Zurich to Luzern will leave at 9.03 tomorrow morning and arrive at exactly 10.05. He is probably right, too. Watches, calendars and computers are devices which not only encourage punctuality, but get us into the habit of working towards targets and deadlines. In a sense, we are 'making the future happen'. We cannot know everything (it would be disastrous for horse racing and detective stories), but we eliminate future unknowns to the best of our ability. Our personal programming tells us that over the next year we are going to get up at certain times, work so many hours, take holidays for designated periods, play tennis on Saturday mornings and pay our taxes on the 28th of each month.

Observers of cyclic time are less disciplined in their planning of the future, since they believe that it cannot be managed and that humans make life easier for themselves by 'harmonizing' with the laws and cyclic events of nature. Yet in such cultures a general form of planning is still possible, for the seasons and other features of nature (except earthquakes, hurricanes, etc.) are fairly regular and well understood. Cyclic time is not seen as a straight road leading from our feet to the horizon, but as a curved one which in one year's time will lead us through 'scenery' and conditions very similar to what we experience at the present moment.

Cultures observing both linear and cyclic concepts of time see the past as something we have put behind us and the future as something which lies before us. In Madagascar, the opposite is the case (see Figure 21). The Malagasy imagine the future as flowing into the back of their head, or passing them from behind, then becoming the past as it stretches out in front of them. The past is **in front of** their eyes because it is visible, known and influential. They can look at it, enjoy it, learn from it, even 'play' with it.

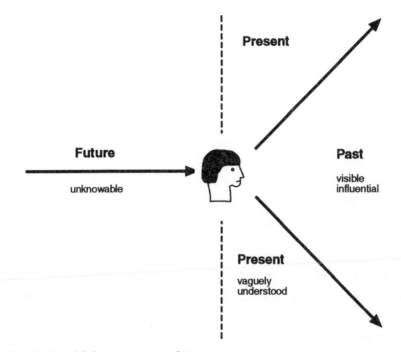

Figure 21   Malagasy concept of time

The Malagasy people spend an inordinate amount of time consulting their ancestors, exhuming their bones, partying with them.

By contrast the Malagasy consider the future unknowable. It is behind their head where they do not have eyes. Their plans for this unknown area will be far from meticulous, for what can they be based on? Buses in Madagascar leave, not according to a predetermined timetable, but when the bus is full. The situation triggers the event. The Malagasy sees this as common sense: the 'best' time for the bus departure is when it fills, for not only does this make economic sense, but it was also the time that most passengers chose to leave. Consequently in Madagascar stocks are not replenished until shelves are empty, filling stations order petrol only when they run dry, and hordes of would-be passengers at the airport find that, in spite of OK tickets, in reality everybody is waitlisted. The actual assignation of seats takes place between the opening of the check-in desk and the (eventual) departure of the plane.

Validity of time concepts

The Malagasy, the Thai, the Japanese, the Spaniard and many others will continue to use time in ways which will conflict with linear-oriented cultures in social and business spheres. The conflict is sharpest in the fields of economics, commerce and industry.

The objective view of time and its sequential effects is, however, favourable to historicity and to everything connected with industrialised organisation. Just as we conceive of our objectified time as extending in the future in the same way that it extends in the past, we mirror our records of the past in our estimates, budgets and schedules. We build up a commercial structure based on time *pro rata* values: time wages, rent, credit, interest, depreciation charges and insurance premiums. In general we are confident (in North America and northern Europe) that we have approached the optimum management of time. Many cultures (including powerful economies of the future, such as China, Japan and South-East Asia) will only allow the linear-oriented concept of time to dictate their behaviour to a limited extent. Industrial organisation demands a certain degree of synchronisation of schedules and targets, but the underlying philosophies concerning the best and most efficient use of time – and the manner in which it should be spent – may remain radically different.

5

STATUS, LEADERSHIP AND ORGANISATION

Cultural roots of organisation

THE BEHAVIOUR OF THE MEMBERS OF ANY CULTURAL GROUP IS dependent, almost entirely, on the history of the people in that society. It is often said that we fail to learn the lessons of history – and indeed we have seen mistakes repeated over hundreds of years by successive generations – but in the very long run (and we may be talking in millennia) a people will adhere collectively to the set of norms, reactions and activities which their experience and development have shown to be most beneficial for them. Their history may have consisted of good and bad years (or centuries), migrations, invasions, conquests, religious disputes or crusades, tempest, floods, droughts, sub-zero temperatures, disease and pestilence. They may have experienced brutality, oppression or near-genocide. Yet, if they survive, their culture, to some extent, has proved successful.

Besides being a creation of historical influence and climatic environment, the mentality of a culture – the inner workings and genius of the mindset – are also dictated by the nature and characteristics of the language of the group. The restricted liberties of thought that any particular tongue allows will have a pervasive influence on considerations of vision, charisma, emotion, poetic feeling, discipline and hierarchy.

Societal training

Historical experience, geographic and geo-linguistic position, physiology and appearance, instinct for survival – all combine to produce a core of beliefs and values which will sustain and satisfy the aspirations and needs of a given society. Based on these influences and beliefs, societal cultural conditioning of the members of the group is established and consolidated (for as many generations as the revered values continue to assure survival and success). Infants and youth are trained by their parents, teachers, peers and elders. The characteristics of the group gradually emerge and diverge from those of other groups. Basic needs of food, shelter and escaping from predators are dealt with first. Social, economic and military challenges will ensue. Traumatic historical developments may divert the traditional thrust of the programming. Japan's *samurai* traditions, discredited in 1945–6, gave way to growing enthusiasm for success in industry and commerce.

At all events, in victory or defeat, in prosperity or recession, a society needs to be organised, adapted or reorganised according to external pressures and its own objectives. Cultural groups organise themselves in strikingly different ways and think about such matters as authority, power, cooperation, aims, results and satisfaction in a variety of manners.

Individual and collective leadership

The term 'organisation' automatically implies leadership – people in authority who write the rules for the system. There are many historical examples of leadership having been vested in the person of one man or woman – Alexander the Great, Tamerlane, Louis XIV, Napoleon, Queen Elizabeth I, Joan of Arc are clear examples. Others, equally renowned and powerful but less despotic (Washington, Bismarck, Churchill) ruled and acted with the acquiescence of their fellow statesmen. Parliamentary rule, introduced by the British in the early part of the seventeenth century, initiated a new type of collective leadership at government level, although this had existed at regional, local and tribal levels for many centuries. Minoan collective rule – one of the earliest examples we know about – inspired a similar type of leadership both in the Greek city-states and later in Rome. In another hemisphere, Mayan and North American Indians held similar traditions.

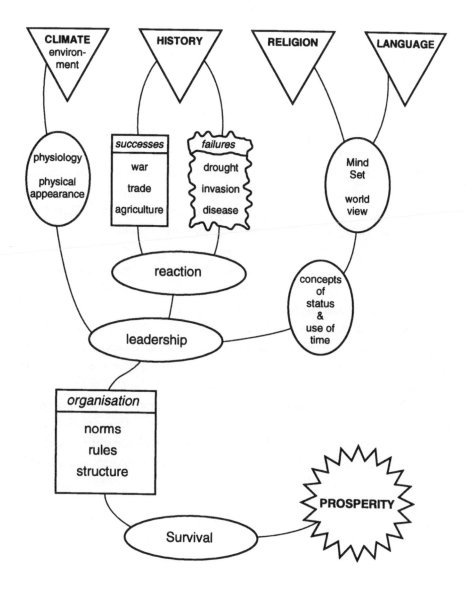

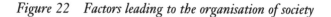

Figure 22   Factors leading to the organisation of society

In the business world, a series of individuals have also demonstrated outstanding abilities and success in leadership – Ford, Rockefeller, Agnelli, Berlusconi, Barnevik, Gyllenhammer, Iacocca, Geneen, Matsushita and Morita are some of them. It is now common for leadership and authority also to be vested in boards of directors or management committees.

The way in which a cultural group goes about structuring its commercial and industrial enterprises or other types of organisations usually reflects to a considerable degree the manner in which it itself is organised. The basic questions to be answered are how authority is organised; and what authority is based on. Western and eastern answers to these questions vary enormously, but in the West alone there are striking differences in attitude. There is, for instance, precious little similarity in the organisational patterns of French and Swedish companies, while Germans and Australians have almost diametrically opposing views as to the basis of authority.

Organisations are usually created by leaders, whether the leadership is despotic, individual or collective. Leadership functions in two modes – one of **networking** and one of **task orientation**. In network mode the concerns, in order of appearance, are the status of the leader(s), the chain of command, the management style, the motivation of the employees and the language of management used to achieve this. In task-orientation mode, the leadership must tackle issues, formulate strategies, create some form of work ethic, decide on efficiency, task distribution and use of time.

Managers in linear-active cultures will demonstrate and look for technical competence, place facts before sentiment, logic before emotion; they will be deal oriented, focusing their own attention and that of their staff on immediate achievement and results. They are orderly, stick to agendas and inspire with their careful planning.

Multi-active managers are much more extrovert, rely on their eloquence and ability to persuade, use human force as an inspirational factor. They often complete human transactions emotionally, assigning the time this may take – developing the contact to the limit.

Leaders in reactive cultures are equally people oriented, but dominate with knowledge, patience and quiet control. They display modesty and courtesy, despite their accepted seniority. They excel in creating a harmonious atmosphere for teamwork. Subtle body language obviates the need for an abundance of words. They know their company well (having spent years going round the various departments): this gives them balance – the ability to react to a web of pressures. They are paternalistic.

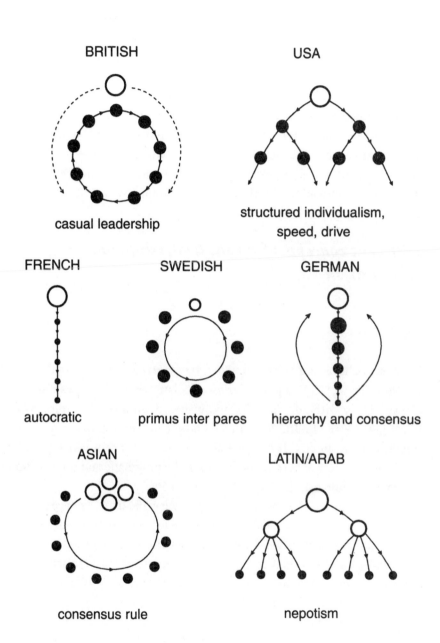

Figure 23 Leadership styles

Because of the diverse values and core beliefs of different societies, concepts of leadership and organisation are inevitably culture bound. Authority might be based on achievement, wealth, education, charisma or birthright. Corporations may be structured in a vertical, horizontal or matrix fashion and may be moulded according to religious, philosophical or governmental considerations and requirements. No two cultures view the essence of authority, hierarchy or optimum structure in an identical light. International exposure and experience will suggest a series of norms, rationalisations and patterns; these will invariably be eroded, even in the short run, by unswerving local beliefs about human values and interaction.

Different concepts of status, leadership and organisation

GERMANY

Germans believe in a world governed by *Ordnung*, where everything and everyone has a place in a grand design calculated to produce maximum efficiency. It is difficult for the impulsive Spaniard, the improvising Portuguese or the soulful Russian to conceive of German *Ordnung* in all its tidiness and symmetry. It is essentially a German concept which goes further in its theoretical perfection than even the pragmatic and orderly intent of Americans, British, Dutch and Scandinavians.

Germans, just as they believe in simple, scientific truth, believe that true *Ordnung* is achievable, provided that sufficient rules, regulations and procedures are firmly in place. In the business world, established, well-tried procedures have emerged from the long experience of Germany's older companies and conglomerates, guided by the maturity of tested senior executives. In Germany, more than anywhere else, there is no substitute for experience. Seniors pass on their knowledge to people immediately below them. There is a clear chain of command in each department and information and instructions are passed down from the top. Status of managers is based partly on achievement, but this is seen as interwoven with the length of service and ascribed wisdom of the individual, as well as formal qualifications and depth of education.

Hierarchy and consensus

German management is, however, not exclusively autocratic. While the vertical structure in each department is clear, considerable value is placed on consensus. German striving for perfection of systems carries with it the implication that the manager who vigorously applies and monitors these processes is showing faith in a framework which has proved successful for all. Few junior employees would question the rules. As there is adequate protection in German law for dissenting staff, most Germans feel comfortable in a rather tight framework which would irritate Americans and British. Germans welcome close instruction: they know where they stand and what they are expected to do. They enjoy being told twice, or three or four times.

German managers, issuing orders, can motivate by showing solidarity with their staff in following procedures. They work long hours, obey the rules themselves and, although they generally expect immediate obedience, they insist on fair play.

In task-orientation mode, German basic values dominate strategies. The use of time resembles the American: meetings begin on the dot, appointments are strictly observed, late arrivals must be signalled by telephone calls in advance, time is linear and should not be wasted. The work ethic is taken for granted and although staff working hours are not overlong and holidays are frequent, the German obsession with completing action chains means that projects are usually completed within the assigned period. Each department is responsible for its own tasks and there is far less horizontal communication between equals across the divisions of a German company than there is in US and British firms. Secrecy is respected in Germany both in business and private. Few German companies publish their figures for public consumption or even for the benefit of their own employees.

Working with Germans

Latins and some Anglo-Saxons frequently experience some difficulty in working or dealing with Germans on account of the relatively rigid framework of procedures within which many German companies operate.

Cooperating successfully with Germans means respecting their primary values. First, status must be established according to **their** standards.

Efficiency and results will win the day in due course, but a foreign national must have adequate formal qualifications to make an initial impression. The German manager with a university degree is promoted on an average every four years and those possessing doctorates have a career path to top management. Punctuality and orderliness are basic. Get there first, avoid sloppiness or untidiness in appearance, behaviour and thought. Procedures should always be written down, for Germans read them, and so should you. While familiarising yourself thoroughly with the rules and processes of the organisation, any instructions you yourself issue should be firm and unambiguous. If you want something written in black ink, not blue, then you should make this clear. Germans want content, detail and clarity – they hate misunderstandings.

It is advisable to strive for consensus at all times, although no one is going to chop and change. Consensus is obtained by clarification and justification, not by persuasion or truly open discussion. Consensus taking creates solidarity, which makes everyone feel comfortable. Each participant in the discussion makes a contribution, but does not query a superior too energetically and certainly does not question their judgement.

Hierarchical constraints necessitate your knowing the exact pecking order in the chain of command; you should also know **your** rung. Superiors generally address subordinates in a low voice, contrary to what many non-Germans believe. German directness enables you to point out when something is being done in an incorrect manner or when mistakes are being made. If the criticism is clearly constructive or designed to help, it will usually be accepted readily. If you are too subtle in your criticism, it may not register at all.

Subordinates in difficulties should be supervised, helped, advised, instructed, monitored. If no help is asked for, or probably not required, then tasks should not be interrupted. Quiet single-mindedness is admired in Germany, so don't try to do six things at once. Don't leave anything unfinished. If you are working hard, **show** it; a casual approach will be misunderstood.

Finally, communication is vertical, not horizontal. Don't go **across** the company to chat with people at your level in other departments. Most of your business ideas should be communicated to either your immediate superior or immediate subordinate. You do **not** have the ear of the chairman, however benignly he may smile at you – unless you are vice-chairman.

FRANCE

French management style is more autocratic than German, although this is not always evident at first glance. German companies are highly structured with clearly visible hierarchies, but these are normally readily accepted and welcomed by the staff. In France the boss often seems to have a more roving role, using '*tu*' to subordinates and often patting them on the back. Such behaviour is, however, quite deceptive, as is the frequent donning of overalls by Japanese company presidents when they visit the factory floor.

Oratorical style

The French chief executive's status is attributed on grounds of family, age, education and professional qualifications, with the emphasis on oratorical ability and mastery of the French language. Preferably he was 'finished' at the *Ecole normale supérieure* – an élitist establishment way ahead in prestige of any French university. French managers can well be described as élitist themselves – all-round *cadres* who are familiar with all or most of the aspects of their business or company, able to deal with production, organisational procedures, meetings, marketing, personnel matters and accounting systems as the occasion requires. They have less specialisation than US or British managers, but generally have wider horizons and an impressive grasp of the many issues facing their company.

The French leader

French history has spawned great leaders who have often enjoyed (frequently with little justification) the confidence of the nation. Napoleon and Pétain are remembered for their heroics rather than for their disasters; Louis XIV, Joan of Arc, Charles de Gaulle, André Malraux were charismatic figures who excited the French penchant for *panache* and smashed the mediocrity and mundanity that surrounded them. Ultimate success in French culture is less important than the collective soaring of the national pulse – the thrill of the chase or crusade. French failures are always glorious ones (check with Napoleon Bonaparte).

While mistakes by German executives are not easily forgiven and American managers are summarily fired if they lose money, there is a high tolerance in French companies of blunders on the part of management. As management is highly personalised, it falls on the manager to make many decisions on a daily basis and it is expected that a good proportion of them will be incorrect. The humanistic leanings of French and other Latin-based cultures encourage the view that human error must be anticipated and allowed for. *Cadres* assume responsibility for their decisions, which they made individually, but it is unlikely that they will be expected to resign if these backfire. If they are of the right age and experience and possess impeccable professional qualifications, replacing them would not only be futile, but would point a dagger at the heart of the system. For the French, attainment of immediate objectives is secondary to the ascribed reputation of the organisation and its sociopolitical goals. The highly organic nature of a French enterprise implies interdependence, mutual tolerance and teamwork among its members as well as demonstrated faith in the (carefully) appointed leader. French managers, who 'relish the art of commanding', are encouraged to excel in their work by the very intensity of expectation on the part of their subordinates.

Role in society

Such expectation produces a paternalistic attitude among French managers not unlike that demonstrated by Japanese, Malaysian and other Asian executives. In the case of the French, emotion is a factor and managers or department heads will concern themselves with the personal and private problems of their staff. In addition to their commercial role in the company, French managers see themselves as valued leaders in society. Indeed, *cadres* see themselves as contributing to the well-being of the state itself. Among the largest economies of the world, only Japan exercises more governmental control over business than the French. French protectionism dates back to the seventeenth century, when increased trade and exports were seen as a natural consequence of French military successes. Modern French companies such as Rhône Poulenc, Aérospatiale, Dassault, Elf Aquitaine, Framatome, Renault and Peugeot are seen as symbols of French grandeur and are 'looked after' by the state. A similar situation exists in Japan and to some extent Sweden.

The prestige and exalted position enjoyed by the French manager is not without its drawbacks both for the enterprise and for the national economy. By concentrating authority around the chief executive, opinions of experienced middle managers and technical staff (often close to customers and markets) do not always carry the weight that they would in Anglo-Saxon or Scandinavian companies. It is true that French managers debate issues at length with their staff, often examining all aspects in great detail. The decision, however, is usually made alone and not always on the basis of the evidence. If the chief executive's views are known in advance, it is not easy to reverse them. Furthermore, senior managers are less interested in the bottom line than in the perpetuation of their power and influence in the company and in society. Again, their contacts and relationships at highest levels may transcend the implications of any particular transaction. A Swedish executive I interviewed who had worked for a French company was appalled by the secrecy of motivation maintained by French senior executives. Information was not allowed to filter down below certain levels. In Sweden authority is delegated downwards as much as possible. In high context France, managers expect that their staff will know what to do – the logic will be evident.

BRITAIN

The feudal as well as imperial origins of status and leadership in England are still evident in some aspects of British management. A century has passed since Britain occupied a preeminent position in industry and commerce, but there still lingers in the national consciousness the proud recollection of once having ruled 15 million square miles of territory on five continents. The best young men were sent abroad on overseas postings to gain experience and to be groomed for leadership. It was the English, Scots and Irish who provided the main thrust of society in the USA – the power which was to assume the mantle of economic hegemony.

The class system persists in the UK and status is still derived, in some degree, from pedigree, title and family name. There is little doubt that the system is on its way to becoming a meritocracy – the emergence of a very large middle class and the efforts of the left and centrist politicians will eventually align British egalitarianism with that of the US and Northern Europe – but it is worth noting that many characteristics of British management hark back to earlier days.

British managers could be described as diplomatic, tactful, laid back, casual, reasonable, helpful, willing to compromise and seeking to be fair. They also consider themselves to be inventive and, on occasion, lateral thinkers. They see themselves as conducting business with grace, style, humour, wit, eloquence and self-possession. They have the English fondness for debate and regard meetings as occasions to seek agreement rather than to issue instructions.

Toughness and insularity

There is a veneer to British management style which hardly exists in such countries as Canada, Australia, Germany, Finland and the USA. Under the casual refinement and sophistication of approach exists a hard streak of pragmatism and mercenary intent. When the occasion warrants it, British managers can be as resilient and ruthless as their tough American cousins, but less explicitly and with disarming poise. Subordinates appreciate their willingness to debate and tendency to compromise, but also anticipate a certain amount of deviousness and dissimulation. Codes of behaviour within a British company equip staff to absorb and cope with a rather obscure management style. Other problems arise when British senior executives deal with European, American and Eastern businesspeople. In spite of their penchant for friendliness, hospitality and desire to be fair, British managers' adherence to tradition endows them with an insular obstinacy resulting in a failure to comprehend differing values in others.

Linguistic arrogance

At international meetings British delegates frequently distinguish themselves by their poise, charm and eloquence, but often leave the scene having learned little or nothing from their more successful trading partners. As such conferences are usually held in English, they easily win the war of words; this unfortunately increases their linguistic arrogance. One huge German insurance firm bought a sizeable British firm lock, stock and barrel. The top and middle executives of the German company were nearly all fluent in English, but advised the managers of the British company to acquire a modicum of German to use in social situations. This was issued in the form of a directive. Two years later none of the senior staff of the British firm had taken a single German lesson.

I recently gave a series of cross-cultural seminars to executives of an English car group which had been taken over by a German auto industry giant. The Germans attending the seminars, although occasionally struggling with terminology, listened eagerly to the remarks about British psychology and cultural habits. The British participants, with one or two notable exceptions, paid only casual attention to the description of German characteristics, took hardly any notes, were unduly flippant about Germany's role in Europe and thought the population and GDP of the two countries were roughly equal! Only one of the British spoke German and that at a very modest level.

Calm approach to tasks

As far as task orientation is concerned, British managers perform better. They are not sticklers for punctuality, but time wasting is not endemic in British companies and staff take pride in completing tasks thoroughly, although in their own time frame. British managers like to leave at five or six, as do their subordinates, but work is often taken home. As for strategies, managers generally achieve a balance between short- and long-term planning. Interim failures are not unduly frowned on and there are few pressures to make a quick buck. Teamwork is encouraged and often achieved, although it is understood that individual competition may be fierce. It is not unusual for managers to have 'direct lines' to staff members, especially those whom they favour or consider intelligent and progressive. Chains of command are observed less than in German and French companies. The organisation subscribes in general to the Protestant work ethic, but this must be observed against a background of smooth, unhurried functions and traditional self-confidence. The contrast with the immediacy and driving force of American management is quite striking when one considers the commonality of language and heritage as well as the Anglo-Celtic roots of US business.

AMERICA

The Puritan work ethic and the right to dissent dominated the mentality of the early American settlers. It was an Anglo-Saxon-Celtic, Northern European culture, but the very nature and hugeness of the terrain, along with the advent of independence, soon led to the 'frontier spirit' which has characterized the US mindset since the end of the eighteenth century.

The vast lands of America were an entrepreneur's dream. Unlimited expanses of wilderness signified unlimited wealth which could be exploited, if one moved quickly enough, without taking it away from others. Only Siberia has offered a similar challenge in modern times.

The nature of the challenge soon produced American values: speed was of the essence; you acted individually and in your own interest; the wilderness forced you to be self-reliant, tough, risk taking; you did not easily cede what you had claimed and owned; you needed to be aggressive against foreign neighbours; anyone with talent and initiative could get ahead; if you suffered a setback, it was not ultimate failure, there was always more land or opportunity; bonds broken with the past meant that future orientation was all important; you were optimistic about change, for the past had brought little reward; throwing off the yoke of the King of England led to a distrust of supreme authority.

American managers symbolise the vitality and audacity of the land of free enterprise. In most cases they retain the frontier spirit: they are assertive, aggressive, goal and action oriented, confident, vigorous, optimistic, ready for change, achievers used to hard work, instant mobility and making decisions. They are capable of teamwork and corporate spirit, but they value individual freedom above the welfare of the company and their first interest is furthering their own career.

Dollar status

In view of their rebellious beginnings, Americans are reluctant to accord social status to anyone for reasons other than visible achievement. In a land with no traditions of (indeed aversion to) aristocracy, money was seen as the yardstick of progress and very few Americans distance themselves from the pursuit of wealth. Intellectuality and refinement as qualities of leadership are prized less in the USA than in Europe. Leadership means getting things done, improving the standard of living, finding short cuts to prosperity, making money for oneself, one's firm and its shareholders.

With status accorded almost exclusively on grounds of achievement and vitality, age and seniority assume less importance. American managers are often young, female or both. Chief executives are given responsibility and authority and then expected to act. They seldom fail to do so. How long they retain power depends on the results they achieve.

Motivation of American managers and their staff does not have the labyrinthine connotations that it does in European and Oriental companies, for it is usually monetary. Bonuses, performance payments, profit-sharing schemes and stock options are common. New staff, however, are often motivated by the very challenge of getting ahead. Problem-solving, the thrill of competition and the chance to demonstrate resolute action satisfy the aspirations of many young Americans. Unlike Europeans and Orientals, however, they need constant feedback, encouragement and praise from the senior executive.

Strict procedures

In terms of organisation, the rampant individualism in American society is strictly controlled in business life through strict procedures and paperwork. American executives are allowed to make individual decisions, especially when travelling abroad, but usually within the framework of corporate restrictions. Young Americans' need for continual appraisal means that they are constantly supervised. In German companies staff are regularly monitored, but German seniors do not hover. In the USA senior executives pop in and out of offices, sharing information and inspiration with their subordinates ('Say, Jack, I've just had a terrific idea'). Memos, directives, suggestions in writing are ubiquitous. Shareholder pressure makes quarterly reporting and rolling forecasts imperative. The focus is on the bottom line.

Americans can be quickly hired and just as rapidly fired (often without compensation). Being sacked carries no stigma, ('It just didn't work out, we have to let you go'). For the talented, other jobs and companies beckon. There is precious little sentimentality in American business. The deal comes before personal feeling. If the figures are right you can deal with the Devil. If there is no profit, a transaction with a friend is hardly worthwhile. Business is based on punctuality, solid figures, proven techniques, pragmatic reasoning and technical competence. Time is money and Americans show impatience during meetings if Europeans get bogged down in details or when Orientals demur in showing their hand.

Europeans, by contrast, are often miffed by American informality and what they consider to be an oversimplistic approach towards exclusively material goals. Eastern cultures are wary of the litigious nature of American business. Two-thirds of the lawyers on earth are American – a formidable deterrent for members of those societies who settle disputes out of court and believe in long-term harmony with their business partners.

SWEDEN

The Swedish concept of leadership and management differs considerably from other European models and is dealt with in some detail in Chapter 20. Like Swedish society itself, enterprises are essentially 'democratic', although a large percentage of Swedish capital is in private hands. Managers of thousands of middle-sized and even large firms have attained managerial success through subtle self-effacement, but the big multinationals have also thrown up some famous executives who might well claim to be among the most far-seeing business leaders in the world: Carstedt, Gyllenhammar, Wennergren, Barnevik, Carlzon, Wallenberg, Svedberg.

Modern Swedish egalitarianism has age-old cultural roots. Although some historical Swedish monarchs such as Gustav av Vasa and Charles the Great were dominating, compelling figures, the Swedish royals, like those of Denmark and Norway, have espoused democratic principles for many centuries, no doubt mindful of the old Viking *lagom* tradition when warriors passed round the drinking horn (or huge bowl) in a circle where each man had to decide what amount to drink. Not too little to arouse scorn; not too much to deprive others of the liquid.

LATINS

The business cultures of Italy, Spain and Portugal are described in later chapters. In Latin Europe, as well as in South America, the management pattern generally follows that of France, where authority is centred around the chief executive. In middle-sized companies, the CEO is very often the owner of the enterprise and even in very large firms a family name or connections may dominate the structure. More than in France, sons, nephews, cousins and close family friends will figure prominently in key positions. Ubiquitous nepotism means that business partners are often confronted with younger people who seem to have considerable influence on decision making. Delegations may often consist of the company owner, flanked by his brother, son, cousin or even grandson. Women are generally, although not always, excluded from negotiating sessions.

Status is based on age, reputation and often wealth. The management style is autocratic, particularly in Portugal, Spain and South America, where family money is often on the line. There is a growing meritocracy in Brazil, Chile and in the big northern Italian industrial firms, but Latin employees in general indicate willing and trusting subservience to their 'establishments'.

Task orientation is dictated from above, strategies and success depend largely on social and ministerial connections and mutually beneficial cooperation between dominant families. Knowing the right people oils the wheels of commerce in Latin countries, just as it does in Arab and oriental cultures. It helps anywhere, but assumes greater importance in those societies which prioritise the nurturing of human relationships over pragmatic, rapid implementation of transactions based on mere notions of opportunity, technical feasibility and profit.

THE EAST

Cultural values dominate the structure, organisation and behaviour of eastern enterprises more than is the case in the West, in as much as deeply-rooted religious and philosophical beliefs impose near-irresistible codes of conduct. In the Chinese sphere of influence (People's Republic of China, Hong Kong, Taiwan, Singapore) as well as in Japan and Korea, Confucian principles hold sway. Thailand is Buddhist, Indonesia and Malaysia strongly Moslem. Although national differences account for variations in the concepts of status, leadership and organisation, there is a clearly discernible 'eastern model' which is compatible with general Asian values.

This model, whether applied to corporations or departments of civil service or government, strongly resembles family structure. Confucianism, which took final shape in China in the twelfth century, designated family as the prototype of all social organisation. We are members of a group, not individuals. Stability of society is based on unequal relationships between people, as in a family. The hierarchies are father–son, older brother–younger brother, male–female, ruler–subject, senior friend–junior friend. Loyalty to the ruler, filial piety to one's father, right living, would lead to a harmonious social order based on strict ethical rules and headed up in a unified state, governed by men of education and superior ethical wisdom. Virtuous behaviour, protection of the weak, moderation, calmness and thrift were also prescribed.

Confucianism entered Japan with the first great wave of Chinese influence between the sixth and ninth centuries AD. For some time it was overshadowed by Buddhism, but the emergence of the centralized Tokugawa system in the seventeenth century made it more relevant than it had been before. Both Japan and Korea had become thoroughly Confucian by the early nineteenth century in spite of their feudal political systems. In the twentieth century Japanese have wholeheartedly accepted modern science, universalistic principles of ethics, as well as democratic ideals, but they are still permeated, as are the Koreans, with Confucian ethical values. While focusing on progress and growth, strong Confucian traits still lurk beneath the surface, such as the belief in the moral basis of government, the emphasis on interpersonal relationships and loyalties, the faith in education and hard work. Few Japanese and Koreans consider themselves Confucianists today, but in a sense almost all of them are.

Confucianism in business

What do these cultural influences mean in terms of status and leadership? The Chinese ideal was rule by men of superior education and morality rather than by those merely of superior birth. Japanese and Korean business leaders today flaunt qualifications, university and professorial connections more than family name or wealth. Many of the traditional Japanese companies are classic models of Confucian theory, where paternalistic attitudes to employees and their dependants, top-down obligations, bottom-up loyalty, obedience and blind faith are observed to a greater degree than in China itself. Prosperity makes it easier to put Confucianism into practice: in this regard Japan has enjoyed certain advantages over other countries. The sacred nature of the group and the benevolence attributed to its leaders, however, permeate Asian concepts of organisation from Rangoon to Tokyo.

Buddhist and Islamic variations

In Buddhist Thailand and Islamic Malaysia and Indonesia, slight variations in the concept of leadership do little to challenge the idea of benign authority. Thais see a strict hierarchy with the King at its apex, but there is social mobility in Thailand, where several monarchs had humble origins. The patronage system requires complete obedience, but flexibility is assured by the Thai principle that leaders must be sensitive to the problems of their subordinates and that blame must always be passed upwards. Bosses treat their inferiors in an informal manner and give them time off when domestic pressures weigh heavily. Subordinates like the hierarchy.

Buddhism decrees that the man at the top earned his place by meritorious performance in a previous life. In Malaysia and Indonesia status is **inherited**, not earned, but leaders are expected to be paternal, religious, sincere and above all gentle. The Malay seeks a definite role in the hierarchy and neither Malaysians nor Indonesians strive for self-betterment. Promotion must be initiated **from above**; better conformity and obedience than struggling for change. Age and seniority will bring progress.

Life in a group

Although Confucianism, Buddhism and Islam differ greatly in many respects, their adherents see eye to eye in terms of the family nature of the group, the non-competitive according of status, the smooth dispersal of power, the automatic chain of command and the collective nature of decision making. There are variations on this theme, such as the preponderance of influence among certain families in Korea, governmental intervention in China, the tight rein on the media in Singapore and fierce competition and individualism among the entrepreneurs of Hong Kong. Typical Asians, however, acknowledge that they live in a high context culture within a vital circle of associations from which withdrawal would be unthinkable. Their behaviour, both social and professional, is contextualised at all times, whether in the fulfilment of obligations and duties to the group (families, community, company, school friends) or taking refuge in its support and solidarity. They do not see this as a trade-off of autonomy for security, but rather as a fundamental, correct way of living and interacting in a highly developed social context.

In a hierarchical, family-type company, networking is relatively effortless. Motivation is the enhancement of the reputation and prestige of the group, which will result in greater protection and support for its members. Managers guide subordinates to achieve these goals and work longer hours as a shining example. As far as task orientation is concerned, immediate objectives are not as clearly expressed as they would be in, for example, an American company. Long-term considerations take priority and the slow development of personal relationships, both internally and with customers, often blur real aims and intent. Asian staff seem to understand perfectly the long-term objectives without having to have them spelled out explicitly. In Japan, particularly, staff seem to benefit from a form of corporate telepathy – a consequence of the homogeneous nature of the people.

What is work?

The work ethic is taken for granted in Japan, Korea and the Chinese areas, but this is not the case throughout Asia. Malaysians and Indonesians see 'work' as only one of many activities which contribute to the progress and welfare of the group. Time spent (during working hours) at lunch, on the beach or playing sport may be beneficial in deepening relationships between colleagues or clients. Time may be needed to draw on the advice of a valued mentor or to see to some pressing family matter which was distracting an employee from properly performing their duties. Gossip in the office is a form of networking and interaction. Work and play are mixed both in and out of the office in Thailand, where either activity must produce fun (*sanuke*) or it is not worth pursuing. Thais, like Russians, tend to work in fits and starts, depending partly on the proximity of authority and partly on their mood. Koreans – all hustle and bustle when compared to the methodic Japanese – like to be seen to be busy all day long and of all Asians most resemble the Americans in their competitive vigour.

Asian management, when organising activity, attaches tremendous importance to form, symbolism and gesture. The showing of respect, in speech and actions, is mandatory. There must be no loss of face either for oneself or one's opponent and as far as business partners are concerned, red carpet treatment, including lavish entertaining and gift giving, is imperative. Ultimate victory in business deals is the objective, but one must have the patience to achieve this in the right time frame and in the correct manner. This attitude is more deeply rooted among the Chinese and Japanese than in Korea, where wheeling and dealing is frequently indulged in.

Is the Asian, 'family model' efficient? The economic success of Japan and the rates of growth in China, Korea, Malaysia and Taiwan, among others, would indicate that it is. Whatever the reality may be, it would not be easy for westerners to convert to Asiatic systems. Individualism, democratic ideals, material goals, compulsive consumerism, penchant for speed, environmental concerns and a growing obsession with the quality of life (a strange concept in Asia) are powerful, irreversible factors to be reckoned with in North America and Northern Europe. The globalisation process and the increasing determination of the multinational and transnational giants to standardise procedures will result in some convergence of aims, concepts and organisational structure, but divergence in values and world view will sustain organisational diversity well into the twenty-first century.

6

HORIZONS AND TEAM BUILDING

Life within horizons

OUR GENES, OUR PARENTAL AND EDUCATIONAL TRAINING, OUR SOCIETAL rules, our very language, enable us to see so far. Any human being can see as far as their horizon, and that is the limit. We can broaden our horizon to some degree by living in other countries, learning foreign languages, reading books on philosophy, psychology, other cultures and a variety of other subjects. Unless we make such efforts, our horizon remains a British horizon, an American horizon, a Japanese horizon or one of many other world views. In other words, each culture enjoys a certain segment of experience, which is no more than a fraction of the total possible available experience. Benjamin Whorf believed that such segments of experience were limited by the vocabulary and concepts inherent in one's language. By learning more languages, especially those with excitingly different concepts, one could widen one's vision and gain deeper insight into the nature of reality. Many graduates in Romance studies feel enriched by being able to see the world through Spanish eyes or using French rationality. Scholars of Chinese or Japanese often develop two personalities when immersing themselves in one of these two languages.

Multicultural people strive towards 'totality of experience' (impossible to achieve in a lifetime) not only by learning foreign tongues, but by cultivating empathy with the views of others, standing in their shoes in their

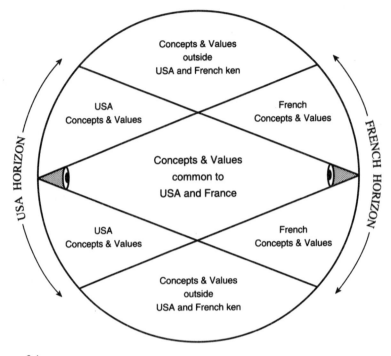

Figure 24

geographical, historical and philosophical location, seeing themselves from that location. But for the moment we live within our limited horizons. Figures 24 and 25 show how Americans and French people look at the world from different standpoints, see some things in a similar light (science, profit, consumerism) while other concepts are visible only to one nationality. A third area, containing a variety of beliefs and philosophies, lies outside the ken of either Americans or French.

Figure 26 shows how two nationalities speaking different languages miss out on several linguistically based concepts. Figure 27 indicates how two cultures united by the same language (England and the USA) are developing different horizons in the twentieth century, where concepts such as subtlety and understatement are invisible to many Americans and 'tough talk', clichés or a certain variety of hype meaningless to most English. In the case of Brits and Yanks, however, the overlapping areas of common experience still dominate the thinking. This is far from being the case with the Americans and Japanese or even neighbours like the Poles and Germans.

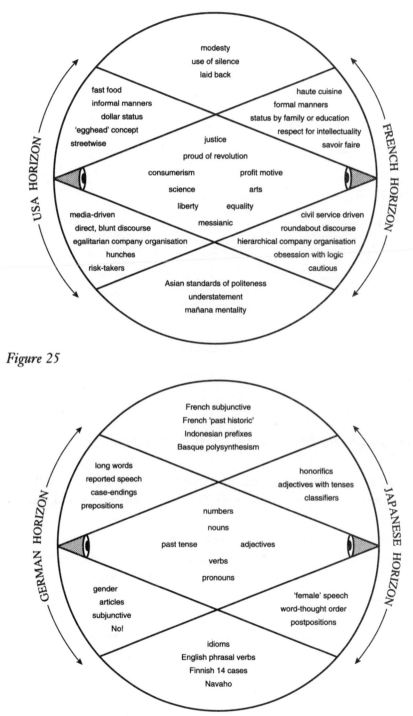

Figure 25

Figure 26

Figure 27

Managing the horizons – teambuilding

As business is increasingly internationalised and globalised, the problem of coordinating individuals or groups who hold quite different world views is constantly highlighted. Teambuilding has long been a subject of study on management courses, even when members were generally from one country or culture; now international teams are with us for good. No multinational company can afford to ignore their special character or neglect their training and nurture.

Many joint ventures get off to a flying start, as the injection of new capital and the synergy emanating from the merging of two layers of experience produce a euphoric honeymoon between the partners. When business is smooth, national 'idiosyncrasies' rarely assume significant importance. Should, however, money or customers be lost, local cultures will quickly retire to their entrenched beliefs and criticise the methods and values of others.

The education factor

We live in an era of improved education and training, but education systems vary considerably from country to country, both as to content and objectives. The French all-round senior manager, carefully groomed in wideranging skills in the *hautes écoles*, views the vocationally trained manager from a German *Volkswirtschaftshochschule* as a highly competent technician. Practical Japanese engineers wonder why their French counterparts evince no inclination to change tyres or fix malfunctioning TV sets. The German *Diplom-Kaufmann* may wonder why his British opposite number seems to have no official qualifications in commerce. Action-oriented American managers, many of whom climbed from the bottom rung of the corporate ladder to the very top through sheer ability, energy and aggressive ambition, may set no store by diplomas of any kind.

Even if all the members of a team have had a 'good' university education, there is no guarantee that this will facilitate international understanding. While universities have revolutionised their teaching of science, mathematics, engineering and medicine over the past two or three decades, there has been little new introduced in the study of social sciences. Only those graduates in foreign languages, literature, philosophy or history are in some ways equipped to interact in a more meaningful way with foreign nationals, and few of these graduates end up in international business.

Language and culture

How can we set about achieving a relatively harmonious and integrated international team? To begin with, one should face the fact that to understand what makes foreign colleagues tick, there is no substitute for learning their language, reading books produced by the culture and familiarising oneself with the country's basic history. This means a sizeable investment not so much in financial terms as in time. To achieve modest fluency in a European language, 250–500 hours of direct teaching will be required, preferably over a three-month period. This should include an intensive course of two to three weeks of full-time (minimum 40 hours) tuition. Japanese, Chinese, Arabic and Russian (to name four other major languages) will require almost double the time. By contrast, study of the country's basic history and main cultural traits could be comfortably dealt with in two or three weeks and done simultaneously with the language training.

Companies which discount the importance of such training do so at their peril. A malfunctioning joint venture with a foreign partner can result in catastrophic financial loss. One large, traditional British company (turnover several hundred million pounds) branched out in three European countries five years ago without giving sufficient attention to cultural diversity. The initial investment was around £10 million. Probably language and cultural training as outlined above for 20 key executives would have cost in the region of £200,000. In 1994 in one European branch alone the British company incurred losses of £100 million. Yet the subsidiary in question was showing a profit at the time of its acquisition!

What had happened? The British parent – vastly successful in the UK – had moved quickly to mushroom the size and scope of the branch operation, applying strategies and policies which had many years of proven success in the UK. Most of the new products and the general monolithic approach found little favour in the local culture. The problems were spotlighted by the local managers who offered polite, guarded criticism and advice. The British, although reasonable, bulldozed on in the firm belief that their name, impressive home record and lengthy experience would carry the day. The locals, in retaliation for the snub, clammed up. The much-heralded synergy was lost.

Executives operating in an international framework must be given a training which will at least exempt them from the charge of complete ignorance of the culture of their colleagues. This implies language training, but also cognisance of some very basic facts about the country concerned, such as politics, history and geography, as well as elementary business behaviour.

Horizons, common ground, divergence

Members of an international team, once they are familiar with the national profile, should be advised as to the cultural traits of their partners. What do the French, German, Japanese see on their horizon? What is essentially (and perhaps irrevocably) different? What overlaps? There are areas of agreement between any two nationalities. Latins are generally considered difficult partners for the British yet Britons can find common ground with French, Spaniards and Italians, although that ground differs in each case.

UK / France	UK / Spain	UK / Italy
sense of superiority	love theatre, plots	flexible
messianic	support underdog	reasonable
long term	vague, 'muddle through'	exports to survive
conservative	humorous	diplomatic, tactful
interest in arts and science	distrust the French	love of art
ex-imperial	dignified	sociable, good at small talk
linguistic arrogance	individualists	uses first names
	poor linguists	compromisers
	out of European mainstream	

It is valuable to focus on common ground; divergences of approach merit no less attention. One's first step towards adaptation must at the very least be to avoid irritants. An Italian, however, well-disposed towards a Brit, finds little subtlety of humour in being reminded that the best-known Italian product is spaghetti. The English may weary of incessant French ramblings at meetings, but they risk hostility if they attempt to quash it as irrelevant. Spaniards, touchy about personal style, do not take kindly to British references to their unpunctuality or overt body language. Japanese and most Orientals should be treated with as much respect and deference as Anglo-Saxons can muster: a good performance will in any case only slightly mitigate their opinion of us as somewhat unsophisticated types. Disruption of harmony and protocol by Anglo-Saxon informality and wise-cracking does not mean that British and Americans are the only miscreants. Latins and Germans alike take liberties in judging Brits as slow-moving, old-fashioned amateurs with no linguistic skills, while Americans are often categorised as dollar-mad salespeople lacking dress sense, tact, finesse and any values other than material.

Building on strengths

Common sense, good breeding and a modicum of unhurried thought are all useful resources for avoiding behaviour which might prove irritable to our partners. If we accept that certain things are not going to disappear (American drive, German seriousness, French sense of superiority, Japanese opacity, Spanish tardiness, Italian deviousness, Norwegian obsti-nacy, Swiss secrecy, Russian sentiment, Arab passion) we may come to the realisation that these very traits can make a positive contribution to our team effort. For example, American enthusiasm harnessed by thorough German planning and supervision could be very effective. Spaniards are slow starters, but can be good finishers, often displaying stamina and verve in the hours leading up to midnight. Italians are generally good deal-makers, finding ways of 'making the business' when others may be too entrenched or even deadlocked. They are valuable, too, in handling other Latins. Managers in experienced multinationals like IBM, Unilever and ABB are skilled at using 'horses for courses'. Unilever recently needed a man to supervise their marketing operations in South America. A Brazilian or an Argentinian might have been resented in some of the smaller countries and certainly in each other's. They chose an Indian, who was given language and cross-cultural training. A keenly perceptive executive, not only did his nationality place him above inter-regional rivalry, but his Indian characteristics of people orientation, subtle negotiating skills and warmth made him someone Latin-Americans would easily relate to.

Teambuilding exercises

There is a wide variety of teambuilding exercises; multinational corporations have tried all of them. At business schools, budding MBAs work together on hundreds of case studies. Promising managers and key staff from different countries are assembled to go camping together, climb mountains, raft down rivers and cross deserts. A basic principle of most teambuilding exercises is that all members shall face some kind of difficulty together, help each other out according to individual ability and with the resources that are at hand. The environmental constraints of a tent, raft, yacht or classroom necessitate working closely together and avoiding needless friction. When the teams are international, interesting things occur. Individuals strive to put their personal skills at the service of the team – sometimes practical, sometimes inspirational, sometimes intuitive. Leaders emerge: different people take charge of provisioning, planning, direction taking, financing, logistics, social affairs, even cooking. A language of communication evolves, as do problem-solving routines. Even on a language course this spirit of cooperation emerges. Latins recognise long literary or scientific words in English easily, but have difficulty with pronunciation; Dutch and Scandinavians pronounce beautifully, but are short on Latin-based vocabulary. Swedes help Finns with unfamiliar prepositions. Germans struggle with English word order. Everyone learns from everyone else.

Back to cultural cooperation: working with someone at close quarters for a protracted period of time enables you not only to observe foreign patterns of behaviour but to perceive some of the reasoning behind them. You also have the opportunity to explain your own actions and concepts (perhaps eccentric for others) as you go along. The talkative Italian, possibly irritating at first, may prove to be the social adhesive holding the group together. The disconcertingly withdrawn, opaque Japanese, sitting quietly in the corner, may later remind the group of things they have forgotten. The hustling American gets everyone to the restaurant on time, the superior Frenchman gets you the right wine, the fussy German has a minibus and umbrellas waiting for you in the rain.

7

BRIDGING THE
COMMUNICATION GAP

Whatever the culture, there's a tongue in our head. Some use it, some hold it, some bite it. For the French it is a rapier, thrusting in attack; the English, using it defensively, mumble a vague, confusing reply; for Italians and Spaniards it is an instrument of eloquence; Finns and East Asians throw you with constructive silence. Silence is a form of speech, so don't interrupt it!

Use of language

ONE OF THE FACTORS LEADING TO POOR COMMUNICATION IS OFTEN overlooked: the nationals of each country use their language and speech in a different way. Language is a tool of communication, delivering a message – but it is much more than that, it has strengths and weaknesses which project national character and even philosophy.

How do the French use their language? Like a rapier. French is a quick, exact, logical language and the French fence with it, cutting, thrusting and parrying, using it for advantage, expecting counter thrusts, retorts, repartee and indeed the odd *touché* against them. French is a good tool for arguing and proving one's point. It is fair play for the French to manipulate their language, often at great speed, to bewilder and eventually corner their opponent, leaving the latter breathless and without reply.

The English use their language differently – to its best advantage, certainly, but they are not quick to attack with it. They will lean heavily on understatement and reservation; they will concede points to their opponent early on to take the steam out of the argument, but their tone implies that even so, right is on their side. They know how to be vague in order to maintain politeness or avoid confrontation, and they are adept at waffling when they wish to procrastinate or cloud an issue. (It is impossible to waffle in French, as each word has a precise meaning.) The English will use a quiet tone to score points, always attempting to remain low key. Scots or the Northern English may emphasise their accent in order to come across as genuine, sincere or warm-hearted, while the Southern English may use certain accents to indicate an influential background, a particular school, or good breeding.

Spaniards and Italians regard their languages as instruments of eloquence and they will go up and down the scale at will, pulling out every stop if need be, to achieve greater expressiveness. To convey their ideas fully they will ransack an extensive vocabulary, use their hands, arms and facial expressions and make maximum use of pitch and tone. They are not necessarily being dramatic or overemotional. They want you to know how they feel. They will appeal, directly and strongly, to your good sense, warm heart or generosity if they want something from you, and often you have to decide there and then whether to say yes or no.

Germans, like the French, rely to a large extent on logic, but tend to amass more evidence and labour their points more than either the British or the French. The French, having delivered their thrust, are quite prepared to be parried and then have their defence pierced by a superior counter thrust. Germans are not; they come in with heavier armour and have usually thought through the counter arguments. Often the best way to deal with a German is to find common ground and emphasise solidarity and reliability in cooperation. The splendid German language is heavy, cumbersome, logical, disciplined and has such momentum that it is invincible in any head-on collision with another language. But that momentum can be deflected by a sensitive negotiator and all parties can benefit.

Scandinavians are something else. In the long dark nights they have thought about matters well in advance and they list all the 'pros and cons' before giving you their conclusion, which they will justify. They will not abandon their decision easily for they believe they have proved their case, but on the other hand they do not ask for too much. Swedes wield their language in a democratic manner with only a modicum of personal deference and with great egalitarian informality. They cut out the niceties and get down to brass tacks. Finns are friendlier and more reticent, but with the same modern equal-footing approach. The Finnish language is much more eloquent and flowery than Swedish, Danish or Norwegian, but the bottom line is still drily factual, succinct and well thought out. You can use any kind of humour with a Finn, linguistic or otherwise. A Dane will go along with you for a while, especially if the joke is at the expense of the Swedes. Swedes will accept your humour if it doesn't affect their profit margin. Never tell jokes about Norway to Norwegians. They don't understand them.

American speech is quick, mobile and opportunistic, reflecting the speed and agility of the young USA. The wisecrack is basic to their discourse. American humour excels in quips, barbed retorts and repartee – short, sharp, smart-alec shafts, typical of the dog-eat-dog society of early America, where the old hands had all the clichés and the answers, and newly arrived immigrants had to learn to defend themselves quickly. Exaggeration and hyperbole are at the bottom of most American expressions, contrasting sharply with the understated nature of the British. In the early days of pioneering, when immigrants speaking many varieties of halting English were thrown together in simple, often primitive surroundings, plainness and unsophistication of language were at a premium. The well-worn cliché was more understandable than originality or elegance of expression. The American language has never recovered from the exigencies of this period. The ordinary man's speech tends to be 'tough talk', rather reminiscent of cowboy parlance or Chicago gangland speech of the 1920s. The nation's obsession with show business and the pervasive influence of Hollywood have accentuated and, to some extent, perpetuated this trend. To make a start is to get the show on the road, to take a risk in a business venture is to fly by the seat of your pants, lawyers are shysters, accountants are bean counters, and, if you have no choice, it's the only game in town.

The Japanese use language in a completely different way from the rest of us. What is actually said has no meaning or significance whatsoever. Japanese use their language as a tool of communication, but the words and sentences themselves give no indication of what they are saying. What they want and how they feel are indicated by the way they address their conversation partner. Smiles, pauses, sighs, grunts, nods and eye movements convey everything. The Japanese leave their fellow Japanese knowing perfectly well what has been agreed, no matter what was said. Foreigners leave the Japanese with a completely different idea. Usually they think that everything has gone swimmingly, as the Japanese would never offend them by saying anything negative or unpleasant.

In English, French and a good number of languages, people often aspire to elegantly polite discourse in order to show respect to their interlocutor. This process is carried on to a much greater degree in Japanese, where standards of politeness are much higher than in the USA or Europe. On all ceremonial occasions, and these may include formal business meetings, a whole sequence of expressions is used which bears little or no relation to the actual sentiments of the individuals present. The language is instead aimed at conveying the long-term relationships which are envisaged and the depth of expectation that each participant has.

When these Japanese thoughts are translated, other nationalities tend to look at the content rather than the mood. Consequently, all they hear is platitudes or, even more suspicious, flattery. There is no doubt that most Japanese businessmen in England and the US are often successful at conveying the idea that they are very agreeable people to deal with. Later, toughness in negotiating appears and seems to contradict the early pleasantries. When at each meeting hosted by the Japanese they go through the ritual of thanking the visitors for giving up their valuable time and for suffering the prevailing weather conditions, Anglo-Saxons in particular feel uncomfortable about the sincerity of their hosts. The Japanese, however, are simply being courteous and caring.

The phenomenon of the different effects caused by national tongues has been noticed throughout the centuries. Charles V of Spain said he thought German could be spoken to soldiers, English to horses, Italian to women and Spanish to God. Vincenzo Spinelli remarked that while Italian is sung, Spanish is declaimed, French is danced and only Portuguese is really spoken.

The whole question of people using different speech styles and wielding their language in the national manner inevitably leads to misunderstanding not only of expression, but intent. Japanese or English may distrust Italians because they wave their hands about, or Spaniards because they sound emotional or prone to exaggeration. The French may appear offensive because of their directness or frequent use of cynicism. No one may really know what Japanese or Finns were thinking or what they actually said, if they said anything at all. Germans may take the English too literally and completely miss nuances of humour, understatement or irony. Northern peoples may simply consider that Latins speak too fast to be relied on. Languages are indeed spoken at different speeds. Hawaiian and some Polynesian languages barely cover 100 syllables per minute, while English has been measured at 200, German at 250, Japanese at 310 and French at 350 syllables per minute.

The communication gap

We have, therefore, a variety of cultures using speech not only according to the strictures imposed by grammar vocabulary and syntax, but in a manner designed to achieve the maximum impact. These different speech styles, whether used in translation or not, do nothing to improve communication in the international forum.

The communication gap assumes three forms: linguistic, practical and cultural. It is with the first of these that we are concerned in this chapter. Practical problems are usually the easiest to solve, as expatriate executives soon learn how to conduct themselves in this country or that. They tip generously in French restaurants, but not at all in China. They use first names in Finland, take flowers to Swedish homes, draw up their rolling forecast for the Americans, and talk business on the golf course in the UK and Japan. (More information on manners and mannerisms is given in Chapter 9).

Of more lasting difficulty for expatriate executives are behavioural differences of cultural or linguistic origin. To be successful, on a long-term basis – to gain the edge over competitors – they must achieve proficiency in both these areas.

Not many people are clever linguists and all over the world thousands of misunderstandings are caused every day through simple mistakes. Here are some examples:

Germany
+ Next week I shall become a new car (*get*)
+ Thank you for your kidneys (*kindness*)
+ What is your death line? (*deadline*)

Japan
+ I have split up my boyfriend
+ My father is a doctor, my mother is a typewriter
+ I work hardly 10 hours a day (*hard*)

Portugal

+ What will you do when you retire? I will breed with my horses.
+ Butchers have been fined for selling monkey meat (*donkey*)

Sweden

+ Are you hopeful of any change? No, I am hopeless.

Finland

+ We are sitting in the glass room (*classroom*)
+ He took two trucks every night (*drugs = pills*)
+ He took a fast watch (*quick look*)
+ How old is your son? Half past seven.

Communication patterns during meetings

We attempt to surmount the linguistic hurdle by learning the language of our partner well or by using an interpreter. The former method is preferable as we get more fully involved in the negotiation and are able to express ourselves better in terms of intent, mood and emotion. When the issues are non-controversial and the agenda is smooth, few obstacles arise. When misunderstanding arises, our language abandons its neutrality and swings back into culture-bound mode.

Italians, who believe in full explicitness, will become more explicit, waxing even more eloquent than before (see Figure 28). Finns, by contrast, will strive to rephrase their statement of intent in even fewer words, as in their culture this is the route to succinctness and clarity (see Figure 29).

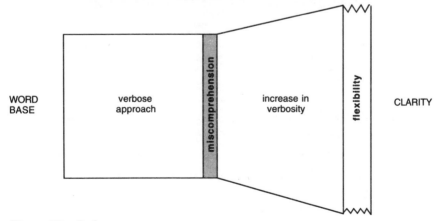

Figure 28   Italy

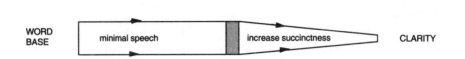

Figure 29   Finland

Germans tend to push resolutely forward in a constant, believing-in-oneself style (Figure 30). The French use a variety of tactics, including imaginative appeal, but invariably adhering to strict principles of logic throughout their discourse (Figure 31).

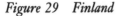

Figure 30   Germany

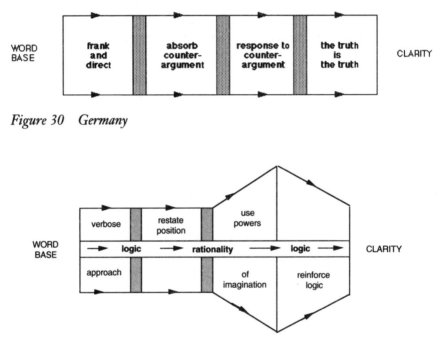

Figure 31   France

English people, like Germans, go steadily forward, but often introduce humour or understatement as negotiating tactics to soften their style (Figure 32). South Americans and Swedes go in for long discussions although in an entirely different manner (Figure 33 and 34).

Spaniards use lengthy discourse to get to know their interlocutor well and to develop friendship and loyalty as a basis on which they can build their transaction (Figure 35).

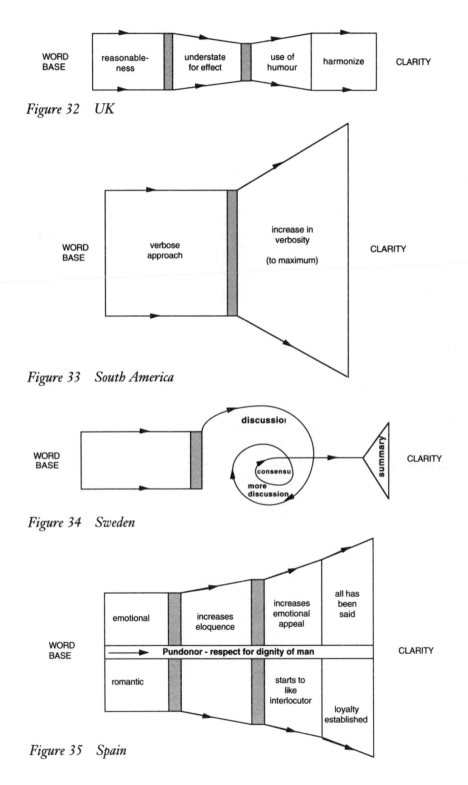

Figure 32   *UK*

Figure 33   *South America*

Figure 34   *Sweden*

Figure 35   *Spain*

Americans regard negotiation as a give-and-take scenario where both sides should put all their cards on the table at the beginning and waste no time beating around the bush. Their style is confrontational and often aggressive (Figure 36).

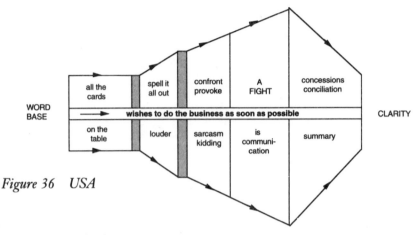

Figure 36   USA

Listening habits

Communication is a two-way process, involving not only the communicative skill of the presenter but, just as important, the listening habits of the customer. Different cultures do not use speech the same way, neither do they listen the same way. There are good listeners (Germans, Swedes) and there are bad ones (French, Spaniards). Others, such as the Americans, listen carefully or indifferently, depending on the nature of address. Figures 37–45 give some indication of the main concerns of several nationalities when they are obliged to listen.

At a recent conference on cross-cultural diversity, a fellow consultant presented a paper in which he gave an account of a problem experienced by Rolls-Royce in their aircraft engine division. A new engine had been introduced and sold with considerable success to their customers around the world. After a certain period the engines started seizing up in a selection of countries, although they worked perfectly well in others. The engine was technically sound, the operating and service manuals were explicit, and highly qualified engineers had taken great pains to make full presentations in all countries which had bought the engine. In view of the problem, these top engineers were sent out again to go through the manuals with the servicing technicians to ensure that things were being done

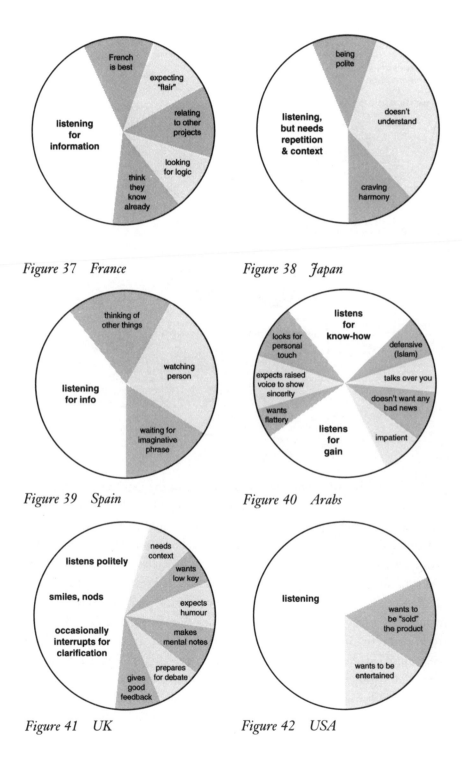

Figure 37   France

Figure 38   Japan

Figure 39   Spain

Figure 40   Arabs

Figure 41   UK

Figure 42   USA

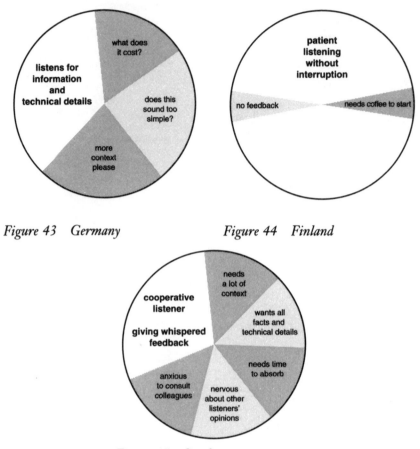

Figure 43 Germany   Figure 44 Finland

Figure 45 Sweden

properly. The British company, conscientious in the extreme, engaged the above-mentioned consultant to interview the engineers. It turned out to be basically a language problem. The well-spoken, highly educated and very experienced engineers explained the manuals in the same professional manner that they employed with British technicians. This met with full understanding in the USA and some other countries where English listening comprehension was high. In other countries, such as Germany, the technicians asked questions when necessary to make sure they had understood correctly. In the instances where the engines were giving problems the technicians belonged to cultures where the level of English, although high, was insufficient to absorb instructions delivered in an idiomatic style. Also their cultures inhibited them from revealing their lack of understanding – to ask for repetition of the presentation would have seemed impolite.

Figure 46 summarises the principal expectations of audiences belonging to different cultures.

US	UK	GERMANY
• humour • joking • modernity • gimmicks • slogans • catch phrases • hard sell	• humour • a story • 'nice' product • reasonable price • quality • traditional rather than modern	• solidity of company • solidity of product • technical info • context • beginning – middle – end • lots of print • no jokes • good price • quality • delivery date
attention span: 30 mins	attention span: 30–45 mins	attention span: 1 hour+

FRANCE	JAPAN	SWEDEN
• formality • innovative product • 'sexy' appeal • imagination • logical presentation • reference to France • style, appearance • personal touch • may interrupt	• good price • USP • synergy with co. image • harmony • politeness • respect for their co. • good name of your co. • quiet presentation • well-dressed presenter • formality • diagrams	• modernity • quality • design • technical information • delivery dates
attention span: 30 mins	attention span: 1 hour	attention span: 45 mins

MED/ARAB	FINLAND	AUSTRALIA
• personal touch • rhetoric • eloquence • liveliness • loudness • may interrupt • want 'extra' talk afterwards	• modernity • quality • technical information • modest presentation • design	• matey opening • informality throughout • humour • persuasive style • no padding • little contexting • innovative product • essential technical info • personal touch • may interrupt • imagination conclusion
attention span: short	attention span: 45 mins	attention span: 30 mins

Figure 46   Audience expectations during presentations

Advertising

The same characteristics which influence the receptivity of an audience naturally have an effect on the way they plan their own advertising and promotion. Information-hungry Germans will issue lengthy brochures for foreign consumption, just as if they were providing information for

Germans. Newspaper or magazine advertisements will be print oriented as opposed to the more pictorial approach of people such as the Spaniards. The German will also tend towards serious, factual persuasion, rather than using catchphrases or slogans common in American advertising. Once when I was at London Heathrow airport in the company of a friend of mine, we contemplated a huge billboard advertisement:

First Bite at the Big Apple

Fly UNITED AIRLINES

My German friend was somewhat puzzled. Big Apple? I explained that that was a fairly common 'nickname' for New York. 'Oh yes,' he said, 'first visit to New York – I see. But why United?' The ad carried little conviction with me, a Brit – no logic in it. For a German it was utter nonsense.

An advertisement for Lufthansa which appeared frequently in a variety of international news magazines with a mainly Anglo-Saxon readership repeats 'serious' concepts such as responsibility (four times), quality (five times), compromise (three times), perfection (three times). Also noticeable is the mention of accurate information – DM 1.1 billion (not 1 billion) – 11,000 technicians (not 10,000). By contrast, an Air France ad shows light French touch and *panache*. It shows a tray laid with cheese and wine and the words 'Flavour of France'. Let's fly Air France and have a bit of fromage *en route*. What a splendid idea. American characteristics take over in this ad for Delta:

DELTA SERVICE
Each year we fly more people than the largest airlines
of Great Britain, Germany and France...COMBINED.
Come Experience Travel That's Anything But Ordinary.

The biggest, therefore, the best. Size justifies the airline to its American mind. A Lucky Goldstar ad, in a different vein, refers to the impressive size of the company in question, but indicates that Korean success has its origins in the age-old traditions of the country's art and taste.

Finnish companies such as Nokia and Valio make frequent use of blue and white in their ads – the colour of the national flag – conveying to the Nordic reader, at least, a sense of Finnish cleanliness and reliability. Swedes tend to use blue and yellow with the same aim.

Firms planning print or television advertising in foreign countries clearly have need for guidance from local advertising agencies to indicate native preferences, pitfalls and taboos. There are some advertising agencies which claim to cater for requirements in any country, but they are few and far between.

The language of management

Different languages are used in different ways and with a variety of effects. Hyperbolic American and understated British English clearly inform and inspire staff with separate allure and driving force. Managers of all nationalities know how to speak to best effect to their compatriots, yet they are in fact only vaguely aware of their dependence on the in-built linguistic characteristics which make their job easier.

German

Germans belong to a data-oriented, low context culture and like receiving detailed information and instruction to guide them in the performance of tasks at which they wish to excel. In business situations German is not used in a humorous way, neither do its rigid case-endings and strict word order allow the speaker to think aloud very easily. With few homonyms (in contrast, for example, to Chinese) and a transparent word-building system, the language is especially conducive to the issuing of clear orders. The almost invariable use of the *Sie* form in business fits in well with the expectation of obedience and reinforces the hierarchical nature of the communication.

As far as motivating subordinates is concerned, German would seem to be less flexible than, for instance, bubbly American English. The constrictive effect of case-endings makes it difficult for German speakers to chop and change in the middle of a sentence. They embark on a course, plotted partly by gender, partly by morphology, in a straitjacket of Teutonic word order. The verb coming at the end obliges the hearer to listen carefully in order to extract the full meaning. The length and complexity of German sentences reflect the German tendency to distrust simple utterances.

Information-hungry Germans are among the best listeners in the world; their language fits the bill.

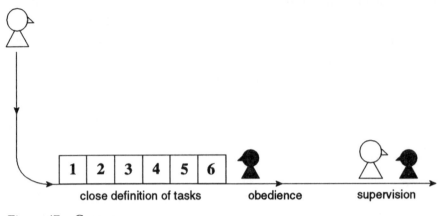
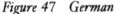

Figure 47   German

American English

In the USA the manager, if not always a hero, is viewed in a positive and sympathetic light, as one of the figures responsible for the nation's speedy development and commercial services. It is a young, vigorous, ebullient nation and its language reflects the national energy and enthusiasm. Americans exaggerate in order to simplify – low-key Britons feel they go 'over the top', but the dynamic cliché wears well in the US.

The frequent tendency to hyperbolise, exaggerating chances of success, overstating aims or targets etc., allows American managers to 'pump up' their subordinates – to drive them on to longer hours and speedier results. American salespeople do not resist this approach, for they are used to the 'hard sell' themselves. Tough talk, quips, wisecracks, barbed repartee – all available in good supply in American English – help them on their way.

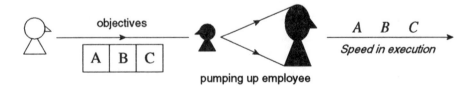

Figure 48   American English

The ubiquitous use of 'get' facilitates clear, direct orders. You get up early, you get going, you get there first, you get the client and you get the order, got it? The many neologisms in American English, used liberally by managers, permit them to appear up to date, aphoristic, humorous and democratic.

British English

In Britain the language has quite different qualities and, as a management tool, is much more subtle. British staff members who would be put off by American exaggeration and tough talk fall for a more understated, laid-back version of English which reflects their own characteristics. Managers manipulate subordinates with friendly small talk, humour, reserved statements of objectives and a very casual approach to getting down to work. You don't arrive on the dot and work round the clock. The variety of types of humour available in the UK enables managers to be humorous, to praise, change direction, chide, insinuate and criticise at will. They may even level criticism at themselves. Irony is a powerful weapon either way.

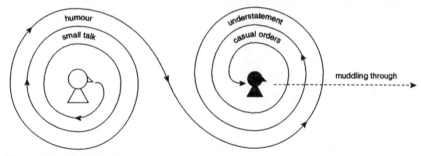

Figure 49   British English

Both British and American English are excellent media for brainstorming, due to the richness of vocabulary, double meanings, nuances and word-coining facilities. American managers and staff often used coined-yesterday business terminologies which neither fully understands, but which unite them in wonder at the spanking newness of the expression. British, in contrast, shy away from neologisms, often preferring woolly, old-fashioned phrases which frequently lead to sluggish thinking. 'Muddling through' is the result – the British are famous for it.

Foreigners follow with difficulty, for in fact they are listening to messages in a code. American or German criticism is blunt and direct; British critique is incidental and oblique. Managers, when praising, may seem to condemn. When persuading, they will strive to appear laid back. When closing a project, they will do so in a casual manner. When being tough they will feign great consideration, even kindness.

Japanese

There is a certain similarity in the language of management in Britain and Japan, although the basic and ever-present indirectness of the Japanese style makes the British, by comparison, seem clinical thinkers! Nevertheless, they have something in common – an aversion to 'rocking the boat'. British managers' understated criticisms, their humorous shafts in attack, their apparent reasonableness of expression at all times, are gambits to preserve harmony in their team. In Japan the drive towards harmony is so strong that it takes priority over clarity, even over truth.

Japanese managers do not issue orders: they only hint at what has to be done. The language is custom designed for this. The structure, which normally stacks up a line of subordinate clauses before the main one, invariably lists the justifications for the directive before it reaches the listener.

'Complete September's final report by 5.30 pm' comes out in Japanese as: 'It's 10th October today, isn't it? Our controller hasn't asked to see September's report yet. I wonder if he'll pop round tomorrow. You never know with him...' The actual order is never given – there is no need, the staff are already scrambling to their books.

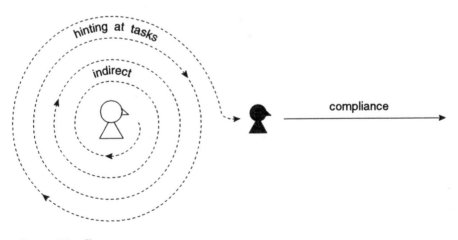

Figure 50   Japanese

Japanese has built-in mechanisms creating a strong impact on the listener. The general mandatory politeness creates a climate where staff appear to be quietly consulted in the most courteous manner. This very courtesy encourages their support and compliance. In fact they have no choice, as the hierarchy of communication is already settled by the status of the manager based on the quality and date of his university degree. The use of honorifics, moreover, reinforces the hierarchical situation. The different set of expressions (again mandatory) used in formulating the subordinates' responses to the manager's remarks closes the circle of suggestion, absorption, compliance.

Other features of the Japanese language which serve managers in instructing and motivating staff are the passive voice, used for extra politeness; the impersonal verb, which avoids casting direct blame; and the use of silence on certain issues, which indicates clearly to the subordinate what the manager's opinion is. Reported speech is not popular in Japan, for Japanese people subscribe to the myth that all one-to-one conversations are delivered in confidence and should not be repeated to others, and indeed the language does not possess a reported speech mechanism.

French

French managers inhabit quite a different world. They are clinically direct in their approach and see no advantage in ambiguity or ambivalence. The

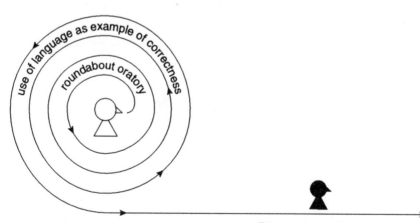

Figure 51   French

French language is a crisp, incisive tongue, a kind of verbal dance or gym-
nastics of the mouth, which presses home its points with an undisguised,
logical urgency. It is rational, precise, ruthless in its clarity.

The French education system, from childhood, places a premium on
articulateness and eloquence of expression. Unlike Japanese, Finnish or
British children, French children are rarely discouraged from being talkative. In the French culture loquacity is equated with intelligence and
silence does not have a particularly golden sheen. *Lycée*, university and *École
normale supérieure* education reinforces the emphasis on good speaking,
purity of grammar and mastery of the French idiom. The French language,
unquestionably, is the chief weapon wielded by managers in directing,
motivating and dominating their staff. Less articulate French people will
show no resentment. Masterful use of language and logic implies, in their
understanding, masterful management.

Other languages

In the Gulf States a good manager is a good Moslem. The language used
will make frequent references to Allah and align itself with the precepts and
style of the Koran. A didactic management style is the result. The inherent
rhetorical qualities of the Arabic language (see Figure 52) lend themselves
to reinforcing the speaker's sincerity. A raised voice is a sign not of anger,
but of genuine feeling and exhortation.

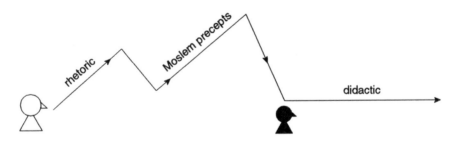

Figure 52   Arabic

Nigel Holden sees Russian, where social distance is encoded in highly
subtle ways, as resembling Japanese as a flexible management language in
network mode. Soviet managers were involved little in such areas as leadership or motivation of employees. The management style utilised threats
and coercion to produce results demanded by socialist 'planning'. How

Figure 53   Russian

Russian will develop as a language of management in the future will depend on modes of address using names and titles and the development of formal and informal mechanisms which do not remind subordinates of coercion and control.

Swedish as a language of management leans heavily on the *Du* form and dry, courteous expressions which clearly stratify managers at the same level as their colleagues or, at the very worst, as *primi inter pares*. I recently heard a TV journalist in his mid-twenties address the prime minister as *Du*.

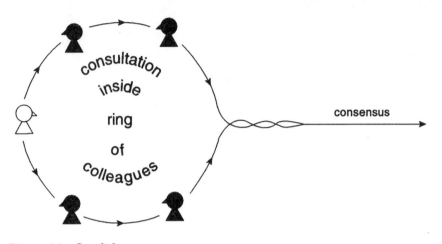

Figure 54   Swedish

To take a very different example, Spanish is directed towards staff at a much more vertical angle. Spanish managers are usually happy to use the *tu* form to subordinates, but the declaimed nature of their delivery, with typical Spanish fire and emphasis, makes their pronouncements and opinions virtually irreversible. Spanish, with its wealth of dimunitive endings, its rich vocabulary and multiple choice options on most nouns, is extremely suitable for expressing emotion, endearments, nuances and intimacies. Spanish managers' discourse leans on emotive content. They woo, persuade, cajole. They want you to know how they feel. The language exudes warmth, excitement, sensuousness, ardour, ecstasy and sympathy.

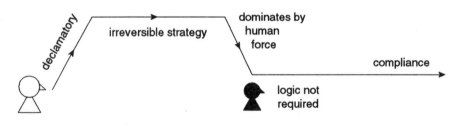

Figure 55   Spanish

8

MEETINGS OF THE MINDS

Meetings can be interesting, boring, long, short, or unnecessary. Decisions, which are best made on the golf course, over dinner, in the sauna, or in the corridor, rarely materialise at meetings called to make them. Protracted meetings are successful only if transport, seating, room temperature, lunch, coffee breaks, dinner, theatre outings, nightcaps and cable television facilities are properly organised.

Beginnings

THERE ARE MORE MEETINGS THAN THERE USED TO BE. JET TRAVEL enables businesspeople to go to a meeting in another continent and often leave for home the same day. It may well be that video-conferencing will reduce business travel in the future, but this facility, too, is a type of meeting.

For the moment, however, consider how people conduct meetings, face-to-face, in different countries. Meetings are not begun in the same way as we move from culture to culture. Some are opened punctually, briskly and in a 'business-like' fashion. Others start with chit-chat and some meetings have difficulty getting going at all. Figure 56 gives some examples of unalike starts in a selection of countries.

Germans, Scandinavians and Americans like to get on with it. They see no point in delay. Americans are well-known for their business breakfasts (a barbaric custom in Spanish eyes). In England, France, Italy and Spain it

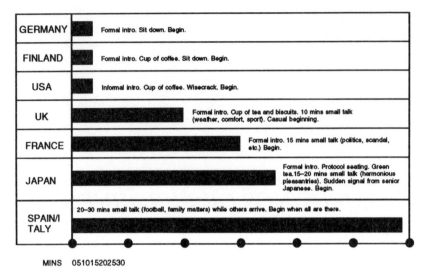

Figure 56   Opening a meeting

would be considered rude to broach the issues immediately. It is seen as much more civilised to ease into the subject after exchanging pleasantries which can last from 10 minutes to half an hour. The English, particularly, are almost shame-faced at indicating when one should start (Well, Charlie, I suppose we ought to have a look at this bunch of paperwork...). In Japan, where platitudes are mandatory, there is almost a fixed period which has to elapse before the senior person present says: '*Jitsu wa ne...*' (The fact of the matter is...) at which point everybody puts their head down and starts. Japanese meetings are conducted in phases:

+ platitudinous preamble
+ outline of subjects to be discussed (language used formal)
+ airing of views (less formal in tone)
+ replies of each party to other's views (more formal and non-confrontational)
+ summary by both sides (formal)

Negotiation

Many meetings between people of different cultures are held to conduct negotiations, and the approach of each side is affected by cultural factors.

Germans will ask you all the difficult questions from the start. You must convince them of your efficiency, quality of goods and promptness of service. These are features Germans consider among their own strong cards and they expect the same from you, at the lowest possible price. They will give you little business at first, but much more later when they have tested you. French tend to give business much faster, but may also withdraw it more quickly. Spaniards often seem not to appreciate the preparations you have made to facilitate a deal. They don't study all the details, but they study you. They will only do business with you if they like you and think you are 'honourable'.

The Japanese are similar in this respect. They must like you and trust you, otherwise no deal. Like the Germans, they will ask many questions about price, delivery and quality, but the Japanese will ask them all ten times. You have to be patient. Japanese are not interested in profits immediately, only in the market share and reputation of the company.

Finns and Swedes expect modernity, efficiency and new ideas. They like to think of themselves as being up to date and sophisticated. They will expect your company to have the latest office computers and streamlined factories. The American business approach is to get down quickly to a discussion of investment, budgets and profits. They hurry you along and make you sign the five-year plan.

Businesspeople from small nations with a long tradition of trading, such as the Netherlands and Portugal, are usually friendly and adaptable, but prove to be excellent negotiators. Brazilians never believe your first price to be the real one, and expect you to bend it later, so you must take this into your calculations.

In short, one gets down to business in different ways, according to the customs of the host country. Concepts of time, space and protocol all play their part. It is only when the meeting gets underway, however, that deeper chasms of cultural difference begin to yawn.

Established principles

Business schools, management gurus, trade consultants and industrial psychologists have focused, for most of the twentieth century, on the goal of reducing the process of negotiation to a fine art, if not a science. Papers have been written, seminars have been held, manuals have been devised and published. The Americans in particular, by dint of their obvious successes in the development of business techniques, not to mention their decades-long supremacy in world trade, have held a dominant position in the expounding and dissemination of the principles of negotiation.

One could be forgiven for assuming that relatively unchanging, universally accepted principles of negotiation would by now have been established – that an international consensus would have been reached on how negotiators should conduct themselves in meetings, how the phases of negotiation should proceed and how hierarchies of goals and objectives should be dealt with. One might assume that negotiators with their common concepts (learned from manuals) of ploys, bargaining strategies, use of data, fallback positions, closing techniques, restriction gambits, mix of factual, intuitive and psychological approaches, are interchangeable players in a (serious) game where internationally recognised rules of tactics, points won and gained, positions achieved would lead to a civilised agreement on the division of the spoils. This 'game plan' and its successful prosecution are not unusual or infrequent in domestic negotiation between nationals of one culture. But the moment international and intercultural factors enter into the equation, things change completely. Nationals of different cultures negotiate in completely different ways. In view of the common information obtainable by all participants and, to some extent, a fair amount of common commercial training and theory, why should this be so?

The problems

These derive from two sources: the professionalism of the negotiating team; and cross-cultural bias.

As far as professionalism is concerned, what is often forgotten is that negotiating teams rarely consist of professional or trained negotiators. While this does not apply so much to government negotiation, it is often readily observable at company level. A small company, when establishing contact with a foreign partner, very often is represented by its managing director and an assistant. A medium-sized firm will probably involve its export director, finance director and necessary technical support. Even large companies rely on the performance of the MD supported by, perhaps, highly specialised technical staff and finance people who have no experience whatsoever in negotiating. Engineers, accountants or managers used to directing their own nationals are usually completely lacking in foreign experience. When confronted with a different mindset, they are not equipped to capture the logic, intent and ethical stance of the other side. Often, when discussing the basic situation executives may be wasting time talking past each other. This leads us to cross-cultural bias.

Cross-cultural bias

When we find ourselves seated opposite well-dressed individuals politely listening to our remarks, their pens poised over notepads similar to the one before us, their briefcases and calculators bearing the familiar brand names, we tend to assume that they see what we see, hear what we say and understand what our intent and motives are. In all likelihood they start with the same innocent assumptions, for they, too, have not yet penetrated our cosmopolitan veneer. But the two sets of minds are working in different ways, in different languages regulated by differing norms and certainly envisaging different goals.

Humanity has a common development up to a certain point and in this respect the negotiators opposite us know what we feel, desire and suspect. Like us, they love their young, feel anger at injustice, fear powers which seek to destroy them, want to be liked and are grateful for favours and kindness. The average Chinese, German, Japanese or American will rarely deviate from this inherited pattern. That can be the extent of our trust, both in a social and business environment. After that we enter a different area — that of learned national culture. Now deviations of attitude and view are certain and we must be on our guard during the meeting to avoid irritants or outright offence, establish mutually understood facts and know when to 'agree to disagree', simply because the other culture cannot accept **or even see** our point of view.

National character and negotiation

Even before the meeting begins, the divergences of outlook are exerting decisive influence on the negotiation to come. If we take three cultural groups as an example – American, Japanese and Latin-American – the hierarchy of negotiating objectives are likely to be as in Figure 57.

US	JAPAN	LATIN AMERICA
1. Current deal	1. Harmonious relationships and 'direction taking'	1. National 'honour'
2. Short-term profit and rapid growth	2. Securing market share	2. Personal prestige of chief negotiator
	3. Long-term profit	3. Long-term relationship
3. Consistent profit		
4. Relationships with partner	4. Current deal	4. Current deal

Figure 57   Negotiating objectives

Americans are deal-oriented, as they see it as a present opportunity which must be seized. American prosperity was built on opportunities quickly taken and the immediate profit is seen as the paramount reality. Today, shareholders' expectation of dividends creates rolling forecasts which put pressure on US executives to deal now in order to fulfil their quarterly figures. For the Japanese, the current project or proposal is a trivial item in comparison with the momentous decision they have to make about whether or not to enter into a lasting business relationship with the foreigners. Can they harmonise the objectives and action style of the other company with the well-established operational principles of their own *kaisha*? Is this the right direction for their company to be heading in? Can they see the way forward to a steadily increasing market share? The Latin Americans, particularly if they are from a country such as Mexico or Argentina (where memories of US exploitation or interference are a background to discussion), are anxious to establish notions of equality of standing and respect for their team's national characteristics before getting down to the business of making money. Like the Japanese, they seek a long-term relationship, although they will inject into this a greater personal input than their group-thinking eastern counterparts.

This 'master programming' supplied by our culture not only prioritises our concerns in different ways, but makes it difficult for us to 'see' the priorities or intention pattern of others.

Stereotyping is one of the 'flaws' in our master programme, often leading us to false assumptions. Here are three examples:

+ French refusal to compromise indicates obstinacy.
  (Reality: French people see no reason to compromise if their logic stands undefeated.)

+ Japanese negotiators can't make decisions.
  (Reality: the decision was already made before the meeting, by consensus. The Japanese see meetings as an occasion for presenting decisions, not changing them.)

+ The Mexican senior negotiators are too 'personal' in conducting negotiations.
  (Reality: their 'personal' position reflects their position of authority within the power structure back home.)

The social setting

French, Spaniards, most Latin-Americans and Japanese regard a negotiation as a social ceremony to which are attached important considerations of venue, participants, hospitality and protocol, timescale, courtesy of discussion and the ultimate significance of the session. Americans, Australians, Britons and Scandinavians have a much more pragmatic view and are less impacted by the social aspects of business meetings. The Germans and Swiss are somewhere in between.

US executives, although outwardly smiling and friendly, generally tend to get the session over with as quickly as possible, with entertaining and protocol kept at a minimum. Mutual profit is the object of the exercise and Americans send technically competent people to drive the deal through. They persuade with facts and figures and expect some give and take, horse-trading when necessary. They will be argumentative to the point of rudeness in deadlock and regard confrontation and in-fighting as conducive to progress. No social egos are on the line – if they win, they win; if they lose, what the hell, too bad.

Senior Mexican negotiators cannot lose to Americans, least of all to technicians. Their social position is on the line and they did not enter into this negotiation to swap marbles with engineers and accountants. Their

Spanish heritage causes them to view the meeting as a social occasion where everybody is to show great respect for the dignity of the others, discuss grand outlines as opposed to petty details, speak at length in an unhurried, eloquent manner, and show sincerity of intent while maintaining a modicum of discretion to retain some privacy of view.

Japanese view the session as an occasion to ratify ceremonially decisions which have previously been reached by consensus. They are uncomfortable both with Mexican rhetoric and American argumentativeness, although they are closer to the Latins in their acceptance of protocol, lavish entertainment and preservation of dignity. As befits a social occasion, the Japanese will be led by a senior executive who sets standards of courtesy and deference. He may have no technical competence, but represents the weighty consensus which backs his authority.

The French view the setting of the negotiation both as a social occasion and a forum for their own cleverness. Their sense of history primes them for the traditional French role of international mediator. Their leader will be their best speaker, usually highly-educated and self-assured. It will require a skilful American, Briton or Japanese to best him or her in debate. The leader will be unimpressed by American aggressive ploys and Cartesian logic will reduce 'muddling-through' Englishmen and belly-talking Japanese to temporary incoherence. This is not a session for give and take, but for presenting well-formulated solutions. Lavish French hospitality will compensate for sitting through lengthy speeches.

Scandinavians, while relatively at home with Americans and Anglo-Saxons and familiar enough with German bluntness and protocol, have little feel for the social nuances displayed by Latins and Japanese. In their straight-forward egalitarian cultures a business meeting is for business to be conducted without regard to social status. Who the other negotiators are, their class, their connections, who they are related to – all these things are irrelevant to Finns and Swedes. Although more polite than Americans, Scandinavians have difficulty in settling down to a role in meetings where social competence dominates technical know-how.

Values & self-image

We see, therefore, how diverse cultures view the negotiating process in a different light, with dissimilar expectations about its conduct and outcome.

Once the talks begin, the values, phobias and rituals of the particular cultural groups soon make themselves evident. For the Americans, time is money and they wish to compress as much action and decision making as possible into the hours available. They rely on statistical data and personal drive to achieve this. The Dutch, Finns and Swiss, although somewhat less headlong, will be similarly concerned with the time/efficiency equation. The Germans will place emphasis on thoroughness, punctuality and meeting deadlines, making sure they always complete their action chains. For this they require full information and context and, unlike Latins, will leave nothing 'in the air'.

The French give pride of place to logic and rational argument. The aesthetics of the discussion are important to them and this will be reflected in their dress sense, choice of venue, imaginative debating style and preoccupation with proper form. The Japanese have their own aesthetic norms, also requiring proper form, which in their case is bound up with a complex set of obligations (vertical, horizontal and circular!). In discussion they value creation of harmony and quiet 'groupthink' above all else. The British also give priority to quiet reasonable, diplomatic discussion. Their preoccupation with 'fair play' often comes to the fore and they like to see this as a yardstick for decision making. Latins place emphasis on personal relationships, 'honourable' confidences and the development of trust between the parties. This is a slow process and they require an unhurried tempo to enable them to get to know their counterparts. This is well understood by the Japanese, but conflicts with the American desire for quick progress.

Self-image is part and parcel of value perception and negotiators see themselves in a light which may never reach their foreign counterpart, although their playing of the role may irritate. English people often assume a condescending, abitrarial role which is a carry-over from the days when they settled disputes among the subjects of Her Majesty's Empire. They may still see themselves as judges of situations which can be controlled with calm firmness and funny stories. The French have an equally strong sense of history and consider themselves the principal propagators of western European culture. This encourages them to take a central role in most discussions and they tend to 'hold the floor' longer than their counterparts would wish.

Latin Americans see themselves as exploited by the US and they display heightened defensive sensitivity which may often delay progress. They consider themselves culturally superior to North Americans and resent the latters' position of power and dominance.

The Japanese, on the other hand, are comfortable with American power – as victors in the Second World War they earned the number one spot. Inequality is basic in both Japanese and Chinese philosophies and the former are quite satisfied with the number two spot for the time being. The Japanese see themselves as far-sighted negotiators and courteous conversationalists. They have no aspirations to dominate discussion any more than they have towards moral world or even Asian leadership. They are privately convinced, however, of their uniqueness of which one facet is intellectual superiority. Unlike the French, they base this belief not on intellectual verbal prowess, but on the power of strong intuition.

Decision making

Negotiations lead to decisions. How these are made, how long they take to be made and how final they are once made are all factors which will depend on the cultural group involved.

Americans love making decisions as these usually lead to action and they are primarily action oriented. The French love talking about decisions which may or may not be made in the future. If their reasoned arguments do not produce what in their eyes is a logical solution, then they will delay decisions for days or weeks if necessary.

Japanese hate making decisions and prefer to let decisions be made for them by gradually building up a weighty consensus. In their case, a decision may take months. This exasperates Americans and many northern Europeans, but the Japanese insist that big decisions take time. They see American negotiators as technicians making a series of small decisions to expedite one (perhaps relatively unimportant) deal. Once the Japanese have made their decisions, however, they expect their American partner to move like lightning towards implementation. This leads to further exasperation.

What westerners fail to understand is that Japanese, during the long, painstaking process of building a consensus, are simultaneously making preparations for the implementation of the business. The famous *ringi-sho* system of Japanese decision making is one of the most democratic procedures of an otherwise autocratic structure. In many western countries action is usually initiated at the top. In Japan younger or lower-ranking people often propose ideas which are developed by middle management and ultimately shown to the president. There is a long, slow process during which many meetings are held to digest the new idea and at length a draft will be made to be passed round for all to see. Each person is invited to attach his or her seal of approval so that unanimity of agreement is already assumed before the president confirms it. He will not do this lightly since he, not middle management, will have to resign if there is a catastrophe. To ask a Japanese negotiator during a meeting to take 'another direction' is quite unacceptable. No hunches or sudden change-abouts here. Drastic swings of intent would force the Japanese team to go right back to the drawing board.

Mediterranean and Latin-American teams look to their leader to make decisions and do not question his personal authority. His decision making, however, will not be as impromptu or arbitrary as it seems. Latins, like Japanese, tend to bring a cemented-in position to the negotiating table, which is that of the power structure back home. This contrasts strongly with the Anglo-Saxon and Scandinavian willingness to modify stances continuously during the talk if new openings are perceived.

French negotiators seldom reach a decision on the first day. Many a British negotiator has asked (in vain) French colleagues at 4 pm, 'Well, can we summarise what we have agreed so far?' French dislike such interim summaries, since every item on the agenda may be affected by later discussion. Only at the end can everything fit into the Grand Design. Short-term decisions are seen as of little consequence.

Ethics

Once a decision has been made, the question then arises as to how final or binding it is. Anglo-Saxons and Germans see a decision, once it has been entered into the minutes of a meeting, as an oral contract which will shortly be formalised in a written, legal document. Ethically, one sticks to one's decisions. Agenda items which have been agreed on are not to be resurrected or rediscussed once a tick has been put against them.

Neither Japanese nor southern Europeans see anything wrong, ethically, in going back on items previously agreed. Chop and change (anathema to Anglo-Saxons) holds no terrors for many cultures. The Japanese consider it would be unethical to insist on a decision which had been rendered invalid or irrelevant by rapidly changing circumstances. How ethical is a share swop agreement if the market crashes the next day? New tax laws, currency devaluations, drastic political changes can make previous accords meaningless.

The French show lack of respect for adherence to agenda points or early mini-decisions. This is due not so much to their concern about changing circumstances as to the possibility (even likelihood) that, as the discussions progress, Latin imagination will spawn clever new ideas, uncover new avenues of approach, improve and embellish accords which later may seem naïve or rudimentary. For them a negotiation is often a brainstorming exercise. Brainwaves must be accommodated! Italians, Spanish, Portuguese and South Americans all share this attitude.

Contracts

Different ethical approaches or standards reveal themselves in the way diverse cultures view written contracts. Americans, British, Germans, Swiss and Finns are among those who regard a written agreement as something which, if not holy, is certainly final. For the Japanese, on the other hand, the contract which they were uncomfortable in signing anyway is, in their eyes, a statement of intent. They will adhere to it as best they can, but will not feel bound by it if market conditions suddenly change, anything in it contradicts common sense, or they feel 'cheated' or legally trapped by it. If the small print turns out to be rather nasty, they will ignore or contravene it without qualms of conscience. Many problems arise between Japanese and US firms on account of this attitude. The Americans love detailed written agreements covering themselves against all contingencies with legal redress. They have 300,000 lawyers to back them up. The Japanese, who have only 10,000 registered lawyers, regard contingencies to be *force majeure* and consider that contracts should be sensibly reworked and mofidied at another meeting or negotiation.

The French tend to be precise in the drawing up of contracts, but other Latins require more flexibility in adhering to them. An Italian or Argentinian sees the contract as an ideal scheme in the best of worlds, which sets out the prices, delivery dates, standards of quality and expected gain, or a fine project which has been discussed. But we do not live in the best of worlds and the outcome we can realistically expect will fall somewhat short of the actual terms agreed. Delivery of payment may be late, there may be heated exchanges of letters or faxes, but things will not be so bad that further deals with the partner are completely out of the question. A customer who pays six months late is better than one who does not pay at all. A foreign market, however volatile, may still be a better alternative to a stagnating or dead-end domestic one.

Propriety

If Anglo-Saxons and Scandinavians have a problem with the ethics of volatility, they have an even greater one with those of propriety. Which culture or authority can deliver the verdict on acceptable standards of behaviour or appropriate conduct of business? If it is recognised that Italian flexibility poses problems for law-abiding Swiss or time-dominated Germans, what are the sanctioned limits of such flexibility?

Italian flexibility in business often leads Anglo-Saxons to think they are 'dishonest'. They frequently bend rules, break or 'get round' some laws and put a very flexible interpretation on certain agreements, controls and reg-ulations. There are many grey areas where short cuts are, in Italian eyes, a matter of common sense. In a country where excessive bureaucracy can hold 'business' up for months, smoothing the palm of an official or even being related to a minister is not a sin. It is done in most countries, but in Italy they talk about it.

When does lavish entertaining or regular gift giving constitute elegant bribery or agreeable corruption? French, Portuguese or Arab hosts will interlard the negotiation sessions with feasting far superior to that offered by the Scandinavian canteen or British pub lunch. Expense-account-cul-ture Japanese would consider themselves inhospitable if they had not taken their visiting negotiators on the restaurant night-club circuit and showered them with the usual expensive gifts.

Few Anglo-Saxons or Scandinavians would openly condone making a covert payment to an opposing negotiator, but in practice this is not an uncommon occurrence when competition is fierce. I once heard an American define an honest Brazilian negotiator as one who, when bought, would stay bought. More recently the leader of the negotiating team of a large Swedish concern tacitly admitted having greased the palm of a cer-tain South American gentleman without securing the contract. When the Swede quietly referred to the payment made, the beneficiary explained: 'Ah, but that was to get you a place in the last round!'

Judgements on such procedures are inevitably cultural. Recipients of under-the-table payments may see them as no more unethical than using one's influence with a minister (who happens to be one's uncle), accepting a trip around the world (via Tahiti or Hawaii) to attend a 'conference', or wielding brute force (financial or political) to extract a favourable deal from a weaker opponent. All such manœuvres can be viewed (depending on one's mindset) as normal strategies in the hard world of business. One just has to build these factors into the deal or relationship.

Compromise

It is not uncommon for negotiations to enter a difficult stage where the teams get bogged down or even find themselves in deadlock. When such situations occur between nationals of one culture (for a variety of reasons), there is usually a well-tried mechanism which constitutes an escape route whereby momentum can be regained without loss of face for either side. Deadlocks can be broken by, for instance, changing negotiators or venue, adjourning the session, or 'repackaging' the deal. Arab teams will take a recess for prayer and come back with a more conciliatory stance; Japanese delegations will bring in senior executives 'to see what the problem is'; Swedish opponents will go out drinking together; Finns will retire to the sauna.

These mechanisms are not always available in international negotiations. The nature of the deadlock, moreover, may be misconstrued by both parties as, for instance, when French insist on adhering to their logic which the Japanese have misunderstood or completely failed to follow. The mechanism used by Anglo-Saxons is usually that of compromise. The British, with their supposedly innate sense of fair play, see themselves as the champions of compromise. The Scandinavians are very British in this respect, while the American willingness to compromise is seen in their give-and-take tactics, deriving from the bartering traditions in US history.

Other cultures, however, do not see compromise in the same favourable light and remain unconvinced of its shining merit. In French eyes 'give and take' is Anglo-speak for 'wheel and deal', which they see as an inelegant, crude tactic for chiselling away at the legitimate edifice of reason they have so painstakingly constructed. 'Yes, let's all be reasonable,' they say, 'but what is irrational in what we have already said?'

For the Japanese, compromise during a negotiation is a departure from a company-backed consensus, and woe betide the Japanese negotiators who concede points without authority. Adjournment is the least they must ask for. Many a senior Tokyo-based executive has been got out of bed in the middle of the night by trans-Pacific telephone calls asking for directives. Delays are, of course, inevitable.

Among the Latins, attitudes towards compromise vary. The Italians, although they respect logic almost as much as the French, know that our world is indeed irrational and pride themselves on their flexibility. They are closely followed by the Portuguese who, in their long history of trading with the English, have acquired close familiarity with Anglo-Saxon habits. The Spaniards' obsession with dignity makes it hard for them to climb down without good reason. South Americans see compromise as a threat to their *pundonor* (dignity) and several nations, including Argentina, Mexico and Panama, display obstinacy in conceding anything to 'insensitive, arrogant Americans'.

Compromise may be defined as finding a middle course and, to this end, both the Japanese and Chinese make good use of 'go-betweens'. This is less acceptable to westerners who prefer more direct contact (even confrontation) to seek clarity. Confrontation is anathema to orientals and most Latins and disliked by Brits and Swedes. Only Germans ('the truth is the truth'), Finns and Americans might rank directness, bluntness and honesty above subtle diplomacy in business discussions. Arabs also like to use 'go-betweens'. The repeated offer of King Hussein of Jordan to mediate in the dispute between Saddam Hussein and George Bush unfortunately fell on deaf ears, even though, as a thoroughly westernised Arab (with British and American wives to boot) he was the ideal middleman for that particular cross-cultural situation.

The problem remains that intelligent, meaningful compromise is only possible when one is able to see how the other side prioritises their goals and views the related concepts of dignity, conciliation and reasonableness. These are culturally affected concepts, therefore emotion bound and prickly. However, an understanding of them, and a suitable step or reaction to accommodate them, form the unfailing means of unblocking the impasse. Such moves are less difficult to make than one might believe. They do, however, require knowledge and understanding of the traditions, cultural characteristics and way of thinking of the other side. What is suitable or inappropriate in their eyes? What is logical and illogical?

Logic

French debating logic is Cartesian in its essence, which means that all pre-suppositions and traditional opinions must be cast aside from the outset, as they are possibly untrustworthy. Discussion must be based on one or two indubitable truths on which one can build through mechanical and deductive processes to clarify further truths and knowledge. Descartes decreed that all problems should be divided into as many parts as possible and the review should be so complete that nothing could be omitted or forgotten. Given these instructions and doctrine, it is hardly surprising that French negotiators appear complacently confident and long-winded. They have a hypothesis to build and are not in a hurry.

Opponents may indeed doubt some of the French 'indubitable truths' and ask who is qualified to establish the initial premises. Descartes has an answer to this: rational intellect is not rare, it can be found in anyone who has been given help in clear thinking (French education) and is free from prejudice. What is more, conclusions reached through Cartesian logic 'compel assent by their own natural clarity'. There, in essence, is the basis for French self-assurance and unwillingness to compromise.

Fellow French people would certainly meet thrust with counter-thrust, attempt to defeat the other side's logic. Many cultures feel little inclined to do this. The Japanese – easy meat to corner with logic – have no stomach for arguing or public demonstrations of cleverness. During the perorations of the other side, their internal telepathy system has been hard at work – their reactions and conclusions are ventral and visceral, emotional and intuitive. They, like some other Orientals, acquire convictions without always knowing why – as occasionally do the 'muddling-through' British.

Anglo-Saxons, particularly Americans, show a preference for Hegelian precepts. According to Hegel, people who first present diametrically opposed points of view ultimately agree to accept a new and broader view that does justice to the substance of each. The thesis and antithesis come together to form a synthesis (compromise). Everything must have an opposite – were it not so, nothing could come into existence. The essence of this cause-and-effect doctrine is activity and movement, on which Americans thrive. An American negotiator is always happy to be the catalyst, ever willing to make the first move to initiate action.

Chinese logic is different again – their background is Confucian philosophy. They consider the French search for truth less important than the search for virtue. To do what is right is better than to do what is logical. They also may show disdain for western insistence that something is black or white, that opposite courses of action must be right or wrong. Chinese consider both courses may be right if they are both virtuous. Confucianism decrees moderation in all things (including opinion and argument); therefore, behaviour towards others must be virtuous. Politeness must be observed and others must be protected from loss of face. Taoist teaching encourages Chinese to show generosity of spirit in their utterances. The strong are supposed to protect the weak, so the Chinese negotiator will expect you not to take advantage of your superior knowledge or financial strength! Another dimension of Chinese thinking is *feng shui* (wind-and-water superstition) which means that the seating arrangements, the position of the furniture, alignment of doors and even the placing of mirrors will have significance for Chinese negotiators. Each individual is also supposed to possess the qualities of the animal of the year he or she was born. For example, the horse means stamina, the snake wisdom, the rat bravery and cleverness – so negotiators, beware!

Language

Negotiators, unless they are using interpreters, need a common language. As English is now the language of diplomacy as well as international trade, they think they have one. English can, however, be a communication link or a semi-invisible barrier. When Americans use in discussion words like 'democratic', 'fair', 'reasonable', 'obvious', 'evidence', 'common sense', 'equitable', 'makes business sense', they often fail to realise that Japanese understand quite different things under these headings and that most Latins will instinctively distrust each word listed above. 'Democracy' has a different meaning in every country; American 'evidence' is statistical, in many cultures it is emotional; in Russia the phrase 'makes business sense' has virtually no meaning. Language is a poor communication tool unless each word or phrase is seen in its original cultural context. This is naturally true also of other languages. Words such as *Weltschmerz* (German), *sisu* (Finnish), *saudades* (Portuguese) mean little to other cultures even when translated, while no westerner could possibly appreciate the spider's web of duties and obligations implied by the Japanese words *giri* and *on*.

The non-verbal dimension

While verbal discussion might occupy 80–90 per cent of the time devoted to a negotiation, psychologists tell us that the 'message' conveyed by our actual words may be 20 per cent or even less. Our understanding, tolerance, sense of comfort and our very mood is more likely to be strongly influenced by other factors (Fisher calls it 'cross-cultural noise').

The **venue** itself may have positive or negative implications. Are we 'home' or 'away'? Are we seated comfortably? (French negotiators are said to arrange lower seats for their opponents!) American businesspeople are used to sitting in a confrontational style, facing their interlocutors across the table and maintaining challenging eye contact, while Japanese by contrast like to sit side by side and stare at a common point (often a blank wall or the floor), punctuating their remarks with occasional sideways glances.

Hierarchy of seating is also important, but of more significance in the early stages of discussion are the negotiators' physical and social attitudes. Each culture has its own concept of the '**space bubble**' – the personal space the individual requires to be able to think, talk and gesture in comfort.

Related to the 'distance of comfort' is the question of **touching**. The Spaniard's grip on your upper arm shows confidence in you, an African may continue to hold your hand when talking to you, but touching of any kind is anathema to Japanese, who regard it as unhygienic; it is little loved by Finns, Swedes, Germans, British and many Orientals.

American informality

Americans are ambivalent in this respect, normally occupying a space bubble equal in size to that demanded by most Anglo-Saxons, but only too frequently indulging in pumping hands, slapping backs and playful punches, which score no points whatsoever with Japanese, Germans and French. Americans in particular, in their eagerness to downplay status and social hierarchy, have created consistent protocolar havoc in business meetings around the world. The last thing the Japanese wants, on first meeting, is to be manhandled (even in a friendly manner); German senior executives have no wish whatsoever to be addressed by their first names; French negotiators abhor people who take their jackets off and loosen their ties during the first encounter. Other American habits such as chewing gum, slouching in their chairs, showing the soles of their shoes as they cross their legs, constitute 'cultural noise' of the first order. Japanese and Finns, on the other hand, can give rise to unease in their counterparts with 'absence of noise' (in their eyes, constructive silence).

Dress, formal and informal, correct and innappropriate, can also give negotiators false impressions of the seriousness or casualness of the other side. **Gestures** (of the Latin variety), can denote overemotion or unreliability to northerners. Impassive faces and absence of body language can cause Latins to suspect cunning or slyness in Japanese, and the lack of feedback from the politely listening Finn can disorientate them.

Silence

Listening habits can clearly play an important part in the negotiating process. Finns and Japanese consider they make an important contribution to the discussion with their culture-oriented silence! 'Those who know do not speak; those who speak do not know' is a second-century Chinese proverb which the Finns, like the Japanese, do not quarrel with. In Finland, as in Japan, silence is not equated with failure to communicate, but is an integral part of social interaction. In both countries what is not said is regarded as important and lulls in conversation are considered restful, friendly and appropriate. Silence means that you listen and learn; talking a lot merely expresses your cleverness, perhaps egoism and arrogance. Silence protects your individualism and privacy; it also shows respect for the individualism of others. In Finland and Japan it is considered impolite or inappropriate to force one's opinions on others – it is more appropriate to nod in agreement, smile quietly, avoid opinionated argument or discord.

The American habit of 'thinking aloud', the French stage performance, the Italian baring of the soul in intimate chatter, the rhetoric of the Arabs – all these are communicative gambits designed to gain the confidence of the listener, to share ideas which can then be discussed and modified. The Finn and the Japanese listen with a kind of horror, for in their countries a statement is a sort of commitment to stand by, not to change, twist or contradict in the very next breath.

Body language

Facial expressions and loudness of voice or manner are also cultural factors which may disturb interlocutors. Members of a Spanish delegation may argue fiercely with each other while opponents are present, causing Japanese to think 'they are fighting'. Orientals are bemused when the same 'quarrelling Spaniards' pat each other like lifelong friends a few moments later. Smiles, while signifying good progress when on the faces of British, Scandinavians or Germans, might mean embarrassment or anger when adopted by Japanese and often appear insincere in the features of the constantly beaming American. Finns and Japanese often look doleful when perfectly happy, whereas gloom on an Arab face indicates true despondency. The frequent bowing of the Japanese is seen as ingratiating by Americans, while the hearty nose-blowing of westerners in public is abhorred by Japanese, who invariably leave the room to do this.

Man is the only animal that speaks, laughs and weeps. Other species we can observe obviously have their own means of communication, but, except for the dolphins, we stop short of saying that they possess speech. Animals growl, bark, grunt and squeal, imparting messages not only to each other, but also to more articulate humans. Inevitably these sounds are accompanied by the appropriate body language – a threatening crouch, hair standing on end, a showing of teeth, imminent flight, submissive posture or cowering, etc. Body language, with its accompanying odours, is probably the principal mode of communication among animals.

Speech as auxiliary to body language

Anthropologists tell us that before humans possessed speech – and possibly in the early days of its acquisition and development – they probably depended as much on body language as do the beasts today. They assume that speech developed to make body language more explicit and that as the former became more sophisticated, gestures became less necessary. The ability to deliver an icy 'I'll break your neck' made club-waving superfluous and 'Would you mind passing me a little more of that delicious cold lamb?' has almost eliminated snatching, at the table or round the camp fire.

The theory that speech – first used minimally as an auxiliary to the basic messages of body language – developed into the main form of communication, gradually reducing body language to the auxiliary role, is a neat one.

Surprisingly, it is not that simple. In spite of the incredible sophistication, subtlety and flexibility of speech, it seems that some humans still rely basically on body language to convey (especially where intense feelings are concerned) what they really mean. Such people are the Italians, South Americans and most Latins, as well as many Africans and people from the Middle East. Others, such as Japanese, Chinese, Finns and Scandinavians, have virtually eliminated overt body language from their communication.

The space bubble

People from reactive and linear-active cultures are generally uncomfortable when confronted by the theatrical, excitable gestures and behaviour of the multi-actives. The feeling of discomfort generally begins at the outset when the 'space bubble' is invaded. Orientals, Nordics, Anglo-Saxon and Germanic people mostly regard space within 1.2 metres of the self as inviolable territory for strangers, with a smaller bubble of 0.5 metres in radius for close friends and relatives. Mexicans (and many of their cousins) happily close within half a metre of strangers for business discussions.

When a Mexican positions himself 0.5 metres away from an Englishman, he is ready to talk business. The Englishman sees him in English personal space and backs off to 1.2 metres. In doing so, he relegates the Mexican to the South American 'public zone' (1.2 metres) and the latter thinks the Englishman finds his physical presence distasteful or does not want to talk business. For a Mexican to talk business over a yawning chasm of 1.2 metres is like an English person shouting out confidential figures to someone at the other end of the room.

Different types of body language

Multi-actives – French, Mediterranean people, Arabs, Africans, South and Central Americans – possess a whole variety of gestures and facial expressions, largely unused and often misconstrued or disliked by reactive, linear-active and data-oriented cultures.

Finns and Japanese do not seem to have any body language – an assumption which administers cultural shock to first-time visitors in Finland and Japan. I say do not seem, because in fact Finns and Japanese do use body language which is well understood by fellow nationals in each country. Finns and Japanese have to be good 'body watchers', as the verbal messages in their countries are kept at a minimum. In the Finnish and Japanese cultures, upbringing and training discourage gesticulations, exaggerated facial expressions and uninhibited manifestations of glee, sorrow, love, hate, hope, disappointment or triumph. In both societies the control and disciplined management of such emotions leads to the creation of a much more restrained type of body language which is so subtle that it goes unnoticed by the foreign eye. Finns and Japanese are able to detect nonverbal messages in each other's culture, as their own nationals behave in a similar manner. As Finns and Japanese are accustomed to looking for minimal signs, the blatantly demonstrative body language of Italians, Arabs and South Americans produces strong culture shock for them. It is as if someone used to listening to the subtle melodies of Chopin or Mozart were suddenly thrown into a modern disco. The danger is, of course, that over-reaction sets in – a judgmental reaction which causes Japanese to consider Americans and Germans as charging bulls and Finns to see French as too 'clever', Italians as over-emotional and even Danes as a bit slick.

The body language of multi-active people often incorporates the following features.

Eyes

Eyes are among the more expressive parts of the body. In multi-active cultures, where power distance between people is greater, speakers will maintain close eye contact all the time they deliver their message. This is particularly noticeable in Spain, Greece and Arab countries. Such close eye contact (Finns and Japanese would call it 'staring') implies dominance and reinforces one's position and message. In Japan this is considered improper and rude. Japanese avoid eye contact 90 per cent of the time, looking at a speaker's neck while listening and at their own feet or knees when they speak themselves.

In great power-distance societies, it is easy for us to detect what the 'pecking order' is by observing people's eye behaviour. Lower ranking people tend to look at superiors, who ignore them unless they are in direct conversation with them. When anyone cracks a joke or says something controversial, all the subordinates' eyes will switch immediately to the chief personage to assess his reaction. This is less evident in northern countries where head-and-eye switching would be much more restrained, sometimes avoided.

Mediterranean people use their eyes in many different ways for effect. These include glaring (to show anger), glistening eyes (to show sincerity), winking (very common in Spain and France to imply conspiracy) and the eyelash flutter (used by women to reinforce persuasion). Eyebrows are also raised and lowered much more frequently than in northern societies, again to show surprise, disapproval, aggression, fearlessness etc.

Weeping is another form of body language little used by monochronic cultures for communication and almost unknown in Finland, Korea and Japan. Weeping is seen frequently in Latin and Arabian societies, even occasionally used in moments of drama in the UK (Winston Churchill was a memorable public weeper). Biologists tell us that weeping is good for us, not only to relieve tension, but tears apparently release excess chemicals from the body and even contain benign bacteria which protect the eye from infections. The Latins know more than we do!

Nose and ears

French and Hispanic people indulge in the nose twitch, snort or sniff, to express alertness, disapproval or disdain respectively. Portuguese tug their ear lobes to indicate tasty food, though this gesture has sexual connotations in Italy. In Spain the same action means someone is not paying for their drinks and in Malta it signifies an informer. It is best to recognise these signs, but not embark on the risky venture of attempting to imitate them.

Mouth

It is said that the mouth is one of the busiest parts of the human body, except in Finland where it is hardly used (except for eating and drinking). This is, of course, not strictly true, but most societies convey a variety of expressive moods by the way they cast their lips. De Gaulle, Fernandel, Saddam Hussein, Marilyn Monroe and James Stewart made the mouth work overtime to reinforce their message or appeal. The tight-lipped Finn shrinks away from such communicative indulgences as the mouth shrug (French), the pout (Italian), the broad, trust-inviting smile of the American, or even the fixed polite smile of the Oriental. Kissing one's fin-gertips to indicate praise (Latin) or blowing at one's finger-tip (Saudi Arabian) to request silence are gestures alien to the Nordic and Asian cultures.

Shoulders

Non-demonstrative people living in another culture for a prolonged period can progress to an understanding of demonstrative gestures. Multi-active peoples have very mobile shoulders, normally kept still in northern societies. The Gallic shoulder shrug is well known from our observations of Maurice Chevalier, Jean Gabin and Yves Montand. Latins keep their shoulders back and down when tranquil and observant, push them up and forward when alarmed, anxious or hostile.

Arms

Arms are used little by Nordics during conversation. In Italy, Spain and South America they are an indispensable element in one's communicative weaponry. Frequent gesticulating with the arms is one of the features which northerners find hardest to tolerate or imitate. It is inherently associated in the northern mind with insincerity, overdramatisation, therefore unreliability. As far as touching is concerned, however, the arm is the most neutral of body zones and even Englishmen will take guests by the elbow to guide them through doorways or indulge in the occasional arm pat to deserving subordinates or approaching friends.

Hands

The hands are among the most expressive parts of the body. Kant called them 'the visible parts of the brain'. Italians watching Finnish hands may be forgiven for thinking that Finns have sluggish brains. It is undeniable that northern peoples use their hands less expressively than Latins or Arabs, who recognize them as a brilliant piece of biological engineering. There are so many signals given by the use of the hands that we cannot consider them all here. Among the most common are 'thumbs up', used in many cultures but so ubiquitous in Brazil they drive you mad with it, hands clasped behind back to emphasize a superior standing (see Prince Philip and various other Royals and company presidents). The akimbo posture (hands on hips) denotes rejection or defiance, especially in Mediterranean cultures.

Legs

As we move even further down the body, less evident but equally significant factors come into play. Northerners participate in leg-language like everybody else. As no speech is required, it inflicts no strain on them. In general the 'legs together' position signifies basically defensiveness, against a background of formality, politeness or subordination. Most people have their legs together when applying for a job. It indicates correctness of attitude. This position is quite common for Anglo-Saxons at first meetings, but changes to 'legs crossed' as discussions become more informal. Formal negotiators such as Germans or Japanese can go through several meetings maintaining the 'leg together' position. There are at least half a dozen different ways of crossing your legs, the most formal being crossing ankles only, the average being crossing the knees, and the most relaxed and informal being the ankle-on-knee cross so common in North America.

When it comes to walking, the English and Nordics walk in a fairly neutral manner, avoiding the Latin bounce, the American swagger and the German march. It is more of a brisk plod, especially brisk in winter when the Spanish dawdle would lead to possible frostbite.

Feet

It is said that the feet are the most honest part of the body: although we are self-conscious about our speech or eye and hand movements, we actually forget what our feet are doing most of the time. The honest Nordics, therefore, send out as many signals with their feet as the Latins do. Foot messages include tapping on the floor (boredom), flapping up and down (want to escape), heel lifting (desperate to escape), multi-kicking from a knees-crossed position (desire to kick the other speaker). Nordic reticence sometimes reduces the kicking action to wiggling of the toes up and down inside shoes, but the desire is the same. Foot stamping in anger is common in Italy and other Latin countries, but virtually unused north of Paris.

Body language in business

Some forms of sales training involve a close study of body language, especially in those societies where it is demonstrative. Italian salespeople, for instance, are told to pay great attention to the way their 'customers' sit during a meeting. If they are leaning forward on the edge of their chair they are interested in the discussion or proposal. If they sit right back, they are bored, or confident to wait for things to turn their way. Buttoned jackets, and arms or legs tightly crossed, betray defensiveness and withdrawal. A salesperson should not try to close his sale in such a situation. Neither should a proposal be made to someone who is tapping with feet or fingers – they should be asked to speak. Italian salespeople are taught to sit as close as they can to their customers when attempting to close the deal. Latin people tend to buy more from a person sitting close to them than from a distance.

Solutions

Cross-cultural factors will continue to influence international negotiation and there is no general panacea of strategies which ensure quick understanding. The only possible solutions lie in a close analysis of the likely problems. These will vary in the case of each negotiation, therefore the combination of strategies required to facilitate the discussions will be specific on each occasion. Before the first meeting is entered into, the following questions should be answered:

1. What is the intended purpose of the meeting? (Preliminary, fact-finding, actual negotiation, social?)
2. Which is the best venue?
3. Who will attend? (Level, number, technicians?)
4. How long will it last? (Hours, days, weeks?)
5. Are the physical arrangements suitable? (Room size, seating, temperature, equipment, transport, accommodation for visitors?)
6. What entertainment arrangements are appropriate? (Meals, excursions, theatre?)
7. How much protocol does the other side expect? (Formality, dress, agendas?)
8. Which debating style are they likely to adopt? (Deductive, inductive, free-wheeling, aggressive, courteous?)
9. Who on their side is the decision maker? (One person, several, or only consensus?)

10. How much flexibility can be expected during negotiation? (Give and take, moderation, fixed positions?)
11. How sensitive is the other side? (National, personal?)
12. How much posturing and body language can be expected? (Facial expressions, impassivity, gestures, emotion?)
13. What are the likely priorities of the other side? (Profit, long-term relationship, victory, harmony?)
14. How wide is the cultural gap between the two sides? (Logic, religion, political, emotional?)
15. How acceptable are their ethics to us? (Observance of contracts, timescale?)
16. Will there be a language problem? (Common language, interpreters?)
17. What mechanisms exist for breaking deadlock or smoothing over difficulties?
18. To what extent may such factors as humour, sarcasm, wit, wisecracking and impatience be allowed to spice the proceedings?

Good answers to the questions in the above 'checklist' will help to clear the decks for a meeting which will have a reasonable chance of a smooth passage. It is to be hoped that the other side has made an attempt to clarify the same issues. French people often hold a preliminary meeting to do just this – to establish the framework and background for discussion. This is very sensible, although some regard the French as being nitpicking in this respect.

9

MANNERS (AND MANNERISMS)

"Manners maketh man". Cross-culturally speaking, they can unmaketh him as well. In a really free world we should be able to wipe our plates with bread like the French, hawk and spit like the Mongolians, belch like the Fijians, drink ourselves legless like the Finns, voice unpopular opinions like the Germans, turn up late like the Spaniards, snub people like the English and eat with our left hand in Saudi Arabia. In theory, there is no such thing as international etiquette, but certain mannerisms are acceptable only at home!

IN OUR OWN CULTURE WE ARE PROVIDED WITH A CODE FOR BEHAVIOUR. There is right and wrong, proper and improper, respectable and disreputable. The code, taught by parents and teachers and confirmed by peers and contemporaries, covers not only basic values and beliefs, but correctness of comportment and attitudes in varying circumstances. The rules may or may not be enshrined in law, but in one's own society they may not be broken without censure or with impunity. Unless we are eccentric, we conform. At home we know how to behave at table, at cocktail parties, in restaurants, at meetings and at a variety of social occasions. We are also fully cognisant of the particular taboos which our own culture imposes.

Comfortable code

The well-brought-up citizen not only feels comfortable with the code, but in the main actually welcomes it. It is a familiar regulatory mechanism which stops people making fools of themselves or being considered outsiders. All societies have outsiders, of course, but most of us prefer to be insiders. Generally speaking, it is less hassle. A problem arises, however, when we go abroad. As a representative of our country, we would like to show what good manners we have. Unfortunately, what are good manners in one country can be eccentricity or downright bad manners in another, as anyone who blows their nose in a beautiful white handkerchief in front of a Japanese will soon find out. International travellers face a dilemma. Should they maintain their impeccable behaviour from back home and risk inevitable *faux pas*, or should they imitate the people they visit and risk ridicule?

Unfortunately, there is no such thing as international etiquette. When someone begins to formulate an international code for correct behaviour, they instinctively look to their own norms as being the logical, acceptable, inoffensive ones. So we are back where we started.

Sincerity helps

Sincerity takes us a long way. Europeans, Asians and Americans meet regularly on business and at conferences and manage to avoid giving offence, by and large, by being their honest selves. The Americans are genial and sincere, the French gallant and sincere, the British reasonable and sincere, Germans and Russians unsmiling but sincere, Finns clumsy but sincere, the Japanese smiling and sincere (although unfortunately Europeans and Americans think their smiles are insincere). The odd dinner or business meeting we carry off well in the euphoria generated by the host's generosity and the guest's appreciative attentiveness. At such initial gatherings *faux pas* are ignored, even considered charming. The question of correct comportment in a foreign environment only becomes pressing when the exposure is lengthened. A protracted host–guest relationship or, even more, an ongoing business relationship, places greater strain on the tolerance and patience thresholds of both parties as time goes by. The American habit of sprawling in chairs at business conferences may seem friendly and disarming to the British, but would place Germans in a constant state of unease either in their own offices or the Americans'. Mexican unpunctuality, forgiven once, becomes unacceptable if endemic. Latin loquacity, engaging at first for Finns and Swedes, soon drives them up the wall. There is a limit to the number of cups of green tea a European can accept in a day.

Learning the ropes

Once the honeymoon of first acquaintance is over, international travellers/businesspeople seek a behaviour pattern which will serve them adequately wherever they find themselves. Some things come easily – handshaking or bowing, ladies first or ladies last, chocolates or flowers for the hostess. Other features give a little more trouble – the use of chopsticks, the texture of local small talk, the concept of time in a particular country. The deeper we delve, the harder it gets. What are the important social norms? What are the core beliefs? The real sensitivities? Above all, what is strictly taboo?

They don't always tell you. Everyone knows that it is inadvisable to send the firm's best-known drinker to represent you in Saudi Arabia and that Arabs do not eat pork, but is one aware that it is bad manners to point one's foot at an Arab in conversation or ask about the health of any of his womenfolk? Did you know that sending yellow flowers to a woman signifies, in some European countries, that she has been unfaithful to her husband?

Let us take a look at the areas where major *gaffes* may cause offence and minor ones some embarrassment – dining table etiquette, cocktail parties, restaurant behaviour, meetings, social norms and finally taboos.

Table manners

An old Malagasy proverb says: 'Men are like the lip of a cooking-pot, which forms just one circle.' By this one might understand that the basic human need for food serves as a uniting factor, at least temporarily. This is more than likely, though what people do around that cooking pot can differ to a startling degree. To begin with, eating is actually more important to some of us than to others. We often hear it said that Americans eat to live and that the French live to eat. This may be an oversimplification, but it is a fact that many Americans have a Coke and burger in the office, the English a sandwich or pub lunch, and Scandinavians are in and out of the company canteen in 30 minutes flat. In contrast, the French attach social importance to the midday meal, which may last from one to two hours. Spaniards, Portuguese and Greeks rarely rush it either.

Eating hours

People also eat at very different times. Nordics, who begin work early, have very little breakfast, but are starving by noon. Finns have lunch at 11.30, while 12.30–1 is a European norm. Spaniards rarely get the meal on the table before 2 and used to carry on until 4 or 5pm, although their membership of the EuropeanUnion is causing the younger executives at least to get back to the office by 3 and cut out the siesta. An even greater variety of eating times is apparent for the evening meal. Finns are starving again around four and they, along with the Japanese 'salarymen' and the British working classes, precede the rest of us to the table around 5.30 pm. Canada and New Zealand, too, take an early 'supper'. The Australians hang on a bit longer, the Americans and most northern and central Europeans sit down around 7.30, while the Spaniards and Portuguese, still digesting lunch, do not want to see food again till 9 or 10pm, often leaving it much later than that. A dinner invitation in Spain or Portugal for 8 or 8.30 means that the main course is likely to be served between 10 and 11. Chinese and other Asians start the evening meal at 8–9pm, although Indonesians have an aversion to dining early.

When invited to dinner at someone's home, most nationalities turn up at the appointed time – it is quite a different matter for cocktail parties. Unpunctuality, is, however, no disgrace in Spain, when an invitation for 9pm means 9.30 in any case.

Protocol

Seating arrangements, when round a table, are often casual and left to the last minute in many countries, although Asians invariably seat the most important guest facing the door. In Europe, the French and Germans are more careful about placing people, bearing in mind their various interests and status. It is the Swedes, however, who behave most formally at table. Swedish hospitality notwithstanding, dinner in Stockholm can be quite an ordeal. The chief guest escorts the hostess to the table and sits on her left, unlike most countries, which prefer the right. Schnapps are served at the beginning and the guest of honour must initiate the toasting. The first toast will be to the hostess and a short speech is required. One raises one's glass, proclaims the toastee's name, looks into his or her eyes, utters the magic word 'skål', knocks back a fair amount of the firewater, holds one's glass up again for another two-second eye contact, then places the glass firmly on the table. As the dinner proceeds each person round the table must *skål* and be *skål*ed in this way. If anyone is forgotten by anyone else, it might not be forgiven easily. The biggest scandal, of course, is if you *skål* the hostess if more than eight people are present at the table. A Swedish couple from the small town of Gävle told me that some years earlier an important French visitor had done this to his hostess and that the people of Gävle had talked about little else since. Swedes are great after-dinner speakers and at large dinners (50 guests or more) lengthy toasts and speeches can take up to two hours. Guests are expected to speak in English, French or German if they can't manage Swedish. You can be either humorous or pompous – both styles seem to go down well.

Bon appétit

In most countries the signal to start eating is given by the host or hostess. In France it is '*bon appétit*', in Germany '*guten Appetit*', in Italy '*buon appetito*' and so on. Anglo-Saxons have no equivalent for this formula and often mutter 'right' or say nothing. This is very disconcerting for French people who invariably come out with 'good appetite'. One Frenchman, on being told one says nothing, waved his spoon hesitatingly over his soup for a moment, then grunted '*Eh bien, alors – bonne nuit*' before tucking in. The Japanese formula is '*itadakimasu*' (I am receiving), although they will probably have preceded this by saying something nice about the appearance of the food. Japanese attach as much importance to the aesthetic arrangement or layout of the food as its actual taste, so in Japan you should not attack a dish without complimenting your hostess on her artistry.

How many courses

Anglo-Saxons are used to eating three courses – starters, main dish and dessert. In other societies, the number of dishes may be far more numerous. The French, for instance, serve many side dishes such as lettuce, *haricot verts*, endives, asparagus and artichoke separately, whereas the British tend to put as much as they can on one plate. In Asia one can lose count of the number of dishes, although in China they will be placed on the table five or six at a time. The Japanese, when seeking to impress, can serve a very large number of dishes one after the other, each containing a small, easily digestible amount. Once hosted by a Japanese college principal, I counted 19 consecutive courses, all paper-thin slices of fish or meat (17 fish to 2 meat) and arranged concentrically overlapping to cover the whole plate. My mother, who was 92 at the time, was worried that the very multiplicity of cuts would be too much for her ageing stomach, but the principal, who was 90 himself, assured her she would be able to digest the lot without any problem. This proved to be true, until they served up the twentieth dish (strawberries) which promptly sent off both nonagenarians to the rest room to be sick.

Customs

According to the customs of the country, meals may be taken sitting or at table, on the floor or on the ground. In Japan it is common to sit on *tatami* matting, in Arabian countries on carpets, linoleum or polished surfaces, in Tonga, Fiji and most of Polynesia on grass or firm soil. When not at table, Europeans and Americans have to decide how to arrange their legs, not being able in general to squat for long in the eastern manner. In Japanese and Arabian households shoes are generally removed and left in the hall. Chopsticks are used in several Asian countries, particularly Japan and China, and Caucasians are advised to acquire enough aptitude with them at least to get morsels into the mouth. Clumsiness is normally overlooked, although goodness knows what they really think of us. We get our own back when some of them use knives and forks. In Arab countries one usually eats with the hand – the right one – as the left is reserved for 'dirty' tasks, whatever those may be. It is not easy to eat a huge leg of lamb oozing gravy with one hand. You need to roll up the right sleeve before you start – the gravy will run down your forearm in any case. Most homes have an adjoining washroom to which you repair periodically to wash the gravy off. The choicest cuts are handed to you by the host – it is bad manners to take a piece yourself or to decline the piece he offers you, too big though it may be. Rice will be squeezed into balls by the host (by hand) and given to you directly. You may squeeze further balls of rice yourself but do not touch the lamb on the serving plate. Don't touch any food with your left hand unless you have informed the host at the beginning of the meal that you are left-handed, in which case remember that your right hand is the dirty one. In Malagasy families the leg of lamb is exclusively the father's portion.

Starters

Starters vary in different countries. Japanese *sashimi* (raw fish) is arguably among the most delicious (and expensive), raw or smoked fish also being popular in Scandinavian countries. French *hors d'oeuvre* often consist of *crudités*. Italians favour *antipasta* (often parma ham). Americans shrimp cocktails and (recently) potato skins, Greeks *tsatsiki* and *taramasalata* and Turks yoghurt. Spaniards like to have a *tapas* session before dinner. Americans whet their appetite with pre-dinner *guacamole* and cheese dips. In virtually all countries, however, soups are a great stand-by and often a particular soup is closely associated with the national cuisine. In Spain, it is *gazpacho*, in France *soupe à l'oignon* and *bouillabaisse*, in Austro-Hungary *goulasch*, in Russia *bortsch*, in China shark's fin or bird's nest, in Nordic countries pea, in Italy *minestrone*, in Germany oxtail and in the United States clam chowder. All of these soups, whether hot or cold, are normally ordered as starters. In Japan *misoshiro* soup is eaten at or near the end of the meal, as is the *sopa alentejana* in the Portuguese province of Alentejo. In the latter case, the peasants used to fill up on soup, as main courses were often inadequate in this once poverty-stricken region.

Soups are normally eaten with metal soup spoons; in China they are ceramic and a special shape. In Japan and Korea one lifts the soup bowl to the mouth and drinks the contents accompanied by legitimate slurping. In these countries rice is also slurped up from close quarters with chopsticks. It is a noisy process, but perfectly good manners. Most Europeans tip their soup dish towards themselves when spooning out the last dregs – in England it is considered good manners to tilt the soup plate away from oneself in the closing stages.

Main courses

Main courses around the world are too numerous and varied to describe here. Strange though many foods may seem, most dishes are edible and even tasty when one has familiarised oneself with them. *Sashimi*, which puts a lot of Anglo-Saxons off at first tasting, is one of the world's great dishes, priceless for its subtlety and delicate flavour. One can hardly say the same of Korean *kimshi*, some Vietnamese fish and eel dishes and various offerings in the small villages along the Yangtse. Fijian *kava* tastes (and looks) like mud to the uninitiated and I would not recommend the

Pyongyang *sake* with a snake in the bottle even to people who owe me money. Finnish *kalakukko* and *mämmi* take a little negotiating, but are good in the end, although *calamares en su tinta* (squid in its own ink) has few supporters outside the Hispanic world.

International travellers should eat as much as they can, to avoid offending their hosts. Americans and particularly English are well placed to get their revenge if they want to by offering their own cooking to visitors on Anglo-Saxon shores. In general, although one offers one's best and tries to follow the good manners of the host country. It is as well to know that an Australian country breakfast may consist of a huge beefsteak with two fried eggs on top and that in Madagascar you should not hand an egg directly to another person, but place it on the floor first. In Tonga and Hawaii you bury meat for a while before you eat it, in Japan you can eat whalemeat and live lobsters (they watch you eat them) and in Finland I have enjoyed succulent steaks of bear, beaver, elk and reindeer. Portuguese mix pork and clams and cook cod in 53 different ways. Malagasy slaughter zebu cattle on sacrificial occasions and put a little blood on guests' heads to integrate them into the festivities.

Unusual table manners are not limited to Third World or out-of-the-way countries. The English take the use of a knife and fork for granted, but Americans do not keep a knife in their hand while eating. First they cut the meat with their knife in the right hand and fork in the left. Then they put the knife down by the side of the plate, transfer the fork from left hand to right, slightly dip the left shoulder and start eating in what to the British looks like a lopsided manner. The British habit of eating vegetables (even peas) with the fork upside down is scorned by the Americans and Europeans. The French – great eaters – use bread as an extra utensil, pushing anything else around with it and eventually employing a chunk to wipe the plate clean and save the dish washers extra effort. It might not look very civilized around Cadogan Square, but what are the French to think of a society which eats its cheese after dessert?

Japanese, westernised in many things, do not usually eat dessert. Neither are they very fond of cheese or lamb, so remember that when you invite them home. In Japan the main things to remember are to say how nice everything looks, keep eating a little of each dish at a time without finishing any off, and lifting up your glass when someone offers to fill it. You in turn should fill up their glass, and any others you can reach. When you have drunk enough *sake*, turn your *sake* cup upside down. In China you should never take the last morsel from a serving plate and never at any time during the meal say you are hungry.

In the Finnish countryside they serve new potatoes with their skins on at the table and you are supposed to peel them before eating. Finns can do this with a knife and fork without touching the hot potatoes, which burn the fingers of the uninitiated. In England we are told not to put our elbows on the dining table and to sit with our hands in our lap when we have finished. Mexicans are told to put both hands on the table during and after the meal; it is taboo to hide them under the table. In Fiji and some other countries it is polite (even mandatory) to belch or burp after completing your meal, to show appreciation. Don't do it in the wrong country. (Swedish hostesses would faint.) In China you know when the meal is ended, for the host stands up and thanks you for coming.

In the United States many Britons have been shocked when on their first helping of the main course, the host asks them, 'Did you get enough?' The use of the past definite (instead of the present perfect, 'Have you had enough?') implies to the Brit that there is no more to be had. In fact the American is offering more, so you may legitimately reply, 'I sure didn't!'

Cocktail parties

There are no fixed rules for cocktail parties, which in themselves are often interesting exercises in cross-cultural behaviour. No one is quite sure what is the best time to arrive, the best time to leave and how long the party should last. Then there is the question of what one drinks, how much one eats and what one talks about. Having a few friends at home for drinks in one's own country is a relatively simple affair. Larger parties with a multinational guest list require considerably more thought.

My wife and I spent five years on the Tokyo cocktail circuit – a very lively one – where attendances averaged well over 50 and involved a minimum of a dozen different nationalities, often more. They were usually held in the homes of business executives; embassies entertained on a somewhat larger scale on National Days and other occasions.

We counted among our circle of friends in Tokyo acquaintances from 20-odd countries as well as a liberal sprinkling of Japanese. Under such circumstances there is no such thing as a cocktail party of short duration. How does one schedule an event where the Japanese will turn up 10 minutes early, the Germans and the Swiss on time, the Americans and British a bit late, the French after them and the Brazilians an hour after the party was due to end? One could put something like 6.30–8.30 on the invitation card, but nobody took any notice of it. Few parties ended before 11 or 12 unless one ran out of liquor.

Another basic problem was how many people to invite. Even among the British and American communities, with which we were chiefly involved, it was likely that there would be half a dozen cocktail parties held every night. Consequently one counted on an acceptance rate of one in three and invited 150. If you were unlucky enough to hit a day when for some reason there were few parties, you might get landed with 100 guests or more – this happened to us on more than one occasion. The problem was further complicated by the fact that Japanese tend not to answer the RSVP – but they usually turn up. Furthermore most Japanese executives do not bring their wives, although some do! One just had to play the averages.

Small talk

Some nationalities thrive in the cocktail party atmosphere and others do not. Russians, for instance, like drinking sitting down, especially as they devote a considerable amount of time to it. Chinese, too – used to mammoth dinners seated at banquet tables – are less at ease shuffling round from group to group of noisy strangers. Americans, with their mobile nature and easy social manners, excel in such a kaleidoscopic ambience. Australians and Canadians, used to formulating strategies for meeting new arrivals, have no difficulty in integrating themselves with circle after circle and conversation always comes easily to them. The British and the French – past masters at small talk – are also practised cocktailers. Yet the very issue of small talk poses a substantial problem for some other nationalities. Germans simply do not believe in it, Finns and Japanese are frightened to death by it, Swedes usually dry up after about 10 minutes. Russians and Germans – more than willing to have long, soul-searching conversations with close friends – see no point in trotting out trivialities and platitudes for two hours to a complete stranger. Swedes – fluent in English and happy to talk about their job and technical matters – find little to say in addition and often admit they become boring after the first half-hour. Finns, unused to chatter, actually buy booklets on small talk (one recently published in Helsinki was a great success).

The Japanese – masters of polite trivia among themselves – are never quite sure what to talk about with foreigners. At Japanese business meetings, there is the obligatory 15-minute session of platitudes and harmonising, after which one can get down to business. At cocktail parties they run up against a void.

Not so the South Americans. Although relatively deficient in foreign language skills, they maintain an incessant patter which often saves the day for Japanese or Scandinavian partners. Mexicans, Peruvians, Argentinians never run out of steam. I once attended an all Latin-American cocktail party in Caracas which began at 7 and finished at 1am. There were 300 people present, very little to eat, nobody stopped talking except to draw breath for six hours flat; I do not remember a single word that was said.

Personal space

At cocktail parties it is sometimes difficult to maintain the integrity of one's 'space bubble', especially when there are a few Latins around. A common sight in Tokyo was a Brazilian or Colombian businessman towering over a diminutive Japanese, gripping his upper arm to show confidence, while the Japanese would back-pedal, striving to keep his glass and himself on an even keel. The Latin in his eagerness pushes ever forward into personal space; in 20 minutes they traverse the length of the room, the Japanese ending up with his back against a wall. The South American notices nothing of the other's discomfort; the latter politely asks the whereabouts of the toilet and flees, drink in hand.

What to drink

For a big party it is necessary to stock a large variety of drinks, although drinking habits are now far more standard than they used to be. This is largely due to the ascendancy of whisky and gin and tonic as international beverages. The French, for instance, who formerly drank Scotch only after dinner, now regard it as an apéritif and import huge quantities of it. English frequently drink it with soda, Americans often on the rocks, Scots neat and Japanese with water ('*mizuwari*'). Gin and tonic sells well on hot evenings and is a favourite with ladies of most nationalities, as is Campari soda or Campari and orange. Germans like white wine, Spaniards and Portuguese red, Russians vodka, Scandinavians anything with a label on it.

When Americans ask for a martini they mean 99 per cent dry gin with just a drop of vermouth in it, often with an olive or cocktail onion for good looks. With the olive it is called a Martini, with an onion a Gibson. When Americans ask for whisky, they mean Bourbon; if they want whisky they say Scotch. When you've worked this out, they ask for whisky sour, so you don't know what to put in it. When you think you're well stocked they will request things like Manhattans, Screwdrivers and White Ladies and see if you know the difference between Tom and John Collins. The British get their revenge at American parties by ringing the changes on Pimms No. 1 Cup, Pimms No. 2 Cup and Pimms No. 3 Cup.

Embassies

Embassy cocktail parties can be long and boring affairs where most of the diplomats talk to each other for hours and leave businesspeople and other lesser mortals to fend for themselves. On these occasions it is advisable to arrive and leave early, as the food usually runs out after the first hour. Japanese embassies provide the best food, the Germans and Americans at least serve enough. Paradoxically the embassies most oriented towards businesspeople were the Soviet, Chinese and Eastern bloc countries, as their attachés were actually the people who developed commercial outlets for command economies.

Leaving

There is no foolproof way of calling an end to cocktail festivities. American businesspeople can get so involved in discussing deals over drinks that they sometimes forget they are at a party, never mind the time. Latins can talk for ever. British, Germans, Dutch, Swiss and Japanese are relatively disciplined cocktail party leavers, but the same cannot be said for Danes, Scots, Slavs and Irish. In Asia it is the duty of a host to end a party, in Europe and the USA it usually depends on the guest. An old English gentleman I knew used to go to the front door at midnight, open it and stand quietly by it. After 10 minutes or so everybody used to get the idea and leave. A Swedish party-giver told me recently that there was only one way to make Finns and Russians leave. Simply announce there was plenty of food left, but nothing more to drink.

Restaurants

Restaurant entertaining plays an important part in the life of the international businessperson. It is not unusual for travelling executives to find themselves being hosted four or five times a week when on a foreign trip. They will be required to reciprocate when their partners or associates return the visit. The choice between entertaining at home or at a restaurant depends on varying circumstances. American, British, Canadian, Australian and New Zealand hostesses are quick to open their homes to foreign visitors. Spaniards, Portuguese and other Latins are less inclined to do so, until firm personal relationships have been established. Dining out is still rather good value for money in Madrid, Lisbon, Athens and Istanbul, whereas astronomical prices in Oslo, Stockholm and Helsinki make Nordics think twice about indulging in this once popular and time-honoured practice.

A deductible expense

Restaurants tend to be packed in the evenings in cities renowned for their gastronomic excellence – Brussels, Paris, Lyon, San Francisco, New York, New Orleans, Vienna, Florence, Bologna and some other big Italian cities are good examples – while nowhere is dining out more popular than in Japan, where restaurant bills are fully deductible items for tax purposes and where companies or fiscal authorities rarely question the validity of entertaining expenses which do not exceed 4 per cent of the firm's turnover. With companies like Mitsubishi, Mitsui and Hitachi footing the bill, that entails substantial activity in eating and drinking! Japanese and other Orientals, furthermore, consider that the relative smallness of their homes in comparison to, say, those of their American or European counterparts, prohibits them from being able to entertain at home in the style the occasion calls for.

Ethnic cuisines

When being entertained by a foreign colleague in a restaurant, one need not be so fully attuned to the table manners of the country, since often the establishment will be chosen on account of its ethnic cuisine, which could be from anywhere. Although Parisians tend to invite you to French restaurants, Germans, Dutch or Swiss executives like to offer you a choice of cooking, while the London executive would have some difficulty in finding an 'English' restaurant once Simpson's and Wheeler's have been used. Americans, too, prefer European or Asiatic cuisine; Japanese executives usually offer you the western or Japanese alternatives.

It is as well to remember that some national cuisines are best represented outside their country of origin. This is certainly true of Russian food, for which Russian restaurants in Paris, Helsinki and Stockholm set standards nearly impossible to reach at establishments within the former Soviet Union. The best Hungarian meals I have ever eaten have been in Vienna, while nothing I ate during my month-long odyssey down the Yangtse even vaguely approached the excellence of Chinese dishes available in London or Hong Kong. London and England in general have unbelievably good Indian restaurants, while the 80-odd Japanese eating places in the British capital serve an expensive but delicious fare which can be bettered only with difficulty in Japan itself. With 50,000 Japanese permanent residents in London, it is not so surprising that such standards have been reached.

Most astonishing of all, Tokyo arguably possesses the best French restaurants in the world! The bounding strength of the yen, plus the traditional Japanese admiration for various aspects of western excellence, has motivated several rich Japanese entrepreneurs (in some cases well-known companies) to set up top French restaurants in Tokyo such as Maxim's and Tour d'Argent, housed in sumptuous premises and staffed by the very best chefs and *maîtres d'hôtel* that Japanese money can buy. These establishments – frequented nightly by expense-account senior executives – have achieved levels of cuisine, service and ambience which could be said to equal or surpass those of competitors anywhere. The variety of dishes on offer cover most of the regional specialities of France. The quality of Kobe beef and Japanese seafood ensure that no ingredients are lacking. Wine is flown in from France – wine lists can include 200–300 of the best vintages from Burgundy and Bordeaux – and it is not unusual for 'good' bottles to cost $3000–$5000 a time. One shudders when envisaging what the total bill might be when half a dozen Japanese executives who know their wines (and they really do) have a good evening out.

Major league and minor league

Somewhat removed from this fast-lane living are middle managers anxious to impress their foreign customers on a night out on the limited budget that their enterprise permits. It is often a good idea to ask the guests which ethnic type of meal they prefer. There are, surprisingly, a very small number of cuisines which can be said to be truly famous internationally. These are French, Italian, Chinese and Indian. Such restaurants can be found in good numbers in almost every city in the world. Most businesspeople automatically opt for one of these styles. There is a growing 'second division league' of ethnic cuisines which are gradually establishing their reputation on an international basis. These include Greek, Mexican, Russian, Spanish, Korean, Indonesian, Thai and now Japanese restaurants, which are bobbing up more frequently in large cities, although they do not rival the 'big four' in general distribution. Other types of cooking such as Portuguese, German, Hungarian, Scandinavian, Vietnamese and Lebanese can be very tasty, especially when a native *gourmand* can guide you as to what to select. One rarely talks about Anglo-Saxon cuisine (American, British, Australian, New Zealand, Canadian), unless one is addicted to pig-meat for breakfast. Dutch, Finnish, Baltic, African, South American and Central and Eastern European restaurants are rarely found in other countries, although Argentinian steakhouses are beginning to gain international acceptance.

Varying ambiences

Given such a variety of eating houses, dining out offers a multiplicity of experiences. In general one adapts to the ambience. Restaurants in Spain, South America, China, Hong Kong and Indonesia are usually convivial and noisy. In England, the USA and Japan the atmosphere is more conducive to quiet socialising or business discussion, while in Sweden and Finland guests are asked to leave if they are too boisterous or unduly inebriated. Moderate intoxication is readily permitted in restaurants in Germany, Austria, Denmark and Greece, while in Japan it is considered good form for the boss to drink more than his subordinates, then perhaps leave early.

In Russia and Bavaria it is not uncommon for strangers to join you at table, particularly where the restaurant is rather large or has certain beer-hall characteristics. In Munich people occasionally bring their dogs and ask if they may sit them under the table.

Lunch or dinner in France assumes much more importance than in some other countries and the choice of dishes, and especially wine, will be attended with considerable fuss and ceremony. Wine has in the last 20 years become much more popular with Anglo-Saxons and Scandinavians and it is as well that you possess a reasonable knowledge of wines from at least France, Spain and Italy if you are a regular host. It is a far cry from the days when Swedes, Norwegians and Finns were not allowed to drink in restaurants unless they ordered another dish with each glass. In the Katarina restaurant in Stockholm, they used to have the *specialrätten* (the special dish) which one ordered with each additional cognac. It was cheap (to ease the strain on the diner's pocket) and was in fact pea soup. One ordered this time and time again with the accompanying brandy, the waiter ceremoniously placing the soup plate in front of the customer. One sniffed momentarily at the soup, waved one's spoon once over it, then let the waiter remove it. You didn't actually eat nine soups, but they would be on the bill.

Japanese modesty

When taking Japanese out to a restaurant one should exercise care that they are not allowed to choose freely from the menu. The reason for this is that the senior Japanese in the group will choose the cheapest thing listed and his colleagues will have to follow suit. In Japan it is good manners, when given the choice of dish, to show that you are not being extravagant with your host's money. This is certainly very meritorious behaviour on the part of the Japanese, but it may not be what you want. Very probably, for business reasons, you wish them to have a costly meal and wind up in your debt. The correct course of action is not to let them choose, but to recommend strongly the most expensive dish on the menu. The *châteaubriand* is what I am having, Mr Suzuki, it's the best dish in this restaurant and I insist you accompany me. He (and his subordinates) will be delighted to concur. It is not a cheap way of doing business, but it will almost certainly get you orders. Suzuki would have no hesitation in treating you with equal generosity in Japan.

Paying the bill

When it comes to paying the bill, it is usual to pay on one's home ground, tickets. Junior managers often agree to 'go Dutch' if they meet frequently. On no circumstances should one propose this arrangement with Asians. In most Asian countries, especially in Japan and China, the question of who pays the bill is quite clear before the evening commences. It is permissible for you to invite them out in their own country, though normally only after they have entertained you at least once. Guests are given the seat facing the door and from this position you should never try to pay. When you have seen the amount on the bill in many Japanese restaurants, it is unlikely you will be eager to pay in any case.

Tipping

Tipping can be such a minefield of error and embarrassment that it is better to ask foreign nationals on their ground what is the accepted custom. Suffice it to say that tips are awaited more anxiously by some waiters than others. The safest situation is when service is included in the bill, although it is not unusual for Latin waiters to expect an additional sum in recognition of smart attention. There is no danger of having to pay for extra quick service in Eastern Europe. Elsewhere, alacrity of service varies enormously according to the establishment, but is noticeably efficient in Portugal, Turkey, Australia, the USA and Switzerland. In most Asian countries the standard of service is excellent, whether you tip or not. In Japan and China tipping is not expected. In France waiters are capable of throwing the tip on the floor if they consider it insufficient.

Home in safety

Once the bill is paid, the waiter rewarded and the appropriate belching (if required) executed, then one is free to leave. In Asia the host generally will include your transport home as part of the evening's obligations. This is not so common in the West, but care should be taken to ensure safe delivery of the guest in such cities as Naples, St Petersburg, Rio, Los Angeles and New York, not to mention spots such as Bogotá and Antananarivo, where not even locals venture out on the street after dark.

Manners in society

In addition to the accepted practices for wining and dining, most cultures have an intricate set of rules governing general social behaviour. These directives are referred to as 'good manners' and are designed to help avoid the embarrassing pitfalls which lie in wait for the uninitiated.

Fortunately, manners are not what they used to be. In England they reached their peak of stringency in the days of Queen Victoria, when gentlemen wore hats just so they could take them off when meeting ladies on the street and inexperienced diners almost starved to death at table for fear of exhibiting inadequate etiquette. Alice Thomas Ellis recently reviewed a terrifying Victorian volume, *Manners and Tone of Good Society, or Solecisms to be Avoided* (circa 1899), which devoted 22 pages to the etiquette of leaving cards and went on to detail suitable instructions for morning calls, introductions, titles, periods of mourning and five o'clock teas.

At the turn of the century, similar behaviour was being advocated in Paris, Budapest, Vienna, St Petersburg and other fashionable metropoles. Good manners, invented by the upper classes theoretically in the interests of smooth social intercourse, in fact developed into a repressive code which put people in their place. Happily, Americans resent being sorted out in this way and shortly afterwards invented bad manners, which saved us all a lot of trouble. In this they were capably supported by the Canadians, with their disarmingly casual social graces, and particularly by the Australians, who, as we all know, don't give a XXXX about etiquette and generally behave as they please.

If some of England's colonies scrapped the tenets of correct behaviour held by the mother country, others imitated them well into the twentieth century. This was particularly true of India, where formality of posture and flowery speech habits even today retain Victorian overtones. Also New Zealanders and many South Africans appear very polite to present-day English people, who, since the Second World War, have largely adopted easy-going American social attitudes.

The Anglo-Saxons, along with the Scandinavians, are probably the most informal societies in the late twentieth century. The Japanese lead the world in standards of politeness, while Asians in general display consistent courtesy to foreigners and to each other. In Europe social ease fluctuates from Spanish warmth and Italian flexibility to Swiss pedantry and German righteousness; the French are probably the most formal of the Europeans.

The problem with observing the manners of others is not so much the degree of formality or informality to adopt (this can be quickly regulated) but to know what the manners are in certain regions. In Japan, for instance, the correct thing to do for a bereaved neighbour is to send them money in a sealed envelope. This custom makes some westerners uncomfortable, but nevertheless has considerable merit. If the family is rich they send the money back, if they are poor they keep it for funeral expenses. What more practical way to help them in their misfortune? To complicate the situation, bereaved Japanese often send you and your wife gifts in appreciation of your gesture.

Gift giving

Gift giving, particularly in Japan and China, is in itself a difficult area to negotiate. In brief, westerners cannot avoid indulging in this practice in the long run without running the risk of Orientals considering them churlish or stingy. Gift giving will almost invariably be initiated by the Asian; when reciprocating, be careful not to outgift a Japanese or a Chinese. It is a game you are not going to win anyway; extravagance on your part will only result in escalating expense on theirs. More important is the thought behind the gift. Something ethnic and tasteful from your own country is the safest (prints, ceramics, lace, illustrated books and so on). In general one should not open gifts in front of Asians and Arabs when an exchange of presents is taking place. The danger of someone losing face is too great.

When in Rome do as the Romans do

In Rome, imitating people's behaviour entails little hardship, as foreign visitors are more often than not quite willing to indulge in the wining, dining and other aspects of *la dolce vita* available in the Italian capital. In some countries and environments, however, one has to use one's judgement as to how far one is expected to 'go native'. Taking one's shoes off in Japanese homes comes easily, but what degree of politeness should one exhibit? For instance, Japanese apologise regularly for personal defects, minor transgressions, even for wrongs they have not done and can be embarrassingly self-deprecating in front of westerners. How much should Americans or Europeans run themselves down or accept Japanese apologies? Paradoxically, Japanese wives, in flower arranging or *origami* classes, speak disparagingly about their husbands, as this is regarded as a sign of modesty and good manners. Should the British wife follow suit? In Japan, Korea and some other countries men walk in front of women and precede them up and down stairs. British, French and Nordic males find this hard to do, though Australians manage it.

Male visitors to Australia are soon disconcerted by being called 'bastards'. An Englishman is a 'Pommie bastard', a Frenchman a 'Froggy bastard' and so on. One realises eventually that this form of address is a sign of affection among Australian males and that if an Englishman is not soon called a Pommie bastard, then the Aussies don't like him. Americans (Yanks) are called septic tanks.

In Russia it is polite to make a short speech with every toast, but it is better not to smash your vodka glass to the floor unless it is evident that your host expects you to. It's the same with plates in Greece – check it out. In Thailand a pale face is a sign of beauty in a woman (don't ask if she is unwell); in Asia one generally wraps up presents in red paper; white, on the other hand, is an unlucky colour associated with death. In Russia people don't answer other people's telephones – they just let them ring. And so it goes on – one just lives and learns how other people behave.

Strange or far out

Some traditions are so unusual that it is not advisable to imitate them. Cattle stealing is a proof of manhood in some African areas and it may be the only route to secure a worthwhile wife. In other, drought-stricken regions it is customary to take soap with you on long journeys, in case opportunities arise for running water. Polynesians bite the head of a newly deceased relative to make sure he has really passed away; it is better to stand respectfully at one side, if you are present.

Chinese decide on how to construct buildings and arrange furniture according to their *feng shui* beliefs, which may mean little to you. Few customs, however, are stranger or more impressive than the Malagasy *famadihana*, which means 'the turning of the bones'. In Madagascar when a relative has been dead and buried for a decent period of time, he or she is exhumed on some suitable anniversary or auspicious occasion, the bones are wrapped in a shroud and lovingly paraded at a family ceremony where a hundred or more people may be present. The bones are examined, fondled, shown to others and even talked to. In Madagascar the dead are considered more important and more influential than the living and the occasion often sees their reinstallation in a costly family tomb which offers considerably more comforts and amenities than the average Malagasy home. A fascinating sideline to this ceremony (to which foreigners are occasionally invited) is the question of taxation. The government taxes the *famadihana* severely, so that not infrequently three or four other families will surreptitiously whisk their own ancestral bones in and out of the tomb, rewarding the 'host' family by sharing the tax levy. This must be the world's quaintest tax fiddle!

Taboos

Taboos exist in every country and we do well to observe them as they are often deep rooted in the history and beliefs of the region. Madagascar again leads the field with a bewildering list of forbidden practices:

+ A woman may not wash her brother's clothes.
+ Pregnant women may not eat brains or sit in doorways.
+ Eggs may not be passed directly to others.
+ Children may not say their father's name or refer to any part of his body.

Closer to Europe, Russians also have an impressive list:

+ Coats should not be worn indoors.
+ It is bad form to stand with your hands in your pockets.
+ You should not sit with your legs apart.
+ No whistling in the street.
+ No lunches on park lawns.
+ No public displays of affection.
+ It is poor form to ask people where the toilet is, and never from the opposite sex.

On the other hand, it is perfectly acceptable to wander round hotel corridors at all hours of the evening or night wearing only pajamas.

In Malaysia it is taboo to point with one's index finger, although one may point with one's thumb. In Indonesia the head is regarded as a sacred, inviolable part of the body and should not be touched by another. You must suppress the desire to pat young children on the head. It is also taboo in Indonesia to have your head in a higher position than that of a senior person. This point of deference is easily engineered while sitting (a low chair or a crouch) but harder to achieve when meeting someone on the street. It is common to see Indonesians bobbing up and down on bent knees as they pass senior citizens or people of authority.

In Korea well-brought-up young people do not smoke or drink in front of elders. In Taiwan it is unthinkable to write messages in red ink. In England, Scandinavia, Japan and China it is bad form to blow your own trumpet, although others seem to see nothing wrong with it.

In Arab countries it is taboo to drink alcohol, eat pork or to ask about the health of a man's womenfolk. You will make an Arab uncomfortable by pointing your feet at him in conversation and you will insult him if you display the sole of your shoe or hold up your hand in front of his face. Do not openly admire his possessions, as he may feel obliged to give them to you. A harmless remark like 'I like that camel' may put you in an embarrassing situation in the Gulf.

Part Three

Getting to Know Each Other

We are normal, they are abnormal. Why do they have to be so devious, unpunctual, unsmiling, unreliable, undisciplined, cunning, lazy, corrupt, two-faced, aloof, distant, inscrutable? Why can't they be more like us? But appearance is not reality. Let's see why they are so pig-headed, etc.

10

UNITED STATES OF AMERICA

The United States of America has the world's biggest economy – four times greater than anyone else's (with the exception of Japan) and ten times bigger than that of Russia. America is first in volume of trade, first in industry, first in food output and first in aid to others. They spend, too, being the top consumers of energy, oil, oil seeds, grain, rubber, copper, lead, zinc, aluminium, tin, coffee and cocoa. They have the four busiest airports in the world and fly three times more passenger miles than anyone else. They have the world's longest road network and longest rail network. They own more cars, telephones, refrigerators, television sets, VCRs, dishwashers and microwave ovens than any other people. They are the top tourist spenders and also gross the biggest tourist receipts (twice as much as popular France, in second place). The USA leads the rest of us as water users, polluters and consumers of newsprint. They also have the highest rates of divorce and murder.

Breakneck pace

The pace of American life is different from that of other countries. In the eighteenth and nineteenth centuries vast tracts of open, unclaimed land to the west beckoned with some urgency to poorer settlers and new arrivals. For decades it was first come, first served – you staked your claim, cleared the land, tilled, planted and defended it. They were days of land grab and gold rush. There was no time to lose as immigrants poured in; out west there were no ruling classes or aristocrats, royal claims or decrees, no constraining ideologies or regulations – only practicality; if it worked, you did it before anyone else did.

One might have assumed that with the majority of goals attained and the visible advent of the affluent society, this frenzied tempo of life would have slackened. It has not. Modern Americans continue at the headlong pace of their nineteenth-century forbears. Work equates with success, time is money. They have to get there first. The chief difference is that in the nineteenth century, everybody knew where 'there' was. Today's Americans, unrelentingly driven by the traditional national habit of pressing forward, conquering the environment, effecting change and reaching their destination, are no longer sure what that destination is.

The rest of the world looks on in awe, for none of us are in the same grip of this achievement fever. It can be argued that Germans and Japanese share the same work tempo as Americans, but the Germans, with their long holidays, social welfare and impressive culture, value quality of life much more. The Japanese, with no more leisure than the Americans, nevertheless achieve what they do at a much more relaxed pace and have created a calm, relatively crime-free society where moral and spiritual values take priority over materialistic goals. The four 'Asian tigers' – Singapore, Hong Kong, Korea and Taiwan, breakneck export powerhouses all – most closely resemble the USA in unrelenting effort, although their eastern philosophies incline them to view success as collectivist as opposed to the American view that the individual must triumph. In America you start at the very bottom, give it all you've got, pull yourself up by your own boot straps, guts it out and get to the very top. It's rags to riches, in a land where everybody is equal. It's a daunting task, but fortunately Americans are unfailing optimists (see human mental programming) and future-oriented.

Americans are not afraid of challenge or competition, although the strain is beginning to tell. Up to the 1970s the economic and political development of the United States had been an undoubted success story. Other nations had had their ups and downs, peaks and valleys, successes and reverses. Only in America had progress been invariably forward, up and one-way. Then came Vietnam, mounting trade balance deficits and the slowing of the economy. Even so, no one in their right mind writes off the Americans. Their industrial, commercial, financial and military assets are of a muscular nature not yet approached by their rivals for twenty-first-century dominance. A greater problem for the American people is not so much the maintenance of their material strengths as the attainment of inner harmony.

How should wise Asians, or Europeans with their variety of ideals, handle this time-keeping, media-driven, dollar-minded phenomenon? Hitch one's star to their wagon and make a fast buck? Or tough it out with them?

How to empathise with Americans

American businesspeople have the reputation of being the toughest in the world, but they are, in many respects, the easiest to deal with. That is because their business philosophy is uncomplicated. Their aim is to make as much money as they can as quickly as they can, using hard work, speed, opportunism, power (also of money itself) as the means towards this end. Their business decisions are usually not affected by sentiment and the dollar, if not God, is considered at least almighty. This single-minded pursuit of profit results in their often being described as ruthless.

Northern Europeans are well placed to deal with Americans successfully. Their reputation as straightforward managers is well-received by the open, frank Americans, who often get seriously irritated by what they see as the 'devious' manners of Latins and Orientals.

At meetings, Americans show the following tendencies:

+ They are individualistic, they like to go it alone without checking with head office. Anything goes unless it has been restricted.
+ They introduce informality immediately: take their jacket off, use first names, discuss personal details, e.g. family.
+ They give the impression of being naïve by not speaking anything but English and by showing immediate trust through ultra-friendliness.
+ They use humour whenever they can, even though their partner fails to understand it or regards it as out of place.
+ They put their cards on the table right from the start, then proceed on an offer and counter-offer basis. They often have difficulty when the other side doesn't reveal what they want.
+ They take risks, but make a definite (financial) plan which must be adhered to.
+ They consider most proposals on an investment/return or investment/timescale basis.

+ Time is always money. 'Let's get to the point.'

+ They try to extract an oral agreement at the first meeting. 'Have we got a deal?' They want to shake hands on it. The other party often feels the matter is far too complex to agree on the spot.

+ They want 'yes' in principle and will work out details later. But they can be very tough in the details and check on everything in spite of apparent trust. Germans, French and others prefer to settle details first.

+ They don't like lulls or silence during negotiations. They are used to making up their minds fast (quick on the draw).

+ They are opportunistic – quick to take chances. The history of the USA presented many golden opportunities to those who grabbed fastest.

+ Opportunism and risk taking often result in Americans going for the biggest possible slice of the business ('piece of the action'), 100 per cent if possible.

+ They often lack patience, and will say irritating or provoking things ('Look at our generous offer') to get things moving.

+ They are persistent. There is always a solution. They will explore all options when deadlocked.

+ They are consistent. When they say 'You gotta deal' they rarely change their mind.

+ They put everything in words. But when they use words like 'fair', 'democratic', 'honest', 'good deal', 'value', 'assume', they think the other party understands the same as they do. This is because US subcultures, e.g. Czechs, Germans, Poles, do understand.

+ They are blunt, they will disagree and say so. This causes embarrassment to Japanese, Arabs, Italians and other Latins.

+ They often reveal brute force as argument, e.g. their financial strength or unassailable position. They will use a majority vote unhesitatingly if they have it and will not spend (waste) much time striving for consensus. They are happy to fire anyone standing in the way of the deal.

+ They assume all negotiators are technically competent and expect to win on their own technical knowledge. They forget the other side may see it as a matter of the status of the chief negotiator. How can a Mexican company president lose to an American engineer?

+ They regard negotiating as problem solving through give and take based on respective strengths. They do not appreciate that the other side may have only one position.

+ Uncle Sam is best. But successful negotiating must enter the cultural

world of the other party. Many Americans see the USA as the most successful economic and democratic power, therefore assume that
American norms are the correct ones.

+ This leads to lack of interest in or knowledge of the foreign culture.
Americans often know little of such matters as saving face, correct dress,
use of business cards, social niceties and formalities important to Arabs,
Greeks, Spaniards etc.

+ In the USA, the dollar is almighty and will win most arguments.
Americans don't always realise that Mexicans, Arabs, Japanese and others will rarely, if ever, sacrifice status, protocol, or national honour for
financial gain.

Calm, pragmatic northerners can live with most of these characteristics.
They, too, are used to informality, first names, humour, persistence, bluntness, technical competence, give-and-take bargaining and general consistency in sticking to what has been agreed. They also wish to conclude the
deal without unnecessary time wasting or labrynthine procedures. Yet care
must be exercised. Americans are fast talking and if the language is English,
there may be certain traps. With Americans one always has to read the 'fine
print', for their apparent openness and trust in the other party are usually
underpinned by tight legal control in their contract, and they will not hesitate to sue you later if you do not comply with every clause you have put
your name to. American law is also quite different from many other legal
systems.

You should always attempt to appear straightforward, honest, but quite
tough in your dealings with Americans, who will respect resilience, open
disagreement, alertness and strong cards. You don't have to 'beat about the
bush' as you would have to with the Japanese or Italians. 'Yes, but what
happens if...?' is a good question with Americans.

If you appear tough often enough, Americans will argue, provoke, certainly push brute strength, but it is all part of their game. They, too, want
the deal. They will use far more words than you are comfortable with, but
your relative quietness will cause them discomfiture and eventually gain
you points. You will only irritate Latins with reticence, but Americans will
respect it. The answer to the oft-repeated 'Have we gotta a deal?' should
be 'Maybe'. Don't be rushed. They, too, are taking risks, but more likely
than not, they can afford to lose more than you can. They are looking at
this particular deal more than the long-term relationship. They have quar-

terly forecasts to satisfy. They want profit now, as opposed to the Japanese, who want your market. Realisation of such American aims helps you in dealing with them. Their friendliness means nothing, although it is pleasant while it lasts. They will forget your name the day after the deal is made.

You have a lot of cards up your sleeve. You know a lot more about Americans and their country than they know about you and yours. Many Americans think Finland is in Canada and confuse Lapps with Eskimos. You can enter their cultural world without difficulty – you have seen hundreds of American films, read many US books and journals. You speak their language and therefore have insight into their thought processes. They will find many Europeans disarming, but also deep. British people deal with Americans by occasionally using Americanisms in their speech, then retreating into British vagueness or semi-incoherence when they wish to confuse. Americans are tough, cunning, but also naïve. You should blow hot and cold with them, appearing half the time to be on the American wavelength and the other half of the time your own person. Americans find this disconcerting; they want to follow the script, or 'scenario' as they often call it.

This is never more apparent than when the Americans are buying – they want to hear your sales pitch. Soft sell is not necessary in the US. Any American walking into a car showroom expects the salesperson to attack him from the word go. He wishes to be told every good point about the car, the true and the peripheral, the fine discount and the personal concession, he then wants to hit back hard with his own demands, finally after much tough talk arriving at the 'deal' neither of them trusts, but both want and fully accept. You can improve on this dialogue by showing all your toughness, but slipping in a quiet injection of 'niceness', even humility.

A certain amount of modesty scores points with Americans. If you are too modest with Latins, you run the risk of their believing you ('They have a lot to be modest about'), but the Americans, as native English speakers, will hear the linguistic nuances and respect your reserve. They, for their part, are incapable of being modest in speech, as American English is irrevocably tough, clever and tending towards the exaggerated and sensational. Learn how to translate your natural modesty into suitable British English:

US	British
Jack'll blow his top	Our chairman might tend to disagree
You're talking bullshit	I'm not quite with you on that one
You gotta be kidding	Hm, that's an interesting idea (disagreement)
That's a beautiful scenario	We might find a way of making that work
I tell you, I can walk away from this deal	We'll have to do our homework
You're going to get hurt	I'm not sure this is advantageous for you
Bean-counters drive me mad	Accountants can be frustrating
It's the only game in town	I have no other choice
We had sticker-shocked the consumers right off their feet	We had overpriced the product
Go for broke	Stake everything on one venture
He'll do his best to make it fly	He'll do all he can to ensure success
If they ever come back from the grave	If they are ever a force in business again
When you scramble, you scramble like a son-of-a-bitch	Speed of action is advisable

Finally, when dealing with Americans, it is advisable to have on your team someone who knows their country well. This applies when dealing with any nationality, but at least many Europeans have spent years in the USA and such 'experts' are readily available. Northern Europeans, with their language abilities and wide knowledge of the Anglo-Saxon world, are today quite close culturally to the British, but often assume that Americans are similar, because they speak the same tongue. But Americans live in a different hemisphere and a different world. They do things their way and people who have lived in the USA know the short cuts in doing business with them.

11

CANADA

In 1565 a ship carrying French explorers sank in Hudson Bay. The survivors, once ashore, encountered local Indians, whom they addressed in friendly terms and asked how they were.

'*Apaizak obeto*,' replied the Indians. They were speaking Basque – 'The priests are better off.'

This startling incident not only pays tribute to the peripatetic initiatives of the Basque people, but is indicative of the early multiculturalism of the huge land mass that the Huron-Iroquois called Kanata.

The groundwork for multicultural Canada was laid more than 30,000 years ago when a diverse range of aboriginals crossed the land bridge between Siberia and Alaska and settled around Hudson Bay and the western and eastern coasts. They were originally inland hunters, but as they moved east across the north they adapted to coastal conditions and began to hunt seal and walrus. Eventually more than 700 groups of Inuit were scattered across the north, each one with its distinct customs and language.

The first contact between these native peoples and Europeans probably occurred about 1000 years ago when Icelandic Norsemen settled for a brief time on the island of Newfoundland. English and French explorers plied the waters of North America in the sixteenth century as they sought a 'North-West Passage' to lead them to the rich markets of the Orient. Although explorers such as Cabot, Cartier and Champlain never found a route to China, they found something just as valuable – rich fishing grounds and teeming populations of beaver, fox and bear, all valued for their furs.

Permanent French and English settlement began in the early 1600s and increased throughout the century. The settlers were obliged to interact with the First Nations people to build a unique Canadian heritage. During the nineteenth and early twentieth centuries, many eastern and northern Europeans emigrated to Canada in search of land and freedom. During this same period, large numbers of Chinese and south Asians also came to work as labourers in the mines, on the railroad or in service industries.

Today Canada is arguably the most multicultural country in the world. In the 1990s over 11 million Canadians, or 42 per cent of the population, were reported as having an ethnic origin other than British or French. Among the larger groups are German, Italian, Ukrainian, Dutch, Polish, Chinese, Vietnamese, Korean, Jewish, Caribbean, Portuguese, Finnish and Scandinavian.

Over 60 languages are spoken by more than 70 ethnocultural groups across the country. The Canadian government is very active in protecting this heritage and multicultural and anti-racist education programmes exist at all levels. Ethnic newspapers flourish across Canada – in Toronto alone there are more than 100. Multicultural radio and television broadcasting thrives. Toronto has a full-time ethnic television station, with a large number of programmes in Italian, Ukrainian, German, Greek, Portuguese and Chinese. Canada's Broadcasting Act (1991) and the Canadian Multiculturalism Act (1988) acknowledge that multiculturalism is woven into the very fabric of Canadian life. Canadians of all cultural origins have the opportunity to contribute to the common goals of equality, national unity, social harmony and economic prosperity.

The story of Canadian multiculturalism is not without its discordant note, however. Inevitably, North America became a focal point for the historical bitter rivalry between England and France. Quebec City was conquered by the British in 1759 and the Treaty of Paris assigned all French territory east of the Mississippi to Britain, except for the islands of St. Pierre and Miquelon, off the island of Newfoundland.

Now under British rule, the 65,000 French-speaking inhabitants of Canada had a single aim: to retain their traditions, language and culture. This endeavour continues today.

When Britain lost her American colony, large numbers of English-speaking colonists sought refuge in Canada. Canada first existed as Upper and Lower Canada, then in 1848 as the Province of Canada with a measure of autonomy, but part of the British Empire. The country subsequently expanded westwards to the Pacific Coast.

Canada played a substantial role in the Second World War and is the only nation to have taken part in all of the UN's major peacekeeping operations. It is the eighth biggest economy in the world; only half a dozen countries enjoy a higher standard of living as far as quality of life is concerned. Canada is assessed in first place on the Human Development Index.

Values

Honest	Fair, gentle
Friendly, easy-going	Generous, parochial
Practical, savers	Pioneers, independent
Humorous	Low key, uncomplicated
Tolerant, but critical of US	Love family, mother nature
Prudish, often traditional	Internationally impartial

Canadians and Americans

Canadians are often defined in comparison and contrast to the Americans, with whom they show an 8000km border and for whom they have conceived a love–hate relationship. Although no other neighbours in the world enjoy such a warm rapport , Canadians love to spell out US-Canadian differences in the following manner:

Americans	Canadians
Self-centred	World awareness
Pushy	Low key
Boastful	Modest
Exaggerate	Understate
Jump to conclusions	Methodical approach
Individual is paramount	The society counts too
Nationalistic	Moderate, even apathetic
Don't respect cultural differences	Multicultural
Distrustful	Trusting
Superiority complex	Occasional inferiority complex
Reckless	Moderate caution
Restless	Internal comfort
Rushing	Measured pace
Expansionist	Conservative, consolidating

Concepts

Leadership

In English-speaking Canada, leading statespeople are generally low key. Not many non-Canadians can remember the name of any Canadian premier except perhaps Pierre Trudeau. Leaders in Quebec have more Gallic flair.

Canadian managers behave in a subdued manner in comparison with their American counterparts and are expected by their staff to be truthful, trusting and egalitarian. Though results oriented, their route to success is governed by common sense rather than aggressive methods.

Status

Canadian leaders have big homes and fine cars, but ostentatious behaviour is definitely frowned on.

Space

Canada is the world's second largest country. Its total area of 9,970,000 sq km tops that of China, the US and Brazil and contains one-third of all the world's fresh water. With only three people per sq km, it has the lowest population density of any developed country except Australia (2 per sq km). Most Canadians, however, live within 50 miles of the US border and the vast expanses of the north (2 million sq km and 20 million lakes) are virtually uninhabited.

Time

Canadians are generally punctual, though the vast expanses of land in the prairies and in the north make people more relaxed about scheduling etc. The Inuits have their own sense of time.

Cultural factors in communication

Communication pattern and use of language

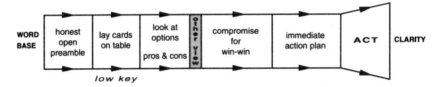

Canadian English sounds pleasing to most ears, being measured, well artic-
ulated and lacking the extreme nasal tones of some US accents. French
Canadians possess more Gallic fervour, but in fact are much more angli-
cised (linguistically) than they would care to admit and are less roundabout
and loquacious than European French.

Listening habits

Canadians are polite listeners and
rarely interrupt a sensible speech
or presentation. It is, however, a
basic tenet of Canadian education
that even young people may challenge the precepts of others.
Canadians excel in courteous give-
and-take debate. Instruction in
schools is less teacher led than student directed.

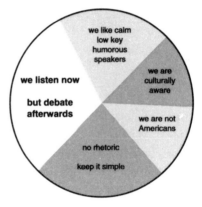

Behaviour at meetings and negotiations

Meetings are essentially democratic and everyone is allowed to air their
own views. Decisions are not rushed and a certain amount of caution is
advised, but Canadians of all origins dislike wasting time. Agreement is
sought rather than dictated and negotiations must lead to a clear action
plan. Pragmatism is the order of the day. Rhetoric or over-tough talk are
not generally appreciated. Humour is always welcome.

Manners and taboos

Canada is a very open society, exercising maximum social tolerance. There are consequently few taboos apart from boasting and other forms of ostentation. Canadians possess easy social graces – they are the world's best cocktail partyers! They invite people readily for supper in their homes where old-fashioned hospitality shows no bounds. Clothing on most occasions is comfortable and tasteful rather than snazzy.

How to emphathise with Canadians

One has to mirror to some extent the typical Canadian values of tolerance, calm, reasonableness and low-key utterances and behaviour. Although they are not very nationalistic, they like you to appreciate the uniqueness of their identity and to distinguish them clearly from Americans. They are easy to deal with, as they are genuinely interested in other countries and are keen on being internationally popular (which they are).

With French Canadians, empathy is quickly gained by speaking French, if you can. They have sustained their isolation from Ontario and the rest of the country by clinging to the bonds of family, language and religion.

12

BRITAIN

ONE EVENING, SWEDISH CUSTOMS OFFICIALS AT ARLANDA AIRPORT WERE puzzled by the behaviour of an elderly gentleman who, long after his cotravellers had passed through the immigration channels, paced up and down with a bewildered look on his face. Finally, one of the Swedes went up to him and asked why he had not come through passport control.

'I don't know where my channel is,' replied the old gentleman. 'There it says "Swedes" and there it says "Foreigners". But I am neither a Swede nor a foreigner, I'm an Englishman.'

The Swedes, like others in Europe as well as Americans and Asians, are well informed as to what Englishmen are like. For decades the British film industry, enriched by the talents of such actors as Alec Guinness, Peter O'Toole, John Gielgud, Ralph Richardson, Alastair Sim, George Cole and Charles Laughton, have put him on the screen for the world to see. The BBC, in such admirable programmes as *Upstairs Downstairs* and *Yes, Minister*, has reinforced the image.

The Englishman dresses in tweeds or a three-piece pin-striped suit and a Burberry mackintosh on rainy days. He wears a bowler hat, carries a tightly furled, black umbrella with a cane handle, has a pink newspaper tucked under his left armpit. He goes to church on Sunday mornings and eats roast beef with Yorkshire pudding for Sunday lunch. He is a man of principle, insists on fair play for underdogs, does things in a proper manner and shows more affection for horses, cats and dogs than for children, foxes and grouse. He probably went to Eton and Oxford (Cambridge?) and frequents Ascot, Wimbledon, Twickenham, Lord's and Wentworth. He believes in the Monarchy, the Empire and the Conservative Party. When not in his Club (no ladies allowed) he sits in the local (pub) with gardeners and game wardens, with whom he sips warm beer called 'real ale'. Often he has tea with the vicar, with whom he discusses the Church of England, farming, poaching, the village fête and his years with the Guards.

Englishmen are fond of cricket, croquet, rugby, sheepdog trials, detective stories and queuing. When queues are slow, one does not complain, as English people must never make a scene, not even if they have a double-barrelled name. The same applies to poor service in restaurants, railway stations and that place where you get your passport.

The antidote to such frustrating situations is the stiff upper lip. When queuing or sitting in a train one does not enter into conversation with others – that is the reason for carrying a newspaper everywhere. When a train was derailed in a tunnel in the London Underground a few years ago, an elderly City gentleman walked half a mile down the line to the next station, where he proclaimed: 'It's horrible down there in the dark. People are talking to each other!'

This powerful stereotype of the British character has been etched on other nations' minds by several generations of British films. Huge populations abroad, including the Japanese, Indians, South-East Asians and Africans, still subscribe to it and send their children to Britain to be educated along the same lines.

The majority of British people bear little resemblence to the stereotype. Not only is the image one of an upper class personage of a former era, but it does not take into account regional differences, which in the UK are extremely marked. If you draw a latitudinal line through the city of Oxford, it is questionable if you will find anyone north of it who behaves in the manner of the stereotype. In the first place, nearly 10 million Britons are Celts (Scots, Welsh, Irish, Cornish and Manx). These people are essentially romantic, poetic and emotional. They, like millions of midland and northern English people in the 'wilds' beyond Oxford, are extremely critical of the archetypal Englishman existing in foreign minds. There is a type of English person who roughly corresponds to the projected image, but he is southern, upper class and almost extinct! Even in the south, we are talking about a tiny, although often highly visible (and audible) fraction of society. Foreigners, often laughing at the eccentric English stereotype, are unaware that 50-odd million Britons laugh at him too. Northern, midland and Celtic Britons feel much more affinity with some Europeans (Norwegians,

Danes, Swedes, Finns, Dutch, Belgians, Germans, Swiss) than they do with the braying figure in tweeds. Britons are supposed to be poor at learning languages – this is a myth. Scots, Welsh, Irish and most people north of Watford learn foreign languages well and often with a good accent.

What are real English people like? The 'world image' bears some resemblance to the reality, but not much. The class system is still in evidence in Britain – an unfortunate anachronism which North America and most of Europe have dispensed with – but in fact most British people could be called middle class. They do not have a strong political party to represent them, although both Conservatives and Labour eagerly pretend to do so. The absence of a moderate centrist party contributes, sadly, to the continuing polarisation of British society.

Polarised or not, how do British people behave? Whatever the status, a pattern can be observed. Yes, we are a nation of queuers and probably the only time British people complain vociferously is when someone jumps the queue. But the stiff upper lip can move – British people today hold nothing sacred. While royalty is respected, the Royal Family is often ridiculed, both in the press and on TV. If the British can laugh at themselves, so can the monarchs – what could be more democratic than that?

Humour is a saving factor in British life – some say it is a product of a fickle climate – and many English people feel that as long as there is humour, there can never be utter despair. It is no accident that the BBC – the most humorous television service in the world – is highly popular in most countries fortunate enough to be able to receive it.

It is true that British people love detective stories. Agatha Christie is the world's most translated novelist and the British easily lead the world in library book loans. Sherlock Holmes is one of the most famous and popular Englishmen of all time. The fact is, the British have a strong conspiratorial streak – they love plotting. The most beloved characters in the extensive British theatrical literature are villains. Guy Fawkes, who was hanged after failing to blow up Parliament, became an instant hero and the nation still celebrates his anniversary every 5 November. The biggest heroes of British naval history were Francis Drake and John Hawkins – both pirates. Apparently polished and sophisticated in diplomacy, the British are masters of intelligence gathering and political blackmail.

And yet British people regard themselves as honest, reasonable, caring and considerate. Their originality often borders on the eccentric, but it is true that throughout history, they have been lateral thinkers with great powers of invention. Often academic and woolly, they can excel in science and technology. Portrayed as a nation of amateurs who 'muddle through' crises, they have shown their visceral strength in the worst adversity.

Their insularity is incurable. Each evening on television British weather forecasters routinely end their message with the prognosis of the next day's temperature: 'The high will be 22 degrees Celsius – that is 72 degrees Fahrenheit.' That after two decades of metric systems!

Don't ask the British to change their double-decker buses or red post boxes, or to drive on the right. Even when they venture abroad, they take their cocoon of insularity with them. It used to be 5 o'clock tea in long dress in the heat of the African jungle; now it's fish and chips and bacon and eggs eagerly provided by Spanish hoteliers on the Costa del Sol.

Fixed habits, fixed ideas, slow to change, unprofessional. How do these characteristics apply to the British way of doing business? How should these eccentrics be handled?

How to empathise with the British

The British feel at home with other English-speaking nationalities, with whom they have little difficulty in establishing an easy-going but effective relationship. They also feel comfortable with Nordics, Dutch and (when they get to know them) Japanese. They think that they strike the golden mean between excessive formality (French, German tendencies) and premature familiarity (American, Australian traits).

Britons, of course, belong to different classes, and foreign people should always bear this in mind. When dealing with the wealthier, more class-conscious southern English, one should stress one's civilised, educated side; when dealing with the more hard-headed northern English, Scots or Welsh, one should lay more emphasis on sincerity and straight, uncompli-cated dealing.

At business meetings, the British are rather formal at first, using first names only after two or three encounters. After that they become very informal (jackets off, sleeves rolled up) and first names will be used and maintained from then on.

British people like to show themselves as family oriented (though less than the Latins) and it is normal for you to discuss children, holidays, reminiscences during and between meetings.

Humour is important in business sessions in the UK and it is advisable for you to arrive well stocked with jokes and anecdotes. People who are good at this should use their talent to the full. British people expect you to match story with story and an atmosphere conducive to doing business will result.

A word of warning: British executives can use humour (especially irony or sarcasm) as a weapon in ridiculing an opponent or showing disagreement or even contempt. Sarcasm is rarely used against Nordics, however, since their modesty and restraint hardly ever deserve it. The British can use humour cruelly against some Latins and overdemonstrative people.

One can learn a lot about the British by observing how they use humour against themselves or their own colleagues. The following uses are common:

+ self-deprecation
+ to break up tension in a situation which is developing intransigence
+ to speed up discussion when excessive formality is slowing it down
+ to direct criticism towards a superior without getting fired
+ to introduce a new, possibly wild idea to unimaginative colleagues (the 'trial balloon')
+ to introduce the unexpected in over-rigid negotiation
+ to laugh at overelaborate or 'mysterious' management priorities and perspective in solemn corporate planning

In short, humour is regarded as one of the most effective weapons in the British manager's arsenal and some people can gain the confidence of the British by showing that they can be a match for them in this area. (A Swiss, Austrian, Turk or German has difficulty in doing this.)

British executives try to show during meetings that they are guided by reasonableness, compromise and common sense. One may find, however, that the British, even in the absence of disagreement, will rarely make a final decision at the first meeting. They do not like to be hurried. Americans like to make on-the-spot decisions when they can, using instinct. The British, more tradition bound, prefer using instinct to logic, but exercise more caution. With them one should suggest, 'Could we have a final decision at our next meeting?'

British rarely disagree openly with proposals from the other side. They agree whenever possible, but qualify their agreement ('Hm, that's a very interesting idea'). Other nationals are more open in this respect. They must watch for hidden signs of disagreement, e.g.:

+ 'Well, we quite like that, however...'
+ vagueness in reply
+ understatement showing, in fact, opposition ('That might be a bit tricky')
+ humour

Some nationalities understand the use of understatement and humour well, but can be irritated by British vagueness. They use it to stall, confuse opponents, or delay the business. Ask them for a decision and they are likely to reply, 'Let me tell you a story'. You listen to the story with interest, for it will probably be a good one. When it ends you will say 'Fine, but what about a decision?' 'I already told you,' the Briton will say. You would do well to show you understand the relevance of the story, or tell one back.

Using charm, vagueness, humour, understatement and apparent reasonableness, British negotiators can be smiling but quite tough for lengthy periods. They always have a fallback position which they disguise as long as possible. You should attempt to discover this position by being equally reasonable, smiling, modest and tenacious. In the end you may find it is similar to your own fallback in most circumstances. The area for bargaining may be somewhat greater with the British (remember they have hundreds of years of experience with India, the Middle and Far East).

Representatives of a British company will make normal use of their firm's reputation, size and wealth in their negotiating hand, and you can do likewise in dealing with them. What they do not reveal so readily is the strength of their behind-the-scenes connections. The 'old school tie', or the 'old boy network', is very much a reality in British executive life and should not be underestimated. It is particularly active in the City, the Ministries and in legal circles, and nationals from a small country should always bear in mind that they may be dealing with greater influences than are apparent on the surface.

The British are generally interested in long-term relationships rather than quick deals. This is a factor you can reckon with and use to your advantage, even though sometimes you may wish to conclude arrangements rather faster.

A lot of business is done in some countries on the telephone. The

British are also capable of discussing terms at length, but nearly always ask you to put it in writing immediately afterwards. They keep thick files.

Finally, there is the question of British insularity. Brits generally have a feeling that 'foreigners' intend to outsmart them.

13

IRELAND

TALK OF 'TWO IRELANDS' USUALLY REFERS TO THE POLITICAL DIVISION between North and South, but another distinction becoming increasingly evident lies in the contrasting image of 'postcard' or 'mythical' Ireland on the one hand, and the enterprising, modernising EU state on the other.

Mythical Ireland suggests the 'little people' and the Emerald Isle, folk music and scenic hills imbued with fifty shades of green. The real Ireland is very different. The youngest country in Europe, it has been vigorously bolstered by EU subsidies, transforming itself from a predominantly agricultural society to a near-urban manufacturing one (one-third of the republic's inhabitants live in Dublin). The darling of EU economies with a high growth rate, particularly among high-tech companies, Ireland has reached (or exceeded) the British standard of living, although it still exports more than 40 per cent of its exports to the UK.

The British Isles

Given the proximity of Ireland and the UK and their relative isolation from mainland Europe, it is not unreasonable to suppose that a close political union might have been realised. Both islands were occupied by the Celts before 300BC and later shared ravaging attacks by numerous Viking raiders in the eighth and ninth centuries. Their historical heritages did not remain parallel, however, since the Romans conquered Great Britain in 55BC but never reached Ireland, having found England rainy enough. Wales and Scotland, like Ireland, remained largely Celtic, but the decisive political development that caused England to diverge from its neighbours was the Norman French invasion of 1066. The more sophisticated Anglo-Norman combination conquered Dublin in 1169 and English power was consolidated later, under Henry VIII and Elizabeth I. Henry's split with Rome left England largely Protestant, while Ireland remained Catholic. The hail of death and destruction left in Ireland by Oliver Cromwell during the English Civil War put an end to acceptable relations between the two countries.

Culture

Values

As a predominantly Celtic nation, Ireland differs culturally from Anglo-Saxon-Norman England. Celts embody both linear-active and multi-active tendencies and are clearly dialogue oriented. The most notable Irish values (some of which are shared by the Welsh and Scots) are as follows:

rural simplicity	poetic tendencies
vision and imagination	love of literature, music, theatre
romance and idealism	warmth, charm
irony, sense of humour	mistrust of British
informality	social anchors of land, church, family

Religion

Many simply think of Northern Ireland as Protestant and Ireland as Roman Catholic. It is not so simple. The Protestant/Catholic split in Ulster is 58 to 42 per cent. While the South is predominantly Catholic (95 per cent) there are over 100,000 Protestants, several of whom have been and are very influential. The republic's first President, Douglas Hyde, was a Protestant, as were three outstanding writers, Oscar Wilde, Samuel Beckett and WB Yeats. Protestant citadels like Trinity College and the Irish Times championed non-sectarian liberalism.

Although Catholicism has long been the backbone of Irish Celtic identity, it has lost much of its influence in the modern republic, largely due to its attitude to women. President Mary Robinson has referred to it as the 'patriarchal male-dominated Catholic Church'.

Cultural factors in communication

Communication pattern and use of language

Irish people speak in a more animated manner than the English and have been described as 'audacious in speech'. This audacity often borders on hyperbole and not infrequent embroidery of the truth. This results in what the Irish call blarney and must be taken into account when conversing with them. Warmly informal at all times, the Irish are great improvisers during discussions and resemble the Italians in their skill at showing apparent agreement and compliance. They are definitely more poetic and philosophical in speech than the British.

Listening habits

When listening, the Irish are courteous and attentive and rarely show open dissent. They often have a strong desire to interrupt (as they are bursting with ideas) but rarely do so. Their feedback is ample enough, but occasionally is rather ambiguous or even devious.

Behaviour at meetings and negotiations

Meetings with Irish people are invariably warm and friendly, but sometimes confusing. They are not great agenda followers and digress enthusiastically when confronted with an interesting idea. Ideas are infinitely more important than plain facts. The Irish have a strong affinity for the abstract, the innovative, the theoretical. In this they are like the French, although less strong on logic. This characteristic causes a certain tendency towards procrastination, while they look at new ways of approaching problems and tasks. It also leads to creativity: they are unconventional and independent spirits who resist structure and routine. Latins find this easier to accept than Germans, English, Swedes or Finns.

How to empathise with the Irish

Be warm, friendly and hospitable, as they are. Show vision and use your imagination. Tell a lot of stories. Think in terms of beauty and aesthetics.

Emphasise simplicity. Don't call them English or praise the English too much. Don't be sarcastic, but accept their gentle irony. Don't show any snobbery or keep them at a distance. Don't be too factual but don't try to pull wool over what you see as rustic Celtic eyes.

14

AUSTRALIA, NEW ZEALAND AND SOUTH AFRICA

A SURVEY OF THE WORLD'S CULTURES WOULD BE INCOMPLETE (DARE I SAY top heavy?) if it did not include some consideration of the cultural forces at work and the fascinating geographical, historical and racial influences observable among the English-speaking countries of the southern hemisphere.

There are a large number of islands and communities in the south Pacific where English is dominant, or a *lingua franca*, or it coexists with melodious Polynesian tongues. Space constrains us to focus on only three of these peoples – Australians, inhabitants of the largest island in the world; New Zealanders, tyrannised by their remoteness; and vibrant South Africans, durable, multicultural, energetically building a new nation in the southern Atlantic.

What cultural traits do these peoples have in common? Is there such a thing as 'down under' solidarity or mentality? Do these English-speaking peoples relate comfortably to each other, taking advantage of similarities in linguistic and literary heritage? Do they respect, envy or dislike each other?

Australians

There is no better clue to the 200-year development of Australian society and culture than the Australian language itself. Australia is the largest English-speaking country in the southern hemisphere. Australian – the sixth largest variety of English (after American, British, Filipino, Indian and Canadian) – is a fascinating, young, vibrant, irreverent, humorous, inventive language.

Newcomers to Australia – who now arrive by jumbo jet, not convict ship – get a distinct impression of southern hemisphere Cockney when they first hear the local pronunciation. The similarity is in fact far from accidental. In the decades leading up to the discovery of Australia, the Industrial Revolution caused tens of thousands of destitute farm workers from Kent, East Anglia and Essex to come tumbling into the East End of London in search of work. They linked together with the dockland people – street traders, hawkers and artisans who had been driven out of the City and West End by the upper and middle classes. This hybrid East End population, crowded together in eighteenth-century slums and cross-fertilising their rural and urban traditions, developed a racy, witty, vulgar type of street English which became known as 'Cockney'.

It was not unnatural that these needy, lowly but fast-living city dwellers provided a sizeable number of candidates for the vessels bound for the penal colonies in Australia. They were joined aboard by town-bred petty criminals from the overcrowded cities of Yorkshire and Lancashire, especially Liverpool which had a large out-of-work Irish population.

Let stalk Strine!

It is an interesting linguistic phenomenon that the Australian language, like Black English 200 years earlier, had its first origins at sea. The officers and crew of the slave ships on the long voyage to America had had to communicate with their charges in Pidgin – a mixture of basic English and several African languages – which gave an unalterable direction to Black English. On the much longer voyage to Australia the melting pot of Cockney, Irish and Northern English dialects led to an on-board fusion of accents, grammar and syntax which formed the basis of penal colony speech as the convicts stepped ashore in New South Wales and Queensland. In this hurly-burly of dialects, Cockney emerged as the clear winner (there were more Cockneys), and the resultant speech variant was larded with dozens of old English dialect forms (*cobber, dust-up, tucker*), with Irish lilt, euphemism and volubility, and with a definite slant towards convict slang (*swag, flog, nick, pinch*). Swear words and vulgar expressions were abundant, as might be expected under the circumstances, but picturesque Cockney rhyming slang also found its way into the mixture and remains one of the fascinating features of Australian English (*trouble 'n strife* = wife; *Bugs bunny* = money; *eau de cologne* = phone).

As the language developed, 'outback' speech was quickly added to the already rich mixture. The language of the outback (or the Bush) had two main elements – Aborigine and frontier inventions. The influence of the former was limited, although picturesque in the extreme. From the Aborigines came such words as *boomerang, kangaroo, wombat, koala, jumbuck, dingo* and *budgerigar*. Frontier words and expressions were more numerous and showed the hardy humour of the explorers: *digger* (= Australian), *amber* (= beer), *banana bender* (= Queenslander), *roo* (= kangaroo), *heart starter* (= first drink of the day), *neck oil* (= beer), *grizzle* (= complain) and *across the ditch* (= New Zealand) are some examples.

The modern Aussie is a townie through and through. Australia is the least densely populated country on earth; it is also among the most highly urbanised. It was in the cities where the Cockneys and the Irish ('both in love with talk') thrived, and it was here that the Australian language gained momentum and vitality. Unused English words were resuscitated (*creek, paddock*), more fossilisms from dialects were prised out – *fair dinkum* (= genuine), *clobber* (= clothes) – and scores of words were truncated with glee – *arvo* (= afternoon), *beaut* (= beautiful), *garbo* (= garbageman), *barby* (= barbecue), *Oz* (= Australia).

Twentieth-century Australian is still undergoing change. There are the pressures of Americanisms, such as *freeway* and *elevator*, and of foreign words brought in by new Australians (*ciao, pizza, kebab*). Some features of Cockney have disappeared (no glottal stops, no dropped *h*s, less rhyming slang), while the 'rising inflection' has become an Australian invention in recent years ('What's your friend's name?' Reply: 'John Bennett?')

Australia is a relatively classless society and so is the language. There are hardly any regional variations, no class pressures on one's way of speaking, and people switch from broad to cultivated Australian at will. There is a tendency, however, for men and women to use different forms, and schoolchildren do influence each other to speak 'broad'. But although Australian speech is in the main uniform, boring it is not. The language of Crocodile Dundee is human, humorous, inventive, original and bursting with vitality. Few languages can come up with similes and metaphors to match – *uglier than a robber's dog, blind Freddie could have seen it, he had kangaroos in his top paddock (he's crazy)*.

Most Australians refer to each other as 'mate', even at the first meeting. Women are called 'love'. 'Fair go' is also central to the Australian outlook, based on common sense, equality and a healthy disregard for authority and ideology. This is why Australians always sympathise with the 'battler' and underdog. They don't like the exercise of power and privilege over the weak. The two deadly sins are *scabbing* and *dobbing* – informing against one's mates.

Communicating with Australians

There is no manual for correct behaviour in Australia, as the country lacks a clearly defined social and conversational map. Most Australians see this as a strength, a licence to be either erudite or rude in any situation. This keeps conversation lively, no one knowing what twist or turn it is likely to take. Will it end up a torrent of abuse, or warm bonhomie and sensitive human exchange, or none of these?

While not entirely true, egalitarianism is a cherished myth and the foreigner must always be very careful not to threaten this notion when talking to an Australian from any background. This egalitarianism is based on the idea of a classless society in which everyone is treated equally – regardless of wealth, education or background.

Working from this 'fair go' premise conversation will be easier, but still fraught with traps. In many countries accent and education will tell you a lot about a person. Not in Australia! The political map has also become very blurred. The longest surviving political party is the Australian Labour Party (ALP) which grew out of the trade union movement. Traditionally, the ALP and its supporters have been pro worker, social welfare and a genuine 'fair go' for the underdog. It was also, until the early 1970s, very isolationist and anti-Asian. Many Labour supporters are very upwardly mobile middle-class professionals living in the most prestigious suburbs of the major cities. They share their political party with single parents and day labourers.

Although the basic fabric of Australian society is complex yet appears deceptively simple, there are certain subjects that are in general 'safe' or 'dangerous'. All sport is generally safe and most Australians respond well to a sporting analogy. They love criticising themselves, but take very poorly to being criticised. This makes it very difficult for you as the newcomer because you will often find yourself in the middle of torrid condemnation of Australia or Australians, but should you agree too enthusiastically or even mildly, you run the risk of being dubbed a 'whinger' (complainer). This could lead to your own country being very negatively compared to Australia. If you persist, you could be told in a variety of ways to 'go back where you came from'.

But Australians also do not like or trust people who constantly or too enthusiastically praise them. They suspect that they are being set up to be either humiliated or deceived. Too much praise raises expectation and puts the high achiever under unsufferable pressure – and Australians hate being pressured. When the Australian cricket team won the coveted Ashes from their arch-rival England, the Captain's first response to being congratulated was not of joy but almost of regret. 'Now everyone will expect us to play as well next time. It has put a pressure on the whole team,' he lamented to a long-faced Australian interviewer.

This tortured form of modesty is greatly respected by most Australians and if it is not observed by the successful they will rapidly fall victim to the 'tall poppy syndrome'. One version of this is: any Australian who achieves success will be brought down to size through a variety of abusive techniques. This leaves them either totally humiliated and regretting their achievements, or packing their bags and heading for those parts of the world where success is allowed to be overtly enjoyed.

Equally, never take yourself or your national symbols too seriously, or a similar fate will befall you. It is a source of great pride to Australians that the Prime Minister is frequently booed at public appearances and that quite a few Australians do not know the words of the national anthem.

Perhaps the greatest strength of the Australian personality, although it is under threat, is their monumental cynicism. Australians are totally cynical of people in power or with too much wealth, respecting the little person, 'the battler', rather than the winner.

If you keep this in mind and don't oversell yourself or undersell your Australian hosts, success, friendship and good times will be yours down under.

Australians in their hemisphere

The world's biggest island is also the smallest continent. Geographical location and climatic conditions play a large part in shaping national character. Australia is the flattest and driest of the continents – when travelling

around it one is impressed by the awesome, mind-numbing, parched flat-
ness. The love of outdoor activities, the ubiquitous beach culture, the fashion for a suntan has led to a national health problem (skin cancer) of major
proportions. The heat produces a tendency towards apathy and procrastination in many areas, expressed in a general *laisser faire* attitude – 'no worries' or 'she'll be all right in the end'. The darker side of Australian life is
not to be discounted – they consume more alcohol and painkillers per
capita than any other English-speaking country. Their racial policy has
been largely unsuccessful and the aborigines are in dire straits as a result.

Yet Australians remain very positive human beings. Few can match their
friendliness and even fewer their spontaneous generosity. Half a million
New Zealanders enjoy the benefits of Australian unemployment benefit,
but resentment is minimal. Aussies see New Zealanders as astute, sometimes tight-fisted individuals, more British than themselves but still possessing a lot of synergy with Australians in terms of sheep, farming and
outdoor activities (sailing, cricket, rugby). There is a sense of solidarity,
particularly with regard to French nuclear testing in the Pacific.

The disadvantages of Australia's geographical remoteness have now
been mitigated by the exponential increase in the capabilities of telecommunications. People in Perth, once the most isolated city in the world
(1500 miles from Adelaide and 3000 miles from Singapore), can now communicate orally, aurally and visually with any business partner in a matter
of seconds. This technology will continue to improve, making inexpensive
locations such as Perth, Darwin and Adelaide far more attractive propositions for multinationals to locate their Asia-Pacific headquarters in than
crowded Tokyo, Hong Kong, Manila or Singapore. Over 100 large companies currently run their regional businesses out of Australia. With the
entry of Britain into the EC, Australia lost its automatic access to traditional markets and was forced to face the reality of its location on the edge
of Asia. Asian immigrants, with no sentimental attachments to British institutions, have accentuated this realisation. Australian schoolchildren now
learn Japanese, not French, as their first foreign language. The fact that
Japanese people are not particularly fond of lamb or mutton may put at risk
the future of the smallest continent's 60 million sheep!

New Zealanders

New Zealanders are more conservative, placid and reserved than Australians. They are more British, not only in their calmness of manner, but in their racial composition. They see Australians as cosmopolitan and somewhat excitable.

The original settlers who in the 1840s founded the then colony of New Zealand were all English speaking – predominantly a middle-class and working population drawn principally from rural areas of England and Scotland. They were literate and, at least during the early settling-in period in the mid-nineteenth century, much of their educational thinking and all of their reading matter came from Britain. As New Zealand's 'foreign' immigrants have always been small minorities, the English spoken in New Zealand has never been distorted (or invigorated) by waves of non-English speakers similar to those which posed a challenge to the English of the USA. New Zealand speech, although affected to some extent by linguistic interchange with Australian, has retained much old rural vocabulary from British dialects and remains, apart from some give-away front vowels ('*pin*' for pen and '*fush*' for fish), resolutely southern English.

The islands of New Zealand are similar in size to the British Isles and not entirely dissimilar in climate. New Zealanders tend to identify more strongly with their insular forebears and regard both Australians and Americans as a different, continental breed. Their stereotype of Australians is as loud mouthed, brash and arrogant, who often interrupt others' speech or talk in tandem, which is frowned on in New Zealand. New Zealanders see themselves as more laid back, certainly more cultured and much more likely to treat women sensitively. Australians often regard New Zealanders as Victorian, outdated, poor country cousins – but New Zealand produces efficient, innovative managers who often do well in Australia, being more adventurous than their Ozzie counterparts. Deregulation has gone much further in New Zealand than in Australia, where business is often seen as a closed shop. Australians are more price oriented than New Zealanders, who are more inclined to value quality.

New Zealanders emigrate in rather large numbers to Australia on account of the scarcity of work in their own country. The things they like about Australia (often referred to as 'The West Island') are the wide-open outback and winter warmth, the cosmopolitan cities and shopping opportunities, the classless society and friendly, helpful attitude of the people.

Australians show a lot of down-under solidarity with New Zealanders, especially in moments of adversity; although on occasions when this bond is broken, the latter feel that they are not the ones who break it.

Many New Zealanders visit Europe and the 'Old Country' once or twice in their life, but are more and more oriented towards the Pacific and spend most of their holidays in Australia or the Islands. They have good relations with Pacific Islanders (Tonga, Fiji, Cook Island) and believe that their Maori policy has been fairly successful. Many Maoris do not share this opinion, feeling they were ruthlessly exploited in the past and that present atonement falls far short of what is morally required. The Maori attitude to white New Zealanders is 'They are guests in our country.' An interesting cultural sideline is that the whites tend to behave like Maoris when living it up, for instance on certain sporting occasions and when singing and dancing. Most whites possess a fair knowledge of the Maori language (without being able to speak it) and sing Maori songs, as well as doing the *haka* with great gusto at ceremonies. This rather engaging symbiotic relationship is noticeably absent in the case of Australians and Aborigines.

South Africans

At the time of writing, the system of government in South Africa is in transition. Apartheid has gone, hopefully for ever. New South Africa emerges into the world limelight as one of the most multicultural nations on earth. It is not a melting pot of immigrants like the USA or Australia, but a society where several communities and races – British, Afrikaans, Malay, Indian, Zulu, Xhosa and other black tribes – will remain as separate and integral forces forging a new union which has aspirations to provide leadership to a depressed and seemingly disintegrating continent.

South Africa possesses the multicultural strengths of a Switzerland, a Singapore, and much more. The rich combination of British, French and Dutch experience, the artistry and ardent aspirations of the blacks, the diligence and tenacity of the Indians and Malays, are ingredients for a dynamic, inspired and unique future. Yet the colourful variety of the country's cultures itself poses a number of problems.

Apart from the friction among the black tribes, the history of warfare between the British and Afrikaans settlers is too recent not to have left a residue of resentment between the two communities. Each group has inherited characteristics from their forebears. English-speaking South Africans are somewhat reserved in nature, proud of their cultural heritage and set great store by good manners, elegant, expressive speech and avoidance of unnecessary conflict. In this respect they differ strongly from the Afrikaners who, like their Dutch ancestors, are blunt (often tactless) and have the American tendency to 'tell it like it is'.

Although British and Afrikaners differ sharply in their style of communication, a white South African lifestyle is discernible. Pragmatism is paramount, but South Africans resent deeply the implication that they are insensitive to the plight of less fortunate human beings. A visitor to South Africa cannot avoid being aware of the eager hospitality and thoughtful kindness of the whites living there. Power corrupts and the years of racial suppression and injustice cannot be pardoned, but there is in fact far less colour consciousness in the country than in many other parts of the world. South Africans have been brought up in a multicoloured society – it is a natural state.

White South Africans are entrepreneurial and decisive in business. At meetings they come well prepared and usually have a few cards up their sleeves. They are familiar with many African cultures and customs, and accept that bribery and accommodation are part of life on their continent if one is to achieve anything. They are, however, flexible in such matters and do not apply the same judgements when dealing with the West. At discussion time they will often sit back to listen and learn, but are not averse to assuming dominance and taking control of a meeting when they perceive an opportunity. In spite of the latitudinal distance, they focus much more on Europe than towards east or west. Africa, the continent they hope to lead, has close connections with Britain and France.

One hears many pessimistic predictions about the deterioration of South African society, in the manner which has been observed in other African states. South African whites recognise that their country can survive only if the blacks play an integral role in the development of the new South Africa. The pool of managerial talent is worryingly shallow: education of the blacks is vital but will take many years. Yet the potential contribution of the black and coloured populations is even greater than that of the 6 million educated, talented, highly organised and relatively wealthy whites.

The Indians, who number about 1 million, are concentrated in Natal and are very industrious and almost completely middle class (traders, professionals, businesspeople, etc.). The coloured population (about 3.5 million) is mostly in the Western and Northern Cape and derives from mixed breeding between white, black, Malay and Bushmen. Occupationally they tend to be farm workers in rural areas, but in urban districts they are either middle class or highly skilled workers and artisans. Sixty per cent of the coloured population speak Afrikaans. Both the coloured and Indian groups are conservative; the great majority voted for the National Party in the 1994 election.

Black South Africans really hold the key to the nation's future. They have many qualities, not least of which are patience, tolerance and a delightful sense of humour. While they are not as well educated as the whites, they are very well educated in comparison with the rest of Africa. They earn better incomes than other Africans and in the 50 per cent which is already urbanised there is a substantial and rapidly growing middle class. Their access to government posts, and the international contact this will bring, will quickly add to their experience and sophistication. Nelson Mandela himself is a shining example of a black South African politician.

South Africa's GDP is already four times that of the combined GDP of the ten other countries of southern Africa. The emergence of a dynamic, stable, prosperous South Africa would be a triumph not only for its people, but for viable multiculturalism itself, following a road which many countries will find themselves on in the twenty-first century.

15

GERMANY

BASIC CHARACTERISTICS OF GERMAN BUSINESS CULTURE ARE A MONO-chronic attitude towards the use of time, e.g. a desire to complete one action chain before embarking on another; a strong belief that they are honest, straightforward negotiators; and a tendency to be blunt and disagree openly rather than going for politeness or diplomacy.

German companies are traditional, slow-moving entities, encumbered by manuals, systems and hierarchical paths regarded by many Europeans and Americans as over-rigid and outmoded. Hierarchy is mandatory, often resulting in exaggerated deference for one's immediate superior and CEO.

The German boss is an extremely private person, normally sitting isolated in a large office behind a closed door. American and Scandinavian senior executives prefer an open door policy and like to wander round the corridors and chat to colleagues. This horizontal communication contrasts with the German vertical system, where instructions are passed down to immediate inferiors only and kept rigidly within one's own department.

In many countries there exists departmental rivalry, but when dealing with the Germans one should remember that they can be especially touchy in this area. Always try to find the right person for each message. Tread on a German executive's toes and he or she will remember it for a long time.

Germans have great respect for possessions and property. Solid buildings, furniture, cars and good clothing are important for them and they will try to impress you with all these things. You should acknowledge the grandeur of German possessions and be unafraid in displaying your own solidity, facilities, etc. Germans wish to believe you are as solid as they are.

When advertising your company's products to Germans, you should put as much as possible in print. Germans are unimpressed by flashy television advertising, clever slogans or artistic illustration. Their newspapers are full of heavy, factual ads giving the maximum amount of information in the space available. Brochures aimed at the German market should be lengthy, factual, serious and should make claims which can later be fully justified. No matter how long or boring your brochure is, the Germans will read it. They will also expect your product to conform exactly to the description you have given.

Germans have their own particular style of conducting meetings and negotiations, and you may find that procedures with big German companies are much more formalised than in your country. It is generally advisable to adopt a rather more formal approach with Germans at meetings and to note the following German characteristics, to which one must react appropriately:

+ Germans will arrive at the meeting well-dressed and with a disciplined appearance. You must match this.
+ They will observe hierarchical seating and order of speaking.
+ They will arrive well informed as to the business and expect you to be also.
+ They will present logical, often weighty arguments to support their case.
+ They often have thought over your possible counter-arguments and have their second line of attack ready.
+ They do not concede their case or arguments easily, but tend to look for common ground. This is often your best approach to make progress. Head-on collision with a sizeable German company seldom leads to results.
+ They believe they are more efficient (*gründlich*) than others and do not change position easily.
+ They compartmentalise their arguments, each member speaking about his or her speciality. They expect your side to do the same.
+ They do not interfere with a colleague's remarks and generally show good teamwork throughout. They do, however, argue with each other in private between sessions. As they are not poker-faced (like Japanese) or simulating (like French) it is often possible to detect difference of opinion among them by their facial expressions or body language.

- ◆ Like Japanese, they like to go over details time and time again. They wish to avoid misunderstanding later. You must be patient.
- ◆ They don't like being rushed.
- ◆ They are willing to make decisions within meetings (unlike the Japanese or French), but they are always cautious.
- ◆ They generally stick to what they have agreed orally.
- ◆ If you are selling to them they will question you aggressively on what are German strong points, e.g. quality of goods, delivery dates, and competitive price. Be ready.
- ◆ They expect, in the end, to get the very best (lowest) price. They may only give you a little 'trial' business even at that. Take it – it will lead to much more business later if they are satisfied.
- ◆ They will look earnestly for deficiencies in your products or services and will criticise you openly (even energetically) if you fail to match up to all your claims. Be prepared to apologise if you have failed in some respect. They like receiving apologies, it makes them feel better. Also you will have to compensate.
- ◆ They can be very sensitive to criticism themselves, therefore you must go to great lengths to avoid embarrassing them, even unwittingly.
- ◆ Use surnames only and show respect for their titles. There are many Doktors in Germany.
- ◆ Do not introduce humour or jokes during business meetings. They are not Americans, they don't like kidding. Business is serious. Tell them funny stories afterwards over a beer. You will find many of their stories unfunny or heavy. Do your best to laugh.
- ◆ They will write up their notes carefully and come back well prepared the next day. It is advisable for you to do the same.
- ◆ Germans generally have good language abilities (especially English and French) but often suffer from lack of knowledge of foreign cultures (they may know a lot less about your country than you think they know). They like to use German whenever they can.
- ◆ They are generally convinced that they are the most honest, reliable and sincere people in the world, also in their business negotiations. Show them that in this respect you are their equal.

Germans are indeed very sincere people and assume that others are too. They are often disappointed, as other people who prefer a casual or flip-pant approach to life do not always give serious answers to serious questions. Germans tend to search long and deep for the true meaning of life and like to spend their time profitably, whether it is to enrich their coffers or their soul.

In their seriousness, they try hard to be dutiful, untroublesome citizens. In a crowded country pressures to conform in public are very strong and Germans do not wish to be seen as mavericks or unorthodox. They have no desire (like many British, French or American people) to be eccentric. Germans try not to make mistakes and generally succeed. If you make a mistake they will tell you about it. They are not being rude – it is their unstoppable drive towards order and conformity. Germans like to be fair and often lean over backwards to show how fair they are.

Germans often appear intense and humourless to Anglo-Saxons, who long for periodic levity in conversation. Germans do not have the British and American addiction to funny stories and wisecracks. They long for deep friendships and have heart-felt discussions of life's problems and enigmas. Anglo-Saxons do not always see the way towards making quick friendships with them, but when they succeed in entering into the somewhat complicated structure of a German friendship, they find rich rewards. A German is generally a loyal and true friend of incredible durability. Outwardly often glum and cautious, they are inwardly desperate for affection and popularity. They want to be cherished just as the rest of us do. When they find that English, American or French individuals – on the surface easy-going and witty – can also be as steadfast as a German, they are delighted and receptive. A German friendship is indeed a very worthwhile investment.

Germans as seen by others

Appearance

Germans are time dominated, punctuality is an obsession.

Germans are slow at making decisions, as they discuss things too long.

Germans give you very lengthy explanations, going right back to the beginning of every matter.

Delays in delivering things are common in Germany. This contradicts their love of promptness.

Germans are not good at providing quarterly financial reports according to the American system.

Americans and Australians find the pace of German business life too slow.

You always have to knock on the door before entering a German's office.

Reality

Time is central to German culture. It is one of the principal ways of organising life.

Germans have a consensus decision-making process, whch requires extensive background research and often lateral clearances.

Germans, when explaining something, like to lay a proper foundation. For them events in the present are a result of the past. Historical context is important.

Germans plan well into the future. They are not preoccupied with immediate results or deliveries.

Germans prefer annual reports. Three months is too short a time frame to be meaningful. Writing quarterly reports disrupts normal work.

Germans like to complete action chains and wish to be thorough (*gründlich*) rather than speedy.

Yes, it is good manners.

Appearance	Reality
Germans are too private. They do not interact well with foreigners and are not mobile. They don't lend things easily.	Germany is not a melting-pot society like the USA or Australia, where people have developed strategies for interacting with strangers. Privacy is important in order to complete action chains without interruption. They don't borrow things easily.
Germans are too formal, using only surnames with office colleagues even after 20 years.	Formality and use of surnames are signs of respect.
Germans are stiff, distant and do not smile much.	In Germany, smiling is for friends. They are more reserved when being introduced to people than, for instance, Americans or Australians. Smiles are not always sincere!
Germans don't like people standing too close to them or touching them.	In Germany, the 'distance of comfort' is approximately 1.2 metres. It is a non-tactile culture.
Germans don't like you entering their office. They get upset if you move a chair or item of furniture.	Privacy is important for concentration on work. Offices (and homes) should be kept in good order. Why move things? The layout has been carefully planned.
There is too much secrecy in German organisations. Information does not flow freely.	Knowledge is power. Also compartmentalisation of German companies hinders lateral information flow. Power flows from the top down.

Appearance	Reality
Germans admire military and economic power more than other kinds.	Not true. They admire intellectual power most. Many heads of German firms have doctorates.
Germans display power and influence through material possessions – fine offices, homes, cars, clothes. They are less modest about those than, say, the British.	Germans like to display symbols of power and success, but handle them with much more grace and reserve than, for instance, Americans.
Germans are noisy people.	True only of German tourists abroad. In meetings, the most powerful person usually speaks in a soft voice.
Germans have too many rules and regulations and do not take human needs into consideration sufficiently.	Germans believe good procedures and processes solve most problems and give order paramount importance to create general well-being.
Germans are too law-abiding, conform too much and are always worried about what others will think.	German sense of order requires conformity. Signs and directions are there to be obeyed. Eccentrics or law-breakers do not gain sympathy as they might do in the UK, France or Australia.
Decentralisation and compartmentalisation represent serious handicaps in German business.	These are structural features in German society. Germany was unified late and dislikes too much central power. The *Länder* are still important. Unlike the French, they prefer dispersion of power.
Germans in conversation and when developing ideas make things too complex	Life is complicated. Germans think Americans and others oversimplify.

Appearance

German possessions, especially furniture, buildings, cars, TV sets, are heavy and lack grace.

Germans have a mania for keeping things in spotless order. They are always washing cars, windows, floors, and constantly servicing equipment.

German neighbours or colleagues criticise you if you do anything wrong, make mistakes or too much noise, transgress any regulation. It is none of their business what I do!

Germans are class-conscious, much more so than in the US or Australia. A class system still exists, especially in top levels of business.

The Germans persist in using 'Sie' when most Anglo-Saxons would start using first names (equivalent of 'Du')

Germans take work too seriously. They have no fun at work. They don't tell jokes during business meetings. They are boring.

Reality

Germans like solidarity in all things. Cars are made to last 10–15 years. Doors, houses, chairs, and tables should be solid – also characters!

Germans do not believe in waste. If you keep things in good order they will last longer. German goods are of high quality and deserve proper upkeep.

In Germany, proper observation of the rules is everybody's business. If every citizen is conscientious, then not so many police will be needed!

This is true to some extent. But top level Germans are very well mannered. They also work very hard and place value on education.

Germans are not casual about friendships. They do not wish to become immediately familiar with strangers.

Germans think business is a serious matter. Why tell funny stories during business meetings? You can tell them afterwards. Why waste time? Being serious is being honest, not boring.

Appearance

Germans are stubborn and lack flexibility. They don't compromise enough.

Germans disagree with people openly and have no tact at business meetings. They are often *too* frank and lack delicacy. They upset people.

Germans make poor conversation partners at cocktail parties. They can't make 'small talk'.

German head offices often fail to react to local conditions abroad and persist in doing things the 'German way'.

Germans are not adaptable. They are unable to effect changes quickly within their organisation to meet changing circumstances.

Germans spend an inordinate amount of time every day shaking hands with colleagues.

Reality

Germans stick to what they believe in. If you want to change their mind, you must show them they are wrong.

Frankness is honesty. 'Diplomacy' can often mean deviousness or not saying what you think. The truth is always the truth. Why pretend?

Germans do not see the point in 'small talk'. They say what there is to say. They discuss business and serious issues very well. They do not wish to open their private lives or opinions to strangers at parties.

There is some truth in this, but German expatriate managers are often successful in convincing HQ of the need for flexibility.

Germans do not like making 'lightning' decisions. They believe an organisation will be successful if procedures are first perfected and then kept in place. Changes in management are less frequent than in the USA.

Shaking hands shows respect for one's colleagues and is the normal way for a German to say 'hello'.

Appearance	Reality
German managers rarely compliment their workers on the job.	Germans are perfectionists, therefore they expect a job to be well done. Why constantly compliment someone who is simply doing their duty? But German managers are very fair to their employees and help them with difficulties.
German advertising is heavy, boring and not visual enough.	Germans like lots of information, therefore they wish an advert to describe the product in detail. They are not impressed by clever slogans, catchphrases or hype. They do not appreciate striking illustrations which often have little to do with the product.
German conventions are long, serious and boring.	Germans regard conventions as occasions where business is done. If one takes the trouble to get a large number of people together it is an ideal opportunity to exchange ideas. They see entertainment as an unnecessary distraction.

16

AUSTRIA

IF WE LOOK AT THE MAP OF AUSTRIA IN OUTLINE WE ARE TEMPTED TO imagine a rump, with a half a leg sticking out to the left. The metaphor, in fact, is not so inaccurate, since the country could be described as a rump state or what is left when others have taken their share. The break-up of the vast Austro-Hungarian Empire hit Austrians hard. The Second World War, with the subsequent four-power occupation lasting till 1955, administered the *coup de grâce* to what was left of their self-assurance. The Austrians, heirs to a glorious imperial past, feel that there is a role for them, but do not quite know where to look for it.

Their search for identity is not an easy one. The dismemberment of the empire caused the loss of many lands and many citizens. Those that are left do not show great cohesion. Austria is compact neither in shape nor in mind. In the West the inhabitants of Vorarlberg would like to be Swiss, but the Swiss would not have them. Salzburg is compelling, but the east is dominated by Vienna – inhabited by large numbers of Czechs, Hungarians, Slovaks, Slovenians and Jews, not to mention recent immigrants from Eastern Europe.

Yet some statistics suggest a prosperous, healthy-minded Austria. Its 21st ranking in world economies is creditable, considering its small population and few resources. Its eighth place in GDP per capita is nothing less than astonishing. It is ninth in car ownership, sixth in tourist receipts and third in health spending. Its only 'gold medal' in global achievement, however, hints at its 'anonymous excellence': it is undisputed first in paper recycling!

Culture

Values

hospitable	traditional, old fashioned
nostalgic	sentimental, romantic
love nature, clean	catholic, pessimistic
respect education	self-deprecatory humour
hypersensitive to criticism	lack self-assurance
chivalrous, charming	class conscious, stylish

Concepts

Leadership and status

In Austria there is a historical respect for aristocrats, not unrelated to the nostalgia felt about the old empire. The country (and especially Vienna) can still be categorised as class conscious. Austria is a democratic republic and business and industry, organised labour and the farming community work closely with the ministries in regulating the economy and political direction.

At business level, leadership is autocratic and authoritarian. Staff listen respectfully to what the boss has got to say, without interrupting. Top managers maintain a sizeable power distance and delegate day-to-day tasks to middle managers, who work harder than they do. Middle managers enjoy authority over the rank and file, but object to the boss's policies at some risk. Workers tend to show exaggerated respect to seniors and are uncomfortable with a system where their voices are rarely heard and where major societal decisions are made behind closed doors. The general lack of self-confidence (observable at all levels of Austrian society) discourages workers from standing up for their rights.

Family connections and private networks are influential and advancement in business and government is less transparent than it seems. The younger generation feel they are inadequately represented. Many Austrians list 'knowing the right people' as the most important factor in advancing one's career; hard work and loyalty to the company come lower down.

Space

In the west of Austria, love of nature and neat, well-nurtured spaces is dominant. Tyrolese keep at a respectful Germanic distance from each other (over a metre) and kissing and hugging in public are rarely seen. Handshaking is mandatory.

The Viennese are much more tactile. Slavic, Jewish and Latin influence is observable in considerable physical closeness and displays of affection.

Time

In the west of Austria people are punctual and hate time wasting. Vienna is different again. The 'coffee house' culture of the capital encourages leisurely gatherings where gossip and networking thrive and clock watching takes a back seat.

Cultural factors in communication

Communication pattern and use of language

Austrians are efficient communicators, using charm and small talk, and on the surface are open and friendly. They are also manipulative, but in an unconscious, natural way, not cold and calculating. They are eager talkers in monologue and are raconteurs who love telling stories and embellishing as they go along. In business discussion their weakness is that they often lapse into a rambling, convoluted style, feeling that they have to fill in all the background and context. Nordic or American directness is disconcerting to Viennese, who find it 'uncivilised'.

Listening habits

Austrian politeness and agreeableness make them attentive listeners on the surface. They are, however, always anxious to speak themselves and, given the opportunity, they often take up where they left off. It is common for them to resume with 'Yes, but...'

Behaviour at meetings and negotiations

Austrians arrive at meetings well dressed in good-quality, smart clothes of a conservative nature. Their manner is formal and titles (*Frau Arkitekt*) are used. They maintain formality, as Germans do, but are less factual than Germans and often introduce personal details, talking about themselves and their emotions, not always with great tact. They attempt to maintain a veneer of self-assurance, but one senses insecurity underneath as they search for an appropriate role to play *vis-à-vis* their interlocutors. They are agreeable to most proposals, but may back out of today's statements tomorrow. They have a tendency to promise more than they can deliver and fall short of German or Nordic reliability in this respect. They avoid confrontation whenever possible and compromise rather than make a solid decision. Their agreeableness can quickly disappear if they are 'cornered' or deadlocked.

It is advisable to check regularly on the performance of Viennese with respect to what they have promised. 'Did you remember...' is a useful start! Unlike Germans, Viennese think short term rather than long; the dismemberment of the country probably has something to do with this. When reminded of their obligations, however, they do their best to comply.

Manners and taboos

Austrians vary in lifestyle – the west is agricultural or tourist oriented and maintains rural and folkloric traditions.

The Viennese, in spite of their underlying insecurity and tendency to be neurotic or melodramatic, are highly cultured people who enjoy a good lifestyle. They are invariably attracted to panache, fame and genius. Their standard of living is good, compared to most Europeans. They have always professed admiration for French grace and style – in their everyday language they use many French loan words.

The suicide rate is high – some victims are children who have failed their exams. Viennese tend to be over-strict with their children, who encounter frequent repression when young and resent it in their teens and later.

Taboo subjects of discussion in Austria are the Second World War, Adolf Hitler, the annexation and criticism of Austrians. As for the rest, Austrians are exciting and knowledgeable interlocutors for whom conversation is a real art. They are extremely hospitable to visitors from abroad.

17

SWITZERLAND

IN TERMS OF CULTURAL COLLISIONS, SWITZERLAND IS A PRIME CANDIDATE for polarisation among its inhabitants, since its citizens speak four languages belonging to four diverse cultural groups, which, during the course of history, have not displayed any particular affection for each other. It is a brave prime minister who attempts to weld Germans, Italians, French and Romansch speakers into a harmonious whole. Perhaps that is why the Swiss settled instead for a council of seven prime ministers and an annually rotating presidency – a suitably weak and humble structure, since all issues of national importance are settled by direct-vote referenda.

Switzerland is the most mountainous country in Europe, with the result that most of its people live in deep and often isolated valleys. They are suspicious of persons who live in other valleys and take refuge in steely, defensive parochialism. The country is divided into 26 cantons (and three half-cantons) where most decisions affecting local people are made – and these include tax systems, welfare schemes, infrastructure, laws, holidays and education.

With such a political system engineered to prevent strong leadership, with even the cantons having to listen to the demands of thousands of communes, with a female population denied the vote until 1971, with over 1,000,000 foreigners on Swiss soil, 150,000 of whom cross the border daily (and go home again), with 48 per cent of the people Catholic and 44 per cent registered as Protestant, with stability only achieved in the twentieth century – one wonders how this improbable state came about, survived and even prospered. Yet the hotchpotch works. Divided by culture, the Swiss are united by force of will.

Switzerland 'began' with a three-cantonal alliance in 1291 between the men of Uri, Schwyz and Unterwalden. The French and Italians joined much later. Formerly a warlike people who took on and defeated French, German and Austrian armies before being eventually crushed at the battle of Marignano in 1515, the Swiss retreated to their mountain strongholds and never left them again. Security and armed neutrality became an obsession, taking precedence over internal squabbles and divisions. As the different cultural groups looked at each other, they realised that disunity and polarisation would herald an early disintegration. In some manner they were able to adapt their inherited traits to produce a mainstream Swiss culture that has more than held its own amid the political and economic turbulence of the last 100 years.

In view of the restricted area available for agriculture, Switzerland has developed an industrial and urban nation. It is particularly strong in metalworking, watches and other precision instruments, textiles, chemical and pharmaceutical products, tourism and international banking. It trades almost entirely with the three countries whose languages Swiss speak – Germany, France and Italy – although 9 per cent of its exports go to the US and 6 per cent to the UK. Unlike its continental neighbours, Switzerland has so far declined to become a member of the EU or NATO (no doubt preferring fierce neutrality). Its prosperity dates particularly from the end of the Second World War.

Some may argue that there is no such thing as a Swiss – one writer described them as a collection of sedated Germans, over-fussy French and starched Italians, all square like their national flag. An analysis of their behaviour, however, reveals a unique and highly independent European.

Culture

Values

As the Swiss have various obsessions – security, punctuality, hygiene, rules and regulations, control, money, saving and perfectionism, propriety etc. – one needs a long list of adjectives to do justice to their qualities!

polite	clean
tidy, punctual	cautious, worrying
over-serious, dull	hardworking, proper

law-abiding, God-fearing	honest
frugal, saving	environmentally sensitive
family oriented, disciplined	pragmatic, perfectionist
obsessed by security, neutral	keen on training and preparation
suspicious of all foreigners	anxious to control

Moreover, the Swiss take their values seriously, backing them up with visible and effective measures. Their neutrality, for instance, bristles with arms. Possessing more weapons per square mile than any other country in Europe, they can mobilise an army of 625,000 men and women in 48 hours. At their disposal are 800–1000 battle tanks, 350 jet fighters, thousands of guns and missiles and an untold number of well-placed landmines. The Alps (their fighting redoubt and base) constitute a veritable fortress with hundreds of bunkers, invisible hangars, nuclear shelters and underground hospitals. The strategy is simple and focused: the Swiss will fight to the last outpost and will blow up bridges, roads, railways, tunnels and even small mountains to cover advancing enemies with rubble! Every Swiss male between 20 and 50 is a member of the armed forces and keeps his weapons at home.

Concepts

Leadership

As in the US there is a deep-rooted distrust of government in Switzerland, and the system of rule resembles the American in its intricate and delicate array of checks and balances. The President has some powers but only one year to exercise them, and is closely bound by the Federal Council of Seven and the frequent referenda.

Status

On account of the quarterly referenda, the common man or woman enjoys a higher status than in most countries. Wealth of course enhances power, but there are few poor Swiss to bully. Material possessions are more common status symbols than other forms of advancement, but as the Swiss say, 'one does not talk about money, one just has it'.

Space

Only a small part of Swiss land is arable and only 6 per cent of the people farm for a living. Space is therefore extremely valuable and cherished. Allied to a strong territorial instinct, this makes personal, communal and cantonal space important issues in Switzerland.

Time

Only the Germans rival the Swiss in their respect for, and submission to, timetables and schedules. Time is not seen as money, in the American sense, but as an important tool in organising daily life and society. Swiss do not rush you, but they do not waste time either. Their accurate sense of timing enables them to predict and forecast events better than most nationalities. In Switzerland things usually happen when they are expected to and spontaneity is not a strong point.

Cultural factors in communication

Communication pattern and use of language

The Swiss are extremely polite conversationists, in both social and business situations. Their desire for privacy and propriety leads them to carry on discourse in a pragmatic and detached manner. They shun inquisitiveness and rarely pry. They are not exciting speakers; even the French Swiss lack the charisma and rhetoric of their cousins in France. Swiss Italians (in the Ticino) are more open but, living in a prosperous area, they display a smugness less noticeable among Italians over the border.

Swiss Germans particularly are cautious speakers, taking care not to offend and adhering to modesty and reserve in most pronouncements and predictions. They speak Switzerdütsch – not a very harmonic tongue – although they will speak real German (or English) if you address them that way.

Listening habits

Swiss are good listeners, not having any great urge to expound ideas at length themselves. They forget little of what you tell them, often taking notes while you speak, and they almost never interrupt. They are conservative in their opinions and it is unlikely that they will be greatly swayed by your advice or persuasion.

Behaviour at meetings and negotiations

The Swiss have a knack of extracting the best deal from opponents without ever appearing demanding or aggressive. They often achieve this on the basis of self-confidence in the quality and value of the goods and services that they provide. Swiss does not come cheap, whether it is watches, precision instruments, pharmaceuticals or ski slopes, but one is often tempted to pay the price.

The Swiss are good at making you feel that you get what you pay for. If you try to bargain with them too hard, they stiffen as if you have made a shady proposal. They are straightforward negotiators who honestly try hard to see matters from an opponent's point of view. One cannot call them inconsiderate – they are quick to make helpful suggestions when it does not hit their pocket. For the most part, they are reliable and efficient and can be counted on to deliver. They are strong on confidentiality.

Manners and taboos

The Swiss are rather heavy drinkers (ninth in the world) and inveterate smokers (sixth). They also are third in drug offences, although this figure may be artificially high due to the efficiency of the national police administration.

The Swiss have a large number of manners, customs and festivals that vary from canton to canton and you cannot be expected to know a great deal about these. They tend to bury themselves in these activities on public holidays and foreigners often feel left out. Taboos include boasting, undue curiosity, invasion of privacy and unpunctuality.

How to empathise with the Swiss

You do not have to be exciting to make a Swiss like you; they are looking for solidity and reliability in the people they deal with. You should show that you are in good control of your emotions, private life and financial arrangements.

Meetings are always by appointment and it is advisable to be there five minutes early. You should be clean and well dressed and always display politeness, even if you are bored out of your mind.

Small gifts are appreciated when you come from abroad, though the Swiss do not make undue fuss. Propriety is much more important than affection, though when Swiss begin to like you, they go out of their way to be friendly.

18

THE NETHERLANDS

HEMMED IN AGAINST THE NORTH SEA BY GERMANY AND BELGIUM, THE Dutch have made the best of the most crowded piece of land in the EU, creating on it the world's largest port and expanding seawards rather than landwards. With the 14th biggest economy in the world, the Netherlands is a small nation with a big clout.

Culturally, the Dutch face north and west (and a bit east) but not south. Their Latin traits are few, but there are striking commonalities with the British, Germans, Swedes and Norwegians, as if at different times they followed different models. Perhaps this partly explains the paradoxical nature of Dutch society. With the Norwegians they share the exceptional characteristic of the national moral dilemma – how can a modern state embrace permissiveness, tolerance, sweeping innovation and pragmatic pursuit of wealth without losing the embedded historical values that served its straitlaced, frugal society so well in the past?

The pervasive egalitarianism in both the Netherlands and Sweden has led to the creation of Europe's two most comprehensive (and expensive) welfare states, with the subsequent corollary of high taxation. In both cases the expense of this luxury has been increased by a generous immigration policy: 10 per cent of Swedes today were not born in Sweden and 15 per cent of those in the Netherlands are not of Dutch descent.

In the business world, both the Netherlands and Sweden have many famous multinational conglomerates (Shell, Unilever, Philips, Volvo, Electrolux, Scania, Alfa-Laval etc.) relative to the size of their economies. This is quite different to the situation in, for instance, Denmark, Norway, Finland and Belgium, where few companies are known worldwide (Nokia and Carlsberg perhaps the only ones).

The proximity of Germany makes it only natural that the Dutch share many traits with their dynamic neighbour. Dynamism, industriousness and work ethic are among the most important of these characteristics. If the Germans are known to be efficient and punctual, the Dutch would claim to be their equals in these respects. Profit orientation is strong and money must be made (but not spent too quickly!). Dutch and Germans are equally frugal, though their governments (especially the Dutch) are less tight-fisted. Only the more conservative, older type of Dutch company resembles the German, but common management traits are frankness, a certain formality with regard to titles and the significance of education as an essential component of leadership. Education is conducted in Holland along German lines, with vocational schools, apprenticeships and on-the-job training major features. Both countries excel in the production of engineers and technicians. Dutch and Germans rival each other in being rights conscious, but compensate by also being very conscious of their duties; rationality is another common factor.

Their forthright Germanic traits notwithstanding, it is perhaps with the British that the Dutch identify most strongly. When conversing with the English they have a confiding air of kinship easily straddling the narrow stretch of water between them. The inhabitants of the Frisian islands speak a language somewhere between Dutch and English. The sea-going traditions of both countries give them a sense of sharing early internationalism, exciting eras of exploration and entrepreneurialism, and huge, rambling empires where durability, administrative skills and religious tolerance were notable features. The Dutch and the English cling to their royals and basic conservatism, but soften this with democratic parliamentary government, love of debate and a quiet, roll-up-your-sleeves self-determinism. Love of home, gardens and flowers are similar in both countries. In business, Dutch and English people resemble each other in dress, exploratory discussion, profit orientation and pragmatism. A surfeit of protocol is frowned on, food is not central to either culture (no three-hour lunches) and internal competitiveness, while keen, must remain covert.

Culture

Values

Dutch economic and geographic paradoxes are comprehensively matched by those of their values:

Conservative	Innovative
Tolerant	Dogmatic
International	Parochial
Materialist	Moralist
Puritanical	Permissive
Opinionated	Consensual
Rights conscious	Dutiful
Consultative	Competitive
Royalist	Egalitarian
Informal	Proper
Entrepreneurial	Cautious
Frugal	Profligate (government)
Self-determined	Cooperative
Frank, open	Jealous of privacy

Concepts

Leadership and status

The hierarchical pyramid in Dutch firms is decidedly flat: managers sit with other executives and decisions are made after lengthy consultation and consensus. As in Japan one diligently avoids the 'tyranny of the majority' and unanimity of decision is sought on most occasions. Individuals may stick to their opinions and cannot be steamrollered, but a great deal of pressure may be brought to bear on persistent lone dissenters.

Cultural factors in communication

Communication pattern and use of language

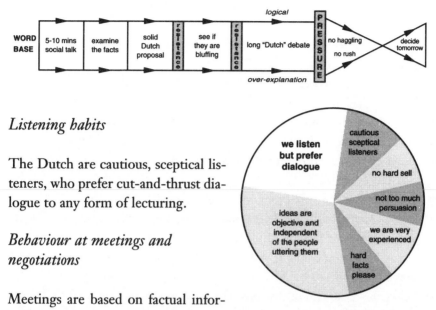

Listening habits

The Dutch are cautious, sceptical listeners, who prefer cut-and-thrust dialogue to any form of lecturing.

Behaviour at meetings and negotiations

Meetings are based on factual information and shows of emotion or ebullience are generally frowned on. Mutual help and dependence are general goals; confrontation is rare and not desirable.

How to empathise with the Dutch

- ✦ Know their history, involvement in former colonies and achievements.
- ✦ Congratulate them on their impressive linguistic abilities, but speak a few words of Dutch now and then.
- ✦ Show that you are punctual, honest, dependable, rational and egalitarian.
- ✦ Back up all you say with facts.
- ✦ Focus on mutual profit.
- ✦ Be willing to brainstorm and endure long debates.
- ✦ Expect and practise verbal agility.
- ✦ Drive a hard bargain, but keep your promises.
- ✦ Be informative, informed and well prepared.
- ✦ Engage in moderate smalltalk before getting down to business.

+ Schedule meetings well in advance.
+ Always appear bold and firm, yet not aggressive.
+ You may be argumentative and sceptical without causing offence.
+ Remember that ideas are objective and independent of the person expressing them.
+ Once a decision has been reached, proceed quickly to implementation.
+ Stick to the agenda.
+ You can offer further opposition if you are outvoted.
+ You can defend your sphere of responsibility.
+ Don't be pretentious – the Dutch dislike the grandiose.
+ Don't be devious. Dutch people are not good at keeping secrets.
+ Don't engage in too much physical contact – about a metre is the normal 'comfort zone'.
+ Don't be late for appointments or waste time.
+ Don't exaggerate overt friendliness (American style) early on. Dutch people consider this an imposition.
+ Don't bargain too much – they are more concerned with quality and reliability.
+ Don't make quick concessions when you meet resistance. The Dutch respect firmness.
+ Don't rush negotiations.
+ Don't exert pressure or use hard-sell tactics.
+ Don't talk about religion (on which the Dutch are divided).
+ Don't pry into family matters.
+ Take flowers to Dutch homes.
+ Don't be ironic or sarcastic, although jocular humour is popular.
+ Don't forget that they probably know a lot more about you than you know about them.

19

BELGIUM

IT IS OFTEN SAID THAT BELGIUM IS NOT A COUNTRY, BUT A COMPROMISE. Belgium was created in 1830 when the Catholic provinces of the Low Countries that had achieved independence from Spain in the seventeenth century broke away from the Calvinist north. Basically there are two nations – a Flemish-speaking one in the north and a French-speaking one in the South. The two do not like each other, particularly since the balance of power is currently passing from the formerly mine-rich French speakers (Walloons) to the *nouveaux riches* and numerically superior Flemish, who are developing the hinterland of Antwerp, Europe's second largest port. To complicate matters further, the city of Brussels is a predominantly French-speaking enclave in Flanders and a German-speaking minority lives along the German border. In Brussels rival linguistic groups occasionally take down street signs in the offending language in the middle of the night.

Political compromise has been reached by the appointment of three prime ministers – Walloon, Flemish and Belgian. Parochial squabbles are numerous, but bad temper rarely escalates into violence. With 66 ministers in the government and political divisions along linguistic lines, one can easily envisage the Belgian capital as a bureaucratic nightmare. As if this were not enough, Brussels has also been appointed the effective capital of Europe; 25 per cent of its residents are well-paid bureaucrats from other countries.

Most Belgians are friendly, hard-working people characterised by an absence of dogma and strong opinions and an earnest desire to earn good money with the minimum of fuss. The Belgians worked hard to realise a Franco-German dream – the union of Europe – and their Europeanisation may have contributed to their relative facelessness compared to other nationalities.

Yet Belgium, in spite of her smallness, has the 20th biggest economy in the world, well ahead of such countries as Sweden, Austria, Turkey, Denmark and South Africa, not to mention Asian Tigers such as Hong Kong and Singapore. Belgium's output equals that of exporting powerhouse Taiwan (which has twice her population). In GDP per capita, Belgium ranks 14th in the world ahead of the UK, Canada, Australia, Italy, Spain and the Netherlands, is 12th on the Human Development Index and is actually the seventh biggest trader in the world, accounting for 4 per cent of total world exports!

An industrial Mighty Mouse, Belgium is hard to evaluate in terms of its cultural influence on Europe and the rest of the world. The impact of its bi-culturalism is diminished by the fact that the intense rivalry tends to neutralise the effect of both sides. There is no such thing as a single Belgian national cultural profile.

Culture

Values

Common values are:

Conservative	Royalist
European oriented	Non-chauvinist
Intellectual humility	Common sense
Avoidance of dogmatism	Flexibility
Compromise	Avoidance of confrontation

Contrasting values can be described as follows:

Flemish values	Walloon values
Egalitarian	Authoritarian
Consensual decision making	Autocratic decisions
Approachable bosses	Large power distance
Delegation of responsibility	Little delegation of power
Relaxed relationships	Vertical structure
Few status symbols	Status symbols important
Dislike speaking French	French speakers
Upwardly mobile	Conscious of rank

Concepts

Flemish	**Walloon**
Leadership	
Bosses are relaxed and low key and it is generally accepted that decision making will be consensual. Responsibility is delegated downwards to a considerable degree.	Leadership is exercised in a manner close to that of the French, where all final decisions rest with the boss. There is normally a general airing of ideas among staff, but this is more a fact-finding exercise than a referendum-style discussion.
Status	
Titles, perks and other status symbols are less important than salary. Authority is normally based on competence.	Rank is important and is demonstrated by car, office space, carpets, job title, furniture, parking space etc. Power distance is great.
Time	
Punctuality is considered normal. Time should not be wasted.	Walloons consider themselves more punctual than the French.

Cultural factors in communication

Communication pattern and use of language

Communication is informal as the boss mixes with staff and often acts on their ideas as well as his/her own. Facts are seen as more important than theories.	Communication goes through official channels, as there is a definite hierarchy in place. Walloons are more imaginative but avoid rhetoric in favour of toned-down style.

Flemish	Walloon

Listening habits

Flemings listen to each other 'in a circle'. They are attentive, as the end result is likely to be an amalgamation of all ideas put forward. Everyone should know the strategy.

Meetings are for briefing, so subordinates tend to listen to superiors rather than the other way round. Staff don't always know what the strategy is.

Behaviour at meetings and negotiations

One is normally dealing with a group. Flemings are non-assertive and welcome compromise. If you are really looking for solutions, there is a good chance of an agreement. They have a pragmatic bent and a calm style. Like most people from small countries, they are adaptable. The bottom line tends to dominate strategy. All members of the group are expected to show competence – nobody is there 'for the ride'.

Walloons are less grandiose and obstinate than the French, largely because they do not have an unswerving belief that they know better than others. One is not dealing with a group but largely with the manager or delegation leader. His views must be analysed. He will also be accountable. He is expected to have charisma, but should also show humility at the right times

Manners and taboos

The most important taboo is speaking French. Others are arrogance, over-assertiveness and pulling rank. They resent having been the lower classes in the past and are still rather annoyed at Brussels being a French-speaking enclave in the middle of Flanders.

Walloons resent being viewed as rather slow-witted French people and dislike the French tendency to make jokes at their expense. They are, however, slower than the French in speech and appear to other Latins to be rather plodding and deliberate.

How to empathise with Belgians

Make it clear that you know that Flemings are not Dutch and that Walloons are not French. The main difference between the two groups is the question of consensual decision making versus hierarchical style, so you should adjust your approach accordingly.

Belgians of both persuasions will be looking for certain qualities in you: pragmatism, profit-mindedness, flexibility, willingness to compromise, ability to respect the integrity and creativeness of a small country. Belgians are very European and assume that you share some of their enthusiasm for Europe (if you are in the EU).

20

FRANCE

IN BOTH POLITICS AND BUSINESS THE FRENCH LIKE TO BE INDEPENDENT (at times maverick) and can appear frustrating to Americans, Japanese and Europeans alike.

French people live in a world of their own, the centre of which is France. They are immersed in their own history and tend to believe that France has set the norms for such things as democracy, justice, government and legal systems, military strategy, philosophy, science, agriculture, viniculture, *haute cuisine* and *savoir vivre* in general. Other nations vary from these norms and have a lot to learn before they get things right.

The French know virtually nothing about many other countries, as their education system teaches little of the history or geography of small nations or those which belonged to empires other than their own. Their general attitude towards foreigners is pleasant enough, neither positive nor negative. They will do business with you if you have a good product, or if you buy, but their initial posture will be somewhat condescending. You may not speak French, you appear to be Anglophiles. That is not a good start in their eyes.

You are not seen as an equal. You may be better or worse, but you are different. The French, like the Japanese, believe they are unique, and do not really expect you will ever be able to conform completely with their standards. What approach should one adopt when dealing with the French? Should one 'gallicise' oneself to some degree, becoming more talkative, imaginative and intense? Or should one maintain stolid, honest manners at the risk of seeming wooden or failing to communicate?

In order to get the best of one's dealings with the French, one has to study their psychology and tactics when they enter commercial transactions. They approach negotiation in a very French manner, which includes the following characteristics:

+ They arrive at a meeting formally dressed, regarding it as a formal occasion.
+ Surnames and formal introductions are used, seating will be hierarchical.
+ Politeness and formal style will be maintained throughout the negotiation if the French 'manage' it.
+ Logic will dominate their own argument and they will be quick to pounce on anything illogical said by the opposition.
+ Their use of logic will lead to extensive analysis of all matters under discussion. Therefore the meeting will be long and wordy.
+ They do not present their demands at the beginning, but lead up to them with a carefully constructed rationale.
+ They reveal their hand only late in the negotiations (this causes people such as Americans to see this as cunning).
+ French try to find out what all the other side's aims and demands are at the beginning. Americans usually oblige by putting all their cards on the table.
+ French are suspicious of early friendliness in the discussion and dislike first names, taking off jackets, or disclosure of personal or family details.
+ They pride themselves on quickness of mind, but dislike being rushed into decisions. For them negotiation is not a quick procedure.
+ They rarely make important decisions inside the meeting. Often the chief decision maker is outside the meeting.
+ They will prolong discussion, as they regard it as an intellectual exercise during which they are familiarising themselves with the other party and perhaps discovering their weaknesses.
+ Their objectives are long term; they try to establish firm personal relationships.
+ They will not make concessions in negotiations unless their logic has been defeated. This often makes them look stubborn in the eyes of the 'give-and-take' Americans and 'muddle-through' British.
+ During deadlock they remain intransigent but without rudeness, simply restating their position.

- ✦ They try to be precise at all times. The French language facilitates this.
- ✦ They can be somewhat touchy if due respect is not shown or if protocol is not observed, but they are less sensitive to questions of 'honour' than the Spanish or South Americans and less worried about losing face than the Orientals.
- ✦ They are perceptive and opportunistic, but in the end always cautious.
- ✦ They believe they are intellectually superior to any other nationality.
- ✦ They often depart from the agenda and talk at length on a number of issues in random order.
- ✦ British and Americans often complain that 'we talked for hours but no decisions were arrived at or action taken'. (The French are actually clarifying their own thoughts through extensive discussion and have not yet decided on their course of action.)
- ✦ They will link the negotiation to other transactions they may be conducting.
- ✦ Personal views will influence their dealings on behalf of the company.
- ✦ Other members of their negotiating team are often close friends, colleagues from university or even relations.
- ✦ Communication style is extrovert, personal, often emotional, but adhering to logic.
- ✦ They arrive at the negotiation well informed in advance, but seeing things through French 'spectacles' often blinds them to international implications. Sometimes they are hampered by lack of language skills.

When dealing with the French, one should behave much more formally than usual, using only surnames and showing almost exaggerated politeness to French senior executives.

One should stick to logic at all times, avoiding American-style hunches or British-style 'feel for situations'. If one contradicts anything one said even months earlier, a French person will pounce on the contradiction.

One should be willing to appear 'more human' than usual, as the French are after all Latins, in spite of their logic and exactness. They like a good talk and observe few time limits for this. If you don't talk enough, they will call you monosyllabic afterwards.

If you want to gain points, you can score by criticizing the English – a favourite French pastime. You need not be unfair to anyone, you just show that you are not entirely in the Anglo-Saxon camp. French do not mind if you have a go at their other neighbours – the Italians and the Spaniards.

Do not criticise Napoleon – he has a kind of lasting identity with the French soul. You can say what you want about De Gaulle, Mitterand or any current French prime minister. They probably won't know who your prime minister is, so they can't crucify him.

The French are often criticised by people of other nationalities and it is not difficult to see why. Essentially argumentative and opinionated, they frequently find themselves out on a limb at international meetings, isolated in their intransigence when all the others have settled for compromise. This naturally leaves them open to charges of arrogance. And yet one must have some sympathy for them. They are clear-sighted, perceptive thinkers who feel that they have a better historical perspective that most of us. They would rather be right than popular. Are they usually right? Like all others, they are fallible in their judgement and subject to bias, but they have great experience in politics, warfare, domestic and overseas organisation and administration and the humanities. Like the Germans, they cannot be accused of taking things lightly. Their long and significant involvement in European and world affairs gives the French the conviction that their voice should be heard loud and clear in international forums. Their political, military, economic strengths may no longer predominate as they once did, but French people perceive no diminishment or fading in their moral and didactic authority. Like the Americans, British and Russians, they have a strong messianic streak. They would not be human if they did not resent the rise of the British after the fall of Napoleon, the decline of the French language as a world tongue, the incursions of the Japanese on the European economic scene, and, most of all, the pernicious Americanisation of large parts of the world, including once-French-dominated Europe and even French culture itself.

Though often seen as selfish defenders of their own territory, it is not inconceivable that with their old-fashioned doggedness and resistance to precipitated globalisation, they might one day emerge as the champions of age-long values and philosophies which Europe subconsciously cherishes. The maverick of Europe may well turn out to be its moral bedrock. At all events, the French merit a closer examination of their apparent obstinacies and negative features.

French as others see them

Appearance

French people are obstinate, always hold a different opinion from everybody else.

They think they are cleverer than anyone else.

They don't like to speak foreign languages, especially English.

They know little about and are not interested in other countries and cultures.

They are overemotional.

Reality

They stick to what they believe is right unless they are proved wrong.

True: the length and magnificence of their historical achievements leave them convinced that their mission is to civilise Europe.

French was once the internationally accepted language of diplomacy and spoken widely in four continents. It is a clinical, precise language; many foreigners also find it beautiful. French people feel sadness at its decline *vis-à-vis* English. England was the traditional enemy. American English often sounds vulgar, anti-intellectual to them.

History lessons in their education system tend to concentrate on French history. They are not very international in their knowledge, but they do know a lot about Asia and Africa and possess extensive scholarship in the study of ancient cultures.

Like all Latins they raise their voice and gesticulate when excited, but they rarely abandon rationality and are not blind to others' virtues.

Appearance	Reality
They are inquisitive, ask personal questions and cannot mind their own business.	French is such an exact language that it is difficult not to be direct when using it. They are often personal, as they are interested in you personally, but they have an innate politeness often unseen by foreigners.
They talk too much at meetings.	A logical argument takes longer to build up than an intuitive one. Cartesian theory requires building blocks. French people also like to consider every aspect of a question before making decisions.
They can't keep to an agenda.	As they inter-relate all the points, they feel they must go back and forth to balance their decisions.
They are finicky.	They generally have a clear idea of what they want and take pains to get things right.
They make grandiose plans.	True, they think big and hate the mediocre. But having established *les grandes lignes*, they are later quite analytical about details.
They make poor team members.	They are very individualistic and not lacking in self-confidence. This, allied to (generally) a good education, encourages them to go it alone. This is counteracted within France itself by a high degree of centralisation.

Appearance	Reality
They can't relax	Relaxing does not come easily to people who are quick, imaginative and culture rich.
They are too quick to attack others.	French people like a tidy universe. They feel compunction to redress what they perceive as injustice, stupidity or laxity. They do not hesitate to intervene.
They prefer ideas to facts and won't make decisions in a normal, straightforward manner.	Statistics can prove anything. Facts are not always what they seem. What is wrong with exploring ideas?
They are cynical.	If you have the British on one side of you, the Germans on the other and the Americans on your TV screen, you have to be.
They are irrevocably chauvinistic	Malraux pointed out that nations usually act nationalistically and are unimpressed by specious internationalisation. Social justice is best obtained in a nation that knows its own ground.
French people are selfish, care little for others	Not true. As Malraux said further, France is never completely effective when fighting for herself. When the French fight for mankind, they are wonderful.
They are messianic.	True. Malraux's brief when being appointed Minister of Culture was the expansion and *rayonnement* of French culture. It is good for us.

21

ITALY

THE ITALIANS ARE CHARMING, INTELLIGENT PEOPLE TO WHOM EUROPE owes a great cultural debt. They are excellent communicators and combine ultra-keen perception with ever-present flexibility. Their continuous exuberance and loquacious persuasiveness often produce an adverse reaction with reserved Britons, factual Germans and taciturn Scandinavians. Yet such northerners have everything to gain by adapting to Italians' outgoing nature, meeting them halfway in their taste for dialogue. There is plenty of business to be done with the Italians, who export vigorously in order to survive. The following remarks attempt to give the northerner a few clues on how some concessions towards extroversion can reap rewards.

Italians like to share details of families, holidays, hopes, aspirations, disappointments, preferences. Show photographs of children, etc. Reveal some of your political or religious opinions – this is normal in Italy, you need not be an island unto yourself. Discuss beliefs and values. Do not be afraid to appear talkative. No matter how hard you try the Italian will always consider you reserved (and talk ten times as much as you).

One characteristic of Italians is that they are relatively non-chauvinistic and do not automatically believe that Italian must be best. This national modesty is rarely seen outside Finland and Italy. Capitalise on this trait by discussing Italy in a frank manner.

Italians, unlike Spaniards, Germans or French, are not particularly sensitive or touchy. They accept criticism and are very flexible. You may speak much more freely with them than with most Europeans, but do not exaggerate directness or bluntness. They are flexible, but also delicate.

Remember that the communication style is eloquent, wordy, demonstrative and apparently emotional. This is normal for them, over-dramatic
for you. Do not be led into the belief that waving arms and talking with the
hands denotes instability or unreliability. They think you, by contrast, are
rather wooden and distant. Make them feel comfortable by showing more
facial expression and body language.

Italians have a different concept of time from that of northerners and
Americans. They do not arrive for appointments on time. Punctuality in
Milan means they are 20 minutes late, in Rome half an hour and in the
South 45 minutes. You will not be able to change this, except in a fixed-
hours factory or office environment. You must therefore adapt. Be prepared to wait 15–45 minutes before your Italian counterpart appears or lets
you into his office. Take a good book or magazine. Alternatively you can
deliberately show up half an hour late, but in fact few northerners are able
to do this. There is also a variance in the concept of space. Italians are used
to being crowded and working in close proximity to each other. This creates an atmosphere of teamwork approximating to that of the Japanese. A
Briton, American or German needs more space or 'elbow room' to work
effectively and this shows itself in such matters as office layout and use of
space both in factories and in administrative areas. Be prepared to 'rub
shoulders' with Italians.

The 'distance of comfort' is greater for northerners than Italians. The
English like to keep a minimum of 1.2 metres between themselves and
their interlocutor. Italians are quite comfortable at 80 centimetres. If you
retreat from such a position, they will think you are avoiding them or that
you find their physical presence distasteful. Make them feel more welcome
by 'standing your ground'.

Italians may touch your arm or shoulder or perhaps hug you if they are
feeling friendly. After some months' acquaintance, they may kiss you on
both cheeks when greeting you or departing. They are showing affection
and you must find some way of reciprocating. At least smile occasionally;
your face will not break (in a southern climate).

Italian flexibility in business often leads you to think they are 'dishonest'. They frequently bend rules, break or 'get round' some laws and put a
very flexible interpretation on certain agreements, controls and regulations. Remember that this is the way they do business and you may well be
able to benefit from this 'flexibility'. They will regard your rather rigid,
law-abiding approach as somewhat old-fashioned, short-sighted or even

blind. In this respect they probably are closer to reality than you are and less ideal bound. They do not consider their approach to be in any way corrupt, immoral or misleading. They will happily take you into their 'consipiracy'. They will share the 'benefits' with you, if you accept. If you stick to the letter of the law, they will go on without you. We are not talking about clear illegalities. There are many grey areas where short cuts are, in Italian eyes, a matter of common sense.

Italians are less private persons than linear-active people and they will borrow your property (or time) with freedom. Eventually they will repay or return your property (calculator, car, report, etc.) so do not be unduly stuffy about it. Remember you can borrow from them whenever you like.

Italians often 'borrow' your money in the sense that they pay late. This is another area where change of habit is very difficult to bring about. The best you can do is try to arrange satisfactory payment schedules in advance and/or take the probability of delayed payments strongly into consideration. Remember the Italians will allow you similar latitude (if they can afford it).

At meetings, Italians do not follow agendas as strictly as do northerners. They will jump ahead to later points or will rediscuss points you think have already been settled. They will talk loudly, excitedly and at length. Often several people will speak at once, and you may find two or three more micro-meetings going on simultaneously. They do not like silences of more than 5 seconds. If you are not running the meeting, there is nothing you can do except sit back and enjoy. If you are in the chair, you have to create some kind of order, but you can only do this by establishing firm rules in advance. One German I know used yellow, red and green cards to discipline people at South American meetings. This humorous but firm approach achieved the desired result.

Italian wordiness v northern succinctness is a constant pain in internal company communication, as both sides wish to achieve clarity, one through many words and the other through short messages and memos. A compromise must be reached. Northerners must teach themselves to be more explicit and explanatory, but also encourage their Italian colleagues to be more concise, economical with words and ideas, and whenever practical to put them in writing. The invention of the fax has been a valuable weapon for Scandinavians and other concise peoples.

Italians are much more polite, on the surface, than northerners, so you will often appear overfrank, blunt and even rude, although you do not intend this. Try to adopt a certain Italian smoothness or delicacy and use flattery more than you normally would. They like it. Open doors for women and stand up and sit down at the right times. You probably do this anyway, but notice how the Italians do it with charm and style. When leaving a room an Italian often says '*Con permesso*'. Try a few tricks like that. If you still feel a bit awkward, console yourself by remembering that to a Japanese an Italian looks clumsy, emotional and often rude.

You will often find it difficult to rid yourself of the impression that the Italians are an unruly, disorganised bunch. They do not seem to plan methodically like you do. Do not forget they are the fifth industrial nation in the world and have outperformed even the Germans and Americans in such areas as domestic appliances and some categories of cars. On top of that they have an enormous hidden or 'black' economy, the extent of which is unknown. Therefore they must be doing something right. Your task should be to discover where they act in a superior manner to you and whether you can learn to do the same. Their efficiency is not as 'obvious' as yours, but it may have something to do with their gregariousness, flexibility, working hours, people orientation, teamwork, quickness and opportunism. Try to get into their shoes.

Italian negotiators are friendly, talkative, and ultimately flexible. They are less direct than northerners and often seem to proceed in a roundabout manner. Italians will discuss things from a personal or semi-emotional angle ('Look at the good relations between our presidents'), while northerners try to concentrate on the benefit for their company and stick to the facts of the particular deal. Northerners should approach negotiation with Italians with adequate time for the exercise and a large store of patience. They must be prepared to discuss at length and maintain calm. An Italian may get overheated on some point, but changes a moment later into the friendliest of negotiators. Italians may quarrel among themselves at the table, but are solid colleagues minutes later. Their starting price may be high, but they are prepared for a lot of negotiating down. The Scandinavian or Briton selling to them must show a first price which allows some room for a reduction later. They will expect it. They must come away from the deal showing they have won or gained something. Each member of their team must be granted something. Northerners will be at their best if they regard the negotiation as a kind of interesting game which must be played with many Italian rules, but which leads to a serious and beneficial result (for both).

22

SPAIN

THERE IS ONLY ONE ENGLAND OR FRANCE, BUT THERE ARE SEVERAL Spains. Spain was plural to the Romans and its multiple aspects are still evident in its clear-cut regions. Castilians are in the majority and continue to dominate, but you would do well to check on a Spaniard's origins when beginning to do business with him or her. Galicians are practical and melancholy, sharing some common ground with some northerners. Aragonese stubbornness finds an echo in Finnish *sisu*. Basques have a talent for industry and commerce and, along with Finns, Hungarians and Estonians, stand apart from Indo-European ancestry. Northerners share the cult of efficiency with Catalans, who face France rather than Spain. On the other hand, they have little in common with two other regions – Asturias, where the people are extremely haughty, and Andalucia, where every one is an orator and timetables are for cats and dogs.

So much for the regions – let us now take a close look at Castile and its people. Castilians are basically Latins and indeed for many centuries they were the guardians of the Roman heritage, preserving its linguistic and literary monuments as well as its traditions of conquest and Empire. Latin characteristics evident in Castile are verbosity and eloquence (the Castilian word '*hablar*' – to speak – comes from '*fabulare*' meaning to invent, to romance, to revel in the joys of conversation). Northerners will hardly feel comfortable confronted by such wordiness, nor with the Spaniard's favourite role of the supreme romantic. Proud of their history and purity of descent, Castilians are at heart crusaders, mystics, impractical individualists who were supreme as *conquistadores* but signally unable to organise their empire. British and Americans may admire Castilian individualism, since it is a trait cherished by them, but individualism in Spain has resulted in refractoriness to authority and organisation, even scorn for government. In the southern part of the country the hot climate reinforces a tendency towards apathy and inertia where laws and regulations are concerned.

The pauper in Spain is considered as noble as the wealthy. Beggars are treated gently, respect is shown to the poor and needy, and an innate aristrocracy is noticed in the very humblest. Personal dignity must be clung to whatever else may be lost. Time, money, even prudence, are of secondary importance.

If pragmatic northerners find this hard to swallow, they will experience even more perplexity with Castilian fatalism. 'Why organise our fate so much?' says the Castilian – all that happens now has happened before and will certainly happen again. While full of boundless energy in the thrill of action or great moments of vision, Spaniards have little taste for the routine, banal tasks of consolidation and coordination. Tomorrow is another day; if it is our destiny to succeed, we shall. Northerners who have little time for fatalism and consider themselves masters of their own fate have little sympathy for this attitude. We may insist that facts are stubborn things, but the Spaniard asserts things are not what they seem. There is a double truth, that of the immediate detail and that of the poetic whole. The second is more important for the Castilian, since it supplies a faith or vision to live by. One must realise the futility of material ambition.

Consideration of these Spanish concepts and credos makes it fairly clear that the Spaniard and the northerner have quite different perceptions of reality. Dialogue between the two is never going to be easy. A grandiloquent, circumlocutory orator and supreme romanticist addresses a passive listener and taciturn pragmatist. There will probably be a language barrier. Yet dialogue there must be, in the world of business.

There are some bridges between Spanish and northern cultures. Castile is a barren land with extremes of cold and heat. The severity of climate and landscape has accustomed Castilians to austerity – a phenomenon not unknown to northerners – and hard times in many countries have encouraged frugality. Although Spain is a land of rich and poor, the egalitarian Britons, Scandinavians or Americans can detect in the Spaniards' protection of the underdog that country's version of true democracy.

People wishing to do business with Spaniards must first accept that they will never act like northerners and that their scale of values is quite remote from the modern age.

Like other people, they buy and sell and are friendly, but they look at you in an old-fashioned way and they are more interested in you than your goods. I once acted as interpreter for three German salesmen presenting their new product to the board of a Madrid company. The Germans had a slick presentation lasting 30 minutes with slides, graphs, diagrams and video. The six Spanish managers facing them hardly watched the presentation at all. They were watching the salesmen. Were these the type of people they wanted to do business with? Did they like them? Were they really human? All Germans give perfect presentations, so why watch it? After the session was over the breathless Germans waited for the response. The Spaniards took them for lunch, which lasted till 4 o'clock. After that everybody took a siesta.

You must work hard at making a Spaniard like you. If you succeed in this, the business will follow automatically. You must show you have a heart and that you do not take everything seriously. Northerners have big hearts, but they are often experts at hiding them. You need to talk to Spaniards with a twinkle in your eye. Their 'distance of comfort' is much closer than that of most Europeans and they like both physical and eye contact. They are more robust than French, Italian or Portuguese people – they are the roughest of the Latins. 'Macho' is a Spanish word and the essential masculinity of the northern businessman stands him in good stead in a Spaniard's company. Northern businesswomen will also be comfortable with male Spaniards, as their relative aggressiveness will score points.

Spaniards are very human. When conversing with them it is best to shed some of your cool tendencies, forget the dictates of time, admit that some roguery actually exists in your country, confess to a few private sins or misdemeanours, ask them some rather personal questions, stay up drinking with them till 3 in the morning and in general let your hair down.

When relaxing in the company of Spaniards, keep one consideration in the forefront of your mind: they are touchy and sensitive. You may laugh at the French and Germans as much as you like, you can even criticise certain Spanish customs such as siestas or the bull fight, but do not in any circumstances say anything that might be interpreted to impinge on their personal dignity or honour. For many Spaniards 'pundonor' (point of honour) is the most important word in the language. They may be poor, but they are noble. They may have been in jail, but they are honest. They may be unpunctual, but they are true. They may owe you money, but they are sure to pay you when they can. They may have failed, but they cannot be humiliated. Like a Japanese or a Chinese, they cannot be made to lose face.

This deference to a Spaniard's dignity, the careful nurturing of their personal, human prowess, the respect shown for their station, personality and soul, is the key to their cooperation, alliance and affection. They will reciprocate in full – if you command a Castilian's loyalty he will be your best friend. He will buy your company's product and send you Christmas cards for 25 years. He will lie and occasionally die for you. He is an honourable man.

23

PORTUGAL

IF THE PORTUGUESE PEOPLE WERE NOT VERY DIFFERENT FROM THE
Spaniards, Portugal would not exist. Looking at a map of the Iberian
peninsula, we have the impression that the roughly pentagonal mass – so
clearly separated from the rest of Europe by the Pyrenees and so narrowly
cut off from Africa by the Straits of Gibraltar – seems geologically formed
for unity: the intermediary between two seas and two continents.

A Portuguese friend of mine likes to play a trick on his Spanish acquaintances. He hints at the patchy quality of Spanish education and challenges
them to draw the outline of Spain. Stung by his insinuations, they invariably put pen to paper and draw the following shape:

My friend plays with them a bit, suggesting that the outline is not quite perfect, whereupon the hapless Spaniards tweak a line or curve here and there, or do the whole outline again with greater care. My friend then does it for them, thus:

Subconsciously most Spaniards think of the Iberian Peninsula as theirs; subconsciously most Portuguese see the Spaniards as potential invaders. There is a parallel situation in the way English, Welsh and Scots feel about each other, although in their case the political union is a fact.

The matter was settled with Spain in 1297 when Portugal won its independence under King Afonso Henriques. For 60 years (1580–1640) the Spaniards reestablished dominion, but since then the divorce has been made final. Geographically, in fact, the division makes sense, just as the separation of Norway and Sweden does. Each party wants its own side of the mountain and the lifestyle has adapted to the environment. Norway and Portugal were forest-clad and coastal, inclining their populations towards seafaring and fishing occupations; in the case of Portugal the fishermen, sailors, foresters and fruit-growers were too unlike the migratory shepherds on the Castilian plateau to share any lasting future with them. Spain has often been seen as a collection of separate provinces. With the advent of Portuguese independence, it counted one less.

Portugal is an Atlantic country, Spain is principally Mediterranean. The Portuguese, with their backs to Spain, face the ocean and the western hemisphere. Cut off from Europe by Spanish land, they had easy sea routes to the British Isles, the African coast, Madeira, the Canaries, the Azores and ultimately the Americas.

Landlocked countries are, in a sense, unlucky. At the mercy of sudden, unexpected attacks by neighbours, their policies are necessarily suspicious, cautious and (when feeling strong) vindictive. They have little freedom of movement, as they are blocked by foreign territory. Those Mediterranean countries without an Atlantic seaboard are to some degree landlocked, as their access to greater seas has historically been barred by Spain, Britain (Gibraltar) and the Moors. Black Sea neighbours Russia, Romania and Bulgaria are unable to proceed even to the Mediterranean without Turkish permission. In the same manner the states bordering on the Baltic had their exit to the Atlantic barred by Viking sea power. Portugal belongs to the luckier maritime countries. If you have stood by Vasco de Gama's statue on the sea shore of his home town of Sines and looked out over the beckoning blue ocean on a fine sunny day, you are left in little doubt as to why the Portuguese sailed forth and sought lands beyond the horizon. The ocean is exhilarating and those people who are substantially exposed to it – Vikings, Britons, French, Spaniards, Polynesians, Dutch and Portuguese – have proceeded literally to the ends of the earth and carved out their own destiny in times when such exploits were still feasible.

Adjoining foreign-held land threatens – it creates an obsession with national security (e.g. Russia). Oceans, on the other hand, are natural defences, providing early warning against foreign aggression and a battle-ground where it may be halted before it reaches your shores. Oceans, moreover, are bridges for easy access to other countries, to bilateral trade and exchange of new ideas without the neighbours getting involved as intermediaries. The Atlantic provided West-facing Portugal with an unhindered link with England, its natural ally against Spain and (later) Napoleon's France. It opened up a country which would otherwise have been claustrophobic, with no contact with fellow Europeans except through the Spanish filter.

Most importantly, the Atlantic gave newly independent Portugal the attractive opportunity for overseas exploration at the very time when large parts of the world were ripe for colonisation. Science, although still in its infancy, was providing an invaluable aid to ocean-going vessels. England, France, Spain and Holland were all gearing up to expand by means of ambitious colonisation. The 500-mile strip of Atlantic sea-coast destined the Portuguese to join these maritime powers and enabled this tiny country to acquire an enormous empire, rivalling in size and resources those of France, Spain and Britain.

In business, although the organisation of firms is based on vertical hierarchy with authority concentrated in the person at the top, Portuguese managers avoid direct conflicts with staff members whenever possible by adopting a benign manner of address and considering the personal problems of subordinates.

The same friendly attitude is observed in their relationship with clients. The Portuguese begin the relationship with the open assumption that trust exists between the two parties. Their manner is so cheerful and communicative that they have no difficulty in establishing this ambience, even in the initial stages of discussion. In Portugal clients are seen as friends, otherwise it is unlikely they will remain clients.

In countries where bureaucracy is heavy – and in Portugal it has this unfortunate characteristic – there is a tendency for the conduct of business to rely largely on good personal relations and mutual confidence of individuals, otherwise there will be no short cuts. In Portugal, as in Italy, the ability to generate close relations, to secure good introductions, to create long-term goodwill, is not only an essential prerequisite to doing business, but is the criterion of efficiency itself! Portuguese executives, who have this gift, make excellent ice-breakers at international gatherings where some of the delegates exhibit initial stiffness.

The Portuguese possess great oratorical skills, but they also like things in writing. This is not only a product of Portuguese bureaucracy (they borrowed heavily from the Napoleonic model) but they consider that well-expressed documents help to avoid uncertainty and ambiguity. There the contrast with Spaniards is startling. Portuguese generally write their language carefully and well; this characteristic serves them admirably in the bureaucratic procedures often required in large multinational companies.

The Portuguese are more formal than the Spaniards who nowadays use the *tu* form all over the place. 'You' in Portugal can be *O Senhor* (*A Senhora*), *tu* or *Você* and these forms can be combined with either first or second names or with titles such as *Professor* or *Engenheiro*. The permutations are many. When in doubt, it is advisable to err on the side of formality. Do not hesitate to address as *Doutor* anyone who appears well-qualified or more intelligent than you are.

Negotiating with the Portuguese

The Portuguese are among the best negotiators in the world. When they negotiated the terms of their entry into the Common Market at the same time as the Spaniards, they obtained considerably better conditions than their fellow Iberians.

Their imperial past and inclination to distance themselves from the Spaniards have made them far more international in outlook than most people give them credit for. Their language abilities are excellent – among the Latins they are easily the best speakers of English, and enrolments on English, French and German courses are staggering. The famous Cambridge School of Languages in Lisbon regularly enrols more than 10,000 students per annum.

Portuguese are easily able to negotiate in English. The following are the chief characteristics of the Portuguese negotiator:

+ They negotiate individually or in small teams. Team members know each other well, and may be related.
+ They will achieve the best agreement for the company, but individual preferences, family and social position will be a background to the decisions.
+ They regard the negotiation result as a credit or debit to personal prowess.
+ Their multi-active nature leads them to link the negotiation to other transactions or business in which they are currently involved. They do not compartmentalise the negotiation.
+ They use surnames and titles, but are friendly, even charming, from the outset.
+ They believe they are smarter than the other side, but try to give the impression they are dumber.
+ They know what they want from the outset, but have an open mind as to the route they will take to achieve it.
+ They are suspicious by nature, but disguise this suspicion.
+ They are quick, perceptive and opportunistic.
+ They exercise maximum flexibility.
+ They often say they understand, when in fact they plan to understand.
+ They make decisions individually or by consensus, according to circumstances.

✦ They begin with a high price to leave room for manoeuvre later, but are quick to modify if they sense tension.

✦ They state what they really want as late as they can in the negotiation.

✦ They argue in a roundabout manner as opposed to French logical build-up or American up-front demands.

✦ They will often change course dramatically during a negotiation and make a platform out of something they didn't come to the table with.

✦ They will often throw an extremely imaginative (wild) proposal on the table to confuse the opponent or gain time.

✦ They rarely turn down any business offered during negotiation, scooping up whatever peripheral or accessorial transactions are available.

✦ Generous by nature, they entertain lavishly in between meetings, often choosing the entertainment themselves.

✦ They expect to pay and be paid promptly.

✦ National honour is not a major factor. They are not touchy about race, religion or colour.

✦ Their communicative style is personal, eloquent, emotional, but more restrained than Italian or Spanish (Atlantic influence).

✦ They come to the negotiation well informed about all aspects of the transaction.

✦ They are experienced on a global scale. Centuries of trading with India, Africa and the Far East have taught the Portuguese to be flexible, devious, realistic and 'good losers'.

✦ A lack of technology and resources often puts Portuguese in a disadvantageous position which they must compensate for with clever negotiation, resulting in a sophisticated approach.

24

GREECE

GREEK CONSCIOUSNESS IS KEENLY AWARE THAT THE GREEK CITY-STATE period laid the basis for Western European civilisation and the liberal democracies. Greece is also a vociferous member of the EU. The collapse of its profitable market in former Yugoslavia (because of the war), the finicky quarrel with neighbouring Macedonia, the unstable position in Russia and the enduring failure to resolve the Cyprus problem have been continuing sources of anxiety for successive Greek governments, which have not always enjoyed unbridled support from EU colleagues, impatient with the Cyprus matter and annoyed at the country's threats to use its veto when it pleases.

Culture

Values

Reason
Freedom
Thrift
Love of the sea

Rational debate
Close family ties
Talent for business

Concepts

Leadership and status

The Greek view of leadership is somewhat similar to the French conception – that is, rooted in rational argument and skill in oratory. Mastery of the language is seen as essential for commanding the respect of subordinates. Family name is very important.

Status is gained in different ways. There is great respect for education, qualifications and intellectual prowess on the one hand, wealth and family connections on the other. There are several powerful family dynasties.

Space and time

Greece is a tactile culture. Its distance of comfort is similar to the Italian, hugging and kissing are common.

The Mediterranean pace of life is slow. Greeks are usually late for appointments, always with a good excuse and warm apologies. They tend to lose all sense of time when engaged in animated discussion.

Cultural factors in communication

Communication pattern and use of language

Greeks are verbose, theatrical and intense. Language is declaimed in a manner similar to Spanish; eye contact during address is the strongest in Europe. Emotion is used as a weapon in discourse. Greeks believe in their own powers of oratory. They use rational argument like the French, but spice it up with emotive content.

Listening habits

Greeks are good listeners, since they wish to be well informed about business. As they are very imaginative, they tend, however, to interrelate the subject under discussion with other matters.

Behaviour at meetings and negotiations

Greeks often display great charm, but they are serious negotiators. The senior person will dominate the discussion, as is the rule in Mediterranean countries. They are shrewd, have great experience and do not give much away. They can talk late into the night and seem to get better as they go along. Their gestures are very similar to the Latin races, but a slight upward nod of the head means 'no' and tilting the head to either side means 'yes, of course'. Occasionally, Greeks smile when they are very angry.

Manners and taboos

The multi-active nature of the Greeks means that they are often late for appointments and, when they give interviews, let them run on endlessly, even if someone else is waiting. Elderly people have a lot of authority and are not kept waiting.

Greeks are excellent hosts and their hospitality can be embarrassing. Flowers or a cake are suitable gifts for hostesses.

Do not mention Cyprus or say anything too laudatory about the Turks. Greeks are also sensitive about other aspects of their foreign policy, e.g. their relations with Macedonia, Albania, Bulgaria and Serbia. Greek businesspeople are much more pragmatic than the politicians and in fact trade with Macedonia and put business before ideals in general. Like the Italians, they are willing to show you 'short cuts' to circumvent bureaucratic delays.

How to empathise with Greeks

Learn the basic facts of Greek history and give them all credit for the 'glory that was Greece'. Personalise business as much as possible and get to know about their private lives, especially with regard to their families.

They will expect your approach, even when discussing business, to be warm and generous. Greeks like to think that the client is a friend. You should indicate trust as early in the proceedings as you can, although you must be watchful. They like eating and drinking, often quite late, and expect you to socialise.

25

POLAND

POLAND SHOULD NOT BE UNDERESTIMATED. BIGGER THAN ITALY OR THE UK, its land area equals that of the Netherlands, Belgium, Denmark, Austria, Switzerland and the Czech Republic combined. In terms of population, there are as many Poles as Spaniards – only Germany, France, Italy and Britain in the EU have more citizens. Its GDP is not small either; its economy is as big as the combined output of Hungary, the Czech Republic, Bulgaria, Slovakia and Croatia.

If Poland were to develop into a pivotal national of considerable political, cultural and economic influence in Central Europe, it would not be for the first time. At the beginning of the seventeenth century, it was the largest state on the continent. Indeed, the celebrated Polish-Lithuanian Commonwealth, founded in 1386, had encompassed Lithuania, Latvia, Ukraine, Belarus and large parts of Russia and stretched from the Baltic to the Black Sea.

Mediaeval Poland saw itself as having a historic mission, that of the defender of Catholicism and the Christian West against the barbarous hordes spilling over the Russian Steppes and attempting to subjugate Europe. As early as 1240, Poland had faced a massive Mongol-Tartar invasion from the East that threatened to overrun the entire continent. In later years Polish armies were called upon to break the Turkish siege of Vienna. In modern times, one could say that Lech Walesa's Solidarity broke the Communist siege of Central Europe and produced a domino effect in Hungary, the former Czechoslovakia, Slovenia, Croatia and elsewhere.

Poles, destined to an historical buffer role between expansionist Russian and German empires, have shown themselves to be *ne plus ultra* fighters down the centuries. Their deep sense of vulnerability has engendered an unquenchable thirst for survival. Their stoicism in adversity, their shining courage and their enthusiasm for battle reached new heights during the Second World War. Polish pilots in the squadron fighting with the British Royal Air Force frequently lost planes through chasing enemy aircraft so far out over the North Sea that they ran out of fuel and were unable to return to their base. Such spirit, bordering on fanaticism, is the key to this vital, proud, sensitive, brave people, the most vigorous and westernised of the Slavs, now turning their face to the West more consistently than at any other time in their turbulent, tragic history.

Culture

Religion

Slavs are divided by religion: Serbia, Bulgaria, Belarus, Eastern Ukraine and Russia are by tradition Orthodox; Bosnia largely Muslim; Croatia, Slovenia, the Czech Republic, Western Ukraine and Poland Roman Catholic. Among Catholic Slavs, however, it is in Poland that the faith assumes disproportionate importance. At the centre of the problem of convergence of cultures, victimised repeatedly by invasion, mass deportations and even genocide, Poles have developed strong feelings of defensive nationalism and determination to survive no matter how devastating an oppression they face. In this defiance, they have consistently benefited from the power of Roman Catholic belief and have unhesitatingly used their religion as a source of identity to protect themselves against non-Roman Catholic enemies.

The fierce adherence of Poles to Roman Catholicism does not mean that they all go to church. They are less enthusiastic churchgoers than, for instance, Americans. But the refusal to separate church and state strengthened both the ecclesiastical and secular sides of Polish nationalism. Neither are Poles intolerant of other religions. There are Jewish, Orthodox, Lutheran, Calvinist and Muslim minorities. Religious tolerance has (like in the Netherlands) been part of the tradition of intellectual freedom down the centuries.

Values

Poles, romantic idealists that they are, believe that they are imbued with so many virtues that it is quite impossible to make a short list.

Polish literature is rich and original; Polish film and theatre directors have achieved fame through their avant-gardism, perceptiveness and resistance to totalitarian systems. Their famous 'cultural underground' performances were staged at major Polish theatres during the communist years. Polish poets, writers, playwrights and musicians are upholding intellectual and cultural traditions going back to Copernicus, Chopin, Paderewski, Joseph Conrad, Rubenstein and Mickiewicz, among many others.

The brilliance of Polish intellectual activity has always been underpinned by another endearing cultural trait – a type of rustic simplicity that derives its strength from a firm attachment to family values, inherent generosity and hospitality. The Pole – a fierce crusader in public – is a soft touch at home and in private. This heart-on-the-sleeve attitude is extended not only to family members, but to strangers and foreigners who give proof of their friendliness and (especially) loyalty. The proud, obstinate Poles show themselves flexible and humble when approached with understanding and open-mindedness. This applies not only to their social interactions, but also to the way they conduct their business.

The family is the basic unit of Polish life, more important than other groupings, church or even feeling for their country. Polish parents keep their children in the sense that they pay for their education, share their lives as much as possible and feed, clothe and house them until they get married.

Concepts

Leadership and status

In Polish history, royals and nobles have figured largely as leaders and organisers. Gentry comprised a high percentage of feudal society and established a chivalrous, romanticist lifestyle. Honour and revenge are living concepts in the Polish mind, as are grace, nobleness of bearing, personal integrity, fearlessness and gallantry towards women, who still get their hands kissed in Poland.

In more recent years, Nazi suppression and 45 years of communism diminished the influence of the leading Polish families. Lech Walesa eventually emerged as a working-class leader of deeply nationalistic convictions. Meritocracy now dominates advancement in Polish society, although nationally the Polish Pope has wielded enormous influence. Status is accorded unreservedly to great intellectuals and artists, both past and present, Chopin and Marie Curie being outstanding examples.

Space and time

The Polish sense of space is typically Slav, inasmuch as they stand or sit closer to each other than Anglo-Saxons or Nordics in conversation and often touch each other to give reassurance. Parents kiss their children well into their teens, often also as fully grown adults. Men kiss women on the hands and frequently male acquaintances on both cheeks. As far as possession of space is concerned, territory has always been a major issue in Poland, in view of the acquisitive tendencies of her big neighbours.

Poles are relaxed about time, but not necessarily unpunctual. One should not steal others' time, but Polish society is not time dominated in the German sense. Poles tend to turn up a little late, but they have an ambivalent attitude to the sequence of events, seeing ultimate reality as not being closely connected with present activity. They are definitely past oriented – the length and significance of their history and heritage provide an indispensable background and launching pad for current action. There is a certain fatalism about their conduct, although they also possess drive and objectivity.

Cultural factors in communication

Communication patterns and use of language

The Polish communication style is enigmatic. They can ring all the changes between a matter-of-fact pragmatic style and a wordy, sentimental, romantic approach to a given subject. When in the latter mode, they are fond of metaphor and their speech is rich in implied meaning, allusions, images and ambiguity. Irony and even satire are used to great effect.

Listening habits

Poles are courteous and rarely interrupt, but listen with calm scepticism and distrust to official announcements. They are quick to detect minor slights.

Behaviour at meetings and negotiations

As with their speech style, in behaviour Poles fluctuate between pragmatism and sentiment. Generally they seem to want a little of both. They are friendly and flexible when well treated, but react strongly if they suspect injustice. Not afraid to confront, they can be quite fiery when under pressure. A particular national characteristic is that they consider aggressive behaviour on their part to be justified when they are severely criticised or insulted.

If they are handled with a combination of frankness and delicacy they try quickly to establish close personal relationships. They have a basic shyness and non-assertiveness born of centuries of not questioning teachers or those in positions of influence and power.

Modern businesses are quickly growing in confidence, but one is still aware of a disarming simplicity in their behaviour towards others. Though personal, Polish negotiations are not particularly informal. A discreet distance is maintained between conversation partners. Often the third person (he or she) is used for direct address. Ideas are often introduced in a roundabout manner and one has to read between the lines.

Manners and taboos

+ Toasting is common and consumption of hard liquor (vodka, cognac) is widespread.
+ First names are for close friends only.
+ An odd number of flowers (unwrapped) is a suitable present for a hostess.
+ Body language is generally restricted, but shrugging of shoulders and slapping of one's forehead to indicate stupidity are fairly frequent.

How to empathise with Poles

Treat such concepts as honour, chivalry and old-fashioned gallantry as meaningful qualities in a Polish context. Show interest in their old culture and considerable artistic achievement. Admire their religious tolerance and general tendency to accommodate the views of others. Show that you perceive their nationalism as a necessary survival mechanism.

Appreciate Polish food and learn some expressions in their language. Don't try to address them in Russian.

26

HUNGARY

AT THE END OF THE NINTH CENTURY, THE HUNGARIANS WENT THROUGH the Carpathian passes to settle the Central Danube basin. There they established an empire that lasted 1000 years, ruling what is now Hungary, Croatia, Slovakia, Transylvania, Western Ukraine and parts of Serbia and Austria. During this period they were devastated by the Mongols in the thirteenth century and endured 150 years of Ottoman rule in the sixteenth and seventeenth centuries. Although fighters by nature, they have not been successful in the conduct of their wars; in fact, they have never won one.

In a national sense, Hungary is somewhat claustrophobic. It is a severely truncated state, compared with the lands that it once ruled. These territories, taken away from Hungary after military defeats, are still inhabited by Hungarians: two million Hungarians live in Romania alone, while another million inhabit Slovakia and Serbia.

Culture

Values

Obsession to achieve
Romanticism
Sense of humour
Vanity
National self-confidence

Bon vivant
Gallantry, chivalry
Sensitivity
Competitiveness
Street wisdom

Concepts

Leadership and status

Under their old aristocracy Hungarians were often led the wrong way. A conspicuous absence of military victories and political triumphs has made Hungarians adopt a cynical attitude to any kind of leadership. The Soviet rule did nothing to change this attitude.

A nation of individualists, Hungarians have gained and encourage status in intellectual, artistic and scientific achievements. Teachers, poets, artists, theatre and film directors, musicians, composers etc. are well respected, though hardly properly remunerated.

Space and time

In personal terms Hungarians sit and stand close to each other. Physical contact is frequent, handshaking mandatory. Conditions are crowded in Budapest and extended families under one roof are common. Buses and trains tend to be packed.

Hungarians are reasonably punctual in arriving for appointments, but lose all sense of time when they get involved in animated conversation. In this respect they act in a very Latin manner, subjecting their behaviour and activity not to the clock but to the psychological dictates of the encounter. The art of conversation cannot be scheduled – subsequent appointments are severely staggered or simply fall away.

Cultural factors in communication

Communication pattern and use of language

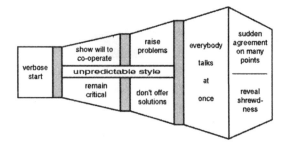

Discussion with Hungarians can be deceptive in the extreme. They possess ample reserves of charm and charisma and give the impression that they are easy going. Smalltalk invariably precedes commencement of business. They truly regard conversation as an art form – they are great storytellers and are not without humour.

Anglo-Saxons and Nordics may soon begin to lose their way. As an argument develops, Hungarians begin to abandon rationality for emotion, logic for rhetoric. Fluency equates with intelligence and they are great with words, often hiding what they are really saying. Exaggeration and flamboyance creep in, mixed with stylishly delivered flattery. Their natural easy-going approach can quickly switch to criticism, however. They are accomplished complainers. Pessimism and melancholy, suddenly introduced, can also be distracting.

Conversations are generally male dominated. Turn taking is problematic, with a tendency for everyone to talk at once. Choose your moment of entry carefully.

Listening habits

Hungarians have rather complex listening habits and require various ingredients to keep their attention.

Behaviour at meetings and negotiations

When holding meetings with representatives of more powerful nations, Hungarians have an initial preoccupation with national honour. They must be treated delicately and not talked down to. They are quite touchy about this, but quickly relax once status has been established. Meetings are, however, generally far from relaxing in terms of negotiating style and duration.

Meetings are rarely quiet and orderly and agendas are not respected. Hungarians are often moody and raise problems without offering solutions; they seem to expect the other party to come up with something. Bargaining is normal, prolonged and popular. In northern eyes, they over-analyse constantly. Often pessimistic, they will lace pessimism with optimistic forecasts of deals to be done. They avoid saying no, but often fail to answers questions directly. You really have to read between the lines.

Business must be carried on face to face, as only in this manner can trust be established. Hungarians are often unable to deliver their promises, but are skilled improvisers, although verbal energy often lapses into physical lassitude. At all times, one must watch one's back. Grandiose in their intentions, they are weak on responsibility and even weaker on implementation.

Manners and taboos

The Hungarian is a *bon vivant*, a drinker of wine rather than beer, a lover of cholesterol-rich food and frequenter of traditional coffee houses where timeless conversation and bitter-sweet Turkish coffee remind one of the Ottoman occupation. Engagement in Hungary is very personal, with much handshaking, strong eye contact and frequent confidences. Women, although sometimes prominent in business, are idealised in the old-fashioned manner. Hand kissing is common and men walk to the left of women (to protect them with their sword). Women precede men into theatres, cinemas and private homes, but follow them into rougher environments such as bars, restaurants and cafés! Hungarian speech uses the third person and has four forms for 'you' in varying degrees of politeness.

How to empathise with Hungarians

Above all, be familiar with Hungarian history and their contributions to the wider world, particularly with reference to science and music. Listen to their complaints and problems, but do not offer any of your own.

Be sensitive to telecommunications and transport failures, which are everyday occurrences. Be patient in following up leads.

Hungarians are impressed by plush offices, cars, clothes etc. and exhibit their wealth. Good clothes are essential and you should strive for immaculate presentation. This, a knowledge of Hungarian and a quick and flexible brain are assets in dealing with Hungarians. Most Hungarians in positions of power are very well educated and they respect strong academic records and intelligent conversation about their own magnificent history. Always refer to Hungary as Central Europe rather than Eastern Europe.

Avoid talking about ethnic minorities, Jews, Gypsies, Romanians etc. unless you are well informed. A sense of humour is essential.

27

THE CZECH REPUBLIC

CZECHS ARE PROUD OF THEIR INTER-WAR RECORD IN A PERIOD THAT SAW them become the tenth industrial power in the world. Democracy flourished under Jan Masaryk and the country seemed to have the rosiest future of the Slav lands.

This fine progress was rudely interrupted by the German intrusion into Sudetenland in 1938 and by the Russian occupation from 1945–89. During the presence of Soviet troops, Czechs offered only passive resistance until Dubcek's audacity produced the Prague Spring of 1968, quickly crushed by Russian tanks.

After the departure of the Soviets, Czechoslovakia wrestled with its internal problem – the growing schism between Czechs and Slovaks. The separation, as might have been foreseen, was civilized and bloodless (in stark contrast to the bloodletting in the former Yugoslovia). Czechs and Slovaks put their house in order in a manner not unlike that of the Portuguese in their 1974 revolution. The election of a playwright and poet – Vaclav Havel – to the Czech presidency crowned this serene political development.

The Czechs have had gnawing problems adjusting to a market economy. Nearly 50 years of being directed by the Soviets had left a legacy of lassitude and avoidance of responsibility observable in other ex-communist states. Soul searching in the Czech Republic is as pervasive as it is in more fortunate countries such as Norway and the Netherlands. The search for Czech identity goes on. Given the many skills and high level of education of the Czech people, there is a high probability that it will be a creditable and inspiring one.

Culture

Values

Individualism, creativity	Sense of humour
Work ethic	Flexibility
Love of learning	Pragmatism, egalitarianism
Tolerance, tidiness, thrift	Rationality
Love of music and theatre	Discipline, steadiness, loyalty
Morality	Lack of self-confidence
Lasting friendships	Passive resistance

Concepts

Leadership and status

Czechs resent power imposed from the outside and never accepted inequality imposed by foreign rulers. The high rate of literacy and general excellence of education over the centuries have enabled Czechs to acquire and enjoy knowledge. Egalitarianism and democratic institutions are instinctively desired. Liberty is seen as something that may be assured by laws, procedures and regulations. Orderliness in society has long been a characteristic of Czech society, though this has often led to excessive officialdom and periods of stifling bureaucracy. The Soviet influence in the Communist period was met by passive resistance rather than by open confrontation.

Space and time

Czechs are not particularly tactile people and kissing, embracing and hugging in public are very rare. Handshaking is mandatory on greeting and taking leave. The 'distance of comfort' is well over a metre.

Bus queues are disciplined and orderly. Czechs arrive on time for appointments and often early for dinner. They are early risers. In the Communist time, factories were in full swing by 7 am or earlier and the working day often finished at 1 or 2 pm.

Cultural factors in communication

Communication pattern and use of language

The Czechs are soft speakers who communicate in a thoughtful manner and in measured tones. Rushing headlong into discussion is not their style and rapid conclusions are rare. They often impress their interlocutors as being phlegmatic and lukewarm rather than just laid back. Their humour is dry and black.

Listening habits

The Czechs are dutiful listeners, always polite and courteous. They rarely interrupt and give little feedback. As they think in a linear fashion, they are uncomfortable with roundabout or digressive discussion and have a low tolerance for ambiguity. Their response, if they are unhappy, can be ironic and contain veiled sarcasm.

Behaviour at meetings and negotiations

Czech negotiations are contemplative, practical and rational. They do not like confrontation and pride themselves on their flexibility and adaptability. They have a gradualistic approach to problem solving, not unlike the Dutch and Belgian styles. Decisions can be deferred until tomorrow, but not indefinitely. Czechs are serious, even moralistic, but show flashes of creativity and unpredictability. They like to think of themselves as entrepreneurs and there are now a very large number of registered, small companies. They believe that sound procedures are good for business and seek common ground with partners, just as Germans do. Their love of structure and regulations and incremental planning makes them poor at handling chaos. A recent survey listed their view of which characteristics are most important for personal success:

1 Ability to solve problems.
2 Concern for the well-being of the group.
3 Being flexible.
4 Persistence.
5 Being organized.

Manners and taboos

Czechs still adhere to old-fashioned concepts of formality and chivalry. Although showing less gallantry towards women than the Poles, they dress up conscientiously when going to the theatre or opera and shake hands with all and sundry in a respectful (almost Germanic) manner. They do not forget to use academic titles when addressing people and respect education and good manners in others. Slouching or disrespectful body language is frowned on and generally they dislike ostentatious behaviour or grandiose comportment. In short, they are (and wish to be) very civilised. They do not invite business associates immediately into their homes, but prove loyal and hospitable friends when acquaintance has matured.

How to empathise with Czechs

Czechs are motivated by people behaving in what they consider to be a civilised manner. They like their creativity to be challenged, and money is a secondary consideration. Brusque confrontation is taboo and they like an approach that leads to calm discussion and the discovery of solutions that suit all concerned.

All kinds of sports and home comforts are good topics of conversation. They have little inclination to talk about war, politics or religion.

28

FINLAND

ONCE UPON A TIME, LONG LONG AGO, THERE WAS A FAR-OFF LAND CLOSE to the Arctic circle – a chilly, bleak patchwork of forests and lakes where bears, wolves, elks and lynxes roamed freely and where Christmases were always white. A strange tribe from faraway arrived in this land where no other people had chosen to live and set about the task of making themselves comfortable there. They cut wood to construct dwellings, they planted crops on open land and they fished the lakes and rivers.

They were an unusual people, of an independent nature, devoted to hard work, yet modest in their aspirations and jealous of their honest reputation. They were clean in their habits, physically fit and enjoyed the outdoor life. They spoke very little, for loquaciousness and especially boasting were taboo. Solitude was the safest and they loved the great space that the new land offered.

Like other peoples, they had jealous neighbours and they had to fight many battles to defend their territory. They did not always win and they were subjugated for long periods. Notwithstanding their suffering and humiliation, they never gave up and in the end they made their land secure and have lived happily there up to the present day.

If this sounds like a fairy tale, it is perhaps because it possesses the elements of one, but we are talking about a modern nation which really exists. This nation, clinging to the old values in the fairy tale, fought a modern giant (state) of 200 million people to hold on to what we today call a democracy. The honest tribe continues to pay off all its debts, protect its environment and vanquish crime, injustice and poverty. The quiet people solve modern problems such as treatment of its minorities, resettlement of refugees (400,000 Karelians) and the struggle against pollution without any fuss.

The tribe is still not very well known in the lands to the south and they are notoriously poor at blowing their own trumpet. Their Altaic language does not calibrate with the majority of the world's tongues, their basic shyness and dislike of exhibitionism lend thickness to an intervening curtain of cultural complexity, voluntary withdrawal and geographical remoteness. They feel a sense of separateness from other peoples.

Yet this tribe is warm-hearted, wishing to be loved and anxious to join the rest of us. They are energetic, essentially inventive and have much to offer others.

The unprecedentedly high degree of national self-consciousness in Finland indicates that the Finns are aware of being a very special people, yet it falls to the outsider to evaluate and quantify just how special they are. Certain peculiarly Finnish characteristics, e.g. contempt for verbosity or an inner, burning desire to rid oneself of debt, seem natural to Finns but rare indeed to the student of comparative culture.

Hero nation

The Finnish character, too, remains mysterious to outsiders. Here we have an outstanding example of a hero nation, one with a virtually unblemished record in its internal and international dealings. To list the Finnish virtues is not difficult. After a long and what must have been arduous migration, the Finns settled the Baltic shores some 2000–3000 years ago. A first testimony to their fortitude is that they have proved to be the only people capable of creating a successful society on territory lying in its entirety above 60°N latitude. (Iceland has also done this on a smaller scale, though most Icelanders went there because they had to, as their blood-stained history indicates.) For hundreds of years the Finns were subjected to foreign domination, yet neither once-mighty Sweden nor monolithic Russia was able to eliminate Finnish customs, language or culture and historical references from both great powers constantly mention Finnish bravery, reliability and diligence.

When the opportunity came to achieve independence, the Finns took it, swiftly and efficiently. They recognised their historical moment and they were fortunate with their leadership at the time. Bloodshed was kept at a minimum, reprisals were few. As quickly as they could, the Finns set about establishing a modern state based on equality and freedoms. Nationalist fervour was high, but arrogant chauvinism has been noticeably absent in Finnish history. Their treatment of the Swedish-speaking minority (now 6 per cent) was scrupulously fair. Swedish is retained along with Finnish as a national language and Finn–Swedes (who feel Finnish, not Swedish) have their own political party, newspapers and equal rights.

For 20 years (1919–39) Finland's progress was steady, at times spectacular. Many athletic triumphs followed – particularly at the 1936 Olympics – women were given the vote and genuine democracy blossomed. Sibelius, Kajanus, Saarinen, Järnefelt, Gallen-Kallela and Alvar Aalto assured the country's representation at the highest artistic levels; intelligent management of the Finnish forest and other resources led to a quickly rising standard of living.

The Second World War was a cruel shock and a severe setback to the young nation, but even defeat was a victory, since independence was maintained and the subsequent fate of 10 East European countries has served to emphasise Finland's good fortune earned by her determination to fight to the end for what she believed in.

After the war, the saga continued. Finland's achievement in resettling 400,000 refugees from Karelia in the space of a few months went largely unrecognised by the world at large. The war-battered country immediately set about the task of paying off unjust war reparations to the Soviet Union – settled in full by the appointed date. The 1950s and 1960s were difficult economically, with Finland starting off as the poor relation in the Nordic family. National diligence eventually triumphed: first Finland surpassed Sweden in cross-frontier investment and eventually enjoyed a boom for the ten years beginning in 1978. A clean, crime-free and poverty-less society entered the ranks of the world's 10 most prosperous countries in the early 1980s. And without ruining the environment.

Pessimism and paradox

Finns sweep their nation's achievements under the carpet in periodic fits of pessimism and self-debasement. Foreigners are cleverer than we are, they say. We are rustic, gullible and easily deceived. We can't learn languages (a myth) and we are rude and clumsy. It is hard for the British and French to imagine a nation which has triumphed over so much adversity fall prey to an inferiority complex! There are a string of such contradictions. Finns are warm-hearted people, but they have a desire for solitude. They are hard-working and intelligent, but they despair openly of emerging from a recession. They love freedom, but they curtail their own liberty with early closing of shops, limited access to alcohol, prohibiting baths after 10 pm and taxing themselves to death. They worship athletics and fitness, but used to eat a diet which gave the highest incidence of heart disease in western Europe. They admire coolness and calm judgement, but drink far too much. They are eager to internationalise but pretend they can't learn languages. They want to communicate, but wallow in introversion. They make fine companions, but love to brood alone by a lake shore. They are tolerant, but secretly despise peoples who are melodramatic or seemingly overemotional. They are essentially independent, but often hesitate to speak their mind in the international arena. They are genuinely democratic, but often let the 'tyranny of the majority' rule. They are fiercely individualistic, but are afraid of 'what the neighbours might say'. They are western in outlook but, like the Orientals, cannot 'lose face'. They are resourceful but often portray themselves as hapless. They are capable of acting alone, but frequently take refuge in group collusion. They desire to be liked but make no attempt to charm. They love their country, but seldom speak well of it.

The Finns, probably on account of exceptional historical and geographical circumstance, have a higher degree of national self-consciousness than most peoples. It is a characteristic they share with the Japanese, Chinese and the French, although the Finns are less chauvinistic.

They are acutely aware of the specialness of their own culture and they are very interested in it. They are also interested in cultural relativism, that is to say, the ways in which they differ from others. They discuss this subject at length and tend to develop complexes which are not always corresponding to reality. The question of 'the Finnish difference' once had its primary involvement in the arts, literature and assertion of political independence. Today it raises its head in the development and conduct of international business.

Finnish qualities

What are the generally accepted qualities of Finnish managers and to what extent are they advantaged or disadvantaged by these characteristics?

Intially, the image of the Finnish businessperson emerges from the general *Suomi-kuva* (Finnish image) which is perpetuated by the Finns themselves and accepted, hook, line and sinker, by foreigners who have little knowledge of Finland. In the Suomi-kuva the true Finn is fair-haired and blue-eyed (in both senses) and is slow, honest, reliable and easily deceived by other peoples. They are a strong, silent type with a rural background and thrive in an environment consisting of forests, lakes, snow, fishing through the ice and minimal conversation with neighbours who live 5 kilometres away. Other pursuits are running, skiing and (now and then) drinking hard liquor. They live in a democracy with a written constitution, are fiercely independent, a true friend, a good soldier, a bad enemy. They have no head for languages and are uneasy with foreigners, but give them strong coffee and take them to the sauna. They are Lutheran, work hard when the money is right and always pay their debts.

The image of the Finnish manager cannot be completely separated from this myth (with its basis of truth). Foreigners expect Finnish businesspeople to behave like Finns. The myth therefore has to be enlarged, to become credible. Finnish executives did not want to learn foreign languages, but disciplined themselves to do so. They prefer to keep quiet, but now and again they speak – and what they say they really mean (it might even be final). They pay their debts, but get their 90 days' credit. They make contracts with the Middle East and southern peoples, but watch their backs and take precautions. They deal with the West, but with Eastern Europe too and this includes the Russians, whom they understand like no other Europeans do. They know Finland cannot compete with the larger countries, but they sniff out niche industries, where Finnish original thinking can score points. Finnish managers insist on up-to-date technology, state-of-the-art factories and offices, and thorough training for all personnel. Profits are speedily reinvested in fine offices, training centres, sports facilities and anything else which will increase productivity.

Finnish strengths

Cold climates inevitably engender cool, sturdy, resilient peoples with an inordinate capacity for self-reliance and instinct for survival. The Arctic survivor must have stamina, guts, self-dependence and powers of invention. In managerial terms, these qualities translate into persistence, courage, individuality and original thinking. Unlike their Scandinavian neighbours, the Finns originate from the East, though they are not Slavic. The uniqueness of their language and their outpost mentality encourage an independent outlook and lateral thinking, which enhances not only Finnish literature, music and fine arts, but extends to brilliance of industrial design and penetrative insight into various branches of technology. It is not by accident that Finland has, in recent times, figured among the foremost innovators in glass, textiles, furniture, imaginative shipbuilding and electronic technology.

Finnish managers, establishing a branch abroad, do not arrive with the heavy feet of the German or the sweeping, complacent logic of the French. They may be regarded as a bit dull, or even gullible, but they are adaptable, ready to learn and compromise.

Their lack of a strong national business culture enables them to consider membership of trade 'clubs' readily and Finland's successful experience within EFTA will undoubtedly be followed by a fruitful association with the European Union. As a bridge between East and West, Finland could blossom into a key EU member, particularly if East European nations such as Hungary, Poland and the Soviet Union gain entry.

Finnish business history is short, but it is replete with a succession of self-made men and rugged individuals who created the companies which are household names in the country today. Such men are less in evidence as business-by-consensus comes into vogue, but their tradition lives on in Finnish respect for the strong leader who plunges onwards. Most Finnish managers make decisions without constant reference to HQ and this agility and mobile management is seen as a David-like advantage when dealing with foreign corporations of Goliathan proportions.

Finns respect, even cherish, the rights of the underdog, so woe betide the Finnish boss who tries to bully or unduly coerce subordinates! This informality of corporate climate facilitates interchange of ideas and development of mutual respect within Finnish companies. The parallel distaste for foreign-imposed bureaucracy has led to Finnish business being seen as a meritocracy and certainly the high level of education of Finnish executives gives them an edge over many foreign counterparts.

From Sweden and, it must be said, from other western countries, Finns absorbed Lutheranism, the Protestant work ethic, a strong sense of social justice, respect for education and social stability (including the establishment of a strong position for women). The solidarity of this background, added to the typical Scandinavian absence of violence in peacetime, facilitated the development of Finnish industry in the twentieth century, culminating in the boom years of 1980–88 and the resultant high standard of living enjoyed today.

Finnish weaknesses

Historical and geographical conditions have also bequeathed weaknesses on the Finns with regard to their bent for business and trade. First, they have been until recent times a rural, agricultural society and their commercial history is young. The Swedes internationalised in 1870, Finland only in 1970. Finnish managers are still living out their first generation in international management, therefore making the mistakes that others have learnt by. Domination by Sweden and Russia has led to a general Finnish belief that they are somewhat backward and even the unquestioned successes of the last decade have not totally eradicated occasional lapses in self-confidence. One sometimes observes a reversal of attitude ('to hell with the foreigners – Finns are best') and this, too, hampers entry into the international arena.

There are obvious weaknesses in the field of communication – Finns speak little, often delay in replying to correspondence, and avoid showdowns with other peoples because of shyness or feeling that they lack *savoir faire*. Clashes between Finnish industry and the Finnish media in the 1970s and 1980s caused many business circles to avoid contact with press and television. This reluctance to communicate has also extended to the foreign media (a pity, because in some countries, eg. the US or Britain, the media can be very helpful in the public relations sphere). Finnish managers, with their reputation as straightforward players, would often be most favourably received by the foreign press.

Europe can manage without Finnish industry, but the converse is not the case. The niche strategy of Finnish companies has proved itself a valuable option for a country severely limited by the smallness of its home market. In the future, Finnish industry cannot afford to neglect any viable overseas markets and there is an urgent requirement to get on trading terms with Europeans, Americans, Arabs, Japanese and other Eastern nations. This also means getting on talking terms, which for the Finn has traditionally been seen as difficult. In Finland, silence is not equated with failure to communicate, but is an integral part of social interaction.

In the Anglo-Saxon world and in Latin and Middle Eastern countries, talking has another function. In Britain the well-known habit of discussing the weather with neighbours or even strangers shows not only the British preoccupation with their fickle climate, but also their desire to show solidarity with and friendliness towards other people. This sociable discourse is even more evident in the USA, Canada and Australia, where speech is a vital tool for getting to know people and establishing a quick relationship.

Their view of language appropriacy isolates Finland and Japan in international discourse. In both countries one hears the same whispers ('foreigners talk so fast – we are slow by comparison – we can't learn languages – our pronunciation is terrible – it's because our own language is so difficult – foreigners are more experienced than we are – they are cleverer and often deceive us – they don't mean what they say – we can't rely on them – we are the truest people'). Having lived many years in both countries, I have great respect for and sympathy with the admirable reserve and obvious sincerity of Finns and Japanese. But the fact is that Pekka Virtanen and Ichiro Tanaka will have to enter the verbal fray. Japan has already set up factories and offices throughout the world and is currently grappling with the cultural and communicative problems of working side-by-side with foreign nationals or actually managing them. Finland, admittedly on a smaller scale, is in the process of doing the same.

Speech-and-thought icebergs

As we all know, most of an iceberg is below the surface. We can also draw the concept of a person's speech-and-thought ratio in the form of an iceberg. In the case of the British and German icebergs the 'section of thought' presented to others in speech is roughly equal. The French iceberg shows more ice visible, corresponding to more speech on the part of the French. South American icebergs break the surface of audibility to a much greater degree. The Finnish iceberg shows a more introspective nature is involved, indicating minimum thought revealed. Japanese tell you even less.

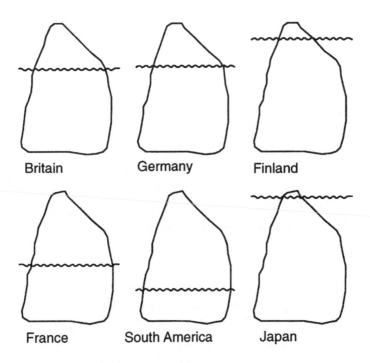

Britain   Germany   Finland

France   South America   Japan

Culture shock

We often hear the term 'culture shock' which many people experience when transferring from one culture to another. Finns first hitting Cairo or Naples will suffer their own version of culture shock. Culture shock is caused by the lack of culture-specific cues, or indications, which tell you how to behave in that society. One of the problems for foreigners new to Finland is that Finnish shyness and silence provide few cultural cues. This causes foreigners to follow their own course and when Finns fail to react openly, newcomers begin to question their role or identity.

To give an example, an Englishman always feels he is a quiet, solid individual when in France, Spain and Italy. He is the typical reserved Englishman, listening to the Latins babbling on. Suddenly, in Finland he is the talkative one. What should he do? Maintain an out-of-character loquaciousness and behave like a Neapolitan, or imitate his Finn and silently watch the sun set over Lake Näsijärvi?

If a northern European questions his image among Finns, imagine how Italians and Spaniards feel as they talk and talk and wave around their arms. 'I feel constantly like an actor on the stage,' said one Italian executive, 'and I have to play the lead role for five acts, night after night.'

Leadership roles

In the business area, this obviously causes problems for foreign managers who have to decide which role or profile of leadership they should adopt among Finnish colleagues. There is clearly room for foreign managers in Finland, in order to bring in fresh ideas and see things from new angles. And yet should they adopt a high or low profile?

Should the French, with their great powers of imagination, attempt to fire and inspire the Finns with their exuberance and enthusiasm, or will they always be regarded as theatrical and overemotional with a lot of wild ideas? Should Germans, with their firm concepts of orderliness and 'Gründlichkeit', try to install solid systems and a greater sense of respect, or will they just be regarded as Teutonic, heavy, inflexible, or even old-fashioned or outdated? Should the Swede emphasise polished management skills within a workers' council framework, or has the more individualistic Finnish approach already bypassed Swedish methods?

Again we must take into account the factor that Finns appear different to various nationalities. The Italians find them wooden, the Spaniards excessively law-abiding. The ultra-polite Japanese see Finns as a bit rude (without knowing it). Danes see them as big drinkers (the women too!) and Swedes often consider them slightly dangerous. The British, with their sense of history, see them as David against Goliath, but otherwise fairly normal, although on the quiet side.

The good, the bad and the ugly

Given these different viewpoints, the life of foreign managers in Finland is probably what they make it. If they look for the good, the bad and the ugly they will probably find all three.

You might say the bad is the tight-lipped, so-called winter behaviour, which causes Finns to hurry by wordlessly on the street (temperature –20°C) and gulp down their Koskenkorva to thaw out their irritability.

Some see Finland as a land full of martyrs, making life difficult for themselves in an already inhospitable corner of Europe which they are reluctant to join. In 1952 there was no alcohol without food, you couldn't have a bath after 10 pm if you lived in an apartment block, you were not permitted to enter good restaurants unless you wore formal attire and the shops usually closed about 10 minutes before your working hours allowed you to get to them. Many of these things have changed, but one still has the worries of prices and taxes being so high that one can hardly breathe. Why do Finns have to build houses of such good quality that you can't pay the rent? In Finland the standard of living is so high that most people can't reach it.

But then there is the good. Finnish leadership practices are sound. Finnish managers, like Finnish army officers, usually lead from the front and they generally strike the right balance between authoritarianism and consultative style.

Although the ice breaks slowly, foreign managers will find that the informal business climate gives them freedom of action. They will not be encumbered by too many manuals, systems or hierarchical paths. Finns leave work early, but they start early and one can have achieved a fine day's work by the time most Britons are heading for lunch. Finnish employees are honest, reliable, punctual and generally loyal and their *sisu* qualities are well documented. Bureaucracy is kept at a minimum.

How to empathise with Finns

Your best starting point is to get it crystal clear in your mind that a Finn is a formidable person. The slow, reticent and apparently backward behaviour often referred to by Swedes, Germans and French among others is no more than a deceptive veneer covering a very modern individual. The more one has to do with Finns, the more one realises that they are, in effect, perfectionists. They defer politely to your cleverness or smoothness but, in fact, they usually upstage you.

The upstaging is done discreetly, but effectively. Your modest Finnish partners, so complimentary of your own attributes, turn out to be highly qualified technocrats with very solid assets. Their office, car and clothes may well be of better quality than yours, their house almost certainly will be. They have *ne plus ultra* standards of cleanliness, honesty, stamina, workmanship, reliability, hygiene, safety and education. In Finland you can drink tap water, doctors know how to cure you if you are ill, buses, trains and aeroplanes leave on time, there are no hurricanes. Newspapers are printed on good quality paper and the ink doesn't come off on your hands; Finnish money may sometimes devalue, but the banknotes have a nice feel to them. Finnish milk and coffee are the best in the world. Food is wholesome, society is solid. The Germans, Dutch, Swiss and other peoples also say how solid they are, but the Finns possess a squat, flat-footed solidity which always makes you feel you know where you are with them.

Finns look for solidity in others. Refer to your own culture's achievements, but always in a modest tone. Low profile works wonders with Finns. Never boast. When you have said your piece, don't expect any feedback. They are thinking about what you have said. They don't think and talk at the same time. Enjoy the silence – not many people give you this luxury. Consider silence as a positive sign, then you can relax. Go to the sauna and have a drink. When working with Finns you should try to set clear goals, define objectives and appeal to the inner resources of individuals to achieve the task under their own steam and to be fully accountable for it. Finns like to demonstrate their stamina in a lone task – they excel in such lonely pursuits as long-distance running, skiing, and rally driving.

Finnish businesspeople wish to have both their responsibility and authority well defined. They don't want one without the other. Self-discipline is taken for granted. Finns do not like being closely supervised; they prefer to come to you with the end result. You should listen well to Finns, for when they eventually have something to say, it is often worth listening to. You have to watch for subtle body language, as they have no other. You may not oversell to them, but charisma is OK. You can be humorous on any occasion, you can talk about the cultural values of others, but don't praise the Swedes too much. Finnish newspapers are among the best and most objective in the world, so they are probably better informed on most matters than you are. Show lively interest in Finnish culture – it is rewarding in any case. Make it clear that you know that Finland and Finnish products are high tech.

If you are managing Finns, remember that they are high on self-respect and inner harmony, as opposed to craving the support of teamwork. They like the idea of profit centres and accountability. They will sometimes be slow in making up their mind but, once it is made up, you are unlikely to succeed in changing it.

Finally, remember they are very dry (this quality, too, brings its delights). The great Finnish composer Jean Sibelius, who occasionally used to go on three- or four-day drinking sprees with other intellectuals, was once phoned by his long-suffering wife asking him for a forecast of when he might come back home. 'My dear, I am a composer. I am involved in the business of composing music, not delivering forecasts,' was the reply.

29

SWEDEN

IN THE WORLD AT LARGE, AND ESPECIALLY IN THE ENGLISH-SPEAKING world, the Swedes seem to be universally popular. Their clean-cut profile as honest, caring, well-informed, efficient plodders, producing quality goods delivered on time, sits well with their frequently well-groomed appearance, good sense of dress and (forgive the stereotyping) blond hair and blue eyes. Their English, grammatically proficient, is clean and crisp, like that of Scots who went to Oxford. In society set pieces, at least, they have impeccable manners and say all the right things for the first 15 minutes.

It is somewhat surprising, therefore, to discover that they are unpopular, often ridiculed and occasionally despised inside the Nordic area. The fact that none of the Swedes' neighbours – Denmark, Norway, Finland – have any undue reputation for aggressivity makes the antipathy all the more unexpected. What is wrong with the Swedes?

This is a question which the Swedes themselves have been trying to answer over the last few decades. Statistically speaking, there is very little wrong with Sweden. Superb medical care has produced the oldest population in the world (18.1 per cent of the population is over 65) and only the Japanese have higher life expectancy (Japan 79, Sweden 78). Infant mortality is the fourth lowest in the world. With a population of 8.6 million occupying an area of 450,000 square kilometres, Sweden's population density is comfortably placed at 19 per square kilometre. Although only the 54th largest country in the world, Sweden is ranked 18th in GDP and a meritorious 5th in GDP per head at $25.487 per annum.

This affluence is reflected in the standard of living – Swedes are first in the world in telephone ownership, fifth in dishwashers, sixth in microwaves, seventh in fridges and videocassette recorders, and tenth in cars. With 99 per cent literacy, Swedes had the second highest percentage of the population in the labour force in 1990–1 (after Zimbabwe!) at 69.3 per cent. Foreign debt is low, foreign aid very high – ninth in the world in bilateral help (fourth as bilateral donors as a percentage of GNP). Sweden occupies a significant position in industrial output (world 14th) and is 15th in world trading. These are excellent figures for a country with a population of under 9 million, considering that Sweden is no 'sweat shop'.

With a slow-growing population (Sweden already has the world's smallest households at 2.2 people per dwelling) and ample land, mineral and energy resources, Sweden would seem to have few material problems. According to the the UN Human Development Index, again Sweden is well to the fore. The HDI, which combines such factors as GDP per head, life expectancy, adult literacy, years of schooling, purchasing power, etc., places Sweden fifth behind only Japan, Canada, Norway and Switzerland in terms of human development standards.

The only significant negative statistics for Sweden are: heart attacks – highest in the world at 37.3 per cent of deaths; murders – Sweden stands 18th; drug offences – second place. Swedish brides are second oldest in the world at 27.6 years and the country has the seventh highest cost of living, but these last two factors may also be viewed as positive.

Sweden is obviously a country that functions well, as the enviable statistics quoted above clearly demonstrate. Why the friction between the Swedes and their neighbours? In the first place, they **are** neighbours: neighbourly love is not a human characteristic. Norway, Denmark and Finland are less impressed than others by the splendour of the Swedish welfare state, as they have similar creations of their own (and there is a growing doubt in all four countries that the system will really work in the very long run). Their cynicism *vis-à-vis* Sweden seems to derive from various historical factors:

✦ Denmark was for a long period a major player in the area.
✦ Swedes often laid siege to Copenhagen.
✦ Swedes ruled Finland for 600 years.
✦ Sweden and Norway shared an uncomfortable union until 1905.
✦ Norway, Denmark and Finland were battered in the Second World War. Sweden was not.

Swedish industry enjoyed a period of prosperity in the the years 1945–60 when Norway and Denmark got off to a much slower post-war start and Finland was badly handicapped by having to pay huge (and unfair) war reparations to the Russians (1945–52). The big Swedish multinationals – Volvo, Saab, Electrolux, SKF, Axel Johnson and so on – boomed during these years, when Swedish steel was reputedly the best in the world. Others' prosperity often gives rise to neighbours' envy, especially when accompanied by a certain complacency. In the Nordic zone, Sweden was seen as big, export-minded, financially strong, well-fed and irritatingly smug.

There is little doubt that the Swedes are much less self-satisfied today than they were in the 1950s and 1960s, but in a recent survey I conducted among 100 Swedish business people, an all-Swedish compilation of their values resulted in the following:

> Conscientiousness, honesty, loyalty, tolerance, equality,
> love of peace, love of nature, cleanliness, kindness, modesty.

It is not without significance that the respondents chose 10 positive values and no negative ones. Laine-Sveiby comments that Swedes fail to see themselves as others see them; in this respect they differ from the more worldly Danes and also from the Finns, who are extremely interested in cultural relativism and constantly worry about what others think of them. Swedes, on the other hand, worry very much about what other Swedes think!

Decision making

Swedish management is decentralized and democratic – the organigram of the typical Swedish company has a decidedly horizontal look about it. Power distance is small and the manager is generally accessible to staff and available for discussion. There will be fewer echelons in a Swedish firm than there would be for instance in France or Germany. There is actually a Swedish law (MBL) which stipulates that all important decisions must be discussed with all staff members before being implemented! The rationale is that better informed employees are more motivated and consequently perform better. This collectivist form of decision making bears an interesting comparison with the Japanese system. In both countries it is seen as important that all colleagues have ample opportunity to discuss projects thoroughly, since the right to debate and express one's opinion is paid for by strict adherence to the company policy once it has been settled. In Sweden, as in Japan, decisions may be considerably delayed, but, once made, are unanimous; everyone in the company will subsequently be pulling the same way. This contrasts sharply with, for instance, the situation in many US companies where individual convictions often lead to internal discord and infighting.

A major difference, however, between the Swedish and Japanese models is that power distance between managers and employees is in reality much greater in Japan. In both systems, prolonged discussion and evaluation leads to good communication of information and generates a feeling of confidence and trust between employees.

The Swedish model is not without its critics. Moran mentions the following as Swedish weaknesses in the implementation of business:

+ avoidance of conflict or taking sides
+ fear of confrontation
+ reliance on the team for initiatives
+ avoidance of competition with others in the company

While employee participation in decision making is clearly desirable in modern firms, the speed at which business is conducted today (enhanced by the facilities afforded by information technology) often requires quick and clear decisions. Probably decision making is faster in the USA than anywhere else; it is slowest in Japan and some other Asian countries. Most European countries lie somewhere in between these two extremes. Sweden is dangerously near Japan. One uses the word 'dangerously' in the sense that while it is an accepted Oriental concept that big decisions take months, it is by no means the case in Europe and the USA. French, British and Finnish managers have experienced frustration, when working with or in Swedish companies, with the constant consultation going on at all levels, the endless meetings, habitual deferment of decisions, obsession with people orientation, ultra-cautiousness, woolly personnel policies, unclear 'guidelines' from managers.

The Swedish manager

Swedish managers are skilled at handling human resources, using charisma, a gentle but persuasive communication style and clever psychological approaches. They are good because they have to be! Their lot is not a simple one. As in Japan, it is not easy to rid oneself of an incompetent, even lazy or less than fully honest employee in Sweden. As it is also unseemly to get rich, managers lack both a carrot and a stick. They cannot fire and they cannot motivate very much with money (bonuses and use of a company car drive up the tax). Consequently they take great pains to get the best out of those they command. Unfortunately they don't command them very much either. They don't issue orders – they are better described as guidelines and are often not more than suggestions. They don't implement even these directives, but delegate authority downwards to have them carried out. If the employee is incompetent or idle, there is a lot of mopping up to do. To be fair to Swedes, one must point out that most Swedish staff members are extremely conscientious, cooperative and loyal. The problem arises (as it often does in Japan) when the task assigned is too big for the capabilities of the individual.

One Swedish professor remarked that in order to exercise power in Sweden one has to create an image of not being powerful. Swedish managers walk a tightrope between undue personal intervention and woolly, ineffective control. They try to establish their line through careful planning and procedures. It is said that detailed planning helps Swedish managers to sleep better!

The feminine society

Geert Hofstede, in his well-known study of business cultures, concludes that of all those covered in the survey, Sweden is the most feminine. In masculine cultures the dominant values are success, money, rewards, objects and possessions. In feminine ones interpersonal aspects, quality of life, physical environment, rendering service, nurturance are considered more important – in short, the creation of a caring society. In the case of today's Sweden, people (including Swedes) are beginning to ask themselves if it is too caring. The welfare system – arguably the best in the world – is very expensive to maintain. Taxes are so high they hurt, and the country is ageing fast. Every year there are fewer breadwinners for more dependants. In a non-competitive world, Swedes might go on selling quality products at high prices to support their living standards, but competition in the twenty-first century will be ferocious. Asians and Americans do not take six weeks holidays plus all kinds of long weekends and rush out of the office at four in summer. The Swedish manager is constantly confronted by requests to take leave for pregnancies, sick children, sabbaticals, right to study, home guard, trade union work, etc.

Capital and industry had been left largely in private hands in Sweden, but the taxation system sees to it that nobody gets rich legally. Those who threaten to do so (Ingmar Bergman, Björn Borg), are forced to go and live abroad to avoid paying tax which might reach more than 100 per cent of income. Monte Carlo has a better climate, too!

One suspects that there is more wrong with the Swedish system than with the Swedes themselves. They are kind, intelligent, steadfast people who want to do well, although it will not be easy for them to eradicate their work-to-rule mentality when things get tougher. An over-regulated society, irrespective of its politics, can engender very boring members, all spontaneity taxed out of them.

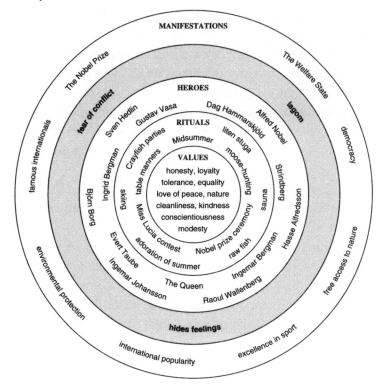

When dealing with Swedes, remember:

+ They believe they are honest and always tell the truth.
+ They don't like to contradict their own colleagues.
+ Authority is delegated down in Swedish companies so you may not be hearing what their boss really thinks.
+ Price may be inflexible, as Swedes believe their starting prices are fair.
+ They may appear inflexible in other respects, as they believe strongly in their group consensus decision.
+ Like Japanese, they find it hard to make changes individually, as it would go against the consensus.
+ They are good listeners and will be sympathetic to your point of view.
+ If they wish to accommodate you, they will need time to arrange it.
+ They are not as profit minded as you are.
+ In spite of their 'caring' nature, they are more deal than people oriented.
+ They are pragmatic as far as technical quality is concerned.
+ Their strong points when selling are quality, design, and prompt delivery.
+ When buying, they also look for quality and are not overly price conscious.
+ They entertain well and generously when this is part of their programme.
+ Like Americans and Finns, they attach little importance to the food at a 'working' lunch and carry on discussing details while eating. French and Spanish people cannot stand this.
+ They can discuss technical details *ad infinitum*, but run out of small talk after 10–15 minutes. Their jokes and anecdotes, however, are first class!
+ They are formal in toasting and expect speeches to be made during and after dinner.
+ They are extremely informal in address, using only the '*Du*' form.
+ Silence in Sweden is not necessarily negative. They are reflective and rather introvert.
+ They are not a 'touching' culture, so don't get too close.
+ They use very little body language and facial expression during business meetings, although they smile much more than Germans and Finns.
+ They remain calm and courteous during discussions and don't quite know how to deal with rudeness or Latin exuberance.
+ They show no particular respect for rank, and address important personages as equals. French, German, South American and Asian people

do not always react well to this very egalitarian manner.

+ They are never overbearing. They do not use brute force, even if they have the upper-hand.

+ Your best approach is to defer to their wish for long, all-round consultation and demonstrate clearly your own patience and understanding, allied to firmness and integrity.

30

NORWAY

I WAS ONCE DISCUSSING CULTURAL RELATIVITY WITH A NORWEGIAN friend and asked him how he would go about categorising nationalities. 'It's simple,' he replied. 'There are only two types of human beings – Norwegians and those who wish they were Norwegians.'

This Norway centredness, so often commented on by Danes and Swedes, is one of the three most striking characteristics of the Norwegian people. The other two are their stubbornness, which serves to reinforce their ethnocentricity, and their immense capacity for national soul searching, which to some extent counterbalances it.

Norway is solvent, secure, well organised and poised for the twenty-first century. Its population of 4.3 million is well catered for in terms of housing, food, welfare and economic opportunity. The 30th economy in the world in size, it is an astounding sixth in GDP per capita and the world's seventh biggest oil producer – enabling it to be the fifth largest exporter of energy. Other assets include its merchant fleet (the biggest in Western Europe) and the quality of its main trading partners. Assured markets are Britain, Germany and the Netherlands. Imports come from Sweden, Germany and the UK, in that order.

Quality of life matches the economic foundation. Norway has the third oldest population in the world and ranks seventh in quality of life, according to the Human Development Index. It is the world's second largest donor of bilateral aid (only Kuwait gives more per capita). The education system is remarkable in that Norwegians study longer than anyone else in Europe (12 years) and have the fifth highest tertiary enrolments, in spite of the difficult terrain and elongated country.

Geographically on the fringe of Europe, Norwegians are greatly admired by two other peoples on the European periphery – the Finns and the British. Opinion polls conducted by the Finnish Ministry of Labour consistently rank Norwegians as the most popular nationality, with the English second.

The warmth of feeling existing between the Norwegians and the British is no surprise. Viking blood flows through the veins of Britons in no small measure. Sea-going people like the English, Norwegians have left thousands of place names in their settlements in the British Isles. The city of Bergen always found the north-east of England more accessible in winter than the rest of Norway and the history of Anglo-Norwegian trade stretches from the Hanseatic era to the present. Britain buys more Norwegian products than anybody else. Other factors binding the two countries are democracy with royalty, the parliamentary system, social justice, love of the outdoors, expeditions to the North and South Poles, Protestantism, seafaring, similarities in philosophic beliefs, calm attitudes and a shared sense of humour, especially in adversity. Norway also has good relations with the US and feels in many ways part of the English-speaking world.

Norway's relations with European nations who are neither Anglo-Saxon or Nordic are more enigmatic. Though viewed as clean dealers, Norwegians are seen by Southern Europeans as distant, excessively introvert, strong willed and disinclined to mix. Germans see them as less susceptible to influence than the Danes, Swedes and Finns. The Slavic nations have had little contact due to the buffer position of Sweden and Finland.

Norwegians remain a proud, independent, reserved, essentially Nordic nation with their house clearly in good order. Their eventual adherence or non-adherence to the EU or other European structures would probably have less import in the economic area than in the cultural sphere. If Finland is rapidly engaged in shedding her image as Europe's cultural lone wolf, it is hard to imagine Norway, with her close historical and cultural ties to her neighbours, continuing to isolate herself spiritually from the common European heritage.

Culture

Values

Norway's secure and comfortable standing, both economic and spiritual, at the turn of the century is further cemented by a comprehensive array of deep-rooted and traditional values deriving not only from the resolutions of Protestant Christianity, but also from the attitudes and culture of the Viking era culminating in the period 800–1000AD. Christianity had some difficulty in establishing its relevance to everyday lives in the far north and for this reason heathen philosophies lived on for centuries.

Others may not be able to make them change their mind, but Norwegians constantly do battle with their own feelings. Like the Dutch they wish to be seen as a progressive, tolerant, modern people, but are reluctant to demolish the traditional pillars of a rather straitlaced society. Thrift, caution, playing cards close to one's chest and strict word-and-deed correlation preclude the flexibility and communicative ease more readily observable in Denmark. Norwegian values can be summarised as follows:

Honesty	Pragmatism
Cautious thrift	Taciturnity
Dislike of extravagance	Obstinacy, introversion
Belief in the individual	Love of nature
Self-reliance	Prudence and foresight
Controlling resources	Norway centredness
Sense of humour	Prefer action to words

Cultural factors in communication

Communication pattern and use of language

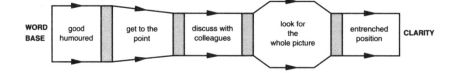

Norwegians' sterling qualities and warm feelings are not readily communicated in their speech style. Cold climates tend to produce introverts and the Norwegians, along with the Finns, are the shyest of Europeans.

Listening habits

Norwegians listen in good humour, but quickly develop strong opinions that they soon expose. They are data oriented and Norway centred.

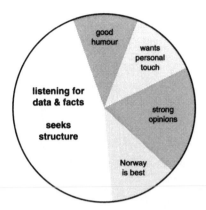

How to empathise with Norwegians

Be frank, direct and strive to appear straightforward. They like clear-eyed, pragmatic dealing in a 'fresh air' atmosphere.

Do not praise the Swedes too much. Norwegians are 'folksier' than Swedes and like a personal touch, although not overdone in the Latin manner.

They are looking for trust, energy and reliability. Always deliver what you have promised. Never appear in any way devious.

Talk about their mountains – they love them. Share outdoor pursuits with them if you can.

31

DENMARK

DENMARK IS A COUNTRY THAT SELLS ITSELF WELL AND ITS CUSTOMERS, moreover, are generally well satisfied. For a land whose area is just over 40,000 sq km (smaller than Latvia or Lithuania and dwarfed by its three Nordic neighbours) and whose population barely scrambles over 5 million, its ranking of 25th in the world's economies (well ahead of Norway, Finland, Saudi Arabia, Hong Kong, South Africa, Iran and Poland, among others) is an economic miracle on a par with those witnessed in Korea, Singapore and Taiwan. Even more impressive than the total GDP figure is the fact that a large part of it consists of quality products, both in industry and agriculture. Danish does not come cheap, but there always seem to be takers. Visible exports usually exceed visible imports.

Trading successes mean that the Danes enjoy a high standard of living. GDP per capita, perhaps the most striking statistic, is just over $32,000, the highest in the EU except for Luxembourg, which enjoys special advantages.

Denmark's population is the seventh oldest in the world and is one of the slowest growing. The country has the smallest households in the world (2.2 persons) and its people are the world's third highest telephone users and seventh biggest drinkers. It also has the highest percentage of the population in the labour force in Europe (55.8 per cent), beaten only by Singapore in the rest of the world.

Why are the Danes so successful? To begin with, they have been around for a long time and the country is only small in one sense. Not only is the Kingdom of Denmark the oldest monarchy in Europe, but it consists of Denmark proper, the Faroe Islands and another not insignificant island landmass in the western hemisphere, namely Greenland. This last part of the kingdom is 2670 km from north to south and 1050 km from east to west. It is not all ice, either, as 16 per cent of the surface is ice free. Greenland was actually a Danish colony until 1953 and has had its own budget since 1979, but remains loyally in the kingdom and is administered by the Danish government. Danes, characteristically flexible, allow the Greenlanders considerable autonomy. They have their own flag, are exempt from military service and have not entered the EU. As in the case of Norway, fishing rights tend to complicate adherence. A similar arrangement exists in the case of Faroese, who have two representatives in the Danish parliament and are also represented on the Nordic Council.

Culture

Values

Danish flexibility, tolerance and business acumen are three of their outstanding characteristics. Danes are mainly Lutheran and many of their values are Protestant ones, shared by their Nordic neighbours. Honesty, cleanliness, work ethic, egalitarianism, social justice, equality for women, and tidy public spaces form the basis of Danish life. But in some respects the Danes vary considerably from other Nordics. Often referred to as the Nordic Latins, they are more readily communicative, easy-going, uninhibited and smoothly international than Swedes, Norwegians or Finns. Consultation with colleagues before making decisions is mandatory, as in Sweden, but Danes get through it faster and then act quickly. After due duscussion they then want autonomy and independence. They believe that they are good at making decisions, more in the Finnish manner, pragmatically and with purpose.

Danes are frequently ironic and sarcastic. As they believe in complete egalitarianism they enjoy using cutting frankness and clever irony. Any form of bragging or aloofness is attacked without mercy, no less than it would be in Australia. Danes are fond of listing their 'ten commandments':

+ You shall not think you are somebody.
+ You shall not put yourself on a par with us.
+ You shall not think you are cleverer than us.
+ You shall not think you are better than us.

+ You shall not think you know more than us.
+ You shall not think you are more than us.
+ You shall not think you are worth anything.
+ You shall not laugh at us.
+ You shall not think that anybody cares about you.
+ You shall not think that you can teach us anything.

However, if these admonitions and warnings seem formidable, remember that you will escape them if you are suitably modest and low key in your dealings with Danes. Indeed, their good humour and apparently laidback business style generally put other nationalities at ease.

Concepts

Leadership and status

Basic Danish assumptions are generally in line with their essentially demo-cratic stance and Protestant fine tuning. Leadership is by achievement and demonstration of technical competence. Leaders are expected to be low profile and benign and to consult colleagues for opinions.

The country has very few huge firms and has over 5000 companies with fewer than 250 employees. Managers in Danish industry tend therefore to be owner-managers, just as there are many owner-captains. Personal involvement in the business results in a favourable view of inward invest-ment and ploughing back profits into companies to improve them further. Other by-products are dynamism and drive.

Status is based on qualifications, competence and results, yet material-ism is downplayed. There is a focus on welfare.

Space and time

The Danish concept of space is that they function best in an ample, airy, well-designed, hygienic environment. Offices are generally very tasteful and colourful.

As far as time-keeping is concerned, they are punctual, without being obsessively so. Danes like early lunches and not-too-long office hours. They spend their spare time creatively.

Cultural factors in communication

Communication pattern and use of language

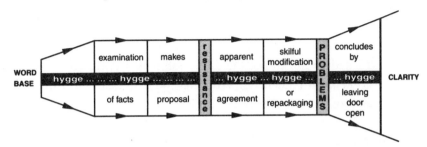

Danes are fluent speakers but calm and low voiced. They are the most loquacious of the Nordic countries, although not obtrusively so. Swedes, Finns and Norwegians consider them somewhat facile and clever. Serious discussions are frequently interspersed with humour. They have a sense of humour that is close to Anglo-Saxon. Linguistic ability is outstanding, particularly in English and German.

Listening habits

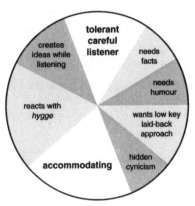

The Danes are good listeners, who rarely interrupt but are quite willing to ask questions afterwards. Questions are good and pertinent, showing that absorption of facts was efficient. They are skilful at establishing a meaningful dialogue.

Behaviour at meetings and negotiations

Danes are among the most congenial of nationalities, being neither too aggressive nor too passive. Like the British, they plot a reasonable line of argument as a basis for progress. They show flexibility in the face of obstacles and do not lack patience in seeking solutions. They show concerns regarding egalitarian procedures and processes – this is the only area in which they refuse to compromise. All members of a delegation will voice their opinion. They are good, level-headed negotiators with the knack of securing good deals without making enemies.

In their own companies and internal affairs Danes are blunt (like the Dutch) and believe that they can negate an opinion without negating the person who expresses it. They expect horizontal communication to be taken for granted and the few hierarchical influences that may come into play to be transparent. Heavy persuasion is taboo and too much lobbying is suspect. Agendas are generally adhered to and time is kept. If no decision has been reached by the end of the day it will be left until tomorrow, but there are no *mañana* tendencies. Working hours are short and overtime will not necessarily produce better results.

Manners and taboos

Danes are generally very hospitable and congenial, quickly creating trust and confidence. *Hygge* – making things 'cosy' for everyone – is an ever-present concern and objective. They are big eaters and under-achieve when hungry. They drink willingly when socialising, but are not noted for over-indulgence.

Handshakes are formal with heels together and a sharp snap down of the head (men), but easy-going informality ensues almost immediately afterwards. Taboos include any attacks on egalitarianism, rights of women, social welfare and various minorities. Danes generally disparage too rapid accumulation of personal wealth and are envious of outstanding individual achievement.

How to empathise with Danes

Danes always appear reasonable, laid back and well balanced. Focus on social progress rather than the benefits of capitalism. Avoid head-on arguments or unpleasant subjects. Danes generally want to hear the truth, but hate abrasiveness or brusqueness. They love anecdotes, particularly those that purport to provide wise analysis of a current situation.

Humour is a key in Denmark. The trick is to introduce informality while at the same time maintaining correctness and properness. They are Anglophile, also firm believers in Nordic cooperation. Military matters and strict political alignments are not favourite subjects. Being a nation of preponderantly small and middle-sized enterprises, they are less impressed by their own big companies than are the Swedes.

32

THE BALTIC STATES

THE DEVELOPMENT OF THE BALTIC REGION INTO A NEW GROWTH AREA within Europe not only harks back to the golden era of Hanseatic cooperation but heralds the prospect – if we include parts of Poland and the St Petersburg hinterland – of a vigorous, cold-climate market of eighty million people. The exploitation of this market, with its enticing mix of such ingredients as high GDP per capita, low labour costs and skilled workforces, could be more attractive and viable in the long term than many areas of southern Europe and elsewhere. The historical opportunity beckons, as the Danes and Swedes link their countries with a land bridge and the eastern Baltic states, encouraged by Finland, seek to revive the old Hanseatic trade routes.

Pitfalls

In the past, the three nations of Estonia, Latvia and Lithuania have rarely cooperated effectively, divided as they have been by language, religion, foreign rulers and dreams of separation and independence. Lithuanians, an emotional and grandiloquent people, feel more at home with Slavic Poles and Russians than they do with Lativians and Estonians. The Polish-Lithuanian Commonwealth was the largest and most powerful state in Eastern Europe in the eighteenth century. Lutheran Latvians, blond and stocky, are more like north Germans, who colonised them as early as the thirteenth century. Estonians, also Lutheran and even more reserved, resemble strongly their Finnish cousins and speak a Finno-Ugrian tongue. Estonia and Finland were connected by a land bridge until 1703, when Peter the Great blocked it by creating the city of St Petersburg and its outlying districts.

Cultural combinations

The composition of international management teams is likely to evolve as Baltic trade proliferates and as its centre of gravity moves eastward. Latvians and Estonians generally accept the Nordic leadership style. The best model for Estonia is clearly Finland, but Estonians often complain that Finns are irritatingly paternalistic.

If the Hanseatic highway and trade routes are to be resurrected – and this would would bring enormous benefit and prolific growth to the region – it will ultimately be vital that the the three small Baltic states cooperate closely with one another, as well as with other nationals on the Baltic shores. A subtle consideration in this regard is the common sprinkling among the Balts of a sizeable number of Russophones. Any exponential increase in the Balts' growth and prosperity can only take place if Russia's economy takes a turn for the good. The part of Russia showing most commercial promise is the north-west, particularly around St. Petersburg, with its huge potential pool of skilled workers, and to a lesser extent the hinterland extending to Minsk and Moscow.

ESTONIA

The smallest of the former states of the Soviet Union, with a population of just over 1.5 million, Estonia lies on the southern shore of the Baltic, her capital, Tallinn, only a few miles across the water from Helsinki. Closely related to the Finns, whom they resemble physically, Estonians speak a Finno-Ugrian language that sounds like Finnish when heard from a close distance. In fact Finns barely understand it when spoken at speed, but most Estonians understand Finnish, since under the period of Soviet domination Suomen Televisio was their 'window to the west'.

Estonians, a proud, organised and individualistic people, do not readily accept a close comparison to the Finns, since they feel that they are more European and that they have more cosmopolitan elements in their culture. Also they complain that Finns patronise them, having gained international experience denied to Estonians in the Soviet years. Third parties visiting Estonia, however, cannot fail to be struck by the similarity that exists between Finnish and Estonian behaviour.

Culture

Values

Work ethic	Home and family
Individualism	Independence and national identity
Importance of nature and its preservation	Skills and education
	Order and cleanliness
Careful with money	Good taste
Introversion	Reserved and non-emotional
Critical	Intellectual
Well mannered	Cynical in attitude to power
Good planners	Honest
Creative and original	

Concepts

Leadership and status

Estonians are very individualistic. Each person prefers to lead, rather than be led. Since the Soviet collapse, they have shown impatience towards those who have tried to tell them how to run a country. They have a deep sense of capability. Of the three Baltic states they were the ones who seized independence most emphatically, with a show of some belligerence (in spite of their smallness and the large number of Russian minority citizens on their soil). They chose incredibly young leaders to guide them through the first delicate years after Soviet withdrawal. They were also the fastest to embrace (rather unpopular) market reforms and resolutely pegged their currency to the German Mark.

Status is gained in Estonia by achievement, decisiveness and energy. They had no former aristocracy to draw on (only foreign occupiers). Status is therefore demonstrated by educational qualifications, money and possessions – car, house, summer cottage etc.

Space and time

Estonians are a particularly non-tactile people. They need body space and cannot bear close contact. A handshake is the maximum – no hugging or kissing in public. Family members are of course exceptions, but even among them physical contact is restrained. Young people are becoming more expressive; rural Estonians are the most reserved.

We see a Northern European attitude towards punctuality, although the Russian minority has a more relaxed view. Estonians do not like to leave tasks unfinished and often do overtime at the end of the day without seeking extra remuneration.

Cultural factors in communication

Communication patterns and use of language

The usual style is slow, drawn-out speech: there is no rush to express an opinion. When asked questions, Estonians allow a significant pause before embarking on the answer.

If asked to describe their own communication style, they use words such as reserved, critical, closed, stubborn and wooden. They believe that questions should be answered directly and summarily, without any extra information being volunteered.

Listening habits

Estonians listen carefully and do not interrupt. Natural cynicism (reinforced in Soviet times) is concealed by evident good manners. After listening they give almost no feedback. Silence can be positive as well as negative. When satisfied with the information received they feel no need to gush. Americans and multi-active Europeans are normally disappointed at the lack of responsiveness; Finns and Swedes understand perfectly.

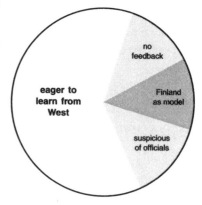

Behaviour in meetings and negotiations

Estonians are reputedly the most skilful businesspeople in the three Baltic states – they certainly speak the best English and face Finns and Scandinavians with confidence. They are calm and level-headed, prizing their ability to show self-control, even when they are not happy with the turn of events. They are tenacious in their arguments, using facts and figures to combat emotive arguments. Although cautious and in no hurry to conclude deals, they have a strong desire to develop Western partners and trade and mop up any business they see lying around.

Once contracts are secured, they impress by their industriousness in production and fulfilling their commitments. For example, the Viisnurk ski factory in Pärnu before independence churned out 800,000 pairs of cheap cross-country skies a year for sale throughout the Soviet Union. When the Soviet Union collapsed, so did that market. Undeterred, the factory stepped up the quality of the product and quickly secured markets in Finland and other Western countries for 250,000 pairs of skies per annum. It then went further and started producing Rossignol skis for the US market.

The versatility of Estonian businesspeople is a quality born of necessity. Although Estonia has several advantages over neighbouring Latvia and Lithuania – it has enormous oil-shale deposits and is a net exporter of electricity – the smallness of its total economy makes it difficult for Estonians to compete in mass markets. Niche products are the solution. In this respect Estonian handicrafts are among the most original in the world.

At meetings Estonians present their products and policies confidently and with frankness. They are well aware that low labour costs give them useful leverage when dealing with Scandinavians, although they are quick to emphasise the high quality of Estonian workmanship. In general, however, self-praise is not considered polite, modesty is a virtue. This sometimes causes problems in that people undervalue themselves.

Manners and taboos

A visitor to Estonia cannot fail to be impressed by the importance of folklore and adherence to ancient customs. As a people they are very self-aware, keenly conscious of their uniqueness and their 5000-year-old occupation of the land. Estonians in previous ages held strong pre-Christian beliefs. The most common themes in folk stories prevalent in the nineteenth century were animistic, place legends where every large rock, tree, body of water or hill were attributed 'souls'.

In social life, as in business dealings, Estonians impress by their orderliness and self-containment. Good manners, neatness and tidiness are mandatory. Young people are relatively well behaved and disciplined. One sees few gangs on street corners and people rarely get drunk in public (although they do in private). Neighbours help each other to build houses and children generally support parents in housework and building activities. Estonians love the sauna, which for centuries has been pivotal in cultural life, often used for giving birth and during illness.

How to empathise with Estonians

Estonians will respect a foreigner who shows respect for them and their flag. They expect no sentimental outpouring or show of affection, only calm admiration for their achievements and capability for survival. In business they expect no favours, just straightforward dealing on the basis that they can be trusted and will perform. Modesty and understatement will carry you a long way.

As in most former communist countries there is little faith in the police or the authorities. The key to doing business is to establish reliable personal connections. It is a small country, where most efficient people already know each other.

LATVIA

Of the three Baltic republics, Latvia has suffered most from Russian infiltration. The last census data before the Second World War listed Latvians as making up 77 per cent of the total population. In early 1994, the corresponding figure was 54.2 per cent, with Russians totalling 33.1 per cent. During Soviet occupation 750,000 foreigners (mainly Russians) arrived in Latvia. Of these, 99 per cent applied for Latvian citizenship! Although present law stipulates 16 years' residence and knowledge of the Latvian language, Russians are not only anxious to secure a Latvian passport, but are extremely supportive of Latvian independence.

This says something about the Latvians' attitude to foreigners. While resentful of Soviet influence, they afford no evidence of systemic discrimination. They are, of course, used to foreigners being in large numbers on their soil; they had seven centuries of Germanic rule. The weight of Russian numbers remains, however, a practical problem. Russians actually outnumber Latvians in the cities and carry on most of the trade. Latvians, traditionally farmers and soldiers, have a problem in reasserting their influence in commercial life. This is an vital issue for the future, as Riga, by far the most important port in the area, holds the key to Latvia's prosperity and international involvement.

Culture

Values

Honesty and loyalty
Arts (especially singing)
Entrepreneurship
Clean, neat homes
Love of books
Conservatism
Melancholy
Individualism

Work ethic
Respect for nature
Family
Education and intellect
Attachment to the land
Old-fashioned politeness
Discipline
Physical strength

Concepts

Leadership and status

Similar to Estonians, Latvians are individualistic. Everybody wants to be not so much a leader, as a manager in his/her own right. However, there is a tendency to respect firm, confident, knowledgeable leadership; Latvians also always want to be on the side that is winning. They are sometimes reluctant to show initiative.

Intellectuals and artists (literature, music, visual art) are popularly known and acclaimed; academics are held to be persons in a respectable position. However, image is also important (as in dress, evidence of financial security or well-being, or having a car, especially an imported brand).

Space

Personal territory is irrelevant in a crowded Riga trolleybus! Otherwise Latvians are not given to flamboyant, public displays of affection; although this is different for family and friends (for instance they will kiss and/or hug on greeting). With strangers reserve is expected; a tactile approach is not likely to be appreciated.

Time

Latvians are usually punctual for actual appointments, but sometimes slow to respond. Occasionally there is a feeling of 'if not today, then tomorrow, why rush?'.

Cultural factors in communication

Communication patterns and use of language

Speech is serious, almost Germanic in its precision and deliberate delivery. Rhetoric is taboo and even outward displays of emotion or lightheartedness are detrimental to the establishment of trust. Latvians do have a sense of humour, but they usually let the other side initiate joking. They are sometimes reluctant to volunteer information. In Latvia they often say 'We measure our cloth nine times, but we cut it only once.'

Latvian speech is not only measured, but is basically very polite. There are hardly any swear words in Latvian, unlike Estonian, which resembles Finnish in its rich store of sonorous curses and oaths. Latvian uses subtleties of expression for effect. This occasionally comes out in their English or German, although such things are not easily translatable.

Listening habits

Latvians are unlikely to interrupt. They will listen closely, not revealing very much.

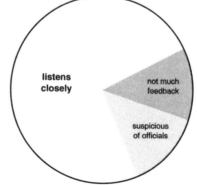

Behaviour in meetings and negotiations

Latvians are similar to Estonians, although less reserved and introverted. Apparently compliant (they hesitate to disagree), they can be stubborn. They may be cool on the first meeting or among strangers, however on acquaintance they become warm and more open hearted. Sometimes they display a slight wistful melancholy and sensitivity. They are not likely to rush into things and some thought and consideration are necessary. They will at times exhibit signs of agreement when that may not be entirely the case, and they are not always easy to persuade or convince.

During negotiations, certain rural attitudes are discernible among managers. These include distrust of lawyers, bankers and marketing types and a feeling that excess profits are illegitimate. The large number of Russophones in business prolongs a tendency to follow the Soviet top-down system, especially with older individuals.

Younger managers are more amenable to change, but they often have a poor understanding of Western management processes: accounting, finance and marketing. Latvians in general have a desire to do things right legally and technically, which gives rise to an over-emphasis on process as opposed to exploring imaginative ideas.

Manners and taboos

Many old-fashioned courtesies still exist: shaking hands on meeting, introductions, no first names unless specifically mutually agreed (similar to the French agreement to *tutoyer*). Latvians open doors for women and allow them to go through first, as well as helping them on with their coats. Women do not smoke in the street (although this is beginning to change), nor do they help themselves to a drink. Men expect to pay; this is a matter of pride.

The custom of holding dinner parties has not caught on yet. Generally the home is open only to family and close friends, except on name days. If you are invited to dinner, a bunch of flowers is obligatory and a bottle may also be welcome.

Impolite, boastful, loud or condescending behaviour is not acceptable, nor is prying or inquisitiveness about personal affairs.

How to empathise with Latvians

Latvians are proud and usually quite bright; they appreciate being treated as intellectual equals. In fact, some tact is required to let them know when they may be wrong. Respect for a unique Latvian identity is important. While there obviously is some lack of what may be termed 'commercial culture', this is not due to any inability on their part but rather to the previously prevailing system (a command economy, with all decisions made in Moscow), which also resulted in isolation from the Western world. Appreciation of the Latvian culture is also important (music, especially singing and choirs, literature, art). Those exploring Latvian culture will quickly gain respect. Language problems (e.g. not always speaking English) are also a vestige of the previous regime and should be evaluated in that light.

LITHUANIA

Western Europeans may consider Lithuania to be a small, insignificant state situated in a remote, far-off corner of north-eastern Europe. Lithuanians would say that they were wrong on all counts. Lithuania is bigger than not only Estonia and Latvia, but also the Netherlands, Belgium, Denmark, Switzerland and Taiwan, not to mention such economic powerhouses as Hong Kong, Singapore and Luxembourg. Secondly, there is nothing insignificant about her history – when she joined Poland through a dynastic union in 1386, the subsequent Polish-Lithuanian Commonwealth was the largest and most powerful state in eastern Europe, stretching from the Baltic to the shores of the Black Sea. If one looks more closely at the map and includes European Russia and the Ukraine as part of the continent, the geometric centre of Europe is in fact just north of Vilnius.

Throughout its history Lithuania has literally, been a European crossroads, absorbing Russians, Poles, Germans, Jews, Belarussians and Ukrainians. In spite of its cosmopolitan nature, it was much more successful than Latvia and Estonia in protecting its national identity during the Soviet era – 80 per cent of its population remains ethnic Lithuanian.

Culture

Values

Preservation of national identity
Generosity
Music (esp. choirs) and dancing
Love of nature
Romanticism

Hospitality
Family
Sentiment
Morality

Concepts

Leadership and status

The Soviet influence has left a legacy of bureaucracy and toeing the party line. Patriots are nevertheless exalted, although former Communist leaders still figure largely in political structures. Lithuania was the only Baltic state that previously had an aristocracy, which lost its influence during the eighteenth century. Association with Catholicism and artistic life endows status. However, political privilege still exists.

Space and time

Lithuania has an agreeable population density and space problems do not arise. They stand somewhat closer to interlocutors than do Latvians and Estonians. They are occasionally tactile, though less so than Latins or Slavs. They are not as punctual as their northern neighbours. Hospitality can drag on into the early hours.

Cultural factors in communication

Communication patterns and use of language

Lithuanians are less reserved than Latvians and Estonians and are regarded by the former as talkative, even loquacious. Poles, however, consider them cold. The level of education is quite high and conversations are inter-

esting, at times riveting. Their opinions are often laced with romantic ide-
alism and nostalgia.

Listening habits

Lithuanians are good listeners, although somewhat impatient if they have
opinions to offer. They are quick to perceive the feelings of others.

Behaviour in meetings and negotiations

They do not follow agendas as strictly as Estonians, although in general
they consider themselves organised and orderly. Good manners are of the
essence, while they tend to be more persuasive than other Balts. Traces of
Soviet-style bureaucracy are sill evident in the conduct of business. When
negotiating, emotion occasionally creeps in.

Manners and taboos

Lithuanians' sense of loyalty involves family, children and friends, although
they have a strong sense of national identity and cultural traditions. Eating
and drinking are considered important; unfortunately alcoholism is a problem. A Lithuanian proverb says: 'Each one drinks as much as he can – not
less or more – until the glass is empty.'

The ancient Lithuanians worshipped the objects and phenomena of
nature and today there are still strong links with the natural world. Most
Lithuanians have a house in the countryside or at least their own garden.
The images of nature are the main themes in literature, visual art and music.

How to empathise with Lithuanians

Treat them as persons and as friends. Show a strong interest in principles,
arts, aesthetic achievement and honest endeavour and play down your
desire to make money as quickly as possible. Give personal opinions, rather
than those of your company, officials or national policy. Develop a personal working relationship based on mutual affection. Show sentiment. Be
willing to indulge in soul searching with them – it is a favourite pastime.

33

RUSSIA

THE DISINTEGRATION OF THE SOVIET UNION HAS ELIMINATED THE gigantic, multicultural phenomenon constituted by the bewildering assortment of countries, races, republics, territories, autonomous regions, philosophies, religions and credos that conglomerated to form the world's vastest political union. The cultural kaleidoscope had been so rich that the mind could only boggle while contemplating it. Its collapse, however, serves to make us focus on something more simple yet unquestionably fecund *per se* – the culture of Russia itself.

It is only too easy to lump Soviet ideology and the Russian character together, since during 70 years of strife and evolution one lived with the other. Stalin – a Georgian – was no Russian, Mikoyan was Armenian, but Lenin, Trotsky, Kerensky – the early Bolshevik thinkers – were all Great Russians, as were Kruschev, Andropov, Molotov, Bulganin, Gorbachev and Yeltsin. Yet Soviet Russians were no more than one regimented stream of Russian society – a frequently unpopular, vindictive and short-sighted breed at that, although their total grasp of power and utter ruthlessness enabled them to remain untoppled for seven decades.

That same society, however, in the same period of time produced Pasternak, Solzhenitsyn, Sakharov, as well as thousands of courageous individuals who supported them. A culture that bred Chekhov, Tschaikovsky, Rachmaninov, Dostoyevsky, Tolstoy, Peter the Great and Alexander Nevsky simply does not vanish into thin air during a brief period of political oppression and drudgery. Its individuality was obliged in a sense to go underground, to mark time in order to survive, but the Russian soul is as immortal as anyone else's. Its resurrection and development in the twenty-first century is of great import to us all.

Some of the less attractive features of Russian behaviour in the Soviet period – exaggerated collectivism, apathy, suspicion of foreigners, pessimism, petty corruption, lack of continued endeavour, inward withdrawal – were in fact not products of the Bolshevik regime. Russia was Communist for 70 years, it had been Russian Orthodox for 1000 years. The basic traits of the Russian character were visible hundreds of years before Lenin or Karl Marx were born. Both Tsarist and Soviet rule were facilitated by the collective, submissive, self-sacrificial, enduring tendencies of the sentimental, romantic, essentially vulnerable subjects under their sway. Post-Soviet Russian society is undergoing cataclysmic evolution and change and it remains to be seen how some eventual form of democracy and the freeing of entrepreneurial spirit will affect the impact that Russians make on the rest of us.

The Russian character has been determined to some extent by unrelenting autocratic rule and governance over many centuries, but the two chief factors in the formation of Russian values and core beliefs were over and above any governmental control. These prevailing determinants were the incalculable vastness of the Russian land and the unvarying harshness of its climate. The figure below shows how the boundless, often indefensible steppes bred a deep sense of vulnerability and remoteness which caused groups to band together for survival and develop hostility to outsiders.

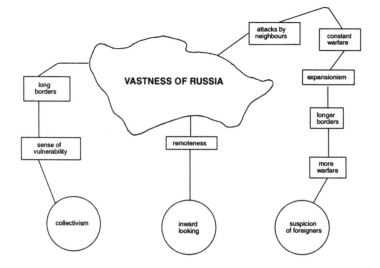

The next figure indicates how the influence of climate (a potent factor in all cultures) was especially harsh on Russian peasants, who traditionally are forced virtually to hibernate for long periods, then struggle frantically to till, sow and harvest in the little time left. Anyone who has passed through Irkutsk or Novosibirsk in the depth of winter can appreciate the numbing effect of temperatures ranging from minus 20–40 degrees Celsius, while the high winter suicide rate in slightly warmer countries such as Sweden and Finland suggests that Russians are not the only ones to wallow in bleakness for a considerable portion of their days.

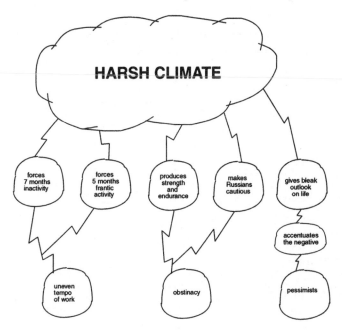

The long-suffering Russian peasants, ill favoured by cruel geography and denied (by immense distances and difficult terrain) chances of adequate communication among themselves, were easy meat for those with ambitions to rule. Small, uneducated groups, lacking in resources and cut off from potential allies, are easy to manipulate. The Orthodox Church, the Tsars, the Soviets, all exploited these hundreds of thousands of pathetic clusters of backward rustics. Open to various forms of indoctrination, the peasants were bullied, deceived, cruelly taxed and, whenever necessary, called to arms. In the sixteenth century military service could be 25 years; in 1861 when serfdom was 'abolished' it was reduced to 16 years! Russians have lived with secret police not just in KGB times, but since the days of

Ivan the Terrible, in the sixteenth century. The figure below shows how oppressive, cynical governance over many centuries developed further characteristics – pervasive suspicion, secrecy, apparent passivity, readiness to practise petty corruption, disrespect for edicts – as added ingredients to the traditional Russian pessimism and stoicism in adversity.

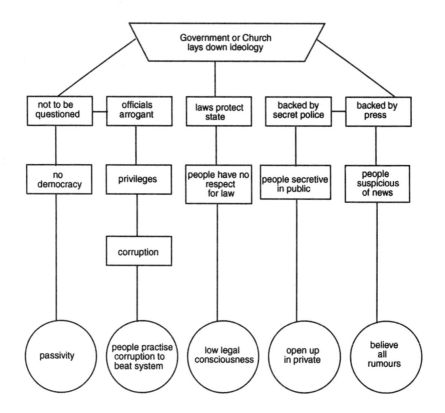

If all this sounds rather negative, there is good news to come. Although resorting to expediency for survival, Russians are essentially warm, emotional, caring people, eagerly responding to kindness and love, once they perceive that they are not being 'taken in' one more time. Finns – victims of Russian expansionism on more than one occasion – readily acknowledge the warmth and innate friendliness of the individual Russian. Even Americans, once they give themselves time to reflect, find a surprising amount of common ground. Rough Russian hospitality is reminiscent of the cosy ambience of the Wild West (or perhaps the deep South) and the Russians, like the Americans, tried to tame a continent. Both peoples distrust aristocrats and are uncomfortable, even today, with the smooth talking of some Europeans. Bluntness wins friends both in Wichita and Sverdlovsk. Both nations, like the French, think big and consider they have an important role to play – a 'mission' in world affairs.

Our familiar 'horizon' comparison shows that while Russians and Americans are destined by history and location to see the world in a very different manner, there is sufficient commonality of thinking to provide a basis for fruitful cooperation. Their common dislikes are as important in this respect as some of their mutual ambitions.

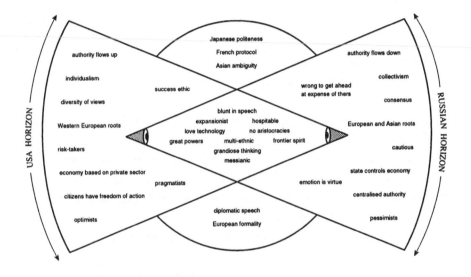

As far as their attitudes to the world in general are concerned, how do Russians see the rest of us and – importantly – how do they deal? While it is clear that they are a society in transition, certain features of their business culture inevitably reflect the style of the command economy which organised their approach to meetings over a period of several decades. Russian negotiating characteristics, therefore, not only exhibit traditional peasant traits of caution, tenacity and reticence, but indicate a depth of experience born of thorough training and cunning organisation. They may be listed as follows.

Russian negotiating characteristics

+ Russian negotiating teams are often composed of veterans or experts, consequently they are very experienced.
+ They negotiate as they play chess, i.e. they plan several moves ahead. Opponents should think of the consequences of each move before making it.
+ Russians often represent not themselves, but part of their government at some level.
+ Sudden changes or new ideas cause discomfort, as they have to seek consensus from higher up.
+ Negotiations often relate the subject under discussion to other issues in which they are involved. This may not be clear to the other side.
+ Russians regard willingness to compromise as a sign of weakness.
+ Their preferred tactic in case of deadlock is to display patience and 'sit it out'.
+ They will only abandon this tactic if the other side shows great firmness.
+ The general tendency is to push forward vigorously as the other side seems to retreat, to pull back when meeting stiff resistance.
+ Delivery style is often theatrical and emotional, intended to convey clearly their intent and requests.
+ Like Americans, they can use 'tough talk' if they think they are in a stronger position.
+ They maintain discipline in the meeting and speak with one voice. When Americans or Italians speak with several voices, the Russians become confused about who has real authority.
+ Russians often present an initial draft outlining all their objectives. This is only their starting position and far from what they expect to achieve.
+ They will, however, concede points only in return for concessions made by the other side.
+ They often make minor concessions and ask for major ones in return.
+ They may build into their initial draft several 'throw-aways' – things of little importance which they can concede freely, without damaging their own position.
+ They usually ask the other side to speak first, so they may reflect on the position given.

+ They are sensitive and status conscious and must be treated as equals and not 'talked down to'.
+ Their approach to an agreement is conceptual and all-embracing, as opposed to American or German step-by-step settlement.
+ Acceptance of their conceptual approach often leads to difficulties in working out details later and eventual implementation.
+ They are suspicious of anything which is conceded easily. In the Soviet Union days, everything was complex.
+ Personal relationships between the negotiating teams can often achieve miracles in cases of apparent official deadlock.
+ Contracts are not so binding in the Russian mind as in the western. Like Orientals, Russians see a contract as binding only if it continues to be mutually beneficial.

A study of the above leads one to the conclusion that Russian negotiators are not easy people to deal with. There is no reason to believe that the development of entrepreneurism in Russia, giving added opportunities and greater breadth of vision to those who travel in the West, will make Russians any less effective round the negotiating table. Westerners may hold strong cards and may be able to dictate conditions for some length of time, but the ultimate mutual goal of win–win negotiations will only be achieved through adaptation to current Russian mentality and world attitudes. The following hints might be of help.

How to empathise with Russians

+ If you have strong cards, do not overplay them. Russians are proud people and must not be humiliated.
+ They are not as interested in money as you are, therefore they are more prepared to walk away from a deal than you.
+ You may base your decisions on facts which are cold to you, emotive to them.
+ They are people rather than deal oriented. Try to make them like you.
+ If you succeed, they will conspire with you 'to beat the system'. They dislike stringent regulations more than you do. They are very Italian in this respect.

✦ Indicate your own distrust of blind authority or excessive bureaucracy as often as you can.

✦ Do them a favour early on, but indicate it is not out of weakness. The favour should be person directed, rather than relating to the business being discussed.

✦ You need not be unduly impacted by their theatrical and emotional displays, but you should show sympathy with the human aspects involved.

✦ When you show your own firmness, let some glimmer of kindness shine through.

✦ They will generally behave collectively, so do not single out any one individual for special attention. Envy of another's success is also a Russian characteristic.

✦ Drink with them between meetings if you are able to. It is one of the easiest ways to build bridges.

✦ They prefer to drink sitting down with time to make frequent toasts and short speeches.

✦ They like praise, especially related to Russian advances on technology, but also about their considerable artistic achievements.

✦ They are sensitive about war talk, considering most Russian wars as defensive ones against aggressive neighbours. They have not been given your version of history.

✦ Their attitude towards America is one of suspicion, tinged with outright admiration.

✦ They love children more than most of us; exchange of photographs of your children is an excellent manner to build bridges.

✦ They respect old people and scorn Americans' treatment of the elderly. In the cruel Russian environment, family love was often the only enduring form of riches. Display your own family closeness, if appropriate.

✦ Indicate your human side – emotions, hopes, aspirations etc. They are much more interested in your personal goals than in your commercial objectives.

✦ During your business discussions, their priorities will be personal relationships, form and appearance, opportunity for financial gain – in that order.

✦ They often appear excitable, but are skilled at keeping their temper.

✦ The eastern and western elements in their make-up often make them appear schizophrenic. Do not let this faze you – the other face will always reappear in due course.

- They have, in their history, never experienced democracy, therefore do not expect them to be automatically egalitarian, fair, even-handed and open to straight debate.
- In this respect, it is advisable to show them clearly how you think about such matters and how you are basically motivated by these factors.
- Terms such as 'democratic', 'fair play', 'profit', 'turnover', 'cash flow', 'public relations', 'goodwill' have little meaning for them in any language, therefore use such words cautiously.
- They like to say they understand when in fact they don't, and also have the tendency to say things they think you want to hear (an Oriental trait), so do not take what is said and heard for granted.
- Anything you introduce as an official directive or regulation they will distrust. Something you indicate as a personal recommendation, they will embrace.
- Russians are basically conservative and do not accept change easily. Introduce new ideas slowly and keep them low key at first.
- Russians often push you and understand being pushed, but they rebel if they feel the pressure is intolerable. Try to gauge how far you can go with them.
- Dissidence in general is not popular with them, as security has historically been found in group, conformist behaviour. Do not try to separate a Russian from his or her 'group', whatever that may be.
- Right and wrong, in most Russians' eyes, is decided by the feelings of the majority, not by law.
- Russians are essentially nostalgic – the present does not dominate their thinking as it might with many Americans and Australians, for instance.
- They love conversation. Do not hesitate to unburden yourself in front of them. Like Germans, they are fond of soul searching.
- They achieve what they do in their own country largely through an intricate network of personal relationships. Favour is repaid by favour. They expect no help from officials.
- Like Germans, they enter meetings unsmiling. Like Germans, they can be quickly melted with a show of understanding and sincerity.
- When they touch another person during conversation, it is a sign of confidence.

Russians' values are essentially human, their heroes universally authentic, their manifestations and symbols richly artistic and aesthetic. To succeed with Russians, one must maintain these qualities in clear focus as opposed to paying too much attention to the enigmatic and often paradoxical aspects of their behaviour and current attitudes.

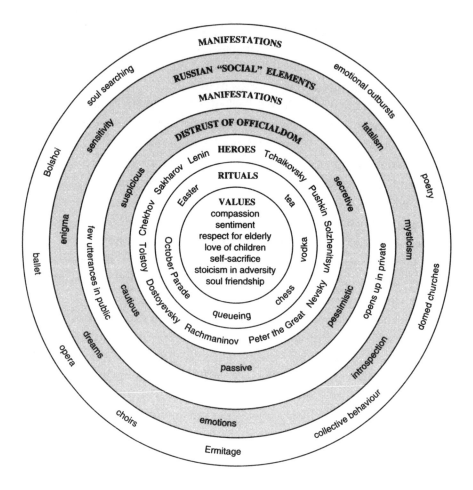

34

CENTRAL ASIA

IN THE SOUTHERN PART OF THE FORMER SOVIET UNION, SANDWICHED between Russia and Iran/Afghanistan from north to south and between the Caucasus and China from west to east, lie six Muslim republics that gained independence when the Soviet Empire disintegrated. These countries – Kazakhstan, Uzbekistan, Kyrgyzstan, Tajikistan, Turkmenistan and Azerbaijan – have become a focus of international interest on account of the wealth of their natural resources.

The geographic location of these states gives them considerable strategic importance. They really do straddle Europe and Asia and when the oil begins to flow (routes are as yet uncertain) the politics of wealth and influence will intensify.

Only Tajikistan has an Indo-European language, akin to Persian. The other five republics speak Turkic tongues that are mutually intelligible. This has inspired Turkey, so far unsuccessful in her application to join the EU, to seek an alternative route to betterment by forming a Central Asian trading bloc of Turkic-speaking countries. This concept has met with cautious approval from the six Muslim republics, ever aware of Russian pressure from the north and the Chinese colossus to the east.

The Soviets had redrawn the map of Central Asia in the 1920s along rough linguistic lines. This divide-and-rule policy was their way of dealing with a large, scattered horde of nomadic and semi-nomadic tribes that roamed the deserts and steppes. These grouped together in settlements and lived in dome-like tents made of felt called *yurts*. They migrated seasonally to find pastures for their herds of horses, sheep and goats. The Kazakhs, for instance, were rarely united as a simple nation under one leader, although they had chiefs. Today there are three levels of identity awareness: first a Kazakh defines himself by his tribe; secondly there is a strong national awareness, third is a supra-national awareness, a sense of belonging to the pan-Turkestani movement. These levels are replicated in several of the republics. Whether the pan-Turkestani dream will ever be realised is highly doubtful, but the cultural backgrounds of the six nations have much in common.

Definitions are complicated. Between the Black Sea and the Chinese border 60 million people live in six countries that were simply part of the Soviet Empire a short time ago. Russian immigration was massive, especially in Kazakhstan, where nearly 40 per cent of the citizens are Russian. So are almost 20 per cent of the inhabitants of Kyrgyzstan. One million Kazakhs live in China, a large number of Uzbeks are to be found in Afghanistan and more Azeris live in Iran than in Azerbaijan. One-fifth of the people of Tajikistan are Uzbeks. This situation is what you might expect where nomads are concerned, but immobilise them inside artificially created boundaries and you have a recipe for friction and conflict. There have been no major explosions to date, but the Turkestani awareness is fading in the face of growing nationalism and divergence of aims with regard to the exploitation of uneven natural resources.

The Central Asian republics share many cultural characteristics on account of their common history. To a greater or lesser extent they are governed by Islamic tenets and profess rather a high level of morality, though pragmatism is creeping in more and more in states that are beginning to realise how rich they may become one day. In general, anti-Russian feeling runs high, not unsurprising in view of earlier Soviet purges.

Central Asians are loquacious, excitable and tough. They have long memories and can be vindictive if they feel wronged or exploited. Males dominate society, as in other Muslim states. Regional rivalries are fierce, as sentiments are often clannish or tribal rather than national. Turkey enjoys a certain popularity as a regional leader, though this may change if it gains entry into the EU. The abundance of oil and gas in the western half of the area suggests closer links to the main European nations in the future and a growing US influence on commercial practices and even culture.

Kazakhstan

Kazakhstan is a vast area (more than twice the size of Texas), sparsely populated, with huge deposits of oil, natural gas, gold, copper, uranium and many other minerals. Kazakhs were mostly nomads until the Russian Revolution, but were subjected to a very brutal sedentarisation programme in the 1930s, although tribal organisation survived and is still perceived by the population as a reality. Kazakhs would like to get rid of their resident Russians; in fact the Muslims are gradually obtaining the upper hand. Kazakhstan is being wooed by oil companies from many nations, not least by the Americans.

Azerbaijan

Azerbaijan has a small population, but large reserves of oil in and around the Caspian Sea. It is being courted by many nations, including Turkey, which has supported it during interim economic difficulties. It is also locked in a protracted war with Armenia over disputed territory, with the Russians supporting the Armenians.

Uzbekistan

Uzbekistan has a relatively large population. Although independent since 1991, it remains in some ways the least changed of the former Soviet republics. The Communist party was renamed and the country is still run largely as a command economy, with farmers obliged to sell their products to the state at well below world market prices. Uzbeks are regarded as the 'businesspeople' among the Central Asians and there is a growing and aggressive Uzbek imperialism, especially felt in Tajikistan where 20 per cent of citizens are Uzbeks, enjoying increasing cultural autonomy. Industry is relatively modern in Uzbekistan. Oil and gas are of major importance and it is the world's third largest producer of cotton.

Kyrgyzstan

Kyrgyzstan occupies the western end of the Tien Shan range and is one of the world's most rugged and mountainous areas. Kyrgyz constitute the rural community, while Russians, Tartars and Uzbeks dominate the cities. Kyrgyz are anti-Uzbek, due to past brutalities when the latter ruled the country in the nineteenth century. There is no hostility towards the Kazakhs, who share a common history. There is a solid anti-Russian tradition and the Kyrgyz have alienated many Russians (many of them have left) by their refusal to accept Russian as an official language. Kyrgyzstan has sought to establish strong relations with Turkey and wishes to establish democracy along the lines of the Turkish model.

Turkmenistan

Turkmenistan has a small population but vast reserves of gas. Created in 1924, it has a unique position among former Soviet Muslims. It constitutes at present a tribal confederation rather than a modern nation. Turkmen society differs from other Muslims of Central Asia by the vitality of various social customs and traditions: sex discrimination and the persistence of polygamy and various traditional marital customs, such as the early marriage of girls, marriage by abduction, *karshylyk* marriage (a sister and a brother married to a brother and a sister), frequent religious marriages, and refusal to let Turkmen girls marry outside the tribe.

Turkmen nationalism is of the most pronounced anti-Russian character. The Turkmen consider themselves different from the other Central Asian Turks, but there are no anti-Uzbek or anti-Kazakh trends in Turkmen nationalism.

Tajikistan

Since the Second World War there is a growing sense among Tajik intelligentsia of their Iranianism, which implies a new feeling of kinship with the Tajiks of Afghanistan and even with the Shi'a Iranians. Resentment is felt against the pushy Uzbeks, fuelled by the memory that some of the hallowed cities of Central Asian culture – Samarkand, Bukhara and Khiva – belonged formerly to the Tajiks. The Tajiks are the most religious of the Central Asian nationalities.

35

TURKEY

TURKEY, AN APPLICANT FOR EU MEMBERSHIP, WOULD MAKE QUITE AN impact if it were to enter. To begin with, it would be by far the biggest country, being approximately three times the size of UK and Italy and out-sizing France, Spain and Germany by more than 50 per cent. It would be second in population after Germany. It is the leader of a Turkic-speaking trading bloc of six former Russian-dominated Central Asian republics, and most of the country is not in Europe. Furthermore, Turkey has not fully satisfied European standards on human rights. It is no wonder that EU members want to take a deep breath before approving entry. Yet where else can Kemal Ataturk's modern, industrialising, secular NATO nation (which, remember, joined the West during the Korean and Gulf wars) go?

Kemal Ataturk

Anyone who has been to Turkey could hardly to fail to notice how dissimilar it is from other Muslim states. The nation's modern character is largely the result of the influence of its founder, Kemal Ataturk.

The future first president of Turkey was born in 1881 in Salonica, then an Ottoman city. In 1905 Mustafa Kemal, as he was then known, graduated from the War Academy in Istanbul. In 1915, when the Dardanelles campaign was launched, he had reached the rank of colonel.

The War of Independence from the Ottomans began in 1919 when Kemal, then a general, rallied a liberation army in Anatolia and convened a congress. This was forerunner of the Grand National Assembly, which was inaugurated in April 1920 with Mustafa Kemal elected president.

He set about transforming his country with unabated zeal, creating a new political and legal system, abolishing the Caliphate and making both government and education secular. The Islamic calendar was replaced by the western calendar, western hats were worn instead of the fez and women stopped wearing the veil.

In 1934 the Turkish parliament gave Kemal the name Ataturk, which means 'father of the Turks'. His emphasis on secularism continues today. 'Turkey is not a land of Sheikhs, dervishes, disciples and lay brothers,' he declared, having developed a lasting hatred for religious fundamentalism. He saw Westernisation and return to Turkish roots as being entirely compatible, inasmuch as Islam was tolerated as a religion but banned as a lifestyle.

Culture

Values

Belief in one's own honesty and reliability

Modified Islamic tenets

Fierceness, tenacity

Hospitality, gallantry

Warmth, likeability

Preservation of heritage

Male dominance

Concepts

Leadership and status

In the Ottoman Empire and for most of Turkish history, power has been concentrated in few hands. Sultans and Caliphs were all powerful and autocratic leadership was a fact of life. Kemal Ataturk changed all that and founded a democratic republic which, in spite of many troubled periods, has worked as well as many other theoretical democracies. It is true that the Army has acted undemocratically on some occasions, seeing itself as 'the guardian of the nation', but after each coup it has handed control back to civilians.

Ataturk gave women the vote in 1934 and there has been one female prime minister, but they still have a long way to go to achieve parity and their position is often under threat from Islamic fundamentalists.

Space and time

Things take time in Turkey and people turn up late for appointments. Istanbul – the largest urban sprawl in Europe – is not easy to move around in and many delays originate from traffic problems.

Turkey is a large country with a low population density. There is generally a 'distance of respect' of more than one metre between speakers. Having said that, Mediterranean Turks are somewhat tactile among friends (this usually confined to one's own sex). In many towns and villages men dancing with men is a common spectacle. Foreigners are often invited to participate – don't be shy!

Cultural factors in communication

Communication pattern and use of language

The Turkish communication style derives from its three main roots, Islamic, Mediterranean and Eastern (Ottoman, Seljuk). The first two are sources of their liveliness – they are in the main both multi-active and dialogue oriented. The third (Eastern) strand is, however, clearly visible – they are more reactive than any Europeans, except perhaps the Finns, and could also be classified as a listening culture, akin to several Central Asian Republics as well as some Confucian societies. Reactive cultures let the other side speak first and slowly try to modify their reply or position to fit in with their interlocutor.

In business circles their style is exploratory – they are very interested in all forms of change that lead to progress. They are polite and courteous (more than Westerners), but they wish to be seen as Western and modern. They show natural exasperation at being rejected by the West, but they are patient and persistent in trying to open and maintain acceptable communication channels.

Listening habits

As reactives Turks are good listeners, wishing desperately to learn from Western colleagues. They control their Mediterranean ebullience and their Islamic righteousness to the extent that they normally refrain from interrupting their interlocutor. Nor do they try to speak over him/her in the French or Arab manner. They listen with some scepticism, but generally impute best motives and are rarely unreasonable unless they feel that they are being duped.

Behaviour at meetings and negotiations

Meetings are usually conducted in a friendly, semi-formal atmosphere. As hosts, Turks are extremely polite and solicitous. They are by no means inexperienced at negotiating, given their immense exposure to trading in the vast, enduring Ottoman Empire. Haggling is normal for them and they are disappointed if it does not ensue. Starting prices bear little relation to the intrinsic value of items. The Turkish salesman who is beaten down, or simply rejected, keeps his cool, showing no sign of anger or annoyance. Doors are kept open for future deals.

Turks are willing to take risks in business, though they exercise a natural caution when investing in new and sizeable projects. Looking at markets, they know the value of their geographic location ('the bridge between East and West').

How to empathise with Turks

A golden rule would be to see them as they are, not as they are described in misleading accounts. They want respect and recognition. They want to play ball. If one refrains from attacking the current shortcomings of Turkish society, if one believes that they are doing their best to cooperate and put their house in order, if one places trust in them and exercises patience, one may end up with extremely reliable and (one day) very influential friends.

36

―――――

IRAN

THIS SIZEABLE COUNTRY (1,648,000 SQ KM) IS LARGELY A PLATEAU averaging 1200 m in elevation and attracted migrating Indo-Europeans, then occupying Europe, as early as 2000BC. Another Indo-European invasion took place (from the Caucasus) around 1000BC, introducing iron, copper and horses, thereby strengthening the area. These factors, as well as an extreme climate that has engendered a tough, vigorous populace, have enabled Persians to enjoy dominance of the region up to modern times.

The Pahlavi monarchy (the Shah) was overthrown in 1979 and the Islamic Republic of Iran was established and endorsed by a universal referendum a month later. Ayatollah Khomeini emerged as the undisputed leader. *Mullah* rule has continued up to the end of the century.

In economic terms, it is important to understand that currently the Iranians are cautious about signing big new contracts with foreign firms. There are big differences in attitude between the private and the public sectors: whereas trade with the private sector can be fast, mobile and present oriented, the state has put on the brakes and is more long term and future oriented in the type of business it will consider. Priorities for acceptance of projects are a willingness on the part of the Western company to invest now, with little financial help from Iran, and reap the rewards later; to create employment for Iranians; and to produce products in Iran, which can also be exported to other countries in the region.

The dawra

The *dawra* are interlocking personal coteries whose style permeates Iranian political life. The word literally means circles. Each circle is an information group of individuals who meet periodically, usually rotating the place of meeting among their members. They may be formed around any number of ties – professional, familial etc.

The *dawra* apparently makes sense because the cultural assumption is that 'real' power doesn't flow from institution to institution, as suggested in the formal apparatus of government, but from person to person and groups of persons who effectively manage to impose their authority. The underlying conception of asymmetrical interpersonal relationships means that Iranians tend to assume that their survival and success depend on their ability to cultivate the right personal contacts and to use those contacts to achieve their goals.

Culture

Values

Iranian, or Persian, culture goes back more than 3000 years and its people adhere proudly to their traditions and sense of leadership and power south of the Caspian. While Muslim, they identify little with the numerous Arab states in the Gulf and carried on an inconclusive but economically damaging war with Iraq ending in 1987. Their cultural classification is multi-active and dialogue oriented, although they are much less loquacious than Arabs.

Iranian values, as itemised by themselves, are chiefly:

Islamic faith and values (as opposed to Western)	Hospitality
	Family
Neighbourliness	Spirituality
Kindness and gentleness	Clemency
Caution in decision making	Academic achievement
Respect for the wisdom of the old	Respect for the Islamic role of
Politeness	women
Seriousness, dignity	Their cultural achievements
Traditional music and literature	Design and pattern
New technology, research, invention	

Concepts

Leadership and status

In general terms, spiritual leadership is dominant. When the spiritual leader Ayatollah Khomeini decided that it was time for the Shah to go, support was massive and immediate (98.2 per cent). In business, the leader may be identified as the last person to enter the room at a meeting and he will sit in the middle. Alternatively, he may show his hospitality by greeting the visitors at the entrance to the room.

Academic achievement is of high importance: in government the Iranian leader must be a 'fully qualified theologian', selected by 'experts'. In business, education and specialist knowledge are what give managers status. Managers may have been educated in the West as well as in Iran.

Space and time

Iranians keep their distance more than Arabs: they are used to this, as the population density is considerably lower than general in the region.

They are perhaps somewhat more punctual than Arabs and would claim to have a greater respect for other people's time. Unpunctuality in Tehran may be blamed, justifiably, on the traffic.

Cultural factors in communication

Communication pattern and use of language

Iranians are talkative (although they appear taciturn to their more talkative neighbours) but respect dignity and seriousness of intent in speech. They can be loquacious, but are not idle chatterers, particularly in business. They have a strong sense of what is appropriate and courteous according to context. They are keen to draw contrasts between what is proper in polite society and situations and what is suitable for the marketplace. They can be persuasive and admire persuasiveness in others. They can tolerate smalltalk, particularly mutual praise of the hospitality of others, but soon wish to turn to the heart of the matter and to show that they have a sharp intellect and that they have something to say.

Listening habits

Iranians like to talk themselves, but will listen attentively if they think that their interlocutor has something new to say. They are greedy for technical knowhow and, with their admiration for 'experts', will listen eagerly to the latest technological ideas. However, care should be taken not to give the impression that the West is superior, as they will respond very negatively if they feel that you lack respect for them or undervalue them. After all, they have a powerful sense of the superiority of their own spiritual values and wish to build a better future for themselves, through technology, without espousing values that they view as decadent and doomed to eventual failure.

With their relatively high respect for other people's space and time, Iranians are not as likely to interrupt as Arabs are, or allow themselves to be distracted from the matter in hand.

Behaviour at meetings and negotiations

Some sort of introduction is required before getting down to business: a good topic is praise for their hospitality and the arrangements made for you. However, they are keen to enter into serious negotiation fairly early on, and will signpost this quite clearly by asking directly for your purpose and intentions. They may evince a certain amount of suspicion until they are absolutely certain what the 'real aim' of the negotiation is. The proceedings are likely to be measured and reserved compared to meetings with Arabs, and Iranians will admire politeness and dignity in the presentation of positions, as well as an openness that does not arouse suspicion of an ulterior motive. This should not err on the side of appearing naïve: Iranians themselves will not readily reveal their feelings or opinions.

It is important to show how the business you are discussing will benefit Iran. Perhaps there is a missing technical link in a project they already have under way in which your company can be of service. Concentrate on this rather than on appearing too greedy to get all the business at once, or you may appear to undervalue their own technical achievements. Try to find out what the missing pieces of the jigsaw are, rather than trying to show you know best. Listen carefully to what they say, as they are prepared to talk at length, and be prepared to analyse the underlying message later as it may not be immediately apparent. However, if you can support your case with plain technical knowhow, modestly presented, they should respond.

Ensure that what is offered to them is absolutely the latest technology: they will not appreciate being offered anything they consider outdated. They are won over by solid information and are likely to take copious notes – so be careful not to contradict yourself later. Once you have won their trust and respect, more business may follow. Emphasise your company name: the fame and reputation of names is of great importance.

The Iranians are very persuasive (note the success of their leaders in winning huge support) and will expect you to persuade them in return. If at first they seem to respond negatively to an idea, this does not mean that you should give up. Try again, about three times. They have immensely strong faith in their ideas and will expect you to have faith in yours. Giving up immediately would arouse suspicions of weakness or lack of conviction. This applies also to invitations – they love inviting and being invited, but will often refuse before accepting.

Iranians are eager to demonstrate that they have a 'sharp mind' unclouded by decadent Western vices such as alcohol, and will not admire vagueness or uncertainty in others. They are very canny, but may come across as indecisive, inflexible and slow moving. Contracts and agreements should be short but complete. Iranians do not appreciate long-windedness.

Be prepared for differences in approach from those managers who have been educated in the West and those whose education has been in Iran. It may be easier to strike a chord with the former.

Remember that meetings may be broken by long prayer sessions, and that it is pointless to arrange business trips to Iran during Ramadan.

Manners and taboos

+ Body language is reserved and limited compared to that of Arabs.
+ No alcohol.
+ Dietary restrictions (especially pork).
+ Don't shake a woman's hand.
+ Use of the left hand is forbidden for 'clean' tasks.

How to empathise with Iranians

The key is to show them respect. A good way to demonstrate this positively, rather than purely by avoidance of areas that are difficult for

Westerners to comprehend, might be to praise their cultural heritage, of which they are justifiably proud. They feel that they have a much deeper culture than that of the Arab world, so any praise of their art, craft and design or architecture (perhaps the easiest areas to appreciate readily) would be welcome. They particularly admire craftsmanship that has been laborious and painstaking, as in their carpets and the interior decoration of their mosques. A sense of pattern and design has been developed as the artistic representation of the human face is forbidden as idolatrous – so when presenting and receiving gifts, which is customary, this should be borne in mind.

The Iranians have long memories regarding slights to their country or faith. You should be aware of your own nation's historical involvement with Iran – they certainly will be. If there is no negative shared history to speak of, then you are starting with a very good advantage.

Avoid humour unless you are absolutely certain that the context permits it. It is particularly important to avoid humour at the expense of others, as this is viewed as unkind. Do not smile too much: they don't.

37

THE ARAB COUNTRIES

WESTERNERS AND ARABS HAVE VERY DIFFERENT VIEWS ABOUT WHAT IS right and wrong, good and evil, logical and illogical, acceptable and unacceptable. They live in two different worlds, each organised in its own manner. Unless one gains a deeper understanding of how these two mindsets differ, one group will end up with an unfavourable impression of the other. It is worthwhile, therefore, to list the main cultural divergences, which go a long way towards explaining why each side sees certain events in a completely different light. The following is only a summary:

+ The West sees Arab society as one which is in decline, propped up temporarily by oil revenues. The Arabs, by contrast, are very conscious that their civilisation once led the world and believe they are capable of doing so again (in a moral sense).
+ The West generally separates Church and State. Most Islamic countries do not and religion strongly influences social behaviour, politics and even business.
+ In the West, the individual is the basic social unit; with the Arabs it is the family.
+ In the West, status is gained by achievement; in the Arab world by class.
+ Westerners like to deal in cold facts; Arabs will not let facts destroy their honour.
+ Westerners want to be fair, but just. Arabs want to be just, but flexible.
+ The West believes in organisations and institutions; Arabs believe in persons (guided by God).

- Westerners in principle wish to modernise. Arabs strive to find a way of adopting modern modes of behaviour without disrupting the traditions they value.
- Most western countries have succeeded in creating equality for men and women. Arabs believe the two sexes have vastly different personalities.
- Western societies differ greatly in their world view. Arabs, by contrast, largely subscribe to the same tenets of morality.
- Arabs move around less than westerners, therefore they are more conservative.
- Westerners must appear to behave rationally. For Arabs, it is important to impress others with their integrity.
- Westerners respect the strong. In Arab societies piety is one of the most admirable qualities: the weak must be respected and protected. This characteristic has been implanted by the Arabs into Spanish cultural attitudes.
- In the West, friends are good company. In the Arab world a friend is a person who cannot refuse your request. Neither can you refuse theirs.
- When introducing themselves, westerners usually restrict the amount of information they give. Arabs tend talk a lot about their family and connections.
- Westerners like to use official channels to further their business interests. Arabs use personal relationships.
- Arabs expect regular praise when they have done good work, whereas westerners are content if they keep their job. Conversely, Arabs are more hurt by criticism than westerners.
- When negotiating, westerners try to find logical conclusions, whereas Arabs use personalised arguments, appeals and persistent persuasion.
- Arabs stand or sit much closer to their interlocutor than does a westerner. It is normal to breathe on them and touch them frequently.
- Arabs are less 'private' than westerners. Visiting and long conversations are frequent.
- Men and women mingle freely in western societies, in most Arab countries they do not. Moslem sexuality is a territorial one. Women trespassing into public places (male spaces) are expected to wear a veil to make themselves invisible. They are rarely seen by westerners indoors.
- Hospitality is more effusive in the Arab world than in the West. They have the tradition of 'open house' even to strangers. A Bedouin will supposedly kill his last camel to feed his guest.

+ Westerners, especially Swiss, Swedes and other northerners, tend to turn up on time to dinner and other appointments. Arabs are much more relaxed in their timing. Social occasions or business meetings need not have fixed beginnings or endings.
+ Unlike westerners, Arabs prefer arranged marriages. On the whole, they are very stable, involving mutual respect.
+ Pork is taboo to Arabs, unlike in the West.

British, Americans and Northern Europeans will realise that they and Arabs are at the two extremes of the monochronic–polychronic scale, therefore communication will not take place in a natural manner. The exigencies of the Moslem religion complicate the interchange of ideas even further. Yet Arabs are used to dealing with foreigners and readily forgive them for not behaving like Arabs. You will even be forgiven for behaving like an infidel, as long as you make certain modifications. The most important thing is to avoid saying or doing anything which they consider insulting or derogatory. This includes the use of alcohol, improper dress, over-familiarity with the few women they allow you to meet, and challenging the basic concepts of Islam.

Foreign women are accepted without veils provided they dress conservatively. They may go shopping and travel alone, but should avoid all-male cafés (which is most of them). Women may not drive in Saudi Arabia.

Arabs are looking for sincerity in your dealings with them and expect to be shown the same respect they show you. If you come across as sincere and true, there is no problem. The natural northern tendency to look down on multi-active behaviour (talkativeness, invasion of privacy, poor time keeping, demonstrative body language) must be firmly suppressed, as the Arabs are not going to change their personality.

It is virtually impossible for multi-active people, especially Arabs, to act like Nordics or Americans. The only solution for good communication therefore is for the linear-active northerner to make some concessions in the direction of extroversion. Many find this difficult, even painful, but the rewards for doing so can be considerable. To begin with, one must stand much closer to an Arab when talking to him than one would with a Briton or a German. If you keep your distance, the Arab will think you find his physical presence distasteful or that you are a particularly cold individual. Arabs speak volubly and earnestly to someone they like, so you must attempt to do the same. They are very dependent on eye contact, so take your sunglasses off when talking to them and look them right in the eye (normally not difficult). Northerners may be uncomfortable with flattery or professions of friendship, but Arabs love these utterances, therefore you should not hesitate to praise their country, their arts, their dress and food (but not their women!).

When talking business with them, you must always do this against an intensely personal background. You want to do the business, but above all you want to do it with him, in whom you must always show close personal interest. If the Arab boasts about his connections and 'network' he is showing you the value of personal relationships, and if his uncle is influential in a government department (or is the Minister) he will expect you to take delight in the possibility of that influence being helpful in the furthering of your business. Do not appear detached and reluctant to accept favours. Your Arab friend will ask favours of you in due course.

Because the family structure is of paramount importance in Arab life, you should pay close attention to all family members he introduces you to. You should enquire regularly about the health (and happiness) of his brothers, uncles, cousins and sons. This would be very unusual in the north, but is a sure (and easy) way to gain your Arab friend's affection and loyalty. When visiting his country it is appropriate to take gifts for all these relatives. Do not expect Arabs to open gifts in front of you.

At mealtimes, eat only with your right hand, take only the food that is offered to you and, while you must praise the food, do not pay too much attention to those who have cooked it. Do not ask to meet the cooks (wives, mothers or sisters) who have laboured so long over the preparation of your meal. Your hosts will offer you the best morsels to eat, which you must accept. They will force too much on you – you will have to overeat a little in order not to upset them. You are not expected to talk much at mealtimes, so in that sense a meal can be a welcome break.

Returning to the subject of words, this is clearly a difficult area for northerners interacting with Arabs. Your shyness, succinctness and reflective silences will gain you no points with Arabs. Your verbal modesty – so much appreciated by Japanese – will be highly disconcerting to them. If you are quiet, they will simply think something is wrong and will fuss around you with all kinds of queries until they find out what it is. Not only do you have to speak **more** when you are with Arabs, but you have to step up the **volume** as well. Loudness of voice, rising pitch and tone, even shouting, all denote sincerity in Arab discourse. You may find this very hard to do. Do your best. Remember the Gulf War took place partly because Bush spoke softly and Saddam did not believe he meant what he said (about declaring war etc.). In Arab society it is quite normal to use speech in a rhetorical, almost aggressive manner to make a point clearly. They are great admirers of eloquence and if you can aspire to eloquence in their presence they will take it as a sign of education, refinement and sincerity, no matter how verbose it may sound in your own ears.

Oaths are quite common in Arabic, so that even if you slip in one of your less vehement ones when you get excited, it would not sound offensive to Arabs, who bring Allah into their arguments in almost every conversation. Arabs do not like discussing unpleasant matters such as illness, misfortune, accidents or death. Do not introduce any. They are even reluctant to tell you bad news about business, so bear this in mind when everything looks rosy. Connected with this habit is the Arab tendency to use euphemisms. Someone who is sick is described as 'tired', teachers magically become 'professors' and slums are referred to as 'low-cost dwellings'.

Arabs have great respect for the written word, especially if it has a religious connotation. Do not wrap up anything in an Arabic-language newspaper – it might have Allah's name on it. If you handle a copy of the Koran, you should show it even more respect than a Japanese business card.

Then there is the ordeal of a business meeting in an Arab country, which for a northerner can be particularly onerous. We have referred earlier to the Arab concept of 'open house' where visitors may gain access at all times. In the twentieth century the concept or tradition has been extended to include 'open office'. This may sound friendly enough, but things can become chaotic if you have the first appointment. Northerners expect to be guaranteed some kind of privacy while they discuss their business matters. In England or Germany, secretaries do not allow bosses to be disturbed by new arrivals during the course of a meeting. It can happen in Portugal, Spain, South America or Sicily, but even there newcomers are often asked to wait. In Arab countries they are shown straight into the office, according to the age-old tradition. Northerners, who normally expect the privilege of speaking without interruption, soon become nonplussed as anything up to half a dozen Arab visitors join the seance.

Not only are northerners unused to hearing several people speak at the same time, but they stand little chance of making their sober tones heard in the general hubbub. Arabs shout and speak loudly for dramatic effect or out of pure joy at seeing friends. They also seem to have the knack of absorbing three or four conversations at once. Even more problematic is how to proceed with the proposals which the northerner has travelled 3000 kilometres to present. Making an appointment for the next day is of no help, since the number of interruptions is unlikely to be less. Recently I asked the Commercial Counsellor at one of the embassies in Abu Dhabi, how one solves this dilemma. He answered as follows: You have to manoeuvre your chair so that you are sitting right next to the man you are doing business with. On the other side of his desk is not close enough – you have to be no more than a foot away and nearer to him than anybody else. When you have secured this position, you then shout down his right or left ear, depending on which side you are on. You continue to pound his ear with your propositions until he agrees with them. He is unlikely to give any trouble as he is suffering from numerous distractions from various angles, and acquiescence is usually the easiest way out. Enterprising multi-actives, such as Italians, often push documents to sign in front of him in these circumstances. You may be unable to do this, but modesty will get you nowhere.

In conclusion, although the cultural gulf between Arabs and northerners yawns wide, there is a fair chance of making a favourable impression. An Arab will admire education and expertise and welcomes representatives of small countries who show less arrogance than Americans, French and British. A Nordic or Dutch person will never be completely comfortable with Arab loquacity, subjectivity, unpunctuality and fatalism, but they can make progress in their relations with Arabs by showing keen personal interest in them, praising and flattering rather than criticising, memorising the basic tenets of their religion, dressing smartly, receiving and extending favours without qualms, showing great respect for old people and traditions and being very flexible and relaxed at all times.

38

INDIA

BY THE MIDDLE OF THE 21ST CENTURY, INDIA WILL HAVE PASSED CHINA IN terms of numbers of inhabitants, making it the most populated nation on earth. Its land area is also immense, with 3,287,000 sq. km. being seventh in the world. Though India's economy is in only fourteenth place (in 1999), the country is developing rapidly in the technological and service sectors and its rapidly growing middle class numbers over 300 million. The origins of the Indus Valley civilisation, with settled agriculture and trade with the Middle East, date from around 5000 BC.

Now the heart of India beats in the densely populated plains of the Ganges, farmed for several millennia. To the north the mighty Himalayan range constitutes the world's most awesome frontier. To the south lies the Peninsula, less fertile than the plains and often politically fragmented. Here the Tamils speak Dravidian languages, far removed structurally from the hundred or more Indo-European languages and dialects spoken in the rest of the country. Hindi, Urdu, Bengali and Gujerati are the most widely spoken tongues in this family, which also included Sanskrit in former times.

Pakistan and Bangladesh, after partition, represent the two other major states on the Indian subcontinent. English serves as a lingua franca in the region, as many of the local languages are mutually unintelligible.

Culture

Values

Indians have a special and unique culture that varies considerably from those of East Asia. Their communicative style is more verbose than the Chinese, Japanese or Korean and they are as dialogue oriented as most Latins. Essentially multi-active, they have created a society where privacy is rarely indulged in and even more rarely sought. They make little attempt to conceal their feelings – joy, disappointment and grief are expressed without inhibition.

Their values revolve around a strong family orientation as well as loyalty to a 'group', which often has to do with their profession. Examples are the diamond trade community or textile merchants. The honour of both family and group is strongly defended and arranged marriages are common within the trade. Further values are material success and creativity. It is important to do well in business and this automatically brings increased status. Creativity is admired, especially in adversity: improved technology often prospers in India during periods when the country is closed to outside influence and benefits. Under such circumstances Indians often shine with a DIY mentality. A keenness to find solutions pervades Indian business – a very positive attitude to experimentation. Honesty is not a major issue as a value, being seen as essentially relative. Stealing crops is seen to be as honourable as growing them and highwaymen – who have their own honour – are recognised as a social group!

Philosophical considerations surrounding values are largely positive. The objective in doing business is success, but one has to play the game well with flashes of brilliance rather than confining oneself to the narrow goal of victory. Fatalism is widespread and gives one a comforting fallback option. If you succeed, you are well off; if you fail, it is destiny that was unkind. These attitudes encourage Indians to be risk takers. The experience gained in many ventures (for failure is no stigma) results in many Indians developing considerable commercial skill. Indians living overseas rival the Chinese in their ability to capture and conduct local business.

The British Raj left both a social and a cultural influence on many Indians. Commonalities with the British include cricket, tea, army traditions, Oxford and Cambridge elite, protection of accumulated wealth, titles of nobility, admiration for (English) literature, democratic constitution, parliamentary rule, early industrialism, class system, the English language as a vehicle of culture and administration, large civil service, legal system, respect for property.

Concepts

Leadership and status

Indians accept a hierarchical system with its obligations and duties. The boss must be humanistic and initiate promotion for his subordinates. In family businesses the elder son rarely decides what he wants to be – he is born to carry on the trade of the father; the father is expected to groom him for the job. First a good education will be provided. The son must study hard, then the next step will be indicated.

A strong work ethic is visible in Indian commerce, especially when people are working in their own or family business. Indians do not work by the clock. There is an easy acceptance of foreigners in business dealings. Indians do not fear foreigners – many invasions have brought familiarity. They are, however, suspicious of the iniquity that the foreigners may bring with them (perhaps a certain fear of division and subsequent loss of national identity).

Nepotism is rife in traditional Indian companies. Family members hold key positions and work in close unison. Policy is also dictated by the trade group, e.g. fruit merchants, jewellers etc. These groups work in concert and come to each other's aid in difficult times.

Space and time

India is a crowded country and people are used to living and working close together. Bus queues are real scrambles. Indians are fairly tactile, but a certain restraint is visible regarding closeness in public. Women are clearly subordinate to men. There is also the question of class consciousness, which lessens the tendency to embrace all and sundry.

There is great latitude regarding punctuality, according to class. The reincarnation factor also influences the Indian concept of time. Opportunities need not always be seized greedily. Time is cyclical, so they will inevitably reoccur (perhaps in another life!).

Cultural factors in communication

Communication pattern and use of language

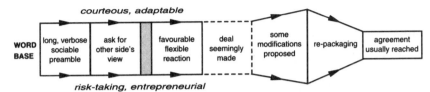

Indian English is old-fashioned, flowery and verbose. It is essentially a human, sympathetic language showing respect and often humility to the listener. It is generous in praise, yet reluctant to criticise, since failure in Indian business may quickly be attributed to bad karma. Indian English excels in ambiguity and such things as truth and appearances are often subject to negotiation. Above all, the language of the Indian manager emphasises the collective nature of the task and challenge. India is far from being a classless society, but the groups will often sink or swim together in the hard world of the subcontinent.

Listening habits

The key to Indian attention is to be eloquent, humble and respectful. They like an extensive vocabulary. They are willing to listen at length, to enable a relationship to develop and their aim, in the subsequent feedback, is to make a friend of the speaker. They do not make a difficult audience, but their sagacity must not be underestimated.

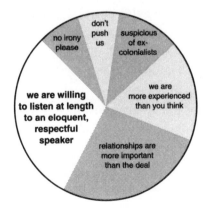

Behaviour at meetings and negotiations

Indians remain polite while modifications are proposed and repackage energetically to reach an agreement. They hate turning any business down. As far as negotiating style is concerned, the Indian has few superiors. Though highly collectivist in his local group, he develops individuality and brilliance when dealing on his own with outsiders. He is clever at buying and selling. The following points indicate just one pattern of negotiation that he employs with great skill when selling: (Each successive step may take place after days or weeks of negotiation.)

1 I don't want to sell at all.
2 This business is the jewel in the crown of all the businesses that my family controls.
3 We don't need the money.
4 I am not intending to sell, but if I ever did sell, I would sell to you.
5 If I should sell, I have no idea whatsoever how we should evaluate such a successful business.
6 If one should try to estimate a price, it would be by analogy with similar deals that were done in the past.
7 A selling X to B was such a deal.
8 A only sold X to B because he needed the money.
9 Perhaps I would like to sell to you, but I shall never be able to carry my family with me.
10 I have heard your proposed price and I have stormed out of the room.
11 I have to tell you in all honesty that we have received a very serious bid from a third party. It is higher than yours.
12 I do not expect you to pay more than they are willing to, but I expect you to match their offer.
13 I am willing to give the deal to you and not them, because I promised to sell to you.
14 I know that this price is not based on the usual multiple of profit, but how do you decide the worth of a business that has 70 per cent of the market?

There are many other ploys that Indians use. Basically, they are disappointed if you do not engage in bargaining with them. Determination of price must come last, after all the benefits of the purchase or deal have been elaborated. Indians use all their communicative skills to get to the price indirectly. When negotiating:

✦ remember they are very skilful and can often fool you;
✦ understand their needs and objectives;
✦ be humble at all times;

- ◆ avoid sarcasm and irony;
- ◆ be patient – few Asians like to decide things quickly;
- ◆ focus on relations; they see this as more important than any specific deal;
- ◆ Indians will accept 'losses' if they mean future gains;
- ◆ their negotiation concept is win–lose, but they are very flexible.

Manners and taboos

Hinduism dominates Indians' social behaviour, with the associated taboos. Women show great deference to men. Dress is opulent, often ostentatious. Brothers and sons generally live under one roof, which results in the fragmentation of land.

How to empathise with Indians

Indians tend to complain openly about the injustices of the colonial period. If treated with respect, they quickly put the past behind them, especially where good business is in the offing. One should play the Indians at their own game, i.e. be reasonable, solicitous and flexible. The country has a magnificent history, which should be referred to and admired. One should know all the basic facts about Mahatma Gandhi and avoid confusing him with Indira and Rajiv Gandhi's family, to which he was not related. A knowledge of Hinduism is also advisable, as is awareness of the geography of India, Pakistan and Bangladesh.

Indians emanate and expect warmth, respect and properness. It is risky to be too jokey with them – they tend to take things seriously. Be flexible at all times. Accept that there is a great deal of chaos and remember that they manage it better than you do.

Learn to cope with Indian bureaucracy, which can be slow and tedious, as well as how to function within constraints and restrictions. Maintain multiple channels of communication, both with government and commercial entities. Develop your own linkages, independent of your partner.

Try to be non-judgmental about Indian failings or limitations. Remember that truth has many aspects – most Asians consider that there is no absolute truth, and truth, facts and appearances are often subject to negotiation.

Show sympathy and empathy whenever you see the other side in difficulties. Never use brute force or gain unfair advantage when dealing from strength.

Recognise the importance of the unwritten word. In Asia oral agreements are weightier than documents. Operate within the context of a medium- to longer-term horizon.

39

SOUTH-EAST ASIA

ALTHOUGH JAPAN, CHINA AND KOREA CONSTITUTE THE THREE GREAT powerhouses of the Far East, the seven major countries of South-East Asia count a combined population of 500 million and have a rapidly increasing significance in terms of future markets, resources of labour and industrial and technological development. Indonesia is the world's fourth most populated state, Vietnam is thirteenth, the Philippines fourteenth and Thailand seventeenth. Malaysia and Singapore are already high tech and actually manufacture a great deal of the technology. Western firms face fewer problems with trading and investment opportunities in most of those countries, which are less inclined to set up protectionist barriers than, for instance, Japan and Korea.

In order for Westerners to do successful business in this area, they have to acquire certain insights into the South-East Asian mindset. National traits vary considerably within this group – Vietnam is the odd one out – but Indonesians, Malaysians, Thais and Filipinos subscribe to a remarkable number of shared characteristics that have little in common with the more austere work-and-duty ethics of Japanese, Koreans and Chinese. The South-East Asia world view is relatively relaxed, time is seen as a limitless commodity, the value of efficiency is often ambiguous – gentleness and virtue are prized above all.

One good way of evaluating the South-East Asian mentality is to examine the Western businessperson's model and put it in perspective in relation to theirs.

Western	South-East Asian
Love of individualism	Fondness for the collective
Personal ego	Personal interests subordinated to the group
Life is a challenge	Security and harmony
Achievement and self-actualisation goals	Our achievements must contribute to group goals
Competitiveness, aggression, direct confrontation	Cooperation, restraint, adaptation to the other
Overt action	Subtle, sometimes ambiguous action
Meetings: climate is one of persuasion, argument, competition	Persuasion is presumptuous, Asian seeks common ground, sharing
Asian view of Westerner: tough, single-minded, demanding	More pliant, takes into account many things, not exigent
Management goals:	
✦ profit maximisation	✦ social responsibility
✦ organisational efficiency	✦ harmonious work atmosphere
✦ high productivity	✦ high performance seen as ruthless
Technological change is rapid	Social and cultural change is evolutionary
External rewards	Internal rewards
Westerner sees SE Asian as timid, indecisive, slow	He is in fact struggling to relate Western techniques to inherited concepts of trust, loyalty, cooperation, compassion, tolerance
Profit sensitive	Sensitive to social pressures
Law, contractual obligations define behaviour	Face saving, face giving define behaviour
Western banter, familiarity, nicknames	Politeness, gentleness, low voice, social rank, mutual respect
Delegates to professionals	Delegates to kinship
Meritocracy	Patronage system
Planning top down	Policies and guidelines top down, tactical plans bottom up

The differences are striking. Westerners are of course generally self-determined and dynamic; the South-East Asian has deep cultural dynamics embedded in deeply rooted practices and customs. He wishes to please his Western partner, but he must remain true to his cultural traditions.

Westerners are really quite unaware of the rough ride that many Asians have when beginning to deal with the West. Let us take the case of an Indonesian gentleman arriving in the US for a business negotiation. The first evening, while he is still suffering from jet lag, he is taken out for dinner by his American partner. After experiencing a crushing handshake, he is made to drink a couple of martinis, then red wine with a huge steak which he manages to get down with difficuly.

The next morning he is hungover, but attends his meeting at the ridiculous time of 9 am. After more excruciating handshakes from other enormous Americans, he is subjected to the indignity of being addressed by his first name (where are their manners?). Smalltalk and friendly socialising at the beginning of the meeting were restricted to two minutes, unappetising coffee was served in plastic (!) containers, and before he had gathered his wits they were straight into the negotiation, giving him no chance to deliver his 10-minute background speech with a view to creating initial harmony between the parties. The negotiating style was confrontational and he was being asked yes/no questions and badgered for quick decisions before he had got his pens and pencils in a row.

The Americans, already physically overpowering, did not seem able to sit at table correctly – they slumped and slouched and showed the soles of their shoes at him in ankle-on-knee crosses. When he indicated polite rejection of some of their proposals by the traditional reluctant-assent method, the Americans took it as 'yes' and threw in more proposals. At times they became very tough, then friendly, then tough again – what a strange custom! They seemed to think that attack was the best method of defence, bluffed shamelessly, then conceded quickly when their bluff was called. Obviously face saving doesn't count! They came out with many slangy expressions, which he didn't understand and which they didn't bother to explain. They used a lot of tough expressions like 'That will blow it out of the water' (what water?) and 'I tell you I can walk away from this deal', when it was quite clear that they wanted to do the deal and make the profit. He wondered what kind of a company he was getting involved with…

The Muslim cultures of South-East Asia

Malaysia and Indonesia share many of the basic characteristics prevalent among East Asian people. However, the fact that Islam is the dominant religion in these two countries gives rise to certain important differences in behaviour and attitudes.

In the following respects the Malaysians and Indonesians are **similar** to the Chinese, Koreans and Japanese:

✦ The family is the basic unit of life. A great deal of time is spent developing interpersonal relationships with family members and close friends.
✦ Harmony is important in social and business life. Head-on confrontation is to be avoided if at all possible.
✦ Loss of face is very serious.
✦ Conversations, including business discussions, are roundabout and indirect in the interest of politeness and avoiding offence.
✦ Society is organised in a hierarchical system based on age and seniority.
✦ Etiquette, good manners, protocol and gentleness are mandatory.
✦ Collectivism prevails over individualism.

The Muslim cultures **diverge** from their Buddhist-Confucian-Taoist neighbours in the following respects:

✦ Their religion affects their social and business life on a daily basis.
✦ Islamic taboos, such as pork and alcohol and the use of the left hand, are observed.
✦ In Malaysia the status and partial segregation of women are in accordance with Islamic practice.
✦ The work ethic shared by the Chinese, Japanese and Koreans is noticeably absent in Malaysia and Indonesia.
✦ Indonesians and Malaysians do not adhere to the same standards of punctuality as their neighbours.
✦ Compared with the Chinese, Japanese and Koreans, the South-East Asian Muslims seem to lack drive and ambition, are less interested in profit and material success.

40

INDONESIA

THE WORLD'S LARGEST ISLAMIC COUNTRY WITH A POPULATION approaching 200 million, Indonesia is the world's largest archipelago consisting of over 13,000 islands. It stretches over 5000 km from east to west and over 2000 kilometres from north to south.

There are fierce independence movements in many islands and Indonesia is described by many as the world's largest colonial power.

It obtained independence from the Dutch in 1945 when the Japanese ceased to occupy the country. Guerrilla warfare delayed total independence until 1949. Sukarno was the country's first President, then Suharto from 1966 untiil 1998. On Sukarno's overthrow, aversion to the influence of communist China led to the slaughter of many Chinese living in Indonesia, where, as in Malaysia, they controlled many aspects of commerce. Chinese today keep a low profile, but are still active in business.

The country is very poor, the per capita incomes not reaching $1000 per annum. About 50 per cent of national income derives from oil.

Bahasa Indonesia, the national language, is closely related to Malay. Dialects are also spoken everywhere and are often mutually incomprehensible.

The position of women is quite different from other Muslim countries:

+ They can vote and have full civil rights.
+ On many islands they hold leadership positions.
+ They have never been veiled or secluded.
+ In Jakarta they shake hands like men, though sometimes they bow with hands folded.

Culture

Values

+ The family is the basic unit and one's first loyalty.
+ Polygamy is permitted, but rare.
+ *Adat* customary law usually prevails over Islam.
+ Friendly hospitality is typically Indonesian.
+ There is no work ethic in the Protestant sense.
+ There is little interest in profit or material success.
+ Unity and conformity are valued above individuality. The present government encourages this.
+ Age is respected.
+ Society is hierarchical.

Concepts

Leadership and status

Leaders are usually from chosen families or emanating from the higher ranks in the army. They are expected to be paternalistic. They often seek consensus, which is the mode followed by all persons.

Status is accorded by age, seniority or military rank.

Space and time

Indonesians live in concentrations and are used to being crowded. They are comfortable in a group and need relatively little personal space.

Time in Indonesia is a 'limitless pool'. It is often referred to as 'rubber time'. Punctuality is not observed. Public or municipal meetings can begin one hour late or more. Indonesians do not like to be hurried. There is little sense of urgency about anything.

Cultural factors in communication

Communication pattern and use of language

WORD BASE				
asks other side ...	modifies own proposal ...	says what you ...	adds	ends in
respect language especially for older people				
... to speak first	... to show deference	... want to hear	polite requests	ambiguity

Communication is dialogue oriented, loquacious, but conducted in a quiet voice and without displaying intensity of emotion. Confrontation is avoided and problems or areas of difference are alluded to in an indirect manner.

Indonesians tell foreigners what they think will please them or what they wish to hear. They also are reluctant to admit that they don't know the answer to a question. They often give wrong directions!

Listening habits

Indonesians listen deferentially and do not interrupt. Speeches at public meetings are long and boring, but people show no dissension. In business meetings they listen carefully to foreigners, but do not always fully understand the content; unfortunately, they do not indicate this. Misunderstandings may arise. The general level of English is quite low.

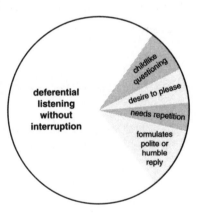

Behaviour at meetings and negotiations

Deferential listening and quiet speaking are aimed at harmony. No one must be made to feel *malu* (ashamed, embarrassed). Everything is negotiable in Indonesia and everything takes time. Bargaining is expected and hard bargainers are respected. There are in reality no fixed prices and starting positions may be way out of line. Indonesians act in a collectivist manner and, like the Japanese, prefer to negotiate in numbers. They are almost never aggressive, but foreigners will need a lot of patience and must forget about time pressures.

Manners and taboos

Respectability in dress is preferred. Women's shorts should reach the knees and should be baggy rather than tight.

Shaking hands with women is acceptable. Men often hold hands. Indonesians touch each other more than most East Asians, but the head remains sacred.

Greetings are always courteous. One's head may not be held higher than that of a superior or older person. This means that Indonesians often bend or lower their head, even duck (or drop shoulders) when passing 'superiors' in the street!

Things are handed over with the right hand or with both hands for added respect. A hands on hip stance is seen as aggressive.

Taboos include Muslim prohibition of alcohol, pork or use of the left hand. It is bad manners to point, ask personal questions or completely finish the food on one's plate. Unfortunately, bribery is common at most levels of society and is called 'speed money'.

How to empathise with Indonesians

Indonesians are very friendly and you should reciprocate this immediate friendliness. Courtesy and gentleness are mandatory. Indonesia will buy from people who treat them with deference and who show they like them. Generally they crave recognition and affection. References to corruption, military influence or other problems or shortcomings evident in the country will only serve to embarrass them.

41

MALAYSIA

MALAYSIA HAS A POPULATION OF AROUND 20 MILLION, OF WHOM 50 PER cent are Malay, 36 per cent Chinese, 1 per cent Indian and 4 per cent other races.

The political structure is a Federation of thirteen states, eleven on the Malay peninsula and two (Sabah and Sarawak) on the island of Borneo. Chief exports are rubber, palm oil, tropical timber, tin, petroleum, cocoa beans and pepper.

Some racial tension exists in the country. As Malay people traditionally have been only little involved in the economic sector of the community, an occupational void was largely filled by the Chinese. When they eventually gained control over the economy, riots occurred. In 1969 a 20-year plan was introduced to increase the Malay labour force at all levels of business and to reduce the foreign share of the Malay market from 60 to 30 per cent by 1990. Due to lack of interest in business by the Malays, these percentages have been difficult to achieve.

The near balance of power between Malays and Chinese requires close cooperation between the two cultures. Currently, due to cultural differences in customs and values, an atmosphere of distrust still exists.

Culture

Values

Respect, courtesy and especially gentleness towards others are the most important elements of ideal Malay behaviour. This is known as *budi*.

Family and friends take precedence over self-centred interests. Love of children is very strong. Malays are motivated to develop deep and lasting relationships with family, friends and worthy, respectable partners. Trust is fundamental to the development of such relationships. Formality at first slowly drops away to informal, trusting attitudes. The most respected people are those who compromise most.

Wealth is not pursued for its own sake. There used to be laws prohibiting the accumulation of wealth by Malay peasants.

Humans are considered basically good by the Malays, rather different from the concept of original sin in Western Christianity. Their strong belief in God (Allah) gives Malaysians a fatalistic attitude towards events. They feel subject to the elements of nature because of their belief in the supremacy of God's will. The Malay language frequently uses the Muslim expression 'God willing'. This favours a lack of motivation for worldly success and of determination to 'get things done'.

In general, Malays prefer to study arts rather than science in college and many of them lack technical sophistication. Again, the contrast with Japan/Korea is striking.

Concepts

Leadership and status

People born in high positions are expected to demonstrate leadership capabilities. A good leader is religiously devout, sincere, humble and tactful.

Status is inherited, not earned, confirmed by demonstrating leadership and caring attitude. A Malay feels comfortable in a hierarchical structure in which he has a definite role.

Work and idleness are not clearly delineated in Malay culture and language. Work is only one of many activities pursued by the Malays. Deepening of relationships and time spent with the elderly may be seen as idle pursuits by Westerners, not by Malays.

Malays are modest and rarely request promotion. They expect it to be accorded by a caring senior when the time is ripe.

Space and time

An adequate distance of comfort is respected. The Malays are environmentally conscious.

There is little attention to the past and the future is regarded as vague and unpredictable (God's will). The present must be spent virtuously.

Cultural factors in communication

Communication patterns and use of language

Conversations are roundabout, avoiding giving offence. Malays are skilled at indirect references. Some British influence is evident in debating. Communication is formal at first, with gradual informality being introduced over time.

Listening habits

Malays are respectful, especially to seniors and elderly people. They make no interruptions. They listen for virtue and caring comments.

Behaviour at meetings and negotiations

Harmony and balanced discussion are sought. Malay indifference to business reduces ambition and competition. There is little attempt to alter the environment (in direct contrast to Singapore, Hong Kong, Korea and Japan). People who compromise most in business negotiations are the ones who are respected most. The Malays are not given to great shows of determination.

Manners and taboos

Most taboos are Muslim. Malays are comfortable in a hierarchical structure, showing deference to seniors and authority. Greetings are important.

It is customary for men and women to shake hands with each other. In the Malay handshake the man offers both hands, but without the grip. He lightly touches his friend's hands, then brings his hands to his breast. This means 'I greet you from my heart'.

Women often *salaam*, bowing very low.

The index finger is not used for pointing. It is more polite to use the right thumb, with fingers closed.

The head is sacred and should not be touched. (No patting children on the head!)

How to empathise with Malays

Malays are more group oriented than many other people. One should try to apply synergistic skills to the relationship. This is a good approach to people who think in terms of divisions between Malay/Chinese/Western or Muslim/Buddhist/Christian.

One should familiarise oneself with the basic concepts of Islam. Show respect for seniors and religious beliefs. Younger Malays are very proud of the modern Malay orientation towards industrialisation and high-tech. One should share this enthusiasm with them.

42

SINGAPORE

Perhaps Singapore never intended to become a tiger. Its name, Singapura, is Sanskrit meaning 'Lion City', but even that description was euphemistic for a port which was notorious as a dreaded pirate haunt and remained a jungled backwater from 1400 to 1800. But better times were soon to come. Singapore is not a tale of two cities, but rather a tale of two men, both remarkable individuals and visionaries to whom the city owes its present prosperity. If you have stayed at Raffles Hotel, you may be aware that it was named after Thomas Raffles, son of an undistinguished sea captain. He joined the East India Company at the age of 14 and in his mid-twenties was posted to Penang where he took the trouble to learn Malay, an initiative which contrasted strongly with the linguistic lethargy of better-educated colonial officials. His common sense and ability to communicate with all manner of people stood him in good stead. He held many important posts as an administrator – at one time he was Governor of Java – but his most significant achievement was the founding of Singapore. A great believer in free trade, he was anxious to establish a British trading post on the China trade route. He selected the site at the mouth of the Singapore river and used his communication skills and personal charm to persuade the local Sultan to grant permission for his base. This was achieved on 6 February 1819 and Raffles set sail for England the next day! He did not return until 1822, by which time it had developed into a booming port with 10,000 inhabitants.

Raffles, who is still greatly honoured in Singapore, was the right man in the right place at the right time. Without any inhibiting social pretensions, he was unusually multicultural for an Englishman and a great humanist to boot. A friend of William Wilberforce, he fought against slavery and piracy and worked unselfishly to bring prosperity (through free trade) to a region which had been hampered by previous Dutch monopolies in the area. Besides Singapore, he founded two other things: London Zoo and The Raffles Institution. It was at this college that the second of the two great men of Singapore was educated – the first Prime Minister, Lee Kuan Yew.

While Raffles fathered the original colony, Lee can truly be described as the father of modern Singapore. His parents were Straits-born Chinese of Hakka origin. After studying at the Raffles Institution, he went to Cambridge where he got a First (with distinction) in law. He set up a law firm in Singapore but became increasingly involved in politics and became Prime Minister in 1959. His tenure lasted 31 years. It was characterised by benevolent dictatorship based on efficiency, honesty, intolerance and an unswerving sense of mission. At the time of its breakaway from the Malaysian Federation, Singapore was considered by many critics to be a non-viable economy on account of its bulging population and complete lack of natural resources. Lee proved them all wrong. He perceived that the teeming inhabitants of Singapore, like those of the Japanese islands, were the country's greatest asset. Unlike the homogeneous Japanese, however, Singaporeans had to be welded into a team. Although all imbued with a desire to create wealth (here they resemble the people of Hong Kong), Singaporeans were of extremely diverse origin – Chinese, Malay, Indian, European and Eurasian. In the space of 25 years, moreover, they had been British subjects, Japanese subjects, Malaysians and Singaporeans. Lee took it on himself to create a sense of national identity, to build a nation, to run it as it should be run. As *The Economist* said, 'Lee ran Singapore like a well-run nursery.' He felt he knew what was best for the country and, showing great political adroitness, he allowed no one to defy him. In his three decades in power he created a powerful economy: Singaporeans who might have wished to oppose or obstruct him were crushed by the sheer weight of the city-state's achievements. In one of his speeches he declaimed, 'The greatest satisfaction in life comes from achievement. To achieve is to be happy... Achievement generates inner or spiritual strength, a strength which grows out of an inner discipline.'

Discipline there certainly was. Chewing gum, littering and (for some time) long haircuts were taboo. Fines were heavy, including ones for failing to flush the toilet. Singaporeans were imbued with Lee's Confucian values – filial respect, duty, moderation and the work ethic were mandatory. Censorship of the media, including television, was strict. Welfare, job stability, good education, cheap housing and affluence were thrust on Lee's citizens. The people of Singapore were going to be happy, whether they liked it or not.

It is only natural that a dictator with such long tenure and puritanical policies should have been heavily criticised. But where would Singapore have been today without him? Ruling even a homogeneous nation is never easy. Lee created a proud sense of nationhood, almost after the Swiss model, among diverse cultural groups who frequently in history have hated and killed each other. It is true that his attempts at state-directed genetic engineering (ostensibly to produce more intelligent offspring) were impractical and unlikely to succeed, but little else he tried failed. The city-state truly bears his own image.

Facts about modern Singapore

◆ The republic consists of the main island plus 57 smaller ones.
◆ The climate varies little throughout the year as Singapore is situated close to the equator. It is generally hot and humid with abundant rainfall.
◆ Independence from Britain was gained in 1959.
◆ The PAP (People's Action Party) has remained in power ever since.
◆ Singapore was a founder member of the Federation of Malaysia in 1963, but left two years later.
◆ Singapore has full employment.
◆ It has the highest rate of home ownership in the world.
◆ It also has the highest rate of national savings.
◆ Foreign investment is ubiquitous.
◆ There is one foreign company for every thousand people.
◆ There is a chronic shortage of labour due to the government's restrictive immigration policy.

How to empathise with Singaporeans

◆ Bear in mind the racial mix and react accordingly:
  – The Chinese dominate and play a big part in running the state.
  – They are efficient, frugal and have an impeccable social/business network that you should respect and try to join.

- Westerners tend to be very experienced (Far East old hands) and are also well connected.
- Eurasians can be sensitive about their origins.
- Indians are mainly Tamils, speaking that language.
- Malays tend to be less ambitious in business than the other groups.

◆ Try to acquire a smattering of the languages spoken in Singapore (other than English): Mandarin Chinese, Malay and Tamil.

◆ Remember and be sensitive to the varying religious beliefs: Christian, Buddhist, Muslim, Hindu and Taoist.

◆ Try not to look or sound like an ex-colonialist.

◆ Be unstinting in your praise for Singapore's economic and social achievements.

◆ Conform in general to the republic's disciplined, law-abiding, some-what sober way of life. Eccentricity wins few medals and erodes your credibility.

43

THAILAND

THE NINETEENTH CENTURY SAW EXTENSIVE COLONIALISATION IN SOUTH-East Asia, but one nation state in the area remained independent. This was Thailand, formerly known to the West as Siam. 'Thai' means 'free', so Thailand is the 'Land of the Free', also known as the 'Land of Smiles' and the 'Land of the Yellow Robes'. The last title vividly describes the religion most widely embraced by the Thai people.

Thailand successfully resisted colonialisation at a time when its neighbours Cambodia, Laos, Burma, Malaysia and nearby Vietnam, China, Indonesia and the Philippines were exploited in various ways by the British, French, American and Spanish governments. The odds against Thailand avoiding falling into either the British or the French sphere of interest were considerable, but various factors combined to enable it to preserve its sovereignty. Thailand was in fact not an easy nut to crack. A nation of successful fighters, it had enjoyed unbroken control over its own territory since 1238, when Thais revolted against the Khmers, whose tradition they share, and established the Kingdom of Sukhothai in the north central part of the country.

Relatively populous throughout the following 600 years, the Thais were no pushover for any power and in fact dominated their neighbours for the period. They also had the territorial advantage of not being adjacent to a nearby colossus – India or China – where British influence was strong. Geographically, they are cushioned by weaker states: Laos, Cambodia, Burma and former Malaya. The fact that they had the colonialist British to the west, but their French rivals to the east, gave them opportunities to play one off against the other and they eventually concluded treaties with both European powers. Neither did they neglect the Americans: the first

American ship arrived in Thailand in 1821; in 1833 the Thai-American Treaty of Amity and Commerce was signed in Bangkok and in the years that followed King Mongkut exchanged correspondence with three American presidents, including Abraham Lincoln. The good relations with the US have been maintained in the twentieth century and the US is Thailand's biggest export market.

USA / THAI HORIZON

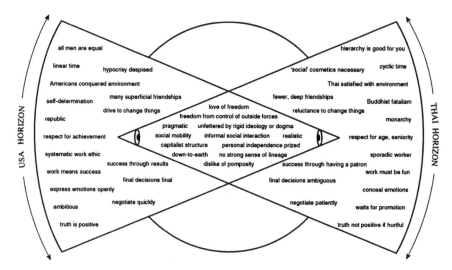

The astuteness of Thai diplomacy, their fiercely independent spirit and the paramount importance of their religion – Buddhism – are the main factors in Thailand's cultural differentiation from the other South-East Asian states.

Thailand is the world's biggest exporter of rubber and, in most years, of rice. Textiles now are a major export item and the nation is also an important exporter of more sophisticated products such as hard disk drives for computers, precision micro ball-bearings and integrated circuits.

Culture

Religion

Of the total population of some 60 million, 95 per cent have declared themselves Buddhists, mostly of the Theravada school. About 4 per cent of the people are Muslims.

In Thailand, Laos, Cambodia and Vietnam, Theravade Buddhism is the most important religion. This is distinct from Mahayama Buddhism, as practised in China, Korea, Japan and the Hanoi area of Vietnam, which has a long history of Chinese influence. Theravada Buddhism is more influential, meaningful and especially visible in the lives of the common people than the Mahayana variant, which is often interlaced with rigid Confucian doctrines.

During many centuries of Thai history, education, which has long been considered a key to national security and development, was almost exclusively in the hands of Buddhist monks. The Thai alphabet was invented by King Ramkhamhaeng (he needed one!) in the thirteenth century. Buddhist monasteries (called *wats*) established schools within their grounds and the monks, in addition to their religious duties, taught reading, writing and arithmetic, as well as other subjects, to local youngsters. Today there are over 30,000 temples scattered throughout Thailand's 73 provinces. In modern Thailand schools are now run by the government, but many of them are still standing within the compounds of monasteries.

To understand the importance of the *wat* and of popular Buddhism in controlling Thai thought, it is necessary to appreciate the multi-functional nature of these monasteries and how much they are used by the common people. Families in rural areas often feel insecure about keeping their valuables in their homes, so they ask the abbot to store them in the monastery. The *wat* is not only the villager's 'safe deposit box', but is a storehouse for documents or artifacts of historical significance. Thousands of Buddha images are also kept there and used for public veneration and objects of meditation.

Travellers may stay overnight in *wats*, especially when travelling to festivals; children sent to schools in Bangkok can use them as hostels, their parents making donations. The young boys live with the monks and assist them with their daily chores, such as washing, cleaning and carrying food containers. They also receive instruction in the Buddhist tenets. Government functions take place in *wats* (elections, conscription); some are used as clinics.

Values

Pragmatism	Simplicity
Fatalism, karma	Love of freedom
Dislike of pomposity	Form and properness
Family, filial piety	Compassion, kindness

Respect, face, deference	Dignity, honour
Contextual sensitivity	Reluctance to imitate change
Satisfaction with nature's tempo	Interest in Western education
Rejection of Western work ethic	Desire for inward comfort
Belief in moderation	

Concepts

Leadership

In 1257 the Kingdom of Sukhothai adopted the paternalistic system of government. The king, while enjoying absolute sovereign power, would, like a father, look after his subjects and personally pay close attention to their well-being. The Khmer system had been based on the concept of Divine Right (not unlike England's). The bloodless coup of 1932 that led to Thailand changing from absolute to constitutional monarchy did little to alter this privilege. Today the king's power emanates from the people, he is head of state and of the armed forces and upholder of Buddhism and all other religions.

In Thailand authority and power are considered natural to the human condition. The holder of power has accumulated merit in a previous life. The best leader is one who empathises most with his subordinates.

Status

There is a clear line of command: king, aristocracy, government officials, priests, doctors, professors, businesspeople, others. The military, while influential, is always in the background. Hierarchy is good for you, subordinates are happy with their rung in the ladder. There is a certain amount of social mobility, but don't challenge the system.

Space

Thais view nature as benign and beautiful and see no real reason to change it. This reduces their drive towards industrialisation, although this has of course inevitably taken place in line with regional development and substantial inward investment.

Time

Buddhists have a cyclical concept of time. Days and seasons succeed each other, as do kings and governments. Opportunities and options recur and multiply irrespective of one's anxiety to seize them. The use of time does not equate with earning a living. Success depends more on luck than timing. Thais dislike deadlines.

Cultural factors in communication

Communication patterns and use of language

+ People who keep cool are respected.
+ Buddhist moderation.
+ When angered, use a subtle method of revenge.
+ Avoid unpleasant truths.
+ Describe only 20 per cent of personal problems.
+ Social cosmetics (giving face to others) are vital.
+ Hypocrisy is not always negative.
+ Humour is used (largely puns).
+ Smiles cover tragic situations.

Listening habits

+ Docile, obedient.
+ Little feedback unless requested.
+ Sensitive discussions must be initiated from the top.

Behaviour at meetings and negotiations

Buddhism discourages competition. Thais therefore are not overly ambitious and are reluctant to initiate change. Easy work with sufficient pay is better than hard work with high pay. Authority is respected when present, but often ignored when absent. Work tempo increases or decreases according to presence of the boss. Discussion of issues is welcomed, but decisions (and blame) are passed upwards.

Social affairs are discussed during work hours, but business is pursued after hours in social situations. There is a patronage system for getting ahead. Decisions are often ambiguous, so that nobody loses face. Negotiations should not be hurried: three or four days of building relationships are advisable first. The central part of business is approached slowly and concentrically. Giggles mean that favour is to be asked for (or withheld).

Manners and taboos

Head-on collisions must be avoided at all costs. Ensure that there is no losing face for anyone. Socialising includes meals, theatre and music, kick boxing, going to the beach, badminton. Care should be taken to observe the pecking order in social and business situations. Superiors are seen as unchallenged, but they generally strive to get on well with subordinates.

How to empathise with Thais

+ Know your Thai history.
+ Emphasise their independence.
+ Be easy going socially.
+ Don't rush them.
+ Learn the basics of Buddhism.
+ Think of time as cyclical.
+ Respect the monarchy.
+ Dress neatly.

44

THE PHILIPPINES

AMONG EAST ASIANS, THE FILIPINO IS A ONE-OFF. HE (OR SHE) IS talkative in the Latin manner; he demonstrates warmth and emotion openly; he is cosmopolitan and travels the world; he is comfortable with Americans and with Westerners in general; he is committed to democratic institutions, including freedom of speech; he distrusts and rejects authoritarianism whenever he is able.

The repressive and corrupt Marcos era was hard on the easy-going Filipinos, not least because the dictator was propped up by the Americans, from whom Filipinos had learnt much better things. Their enthusiasm for liberty, their will to debate, their commitment to free enterprise, their open borders were all part of the US legacy. On the overthrow of Marcos in 1986, Corazon Aquino introduced political reforms. Her successor, President Fidel Ramos, proved more adept and, though formerly an autocratic figure, kept the country firmly on the path of reform. He perceived clearly the effect of Western countries on Filipino thought and pointed out that his people could not be governed in the same authoritarian manner as the Japanese, Chinese, Koreans and Singaporeans.

For example, over 100,000 Americans live in the Philippines and almost two million Filipinos are in the US, where they are the fastest-growing Asian minority. Some 50,000 visas are granted a year, second only to the Mexicans. A Filipino governor was elected in Hawaii.

The 'non-Asianness' of Filipinos derives not only from their 100-year contact with the Americans, but also to a great degree from the 350-year period of Spanish colonialism. Indeed, the islands were named after Philip II of Spain!

THE PHILIPPINES – COLONIAL INFLUENCES

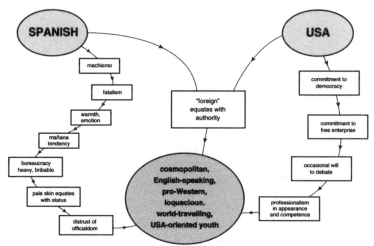

Culture

Values

Family most important
Education highly valued
Respect for old people
No criticism in public
Avoidance of change to minimise
    risk of shame
Love of gambling and games of chance
Loyalty sought and reciprocated
Personalisation of business essential
Roman Catholicism

Hospitality
Authority highly valued
Hiya (shame) must be avoided at
    all costs
Fatalism
Machismo
Sensitivity to overly aggressive
    behaviour (American)
Flexibility

Concepts

Leadership

Leadership is based on family name, age and connections. Subordinates are
generally obedient and avoid dissension.

Status

Status is established by family name, connections and education. In spite of the Filipino love of democracy, senior and even middle-ranking Filipinos can be hypersensitive in matters of status and quickly take offence if there is an imagined slight.

Space

The distance of comfort is closer than that of most Europeans but similar to that of Spaniards. The everyday greeting for acquaintances and friends is a handshake for both men and women. A pat on the back was inherited from the Spanish.

Time

A *mañana* tendency has also been inherited from the Spanish. When making appointments, it is advisable to ask if they are 'American time' or 'Filipino time'. In the case of the latter, one or two hours late is not unusual.

Cultural factors in communication

Communication patterns and use of language

Filipinos' dialogue-oriented, rather emotional communication somewhat resembles Spanish, but is less forceful and exuberant. Oratory is valued and speeches can be lengthy. Though Tagalog is used throughout the country, the Philippines is, at a functional level, the second-largest English-speaking nation in the world.

Listening habits

Although somewhat excitable and scattered in thought, Filipinos' Asian side makes them good, polite listeners. They like warm but modest speakers.

Behaviour at meetings and negotiations

Politeness, especially to older people and persons of senior rank, is absolutely essential. The tone of discussion is generally conciliatory and avoidance of heated discussion or opinionated expression is advisable. Filipinos like to be conformist and rarely say no openly. They conceal their feelings well and one should try to read the hidden signals that they give at meetings. The fatalistic phrase *bahala na* (God wills it) is often heard – one can even use it on them if one wishes!

Raising the eyebrows or jerking the head upwards are both affirmative. A jerk of the head downwards means no. If someone says yes while putting their head downwards, you can be reasonably sure that they really feel negatively about the matter. Filipino body language is generally more overt than with many Asians, but more restrained than that of Latin people.

There is a general commitment to free enterprise and friendly relations with the West. Business efficiency, however, is affected negatively by having to seek contacts in high places to cut through bureaucratic red tape. Bribery is not unknown.

Manners and taboos

In restaurants men still hiss to attract waiters. Women often signal with their fans. Filipinos are extremely hospitable and love parties, singing, dancing and good food. Flowers are a suitable gift when visiting their homes.

Men usually wear the *barong tagalog*, a loose, frilly, white or cream-coloured shirt with tails out, no jacket or tie. Most foreign men do the same after a while.

Taboos include confrontation and topics such as corruption, foreign aid, religion and poverty. Public criticism of any person must be avoided. Gift giving is fairly common, but one is not allowed to accept a gift (or any other service) without first refusing it twice.

How to empathise with Filipinos

As Asians, Filipinos expect modesty, gentleness and courtesy. Because of their Spanish influence, they expect warmth, respect and close personal relations. Try to make them like you – if they do, then price, although still important, becomes secondary.

Adapt to their time concept – they will not change it. Show respect for their education and qualifications, connections and personality. Be very polite to all senior people. Above all, ask continually about their family and their well-being.

Speak calmly, sensitively and in a low voice. Shake hands briefly and without too much firmness or energy. When criticising, praise other things at the same time. Leaving something unsaid can also be a subtle way of indicating mild disapproval. Take an interest in Filipino culture and language. Always be professional in look, manner and competence: they expect it.

45

VIETNAM

EVEN THOUGH IT HAS BEEN DEVASTATED BY WARFARE AND ECONOMIC chaos, Vietnam must ultimately emerge as a major player in the South-East Asian region. Its substantial land area of 330,000 sq km (considerably bigger than Italy or the UK) is occupied by 75 million hard-working, frugal, relatively well-educated people. It is the 13th most populous nation in the world and is also arguably the most schizophrenic. The densely inhabited areas of the Red River Delta in the north and the Mekong Delta in the south are not only 1500 km apart, but are separated by a slender bottleneck of mountainous terrain where it is difficult to obtain anything beyond life's basic necessities, mobility is minimal and English is rarely spoken.

Two very different Vietnams have existed for centuries. Chinese colonisation of the country from 208BC to 939AD left behind it a neo-Confucian *yang* subsystem that has persisted in the north up to the present. The more free-wheeling, commercially minded south was always the bastion of *yin* reaction – more open villages, more tolerant of individual initiatives and cultural heterodoxy. The *yang* concept was embedded in age-old Vietnamese traditions, expounding Confucianism, order and discipline, male dominance, common welfare, replication of uniformity. The *yin* concept was directly opposed: Taoism, Buddhism and Catholicism being more liberal, supporting freedom rather than excessive discipline, individual rights against collectivism, organisation of diversity against uniformity and promoting women as influential members of society.

The *yin–yang* struggle was launched with the flourishing of Buddhism and the founding of a national university (1076) and was fought passionately in the nineteenth century between the national bureaucracy, organised around the 'closed village' system (easy to control), on the one hand and an assortment of writers, intellectuals, women, Buddhist monks, teachers and would-be entrepreneurs on the other. From 1932 Vietnam consciously and vigorously strove to create a viable modern identity. The first part of the twentieth century witnessed an extreme case of social conflict over the setting of the *yin–yang* thermostat; it is easy to forget that the Vietnam war was fought mainly by Vietnamese against other Vietnamese.

Vietnam lost ground, economically and politically, due to 30 years of war and its struggles with the French. Its neighbours progressed greatly during this time. Former premier Van Linh is seen as the 'Vietnamese Gorbachev', but democracy has never fared well in Vietnam. Today the Christians and Buddhist monks seek human rights and freedom of expression; a growing middle class seeks political freedoms; an entrepreneurial class (especially in the South) seeks accelerated economic reforms.

Currently the Vietnamese are trying to solve their problems by following the Chinese model rather than the Russian, i.e. to liberalise the economy as quickly as possible and encourage investment, while at the same time maintaining strict political control (communism).

Culture

Values

The following list of values and core beliefs straddles northern and southern concepts (still in the process of adaptation):

Confucian: work ethic, duty, morality   Respect for learning
Filial piety (pre-Chinese)   Theme of sacrifice
Resistance to foreigners   Resilience, tenacity
Nationalism   Restraint
Forbearance   Sense of proportion
Collectivist (society over individual)   Women play important role
Pride, self-respect (esp. North)   Entrepreneurism (esp. South)
Pro-Westernism

Concepts

Leadership and status

There is a tradition of collective leadership according to Confucian tenets. Currently leaders must possess a good war record and adhere to socialist thinking. Old Vietnamese society was organised along hierarchical feudal lines. Tribal chiefs – civil, religious and military – were often large landowners and controlled serfs. Power was hereditary. A *shogun*-like figure was usually 'king'.

Space and time

Vietnamese are a group-oriented society used to living and working in close proximity to each other. The Red River Delta, with over ten million inhabitants, is one of the most densely populated areas on earth. Nevertheless, the Vietnamese are not tactile.

Their sense of time, basically Asian and cyclic, has been affected by French and American influences, so that *mañana* tendencies observable in the Philippines and Indonesia are less of a problem in Vietnam.

Cultural factors in communication

Communication patterns and use of language

French influence is readily observable. Facial expression is much more evident than in, for instance, Japan, Korea or China, and some body language reminiscent of the French is to be seen. Emotional factors can be used in argument. Good education and a high rate of literacy lend people confidence in communication. The literary tradition is strong, particularly in poetry. People in the South tend to be more open and frank than many Asians (no doubt due to prolonged contact with the Americans).

Listening habits

Vietnamese are good listeners, expecting speakers to be clear and logical. They are well versed in French-style debate.

Behaviour at meetings and negotiations

In essence, the style is a combination of French rationality and Vietnamese tenacity. Although basically courteous, negotiations are cautious and give little away. The Vietnamese have no immediate trust for Chinese, Japanese or Westerners, being suspicious of all. The current relaxation of hostility to Americans is because they see the US as a political counterweight to China, as well as an economic counterweight to Japan. They are opening up to ASEAN countries for the same reasons.

Decision making is by consensus. Political (socialist) considerations have up to now dominated business, but the *doi moi* (renovation) process has done a great deal to liberalise the economy and to soften attitudes. Ideals of equality have been abandoned. Salary differentials have been vastly widened. Bureaucracy is, however, still tortuous and corrupt, according to most standards.

Manners and taboos

The age-old tradition of respect for the elderly is reflected in the leadership. Traditions (especially in the countryside and mountains) – adhering to totemism, animism, tattooing, chewing betel nuts and blackening of teeth – have little application to modern city life but indicate the cultural affinities of the Vietnamese to the Khmer and Melano-Indonesian peoples and stress the non-Chinese side of their culture. Music and the water puppet theatre are strong elements of folklore. Political dissension is, of course, currently taboo.

How to empathise with Vietnamese

Consider everything from the Vietnamese viewpoint – their long struggles against the Chinese, French and American 'invaders'; their duty and morality in resistance; the provocations they suffered at the hands of the Khmer Rouge; their current economic difficulties. Asians can probably handle them well, but should remember that they have some Western characteristics, including French rationality and emotive behaviour as well as occasional American free-wheeling traits.

Self-respect and loss of face are very much on their mind. They are not dealing from strength, but have great pride and will not be humiliated.

Their 'old men' must be deferred to and in any case are currently in control. They are always tenacious and only surrender anything with reluctance. One must always appear just in their eyes.

46

CHINA AND HONG KONG

CHINA IS NOT ONLY THE WORLD'S MOST POPULATED COUNTRY, IT ALSO boasts the planet's oldest civilisation – an agriculture-based society formed on the Yellow River 5000 years ago. During this long period – practically all of recorded human history – China, essentially an isolated country, cut off from other peoples by a vast ocean to the east, jungles to the south, towering mountain ranges to the west and freezing steppes to the north, has never formed a lasting, friendly relationship with a distant country. For two millennia the Chinese Empire was its own universe, sucking in Korea, Vietnam and other neighbours, while exacting tributes from others, including Japan. Its unbroken culture spread itself over many centuries throughout East Asia, where its influence is manifest in music, dance, paintings, religion, philosophy, architecture, theatre, societal structure and administration and, above all, language and literature.

Westerners who see China as a Third World, relatively backward nation in terms of crude technology, sparse infrastructure, appalling hygiene, rampant pollution, outdated politics and inadequate communication fall into the trap of misjudging, underestimating and misunderstanding the power and impact of the Chinese people on their neighbours and, in another sense, the world at large. China sees herself as *Chung-Kuo* – the middle kingdom, the centre of the universe and venue of the world's oldest lifestyle. A visitor from the Tang Dynasty (China's golden age) would see its legacy intact in the streets and fields of China today. The Chinese, a billion strong, see no diminishment of their moral authority – exercised with such power for thousands of years – and their sense of cultural superiority is greater than even that of the Japanese, whom they civilised. Foreigners in the eyes of Chinese are inferior, corrupt, decadent, disloyal and volatile, frequently hegemonistic, barbaric and, in essence, 'devils'.

Once you are fully aware how Chinese view you, you will find it easier to deal with them. They did not make these assumptions lightly. In the 'Opium Wars' between 1839 and 1860 Britain forced Bengal opium on the Chinese, annexed Hong Kong and claimed enclaves in several Chinese ports, including Shanghai. France, Germany and Russia soon followed the British, while the Japanese, imitating the West, smashed China in the war of 1894–5 and annexed Taiwan. This proved merely a prelude to a full-scale invasion of the mainland, followed by civil war after the Japanese withdrawal, culminating in victory for Mao's forces in 1949. The foreign 'devils' had to abandon their profitable ghettoes in Shanghai and other cities, leaving only Hong Kong in alien hands.

That xenophobia might be an understandable reaction to the events cited above can be readily perceived. Whether the Chinese actually possess cultural superiority over the rest of us is another matter. They believe they do. The numerous and magnificent spiritual and artistic achievements and accomplishments of Chinese civilisation do not go unrivalled in other parts of the world. While the brevity of the European occupation of the Americas might disqualify them from serious competition, the clear think-ing and spiritual values of the Ancient Greeks must put them in contention; the organising abilities and breadth of conquest of the Roman Empire matched the Chinese; above all the Italian Renaissance threw up artistic giants who might be considered to have equalled (or even surpassed) Chinese aesthetic masterpieces, whether in the field of music, painting, opera, dance or architecture. Leonardo, Michelangelo, Titian, Raphael, Verdi, Rossini and Dante are a hard act to beat.

The Chinese would not deny this. They are capable of expressing admi-ration for European artistic creation, *dans son genre*, just as they appreciate the efficiency of American, British and French political systems and tech-nological progress. Where they feel superior is in the area of moral and spiritual values. In as much as most nations feel that their norms are the correct ones – that their behaviour alone is truly exemplary – this is not surprising in itself. The Chinese, however, like the Russians and the Muslims, combine their sense of moral righteousness with fierce criticism of western societies. The large European nations of former imperial glory – Britain, France, Spain and Portugal – they see in decline, decay and spiritual disintegration. They see the American culture as having begun to decline before it reached its peak. The Japanese, once earnest students of Chinese philosophies and precepts, have succumbed to materialism and consumerism. Russia was never admired.

What are these superior Chinese values? They are not slow to tell you. They list them as follows:

modesty

tolerance

filial piety, courtesy, thrift

patience, respect for elderly

sincerity, loyalty, family closeness, tradition

trustworthiness, stoicism, tenacity, self-sacrifice, kindness

moderation, patriotism, asceticism, diligence, harmony towards all

resistance to corruption, learning, respect for hierarchy

generosity, adaptability, conscientiousness

sense of duty, pride (no losing face)

being undemanding, friendships

gratitude for favours

impartiality, purity

gentleness

wisdom

A westerner, ploughing through this list of self-ascribed values, might wonder about modesty and impartiality, but, in the main, the Chinese do go about their daily lives, especially at the individual level, exhibiting many of those characteristics. Whatever they might think of us, we can hardly fail to see them as hard-working, conscientious, patient, undemanding and thrifty. They seem generally to be in harmony with each other (good team members) and towards us they are usually courteous and compliant.

To understand why individual Chinese go about their affairs in an orderly, respectful fashion, we would do well to examine some of the basic tenets of their beliefs and philosophies. The most important influence is that of Confucianism.

Stability of society in China, according to Confucian views, is based on unequal relationships between people. This is almost diametrically opposed to British, American and Scandinavian ideas, but it is hardly questioned in China. The five relationships basic to ethical behaviour are:

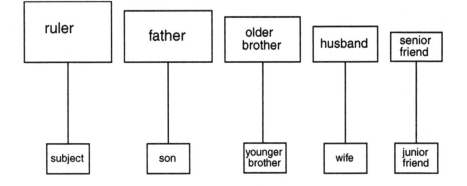

The Chinese believe that non-observation of these relationships is responsible for disorder, crime and lack of societal responsibility in many western countries, where only the husband–wife relationship (now threatened by frequent divorce) is generally adhered to, apart from occasional respect granted to a ruler here and there.

Unequal relationships do not simply imply unlimited advantages for the superiors. While their authority must not be questioned, their obligations are also mandatory. They must protect and exhibit kindness to those who show them obedience and allegiance. The basic teaching of Confucius can be summarised as:

+ The observance of the unequal relationships.
+ The family is the prototype of all social organisation. We are members of a group, not individuals.
+ One must behave in a virtuous manner towards others. Everbody's 'face' must be maintained.
+ Education and hard work must be prized.
+ One should be moderate in all things. Save, stay calm, avoid extremes, shun indulgence.

Confucianism exercises a strong influence on the daily lives and business cultures in China, Japan, Korea, Taiwan, Singapore, Hong Kong, and, to a lesser extent, other East Asian countries. Westerners wishing to deal with these Asians should take this into account and adapt accordingly.

The Chinese are also influenced by several other factors which do not feature in the western mindset. These are, among others:

- **Taoism** – insistence on healthy lifestyle, adequate vegetarianism, generosity of spirit.
- **Buddhism** – harmony through meditation.
- **Ancestor worship** – past figures strongly influencing present action.
- **Feng shui** – 'wind and water' superstition, affecting decisions on building and arrangement of furniture, mirrors and doors.
- **Herbal medicine and acupuncture** – frequently used and believed in.
- **Animal years** – giving an individual the qualities of the animal.

What might seem old-fashioned superstition to Europeans is present-day reality to the Chinese. If you were born in the year of the Horse, they will conclude you have stamina and they will not try to outlast you. If you are a Rat they will exercise great care in dealing with you, as you are smart, brave and clever. They may consider that you will be unlucky, as your office has two doors in a straight line, but their natural courtesy will make them refrain from telling you. They will agree in a compliant manner to most of your business proposals, especially if you show great keenness in making them. They wish to avoid a discordant note. They will let you wait half an hour at the bus stop rather than disappoint you with the news that the bus had left just before you arrived.

Collectivism is very strong in China. It originated in the early agrarian economies and is enhanced in the teachings of Confucius; it is not a product of Communism, although the Communist regime found it useful. A Chinese belongs to four basic groups in each of which he or she is, to some degree, a prisoner – the work unit (*danwei*), family, school and community. Their obligations to each group, from which they may not distance themselves, mean that they have virtually no social or geographic mobility. No westerner labours under such constraints, therefore finds it hard to understand to what extent a Chinese's hands may be tied when it comes to making a decision requiring sudden change or independence of action. Lack of mobility also gives the Chinese an added problem as to the question of losing face.

An American who lands in disgrace in New York can begin again next week in California. The Chinese who loses face may well have to guts it out for the next 40 years in the same community, workplace or academic environment. Neither do they just have one face to maintain. Their different social obligations (laid down by Confucius) force them to be many things to many people.

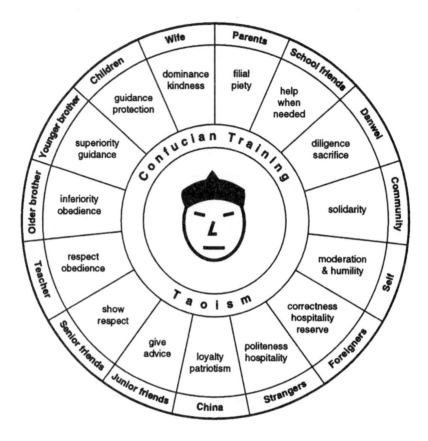

Traditionally the Chinese have been locked into the 'extended' family system where links between children and parents, uncles and aunts, cousins, grandchildren, husband's and wife's families and a host of distant relations both in China and overseas are much closer than anything we experience in the West. The 'networking' advantages of such a system are obvious, although the acute interdependence involved can cause considerable stress. Additional responsibilities towards school friends, teachers and neighbours increase the strain. Under the Communist regime it was, however, the individual's involvement with the '*danwei*' or work unit that pinned them down to the greatest degree. The relationship went much deeper than simply paying wages for a job done – the *danwei* solves disputes, administers government regulations, sees to housing, medical care, day care and kindergarten, arranges recreation, picnics and holiday homes, and makes funeral arrangements.

Americans, British and northern European people, unused to paternalistic companies or 'work units' and jealous of individual rights and privacy, abhor this type of group interference. Yet western insistence on individualism at all costs is blamed by the Chinese for their problems of crime, addiction and family breakdown. China is not alone among Asian nations in evolving an alternative philosophy – that of 'group rights', where the extended family is seen as more important than the individual. According to Confucius the individual owes as much to society as the other way round and, if these duties are scrupulously carried out, the resulting social cohesion, mutual protection of face and continuing harmony will lead to economic success.

This leads us to the question of human rights. Virtually all European countries see these as a prerequisite to other areas of development, while in the USA they are the bedrock of the constitution itself. There is nothing Americans hold more dear. China, in company with some other Asians, have a different set of priorities. 'Starving people are not in a position to exercise human rights' is the argument.

The West may well argue that after 5000 years of civilisation China should already be further along the road towards individual prosperity than she is today. Chinese answer that their late development is partly due to nineteenth-century western colonialism (look how Japan has prospered) and that with one billion persons speaking umpteen different dialects, group prosperity and cohesion are safer goals. Each nation shies away from the problems of its past history and takes steps to avoid their repetition. Russia, Poland and Finland fear invasion, Japan humiliation and nuclear bombs, Korea and the Baltic States foreign occupation, Mexico exploitation, Germany inflation and conflagration, America slump, China anarchy and foreign devils.

Chinese core beliefs and their consequences in business

Chinese people cannot adhere to their strong Confucian beliefs and other age-old traditions without their business culture being affected. Some of the consequences are listed below:

✦ Power distance is large. 4000 years of centralisation result in a tradition of obedience.

- ✦ Inequalities are expected and desired.
- ✦ Less powerful people should be dependent on the powerful who must protect them and take care of their careers and welfare.
- ✦ Parents, teachers, bosses, must all be obeyed.
- ✦ Age brings seniority.
- ✦ There is a wide salary range between the top and bottom of the organisation.
- ✦ The ideal boss is a benevolent autocrat.
- ✦ Privileges for managers are expected and popular.
- ✦ Subordinates expect to be told what to do.
- ✦ Individualism is taboo.
- ✦ Relationships are more important than tasks.
- ✦ Confrontation is avoided, harmony and consensus are ultimate goals.
- ✦ The search for virtue is more important than the search for truth. A and B can both be right if both are virtuous.
- ✦ Long-term orientation and goals.

Chinese behaviour at meetings and negotiations

- ✦ Chinese prefer meetings to be formal, although dress is usually comfortable.
- ✦ Seating will be according to hierarchy. Business cards are exchanged.
- ✦ The senior man must be shown great respect and attention at all times, even though he takes little part.
- ✦ The deputy or vicechairman is often the decision maker.
- ✦ The real decisions will be made outside the meeting, which is principally for information gathering.
- ✦ The pace will be slow and repetitious. The time frame is too long for westerners who may see the slow-down techniques as bargaining ploys.
- ✦ Politeness is observed at all times. Confrontation and loss of face (for both sides) must be avoided.
- ✦ Chinese rarely say 'no' – only hint at difficulties.
- ✦ A collective spirit prevails, nobody says 'I', only 'we'.
- ✦ In a collectivist culture, accountability for decisions is avoided. Authority is not passed downwards from the leaders.
- ✦ Decisions have a long-term orientation. Negotiations in China are important social occasions during which one fosters relationships and

Accountability

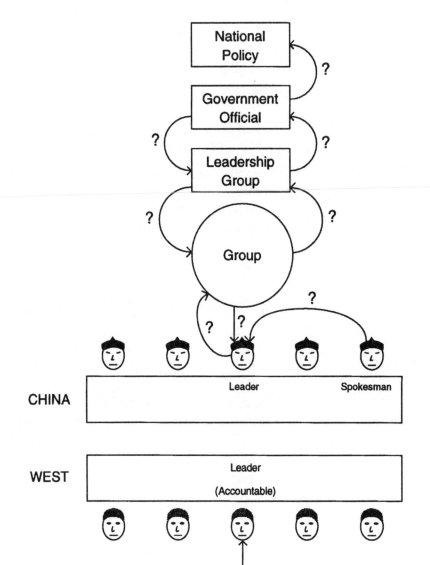

decides if the people on the other side of the table are suitable partners in the long run. The Chinese, who have been doing business for 4000 years, certainly are.

+ They consider you technically competent, otherwise inexperienced in business relations.

+ They negotiate step by step in an unhurried manner. They prefer to open proceedings with a discussion of general principles of mutual interest. That is probably enough for the first day. They dislike US eagerness to sign a contract.

+ Deal-oriented Americans and many Europeans agree to perform specific tasks over an agreed period of time. Chinese, looking beyond the deal, prioritise mutual trust in the long term.

+ They are thrifty, cautious, patient. You will have to match their patience and stamina, otherwise deals and opportunities will be lost.

+ They combine flexibility with firmness and expect both these qualities in you.

+ Once they have decided who, what, when and how is best, they are very trustworthy.

+ They know the size of their market and use this in their pricing strategy.

Etiquette

Chinese are basically very welcoming people who extend generous hospitality and courtesy both to Asians and 'barbarians'. Sit-down dinners are the norm, usually lasting about two hours and ended by the host standing up. On these occasions you should try all the delicacies put in front of you by your host, without actually leaving any dish empty. Protocol is easygoing. Chinese slurp and make all sorts of noises when eating, they also indulge in smoking at the table and have been known to spit on the floor. You are unlikely to disgrace yourself unless you are particularly inept with chopsticks, handle food with your fingers – or insist on paying the bill before your host has the chance to do so.

As far as meetings are concerned it is often necessary to make appointments one or two weeks in advance with officials, only a day or so with entrepreneurs and acquaintances. You should turn up on time. Individual Chinese often arrive 15 minutes early and say they can finish the business before the meeting was scheduled to begin, so as not to waste your time.

You need not take punctuality to these lengths but you should not be late.

When saying farewell, Chinese mention their imminent departure early on in the meeting, as opposed to westerners who delay it till just before leaving. A Chinese prolongs the farewell on the street, perhaps accompanying you part of your way.

Guanxi and gift giving

Guanxi means the linking of two people in a relationship of mutual dependence. It involves reciprocal gifts and favours. While this is a charming custom, it can also be fraught with danger as the recipient of an usually expensive gift will almost certainly be asked shortly for a huge personal favour. It may well compromise a business situation and cause embarrassment to those who are closely restricted by their companies in the area of discounts, arbitrary pricing, etc.

Humility

Courtesy in China also involves excessive humility and self-disparagement. All good Asians are self-effacing, but Chinese take it to ridiculous lengths. You may try to fit into the picture by being a good listener, using deference and understatement in your replies, never mentioning your impressive business or academic qualifications, and trying to get in the back row when someone takes a photograph.

The twenty-first century, the People's Republic of China and you

Asians are destined to be world leaders in industrial, economic and trade growth in the twenty-first century. China with her mammoth population and land area will be the dominant force in the region. Japan will also be a major player, but China has 10 times Japan's population and 25 times its land area. Breathtaking development and growth in China are only a question of time – the West would be wise to start establishing meaningful and durable links and relationships **now** while the Chinese currency is relatively weak and investment is cheap.

The return on investment, provided it is long term, may well be staggering. One should foresee the biggest economic development in world history. What happened in Japan between 1954 and 1990 is bound to happen in China, but on an unimaginably greater scale. Forecasts indicate that average production per head in China will rise from $350 at the beginning of 1992 to $12,000 in 2050. A country with a GDP of $10,000 billion a year will be the world's biggest market and possibly leading exporter. Americans, Europeans and other Asians will compete ferociously to sell into that market.

How can one go about establishing one's position and image in Chinese eyes? Policy and direction taking must be long term, otherwise one wastes one's time on relatively unimportant ventures. Westerners should bear in mind the following factors:

+ You are dealing with people who place values and principles above money and expediency.
+ The Chinese will not stray from their reverence of Confucian views on order, family and consensus. Show unqualified respect for these.
+ The Chinese see their language not only as a cultural tool which has historically influenced Japan, Korea, Indo-China and other areas, but as a repository for transmitting cultural values. The undisputed link between language and culture gives them a strong motive to increase the currency of the Chinese language, at least on a regional basis. You would do well to have one or two individuals in your company or organisation develop reasonable fluency in Chinese.
+ Britain in particular has long experience in China and many connections in East Asia. Chinese also react favourably to Nordic calmness, German technology and French *savoir faire*. Europeans should study Buddhist and Confucian behaviour and show compassion for Chinese difficulties. It will pay off.
+ Final golden rules – be extremely deferential at all times, combine courtesy with firmness, show humility and respect for age and rank, don't overdo the logic, prepare your meetings in detail, don't speak in a loud voice or rush them, know your Chinese history, always keep your calm and remember that patience and allowing adequate time for reflection are the keys to making progress, however slow it may seem.

Hong Kong

Hong Kong was acquired by the British government by way of a 99-year lease from China which expired in 1997. The seventh biggest port in the world, its historic function was to serve as an *entrepôt* for trade between China and western countries. In this role it developed successfully up to the Second World War, but when, in 1950–1, the United Nations placed an embargo on trade with China and North Korea during the Korean War, Hong Kong could no longer survive on trade alone. The colony was forced to change from a trading to an industrial economy; rapid developments were effected in garment and textile industries, electronics, shipbuilding, steel rolling, cement manufacture, aluminium extrusion, and a variety of light products from toys and wigs to plastic flowers.

From the very beginning Hong Kong had a clear *raison d'être* – to make money. It certainly succeeded. In the absence of any significant natural resources, Hong Kong's wealth, like that of Singapore, Japan and Korea, is created by its one asset – industrious people. In this case 99 per cent of them are Chinese, about half of whom immigrated from the neighbouring Chinese provinces of Kwangtung and Fukien. The other half are native Hong Kongers. The dominant Chinese dialect in Hong Kong is Cantonese – quite different from Mandarin.

The major non-Chinese elements in the population are from Britain and the Commonwealth, the USA, Portugal and Japan. As in the case of Singapore, the combination of western commercial knowhow and eastern diligence has produced several decades of impressive productivity and prosperity.

The seemingly unending boom has been facilitated by several factors. Although China coveted its 'South Gate', the colony functioned as an excellent point of contact with the West, even at the most critical periods of the Cold War. Trade between Hong Kong and China flourished. In 1994 China exported $72 billion worth of goods. Of these 45 per cent went to or through Hong Kong which, in turn, sent 30 per cent of its exports to China.

Hong Kong is valuable to China as a conduit for trade, investment and technology transfer. Its existence enables China to trade extensively with two other Tigers – Taiwan and South Korea – without having to compromise her political stance. Western confidence in the ability to continue trading strongly in the area after 1997 is reflected in the rising value of real estate, the frenetic construction in both Hong Kong and Shenzen and the increasing number of foreign companies actually entering Hong Kong. There are more than 500 American trading companies doing business with China from Hong Kong and Kowloon.

Hong Kong is many things that Singapore is not, and vice versa. Both Tigers take gold medals for industriousness, tenacity, risk taking and efficiency. Both have made their fortunes by shrewdly combining strengths from East and West. Both populations are predominantly Chinese, who have demonstrated their infinite potential and talent, given the right conditions for development. After that the comparison becomes more of a striking contrast.

Hong Kong has expensive housing, high salaries and job mobility, little red tape, no inhibitions and people who live from deal to deal. Singapore, in contrast, has cheap housing, moderate salaries and job stability, strict regulations, decorum and long-term planning. Opinions vary, among both westerners and Orientals, about which is the better place to live and work. Singapore impresses with its discipline, racial tolerance and successful multiculturalism. Westerners frown on the direct control exercised by parliament over 600 companies, but admire the overall efficiency and honesty of conduct. Hong Kong dazzles you with sheer, unbridled energy, single-mindedness and pluralism. It is interesting to note that, although Hong Kong is 99 per cent Chinese, Singapore generally enjoyed better relations with China than the former colony did. China finds pluralism hard to understand; Singapore speaks with one voice – a more traditional oriental practice. Moreover, the voice is in Mandarin, better accepted in Beijing than singsong Cantonese!

There is naturally a questionmark against Hong Kong's future. The reincorporation of a 99-year-old British colony into a motherland possessing 5000 years of unbroken heritage is truly a collision of cultures, in spite of racial commonalities. Communication styles and listening patterns are far apart.

Hong Kong, with entrepreneurism in its blood, sense of urgency, driving always in the fast lane, stands in close comparison to the bustling USA. It remains to be seen what the cultural collision with the bureaucratic motherland will produce, although China has done little to interfere with the East–West flow of business since devolution.

Communication patterns

People's Republic of China

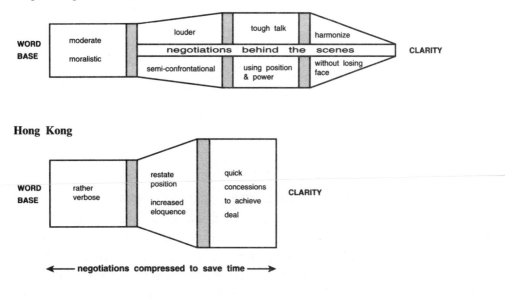

Hong Kong

WORD BASE — rather verbose — restate position, increased eloquence — quick concessions to achieve deal — CLARITY

← negotiations compressed to save time →

Listening habits

People's Republic of China

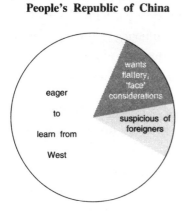

Hong Kong

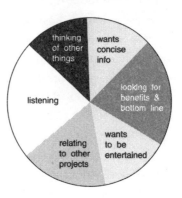

47

KOREA

KOREA IS THE ONLY (OFFICIALLY) STILL DIVIDED COUNTRY IN THE WORLD. Both Koreas are armed, dangerous and technically at war. This chapter focuses principally on South Korea (often referred to as the ROK), but in terms of deep-rooted culture all Koreans are the same. Differences in the political structure between the communist North and capitalist South have, since 1945, obliged North and South Koreans to lead very different lives, but the Korean core beliefs of *kibun, hahn*, Confucianism, tenacity and obsession with survival dominate thinking on both sides of the border and distinguish Koreans strongly from their Chinese and Japanese neighbours.

Korea will eventually be reunified and when that happens the combined population of more than 70 million will put it on a par with Vietnam and increase its clout in East Asia. South Korea's influence is already remarkable. On a limited land area less than half the size of the UK, South Koreans have built the third-largest economy in Asia, based on low-cost, high-quality export production. Its GDP (1999) of nearly US$500 billion dwarfs those of the three other Asian Tigers – Taiwan (US$260billion), Hong Kong (US$142 billion) and Singapore (US$85 billion). South Korea is the 13th largest trading economy in the world and actually grew at an average rate of more than 15 per cent between 1960 and 1995!

The South Korean miracle is beginning to show signs of both maturity and age and is changing the focus of its economy from low-cost, low-technology production to high-tech, high-value-added, capital-intensive products. The strength of ROK's large conglomerates (the *chaebols*) and the industriousness of its businesspeople and workers suggest that it will successfully make the transition to a new economy appropriate to twenty-first century conditions.

On account of its proximity to China, Korea has been, and still is, strongly influenced by the teaching of Confucius. A description of the basic tenets of Confucianism is given in the chapter on China. *Hahn* is something different and more peculiarly Korean. This is the word used to describe the pent-up energies and frustrations that developed in the Korean psyche under conditions of extreme hardship and oppression. We must remember that Japan occupied Korea from 1895–1945 and the Korean War of 1950–53 caused unimaginable suffering throughout the peninsula. *Hahn*, which stems not only from foreign occupation but also from social immobility, sexual discrimination, family vendettas and abject poverty, has translated into extreme nationalism, release of energy and in the end to Korean prosperity.

Kibun, roughly translated as 'face' or 'reputation', is a more sensitive issue in Korea than perhaps anywhere else in the world. For a Korean, *kibun* is an intuitive feeling for social balance and correct behaviour. Koreans are able to deal even with people they dislike under a veneer of courtesy and benignity. Foreign people dealing with them can easily be fooled into thinking that Koreans are easy going and good natured.

The chaebols

The *chaebol* in Korea is the rough equivalent of the *keiretsu* or former *zaibatsu* in Japan. It is a conglomerate of a dozen or more companies owned by or closely linked to a prominent family. Personal and family connections are extremely important in Korea, where clans are seen as bastions against the outside world. The very size of the *chaebol* in modern Korea has necessitated the employment of a large class of well-educated professional managers. Even they, however, generally have close personal ties with the owning family.

Foreigners working with Koreans do well if they can cultivate good relationships within Korean power structures. This is difficult to do and third-party introductions are both advisable and necessary.

Culture

Values

Confucian ethic	Protection of *kibun* (inner feelings)
Vertical society	Respect for elders

Observance of protocol	Competitive spirit
Toughness	Obsession with survival
Creativity	Adaptability
Tendency to violence	Suspicion of neighbours (China, Japan)
Tenacity	Dislike of foreigners in general (*hahn*)
Nationalism	Willingness to suffer hardship for the good of the country

Concepts

Leadership and status

Leadership is Confucian in essence, but the importance, influence and power of certain families are more in evidence than in Japan and China. Power, once acquired, is not easily conceded and the history of violence between the authorities and the people is top down in Korea, as opposed to frequently being bottom up in Japan. Family name, wealth and the power of the *chaebols* decide status.

Space and time

Korea is a crowded country and space, especially in the big cities, is at a premium. Koreans are used to working close to each other, but require clearly defined personal space in formal situations. They are non-tactile. Koreans are very hard working (they try to outperform the Japanese) and rarely waste time. They are relatively punctual and have an American-like attitude to packing as much action as they can into a given time period.

Cultural factors in communication

Communication patterns and use of language

Koreans are energetic conversationalists, very intense when serious, occasionally displaying Western-style humour when trying to charm. In Korea truth is elastic.

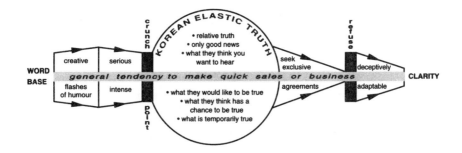

Listening habits

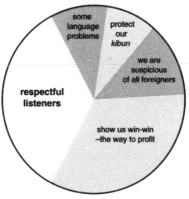

Koreans are courteous listeners in true Asian style, but often give the impression that they know in advance what you are going to tell them.

Behaviour at meetings and negotiations

It can be more difficult to create a lasting agreement with quick-moving Koreans than with the highly structured Japanese or bureaucratic PRC officials. Historically, their collective experience is that compromise leads to defeat, second place spells disaster. This makes them extremely competitive and continually on the look-out for further advantage. This is annoying to the Westerner who is trying to negotiate a win–win situation.

Negative aspects of doing business with Koreans include the following:

✦ Deception: they will tell you this or this has been done, while not actually doing anything.

✦ When they wish you to withdraw from a deal (to leave them in sole charge) they often create difficulties for your staying with it. These difficulties can sometimes be arranged with official or government compliance.

✦ They show foreigners a good time and send them home happy, but fail to implement the agreement signed in the cordial atmosphere that they create.

+ They often seek long-term, exclusive agreements. It is better to sign agreements for the short term based on Korean performance!
+ Koreans often break a relationship suddenly if they find a better deal elsewhere.
+ Knowledge is power – they tend to keep it to themselves.
+ If selling to you, they may let quality fall if they get bigger orders elsewhere.
+ When buying, they tend to look at price rather than the useful life of your product.
+ They prefer quick sales to development of solid business relations. (This is due to Korea's chronic instability, historically.)

Positive aspects of dealing with Koreans include:

+ They are willing to experiment and take risks.
+ They hustle and bustle.
+ They are creative and show initiative.
+ They are accessible.
+ They are adaptable and amenable to last-minute changes.

Manners and taboos

Protocol is extremely important. If you fail to give a Korean the respect due to his rank or status, he will withdraw and avoid you in the future. If you fail to observe the basic rules of social exchange in Korea, you become an 'unperson' and Koreans will henceforth have no concern for your welfare. They can be violent to 'unpersons'. Foreigners, unless showing constant and proper respect, are quickly relegated to 'unperson' status – although politeness will be maintained.

Touching another person is an affront. Businessmen now shake hands to show that they are modernised, but often bow at the same time. They sometimes become more affectionate after a few drinks, but usually apologise for being drunk (the same evening and again the next day).

Punctuality is less important than in China or Japan. When in their office or in contemplation, Koreans build imaginary walls round themselves, then take off for a time. You can break through this wall by coughing discreetly at a distance of three to five metres.

They don't introduce others formally but say to strangers 'I am seeing you for the first time'. The elder then suggests introducing, whereupon both mumble names unclearly and exchange cards. Koreans avoid calling each other by name, preferring titles.

Table manners include serving the guest, slurping soup, smacking lips and belching heartily to show appreciation of the meal.

How to empathise with Koreans

Koreans consider themselves very different from the Chinese and Japanese and due respect must be paid to their long history, artistic riches and national uniqueness. They believe that they can handle westerners better than other Asians. Your reactions should be willingness to go along with their ideas, sharing humour with them whenever possible, but maintaining a firm, pragmatic stance at all times. They respect toughness; they will exploit gullibility.

Pay great attention to protecting their *kibun* – loss of face in Korea is more serious than anything else. Do not overemphasise your Japanese connections and do not refer to the Korean language as an offshoot of Japanese.

48

JAPAN

THE JAPANESE ARE CULTURALLY VERY DIFFERENT, THEIR UNIQUENESS probably deriving in the main from three principal factors: their history of isolation; the crowded conditions imposed by their geography; and the Japanese language itself.

Isolation

Although Japan for many centuries had a close cultural connection with China, the period of autocratic Tokugawa rule beginning in 1603 led to almost complete isolation from the rest of the world until the advent of Commander Perry of the USA in 1853. For 250 years Japan, cut off from foreign stimulus, developed a distinct society and culture which has no equal in terms of group cooperation. The main organisational features developed in this closed period remain characteristic of Japanese society today in spite of the evident changes occurring in the twentieth century. Packed together in large numbers in big cities they developed complex social skills which led to the phenomenon known as the 'web society'.

A web society

A web society is one where there is great interdependence between all members of a group and an abundance of moral and social obligations, both vertically and horizontally. It all begins at birth. Whereas western babies are soon separated from their mothers and put in a room of their own, Japanese children are kept close to their parents' side day and night, for two or three years. Western children quickly develop an intitiative of their own and gain early experience in problem solving. Japanese children, by contrast, are encouraged to be completely dependent on human beings close to them and develop a sense of interdependence which stays with them throughout life. They can demand favours from people in their group and these have to be granted. Their first 'group' is the family, but later it becomes high school, then university, then the company. Age and seniority have their priorities, but also their obligations. The Japanese language has separate words for elder brother and younger brother etc., since the duties of one to the other are different and must be sharply defined. Protection can be demanded from those who have 'gone before'. Section leaders will unashamedly demand promotion for mediocre employees in their section, simply because they are under their wing and have remained loyal. It is almost impossible for a general manager to resist these demands.

The 'web society' structure brings advantage to the Japanese businessperson in terms of what many westerners today call 'networking'. Japanese, although great respecters of privacy, are very gregarious in business situations. Consequently the 'spider's web' of which they are part provides them with a unrivalled high context information network.

The Japanese language

Japanese behaviour is also strongly affected by the nature of the language. According to the Benjamin Whorf theory, the language we speak largely determines our way of thinking. The Japanese themselves use language in a completely different way from the rest of us. Japanese is often described as a vague or ambiguous language. For instance, the verbs are impersonal, so often you do not know who is being referred to. This vagueness is frequently used on purpose by Japanese conversants who wish to absolve anyone of possible blame and demonstrate politeness. The well-known honorific terms in Japanese enhance this politeness, while often adding to the vagueness. Long indirect clauses usually precede the main statement. Everything must be placed in context in Japan, therefore, blunt language is too brief and out of place. No Japanese boss would say 'Tidy up the office.'

They are obliged to say to their subordinates, 'As we have some important visitors coming at 12 o'clock and since we wish them to get the best impression of our company, perhaps we could improve the orderliness around here.' Another way in which the language reflects the society is that there is no reported speech mechanism in Japanese. Japanese people do not like to report other people's statements, as failure to be accurate could result in embarrassment or injustice. My secretary in Japan always refused to describe the contents of telephone calls made in my absence and invariably asked me to ring back the caller to get the message.

Japanese business climate and practices

The Japanese is therefore conditioned by exceptional historical and geographical constraints as well as by their thought processes in a language very different from any other. How does this affect foreign businesspeople dealing with them? Let us consider a few well-known eastern phenomena.

At the beginning there is the first meeting. Japanese, unlike westerners, do not like meeting newcomers. In their own web society Japanese executives know exactly the manner they should use to address superior, inferior or equal. Americans who stride across the room and pump their hand are a source of great embarrassment to them. First, unless they have been properly introduced, they are unable to define their stance. Secondly, it is likely that westerners will initiate a person-to-person exchange of views, which poses an even greater danger to the Japanese. They represent their group, therefore cannot pronounce on any matters there and then without consultation. The exchange of visiting cards is a familiar ceremony in Japan, although the information gained from these will be insufficient without prior knowledge.

Westerners are individuals, but the Japanese represent a company, which is part of a group, which in turn represents Japan. In these circumstances, how can they deal face to face, alone? Westerners show their priorities on introducing themselves – 'My name is Bill Robinson, Export Manager, Threadwell Textiles Inc.' The Japanese replies, 'Mitsubishi's General Affairs Section, Assistant Manager, Yamamoto I am' (putting things in the correct order).

Westerners often complain that on six visits to a company they will be met by 18 different people in groups of 3 and will have to say the same thing six times. This is time-consuming, but necessary for the Japanese, as all the members of the group have to become acquainted with them.

After this ordeal, Westerners often press for a quick decision. They will not get one. If they impose a time limit, the Japanese will back out quietly.

Losing face

As we all know, orientals do not like to lose face. I had a striking example of this during my first week in Japan when a colleague and I were negotiating for the lease of a building. After some trouble we had secured an appointment with the president of the company which owned the building and he – a 70-year-old man – spoke for half an hour (through an interpreter), explaining the merits and high reputation of the building, terminating his remarks with the price for the rental. It seemed a little on the high side to me; my colleague, who had been brought up in an Arab country, promptly offered him half. The elderly President and the interpreter immediately rose to their feet, smiled and bowed simultaneously and left the room. We never saw them again.

Japanese politeness

The Japanese do in fact negotiate, but not in the Arab manner. Face must not be lost and politeness must be maintained at all times. The Japanese go to incredible lengths to be polite. I was once having dinner at the home of a very elegant Japanese lady in the seaside resort of Atami. The dinner party consisted of about 16 people – Japanese, British and American. In the middle of the main course the phone rang and our hostess went to answer it. She spoke Japanese, which most of us understood, and we listened idly to what she said. Someone was obviously asking her about property prices in Atami, for she indicated what she had paid for her villa, how prices increased as you went up the slope and how they decreased if you went too far up or too far to the left hand side. She discussed inflation and the advantages of investing in property, as well as the general state of the property market in Japan and in Atami in particular. She was a knowledgeable woman and the call took 10 minutes. Finally, with a lot of bowing on the phone she concluded the conversation and hurried back to the table with her apologies to the guests. 'Who was that?' asked one of her friends. 'Wrong number,' she replied.

Japanese politeness can take many strange forms. Their reluctance to say 'no' is well-known. If you say to a Japanese 'I want you to lend me a hundred dollars,' they will say 'yes', without actually offering the money. What they mean is, 'Yes, you want me to lend you a hundred dollars.' If they do not wish to enter into a deal with a foreign partner, they will not come out with a negative reply. However, you will not be able to get in touch with your contact in that company thereafter. He or she will always be ill, on holiday or attending a funeral.

A German sales executive spoke to me recently about the behaviour of a Japanese company president into whose office he had penetrated after months of trying. He had been told he had only 10 minutes to deliver his presentation and he did this in good English. The Japanese closed his eyes after the first minute and kept them closed for the rest of the time. The German asked me if this was impolite or had the company president actually fallen asleep? I had to reassure him that this was the Japanese way of indicating that he was listening intently to what was being said.

Another incident illustrating Japanese politeness occurred once during a course I taught in a British university. Three of us had invited Mr Suzuki out to dinner and we arranged to meet him at eight o'clock in the Common Room Bar. Knowing he was rather formal, we had all put suits on. Entering the bar, we saw him at a distance in a casual shirt and slacks. We quickly exited before he saw us and went back to our rooms to change into casual attire. We rushed back to the bar, where Mr Suzuki stood awaiting us in his best blue suit (he had caught a glimpse of us).

Japanese negotiating characteristics

+ The first person you contact in a Japanese company (or who contacted you) will be present throughout the negotiating period.
+ Japanese normally negotiate in teams, each member of which has a different speciality.
+ The members of the team may change or be increased, as the Japanese wish as many members of their company as possible to get to know you.

- They usually outnumber opposing teams.
- There will be a senior staff member present who will dictate tactics, but he is rarely the one who does the talking. Each member will ask questions within the field of his or her competence, using the best linguist as the interpreter.
- Their questions constitute an information-gathering process. They are not about to make a decision on hearing your answers.
- Their decisions will eventually be made by consensus, therefore no person will display any individuality. They use the name of their company or 'we' – never 'I'.
- However strong the team, they will have to refer back to head office. Therefore no decision will be made at the first meeting and probably not at the second.
- New faces almost invariably appear at the second meeting, as someone in head office will have requested a 'second opinion'.
- The second meeting tends to go over the same ground as the first, but the questions will be in more depth.
- The Japanese negotiators bring their company's position to the table with little authority to change it. Therefore there is little flexibility.
- Flexibility is more evident between meetings, when they have checked with head office.
- Japanese are willing to go over the same information many times to avoid later misunderstandings and achieve clarity, although the ambiguities of their own speech style often leave westerners far from clear on their intentions.
- They are cautious, skilled in stalling tactics, won't be rushed. They need time to reach their consensus.
- Their decisions are long term, e.g. Do we want these people as partners in the future? Do we trust them? Is this the right direction for the company to be heading? Big decisions take time. They see American negotiators as technicians making a series of small decisions speedily to expedite one (perhaps relatively unimportant) 'deal'.
- Once the Japanese company has made its decision, the negotiating team then expects quick action and many criticise the partner if there is a delay.
- Japanese negotiators are invariably polite, understanding of others' problems and good listeners.

- ✦ They will break off negotiations if the other side is too blunt, impatient or fails to observe protocol.
- ✦ They must never lose face. If insufficient respect is shown or if they are cornered by ruthless logic, there will be no deal.
- ✦ If great respect and very reasonable demands are shown, they are capable of modifying their own demands greatly.
- ✦ They go to great lengths to preserve harmony throughout the negotiations. They strive to bring the two 'respectable' companies closer together. They are happy to socialise in between meetings.
- ✦ They never say 'no', never refute entirely another's argument, never break off negotiations as long as harmony prevails. This leaves them room for renegotiation some time in the future if circumstances change.
- ✦ They will cancel a meeting if they think the conditions on which it was set up have changed.
- ✦ They will show exaggerated respect to your senior negotiator and expect you to do the same to theirs.
- ✦ They will sometimes bring to the meeting a very senior person (e.g. former minister) who is only a consultant to the company, but commands (your) respect and deference.
- ✦ They will use a middleman or go-between if they can find one. After all, if both sides trust him, then there must be harmony.
- ✦ Negotiating style will be non-individualistic, impersonal and unemotional, but emotion is important (it is just under the surface). Logic and intellectual argument alone cannot sway Japanese. They must like you and trust you wholeheartedly, otherwise no deal!

The company is sacred

We all know that in Japan the company is sacred. Once employees are accepted, they show complete loyalty to the company and there is no clear dividing line between life and job. Their loyalty is rewarded by lifetime employment and regular promotion. They steadily climb the ladder in a vertical society and are completely satisfied with their status on every rung. Their fidelity and long hours will guarantee them promotion to important positions, whether they are intelligent or effective or not. This often leads to problems in companies which are anxious to make good profits.

Japanese success

Why have Japanese companies been so successful in the last few decades? This is a question often asked by westerners to which there is no single answer. Hard work, good education, unpaid overtime and short holidays all play their part. But if there is one key to Japanese success it is their ability to conduct a company's internal affairs in a spirit of harmony and cooperation. Americans and Europeans seem to have more energy as individuals, but often are pulling in different directions within a company. There is certainly submarine infighting in Japanese companies, but once unanimity of agreement has been reached (and the president insists on it) then everyone pulls the same way. Japanese will discuss and discuss until everybody agrees. They will not permit what they call the tyranny of the majority. Endless discussion often results in slow decisions, but the Japanese think the gain in solidarity is worth it. Results seem to show that they are right.

Tension

All this is not without its tension, since Japanese executives frequently have to submit, even if their ideas are good ones. One evening in Tokyo I was watching a boxing match on television for the Featherweight Championship of the World. Sitting next to me was a Japanese business friend of mine, Okada, who was eagerly supporting the Japanese boxer involved. It was a close fight and after 14 rounds both men were still on their feet. At this point Okada rushed out of the room. I watched the deciding 15th round, which was thrilling in the extreme, alone. A few minutes after the fight had finished, Okada came in again and asked me who had won. I told him. I also asked him why he had to dash out just before the last round. 'I couldn't stand the tension,' he replied. This incident serves to illustrate how two individuals sharing the same experience may react in different and surprising ways. Anyone observing Okada and myself during the fight would have said I was the more excited of the two. I, for my part, was quite unaware of the degree of his inner tension.

Complexes

A lot has been said about the Japanese having an inferiority complex and their readiness to imitate foreign models is usually quoted as an example of this. The Japanese seldom refute the accusation of being imitators and indeed Japanese company presidents have occasionally apologised to foreign firms who have shown them a new product for having copied and improved it and quickly put it on the market at half the price. The Japanese approach is strictly pragmatic. Why waste money on research and development if it has already been done? Their own contribution is improvement and higher productivity. A discussion on the Japanese inferiority complex can quickly lead to the opposite conclusion – that they have a superiority complex. This is reflected in their racist attitude to blacks and Indians and in periodic arrogance regarding their economic might. They are fully aware that they are second in the world in GNP, first in shipbuilding, first in longevity and probably first in their ability to save. Perhaps their feelings of superiority and inferiority might best be described as national self-consciousness. The pendulum seems to swing between frantic efforts to catch up with the West in technology and equally energetic assertations of national independence and true Japanese values.

Japanese translators

Their attitude to foreigners, even educated people and high-ranking businesspeople, is clear. You are always an outsider. Your efforts to speak Japanese will be smiled on, but seldom taken seriously. As many senior Japanese do not speak English, Japanese translators are often used. They can be unbelievably bad and seldom give real translations when Americans or Europeans wish to be blunt. Often the message, lost in an endless labyrinth of polite vagueness, will not get across at all. The translator in Japan has an unhappy lot. Usually they will be abused by westerners for not translating properly and criticised by their own superiors for being unclear. They are not really trusted anyway, as they speak two languages.

The language curtain

Japan exists behind a language curtain and is unfortunately unaware of her intellectual isolation. While millions of Japanese attempt to learn English, results are generally poor and consequently Japan's voice in the world is not heard to the extent which her economic might justifies. Few Japanese politicians have understood this problem, although business leaders are beginning to realise more and more the disadvantage they are at. One great barrier is the Chinese script, unfortunately adopted by the Japanese early in their history. This makes it extremely difficult for foreigners to learn Japanese and Japanese schoolchildren lose valuable time mastering two or three thousand complex characters, when they could be learning English.

Why don't the Japanese simply switch to the Roman alphabet? First, they would cut themselves off from their literature and calligraphic art. More important still, Japanese people are bound up emotionally with the visual aspect of the written characters. They have a kind of magic quality. A European text written in Roman characters can only be linear or factual. A complex Chinese character, with perhaps 10 or 15 strokes, conveys not only the meaning but has an aesthetic value. Visual aspects are important for the Japanese, as can be seen in their pretty ways of arranging food. Where westerners often imagine things in words, Japanese can imagine them visually. This is difficult to explain to anyone who has not studied written Japanese, but let me try to give you a practical example, which in fact has nothing to do with writing. You probably know that in most Japanese shops the attendants will calculate your purchases not on a calculator but on an abacus. They can do this extremely quickly and rarely make mistakes. What is astonishing is that when they do not have an abacus nearby they go through the motions on their open palm, look at it and tell you the amount. This always used to surprise me and once, out of interest, I challenged my local shopkeeper as to the accuracy of his calculation. He actually stared at his hand again and then looked at me and insisted he was correct. He even showed me his hand! The physical memory is in his fingers which have flicked the imaginary beads, just as it is in the fingers of an English typist who can imagine linear Romanic script by pretending to type certain words.

Japanese as seen by others

Appearance	Reality
They are aloof.	Extreme shyness makes it difficult for them to initiate conversation.
They are short on words.	True. Japanese distrust words. Also they may have poor command of the language you speak.
They deafen you with silence.	Silence shows respect for the speaker.
They often look glum.	In Japan, happiness hides behind a straight face.
When they smile, they don't look sincere.	Japanese often smile to make you feel comfortable. You should be thankful – if they don't like you a smile is still better than a scowl!
They say 'yes' when they mean 'no'.	They don't like to offend you by showing open disagreement or refusal.
We can never tell what they really thinking.	By generally keeping a straight face, Japanese are rather impassive. They are not trying to deceive you.
They never look you right in the eye.	Japanese are taught that it is rude to stare.
They sit up straight all the time and don't seem to relax in meetings.	Japanese don't like to slouch. Maintaining correct posture is polite.
They go to sleep during meetings.	Not often. When they close their eyes it means they are concentrating on what you are saying.
They delay in making decisions, don't answer letters and faxes when we press them.	They don't like to be rushed. They must complete their consensus.

Appearance	Reality
They never make decisions during meetings.	Japanese regard meetings as information-gathering sessions or occasions to state their position. They make decisions outside meetings, seeking the consensus of their colleagues.
They lack individualism and all behave the same way.	They prefer teamwork and group decisions to individualism. Homogeneity makes them act alike.
They talk Japanese during meetings so we can't understand them.	It is their language! Also they may find it difficult to concentrate for long periods in a foreign language.
They are often ambiguous. We are never quite sure what they mean.	Japanese is an ambiguous, vague language which carries over into the English translation. Also their language level may be low.
They delay in making an order for six months, then they expect you to deliver tomorrow!	Japanese companies tend to proceed with implementation while they await an order. That way they are never caught flat-footed.
Sometimes they don't seem interested in immediate profit. This is annoying to westerners.	Japanese shareholders do not press for dividends. They believe more in increasing market share, improving share price and eventually making capital gains. They think long term.
They often talk and act like 12-year olds.	General McArthur made the mistake of saying and believing this. The low language level gives this impression.

Appearance	Reality
They are tough negotiators, often refusing to change their position.	Tough negotiators are good ones! Japanese meet force with intransigence. But when treated with respect, they are often willing to modify their position considerably.
They don't like foreigners, believing they are a superior race.	It is true that Japanese people consider themselves unique, but they have often been willing to learn from others. In Japan they treat foreigners very well. Their hospitality is unsurpassed.
They don't mix easily with other nationalities.	Those Japanese who have had little contact with foreigners are often afraid to mix with them, as they feel they won't know how to behave.
They are noisy in groups and behave badly when abroad.	In Japan there are very strict rules on social behaviour. When abroad the relaxation of these rules tends to make them let their hair down and be boisterous. Also they tolerate alcohol badly.
They try to bribe westerners with gifts.	Not true. Gift giving is a tradition in Japan and applies also to foreign guests. You can reciprocate.
They do not always respect contracts, often asking for renegotiation after several months.	They respect oral contracts and the spirit in which they were made. They wish to renegotiate if market or other conditions have changed.

How to empathise with the Japanese

What advice should one give to a foreign businessperson who goes to Japan? First, restrict your body language. Do not wave your arms, do not touch people unnecessarily and above all do not put your arm round their shoulders as you pass through doorways. Do not report conversations you have had with Japanese to third parties unless it is clear that you may do so. Do not mention business for the first 15 minutes of any conversation unless the Japanese says '*Jitsu wa ne...*' which means 'the fact of the matter is...' Never address any Japanese businessman by his first name and never, never talk about the war. (Germans, on the other hand, like talking about the war.)

If you are dealing with a group of Japanese (and they usually come to see you in groups), address your remarks to the senior man and bow to him as low as he bows to you. You may talk about golf or ski jumping as much as you like, but do not tell jokes unless they are at your own expense and can easily be understood.

It is not a good idea to ask to see a Japanese home, since even important businesspeople often live in tiny apartments – a fact which causes them some embarrassment. They are quite happy to go to your home, however, since you are likely to have more space. Do not shake hands with them more than necessary as they regard this practice as unhygienic. On the other hand, you should always present your visiting card immediately at the first meeting.

It is essential to remember that a Japanese likes doing business in a harmonious atmosphere, therefore you should do nothing which reduces harmony. The Japanese rarely criticise each other or even third parties and never say 'no' directly. Excessive frankness is therefore usually out of place.

When dealing with a Japanese company which may superficially resemble your own, do not assume similarities that are not there. Japan has **modernised, not westernised**, and true similarities are mainly only technical. Don't assume that they mean the same as you do when they use words like 'leadership' or 'motivation'. They have something quite different in mind. Also 'machine' means sewing machine, 'green car' means first class railway carriage and 'Arbeit' means part-time work.

If there seem to be a lot of 'don'ts' with regard to your behaviour when dealing with the Japanese, there is also a list of 'dos'. Above all you should be modest and reserved. Bow if you can manage it and begin your conversation by asking about their families. It is quite correct to enthuse over the Japanese economic miracle, as well as their reputation for honesty and lavish hospitality. Another positive subject is the long unbroken history of Japan and its achievements in the arts.

It is also quite correct for you to apologise for your rudeness when you last met. Japanese always do this whether they were rude or not. What it means is that you speak in a disparaging manner about your unpunctuality or poor hospitality or any other personal defect you can think of. For instance, Japanese apologise regularly for having had a cold, having taken you to see a poor film, having given you a ride in their noisy car or having beaten your country at karate.

Finally, if you want to do business with the Japanese you must also try to look the part. Remember that normally all Japanese executives dress conservatively in blue or grey with a white shirt and dark tie. A Japanese businessman looks at you in a manner not unlike that of the Spaniard. He must like you and he must trust you, otherwise no deal. He likes people who are clean, well-dressed, not too hairy, not too young, modest and of quiet voice and above all, polite. You must also convince him that you are respectable. For a Japanese, respectability comprises a certain age and several of the qualities just mentioned above, but also a proven record in business, an absence of any doubtful partners or deals and evidence of unquestioned solvency. Many Japanese businesspeople will ask you openly at the first meeting who are your board of directors, what is the capital of the company, who your chief customers are and if you have a chairman's report to show them.

How to win friends and influence people from Japan

+ Treat them quietly.
+ Be ultra-polite at all times. This involves often standing up when you would normally sit down, perhaps bowing when you would shake hands and apologising several times for rudenesses you have not committed.
+ Entertain generously with splendid meals which you apologise for afterwards.
+ Never say 'no' or 'impossible' or 'we can't'.
+ If you disagree, just be silent.
+ Never corner them or make them lose face.
+ Open business discussions only after 20 minutes.

+ Flatter them a lot. They like it.
+ Give them your business card at the first meeting and show great respect for theirs. Put it on the table in front of you and look at it regularly during conversation.
+ Show great respect for their company.
+ Emphasise the size, age, wealth and reputation of your own company.
+ Don't tell jokes during business meetings. You may afterwards, they won't understand them anyway.
+ Remember that anything you say they take literally. Flippant remarks such as 'This is killing me' or 'you must be kidding' would be misconstrued.
+ Be less direct in your utterances that you would be with others. Remember the Japanese do not admire bluntness and strive at meetings to achieve 'harmony' on which they can build long-term relations.
+ What you say matters little to them. It's how you say it that counts. You must never hurt their feelings. Remember this and the business will probably come automatically. Show great respect for their 'leader' and/or anyone over 50 who is present.
+ Learn some Japanese and show you have an interest in their culture. Don't overdo it – they don't like foreigners who speak fast Japanese.
+ When speaking English (if this is your common language) speak slowly and distinctly. They smile and nod constantly but understand only 30 per cent of the time.
+ Be prepared to say everything five times at a succession of meetings and anything vital at least ten times.
+ They prefer oral agreements to written ones, so don't push documents at them until they are ready.
+ If they make an oral agreement, they will stick to it. They do not necessarily want to shake hands on it. A nod or slight bow is much better.
+ Try not to extract decisions from them at meetings. Remember they have to check with head office Tokyo.
+ Things are often agreed between meetings, so be prepared to talk business during socialising.
+ Imitate or adapt to their pace, manners and demeanour as much as possible, satisfy all their requirements and desires if you can. Meet them halfway in concessions and style, but remain yourself, as they probably respect your country's historical record, and way of life.
+ Find common ground when you can. They love sharing.

49

LATIN AMERICA

ONLY 500 YEARS HAVE PASSED SINCE THE BEGINNING OF THE IBERIAN conquest of South America – a mere blip in relation to the history of human activity there. It is clear, however, that the Hispanic-Portuguese arrival, devastating the indigenous cultures that preceded them and imposing their own civilisation, had a decisive impact on the moulding of Latin American life. But Latin Americans are not Spaniards or Portuguese. They are a distinctly separate breed and we should be remiss in our assessment of them if we were to ignore not only the bloodlines of some of their ancestors as well as their unique cultural achievements, but also the vast, inaccessible stretches of wild and savage terrain that for tens of millennia challenged and developed the pioneering migrating 'Indians' as they pressed inexorably southwards. The *porteño* (citizen of Buenos Aires) looks and feels as European as a Parisian or an Italian, and the city-dwellers of Santiago and Montevideo are rather similar – but beyond these enclaves, signs of the rich *mestizo* blend are in great evidence all the way from Tierra del Fuego to the Rio Grande.

Such a blending of races and ancestry, such an exciting mix of pioneers, adventurers and warriors, such a vast, wild exhilarating geographic environment, in a southern ocean setting of relative isolation (even in the twentieth century) produces a special human type with which Europeans are not yet fully familiar. 'Types' in the plural is more appropriate, since the twenty-odd republics of Latin America vary to a considerable degree in their world views and lifestyles, but there is a common quality distinguishing the Latin American from the rest of humanity. Their psychology is somewhat elusive, not easily defined or qualified, perhaps not yet fully exploited or applied.

When we attempt to define or evaluate a distinctive Latin American culture, it is inevitable that we take Hispanic traits as our starting point. The *conquistadores*, at least in the early years of conquest, ruthlessly imposed their own type of civilisation on the indigenous peoples. If the driving force of conquest was greed, it came disguised as a crusading faith – Catholicism – with the backing not only of the Pope and two Iberian monarchies, but with all the trappings of south-west Europe: merciless soldiering, bureaucratic impositions, taxes and levies, zealous missionaries, churches, schools, courts, even the Spanish Inquisition itself. The indigenous cultures were occasionally exploited (to seek allies) but in the main crushed, destroyed or, in the case of inaccessible terrains, ignored.

The Latin American displays Romanic-Mediterranean characteristics in no small degree: he (or she) is an emotional, exuberant Latin. The Hispanic qualities that the Spaniards inherited from their non-Roman conquerors were also imported into Central and South America in the cultural baggage of the *conquistadores*, many of whom came from Moor-influenced Andalucians and Extremadurans. *Machismo*, double truth, *mañana* tendencies and chauvinism are prominent among them.

The influence of the American Indian cultures causes Latin Americans to differ from their Spanish cousins. The invaders rapidly acquired the ability to adapt themselves to the strange and exotic environment of the Indians. They slept in hammocks, paddled canoes, smoked tobacco, ate maize and potatoes and married local women. They shared the Indians' attachment to the land; they were equally exhilarated by the vast expanses of the wild continent. Mingling with the natives, they acquired a deep and new understanding of human suffering that widened their world view and made them see exploitation from another angle. They learnt to resent European authority and felt the incongruity of the norms of an old society imposed on new lands and situations. Optimism, engendered by the limitless spaces and opportunities, joined hands with native fatalism. If one trusted in bountiful nature, all would end well.

Latin American characteristics

Trait	Origin
Love of space	Geographic
Optimism bordering on arrogance	and
Impatience with European caution	environmental
Isolationism	
Lack of international experience	
Rural habits	Indian
Attachment to the land	
Poor cooperation with authorities	
Sense of fatalism	
Periods of inactivity	
Understanding of human suffering	
Compassion	
Resentment against exploitation	
Fear of the unknown	
Indecisiveness	
Imitation	
Fatalism	Moorish
Machismo	(via
Mañana	*Conquistadores*)
View of women	
Crusaders	Hispanic
Idealism over materialism	
Art of conversation prized	
Feel culturally superior to North Americans	
Good grasp of human values	
Theatricality	
Catholicism	
Importance of status	
Human beings are more important than rules	*Conquistadores*
Little correlation between law and actual life	
Little aptitude for parliamentary rule	
Lack of internal discipline	

50

ARGENTINA

OF THE 18 INDEPENDENT REPUBLICS OF SPANISH AMERICA, ARGENTINA IS the largest, the richest, the most influential, arguably the most scenic and colourful, certainly the most enigmatic. With 2.8 million sq km of territory (the eighth largest in the world), gifted with enormous resources in the form of oil, minerals, gas, cotton, sugar, timber and tobacco, with pampas covered by a topsoil reputedly three to six metres deep capable of supporting 55 million head of cattle and 30 million sheep, with a 95 per cent literacy rate and an extremely sophisticated well-educated middle class concentrated in a strikingly beautiful and smoothly functioning capital of over 10 million people, Argentina still struggled in the 1990s to achieve a GDP barely superior to Belgium and a GDP per capita only a quarter of that of Denmark.

In 1936 Argentina was one of the wealthiest countries in the world, chasing a standard of living barely inferior to that of France. In the 30 years from 1945 to 1975 inflation averaged 30 per cent. In the mega-crisis of 1989–90 hyperinflation actually touched 5000 per cent, easing to 1350 per cent in 1990. In the same period Germany, Japan and Korea wrought economic miracles of an entirely different dimension. Why have the Argentinians, so intellectually brilliant and analytical, failed to realise their beckoning potential?

The factors are many and complex, although 40 years of political squabbling and glaring economic errors would seem to point the finger of blame at atrociously inefficient and corrupt government. But what of the Argentinians themselves?

While the demographic make-up of Argentina is a diverse mix of nationalities, the continuing dominant position of the capital Buenos Aires in Argentinian commerce means that international business partners will normally have to deal with *porteños* (inhabitants of the city) in their activities in or related to Argentina. Consequently, one must focus on the *porteño* mindset to enable one to deal successfully.

Values

To begin with one must examine the Argentinian national malaise, which is particularly evident in Buenos Aires. This somewhat melancholy phenomenon, which parallels national soul searching in the Netherlands and Norway, pervades *porteño* thought, leading to indecisiveness and over-analysis that is often mocked by other South Americans.

Cultural factors in communication

Manners and taboos

Buenos Aires reputedly has more psychiatrists per capita than anywhere else in the world. It is probable that the acute slipping in the standard of living has undermined people's confidence. To foreigners *porteños* are the kindest people on earth, but they admit that they are more testy among themselves, that they look down on their rural cousins and that they feel intellectually superior to all other Latin Americans who, in turn, call them arrogant.

The *porteño* is a compassionate human being with impeccable manners indoors and out. In restaurants he is quiet and on the street he is a considerate pedestrian and citizen. All pavements in Buenos Aires are flattened on pedestrian crossings to help people in wheelchairs, and water and orange juice are supplied free of charge when one orders a coffee. Waiters and taxi drivers, hotel staff and most people in public offices do their job efficiently and one does not see the 'chip on the shoulder' so common among poorly paid people in southern Europe. One can score points by reciprocating courtesies with *porteños*, though one has to make allowances for their idiosyncrasies. They are extremely sentimental, emotion often creeping into business dealings.

They are certainly over-politicised and one may have to listen to their woes more than is desired. About 80 per cent of their national and local newspapers are devoted to politics and hardly make fascinating reading for those foreigners who have taken the trouble to learn Spanish. Corruption at high levels is endemic and one tires of wondering how long it will take Argentinians to rid themselves of bad government – when did they have a good one? At least the power of the military establishment over the political process seems to have been restrained, but scandals among elected administrators continue.

The *porteño* is a good Catholic and resembles the Italian in his attitude to extended well-knit families. He feels European, but knows relatively little about Europe, which seems very distant and expensive to reach. In reality his waking hours are filled with animated discussions of the exciting life of the thronged capital – politics, scandal, crime, business, football and other sports, theatre and cinema, the tango (an obsession) – as well as cultivating a lively social circle where wining and dining attain a standard unrivalled in most countries.

51

MEXICO

ARGENTINA AND MEXICO, THE TWO SPANISH-SPEAKING GIANTS OF LATIN America, both have to contend with a culturally different 'colussus' to the north. Argentina, relatively isolated in the southern ocean and at the bottom end of the continent's cone, has surprisingly little contact with Brazil and is visited by fewer than four million people per annum. The US is far distant in another hemisphere; consequently Argentinians have had the leg room to fashion their present-day culture along preferred European lines.

Mexico, by contrast, has its 2500 km northern border crossed 20 million times each year, mainly by Americans, who accept 85 per cent of Mexico's exports and account for 70 per cent of its imports. To put this into clearer perspective, Canada is Mexico's second biggest export market with 2.4 per cent of products and Japan is second in Mexican imports at 4.6 per cent!

Mexico's involvement with the US, and particularly the loss in 1845–6 of its territories that are now California, New Mexico, Arizona, Nevada, Utah and part of Colorado, has had a decisive influence on the history of the nation and the shaping of Mexican mentality. For every Mexican, the Aztec legacy and the *Yanqui* trauma are ever-present realities, shaping their thoughts, attitudes, actions, values, plans and unique mindset.

Culture

Values

Personal dignity	Uniqueness of the individual
Hypersensitivity	National honour
Exaggerated emotion	Passion, rhetoric
Mysticism, fatalism	Apathy, passivity
Obedience to authority	Group loyalty
Family	Deference to age
Face saving at all costs	Resentment against exploitation
Acceptance of stratification of society	Demoralisation, inferiority complex
Idealism as reaction to defeat	Dual truth and reality
Concern for status and appearances	*Machismo*
Historical perspectives	*Mañana*, cyclical time
Disdain for menial labour *per se*	Human relations orientation

Concepts

Leadership and status

In many Western societies status is achieved through hard work, accomplishment and sometimes wealth. In Mexico it is less a matter of achievement than of completeness. The Mexican leader may have acquired his position initially by birthright or nepotism, but he will not be successful unless he takes great pains to develop a huge network of friends, business partners and officials who will help him to consolidate his power base. These relationships are built on complex personal ties that allow favours to be sought, usually granted and ultimately reciprocated.

In business, a senior manager will command unquestioned obedience and respect from his subordinates, but, as in Confucian systems, he is obliged to reward them with loyalty, courtesy and protection. The *patrón* wields his power openly and with *machismo*, but he will show immediate compassion for a worker's misfortunes and come readily to the aid of the family in the case of undue hardship or bereavement.

Time

Much has been written about the Hispanic *mañana* syndrome, which, though perhaps originating in Moorish Andalucia, is associated more closely with Mexico than any other nation. At all events, punctuality is not high on the list of Mexican priorities.

In most hierarchical societies it is accepted that the powerful make others wait. Easy access to the presence of a superior casts doubt on his status. In Mexico, life is not organised around a clock – a mere machine – but around a succession of encounters and relationships that are qualified and quantified not in linear fashion but in terms of depth of personal involvement, excitement, opportunity or caprice. Human transactions must be satisfactorily completed – not interrupted by the ringing of a bell or a knock on the door.

This is one aspect of time keeping. The other aspect, which concerns late deliveries or tardy payments, often accompanied by paucity of communication, is an unending source of irritation to linear Americans, Germans or others, who accuse Mexicans and Spaniards of laziness. But they are not lazy – they cannot afford to be! Delays may be caused by the necessity to juggle options or assets due to lack of resources, or simply because one is not ready to make one's move yet. Mexicans recognise that fate has many things in store for us that we cannot foresee, that the sequence of events in God's calendar may not correspond to human schedules and deliveries. Sometimes one has to make changes to accommodate changes elsewhere – one has to choose one's priorities.

Cultural factors in communication

Communication patterns and use of language

Of all the varieties of Spanish, Mexican, with its abundant use of diminutives and colourful imagery, is perhaps the most flowery. Like Italians, they leave little unsaid, are generous in their praise and flattery, and when talking to foreigners, rarely say anything that you do not want to hear. In Mexico people are expected to discuss issues at length, seeking the agreement or conversion of the other and leaving no stone unturned to make oneself clear. As with most Latins, conversation is regarded as an art and they fully expect you as their partner to give as good as you get.

Feelings are more important than facts and any statistical description of a business activity fails to take into account the complex web of human entanglements surrounding a project. A Mexican in the full fling of rhetoric may seem to many foreigners to have his emotions barely under control. Yet passion and eloquence are central to a Mexican's style of delivery and his oratory is designed to show his extensive understanding of a complex issue.

Behaviour at meetings and negotiations

Meetings are always preceded by friendly smalltalk and only begin when the time feels right. The Mexican leader of the delegation will be highly visible, have priority of seating and will probably be the chief spokesman. Initially, great politeness will be displayed by all and surnames with formal titles will be used. Any relaxing of formality as the meeting progresses will be initiated by the senior Mexican.

Clothes are important – usually neat, conservative and of good quality.

The Mexican delegation will expect its leader to call the shots, always concur with him and protect his status through attention and deference. Mexican specialists or experts will make contributions, but this will be coordinated by the leader. The other side should address all remarks to the senior Mexican, not to an interpreter and only briefly to specialists.

Mexicans rarely tend to discuss details at plenary sessions. The senior Mexican is expected to outline the background to the project in clear, broad terms and to convey his approval of general principles without taking up any fixed position. The delegation leader will be skilled in exhibiting a detached approach to any issues that appear thorny, so as to avoid unpleasantness.

Foreigners must remember to satisfy the Mexican 'national honour' at all times. Mexicans are descendants of the Aztecs and know all about power and superiority/inferiority issues. They may accept the superior firepower of the other side, but must never be humiliated. This is not always easy for Americans and some other nationalities. Because of the need for face saving, clear escape routes should always be signposted during negotiations.

Abstract principles count little for Mexicans if they contradict or clash with the views of one of their leaders. Credibility is the most powerful factor in persuading Mexicans to do something. It is unlikely that you will be able to out-talk them or win by wheeling and dealing.

Mexicans do not follow agendas rigidly and feel that they can discuss any point when it seems opportune. They are less concerned about the completion or profitability of the deal under current discussion, thinking much more long term. For them, successful business is all about creating a large number of long-lasting and reliable alliances. Insistence on deadlines and over-meticulous items in a contract signifies (for the Mexicans) lack of trust.

Advantage may be gained when the strengths of each party are roughly equal by according to the Mexican leader the status of *patrón*. As such he will have to grant courtesies and some privileges to the 'client'.

Manners and taboos

Mexicans are extremely warm-hearted and hospitable people who are not slow to invite you into their homes, where you will encounter strong family ties and an unequivocally moralistic ambience based on Catholic principles. The father is the head of the family, his wife and children are normally happily obedient; he is also devoted to his mother. Mexican women take great pains to enhance and preserve their considerable beauty, they normally use heavier make-up than European women and are fond of gold and silver jewellery. Like their husbands they are animated and charming conversationalists; Mexican eye contact is very strong and of course body language in general is extrovert. The distance of comfort is close, men particularly hug other men (even foreigners when they get to know them), slap backs affectionately and grip elbows to show trust. Dining is late; home or restaurant entertaining can drag on until the early hours of the morning.

No account of Mexican customs would be complete without reference to *la mordida*. While Mexicans give freely to their guests, the conduct of business and obtaining many social services incur a cost that is normally obviated in US and northern European societies. Mexican civil servants, officials and police are paid very little and usually seek to augment their meagre salaries by accepting what Americans call bribes to facilitate the granting of permits and other services. Mexicans consider this to be rather normal and not unreasonable. The custom sits well both with the traditional Spanish willingness to help the underdog ('There but for the grace of God go I') and the historical precedent of the Aztec system of exacting tributes. The dilemma for the foreigner lies not in knowing whether he should pay or not, but in how much he should pay. There is a going rate for everything, whether it is securing a government contract, an import permit, or quick access to the head of a queue in a post office. Mexicans are familiar with expected rates and it is often wise to consult them.

How to empathise with Mexicans

Mexicans are not difficult people to get along with as long as you bear in mind their preoccupation with personal and national honour and take great pains to protect their face at all times. People used to handling Japanese will have no problems with Mexicans. However, it is even better to be proactive in terms of improving relations.

The basics are the same as in other countries – learn the language, study their history, familiarise yourself with the national literature and world of the arts. In Mexico this procedure brings glowing rewards, as the museums, murals, paintings, mosaics, architecture, music and ballet possess unique riches, not to mention the Aztec and Mayan constructions. While you may indicate fully your knowledge of the splendours of the indigenous empires, it is not advisable to dwell on the unique fusion of cultures and ask a Mexican how much Aztec blood flows in his veins. As Indians currently are placed on the bottom rung of the social ladder, even a descendant of Moctezúma himself would be reluctant to claim his full kinship. Other subjects to be avoided are political views implying criticism of the PRI majority party, corruption in high circles, killings and unrest in Chiapas and other oppressed areas, and Mexican loss of territory to the US.

52

BRAZIL

BRAZILIANS – THE ONLY NON-SPANISH-SPEAKING PEOPLE OF LATIN America (Haiti excepted) – act quite differently from other South Americans because their mother country is Portugal rather than Spain.

The Portuguese 'conquest' of Brazil was almost laughable in its casualness. Pedro Alvares Cabral discovered the country by accident when he seems to have strayed off course on his way to India in 1500. At least he took the trouble to raise the Portuguese flag while he was there, but the Portuguese court was much more interested in extracting spices from the East. Spain consequently completed the conquest of most of South America by 1550, the Portuguese barely hanging on to their huge colony. However, Jesuit missionaries lent the occupation more seriousness. Negro slaves were imported from Angola and Indians were enslaved to help work the sugar plantations. The Portuguese settlers cohabited with the Negroes and Indians, producing *mulattos* and *mamelucos* respectively. Thus the bloodlines of the new nation were rapidly being established.

The diverse, illiterate populations of early Brazil, scattered along huge coastal plains, plateaux, rivers and jungles, rendered orthodox parliamentary government impossible. Monarchs and dictators were always necessary. Fortunately, many of them were benevolent. The Portuguese-Brazilian genius for compromise has continually enabled the nation to make tolerance and exploitation compatible. Autocratic rule is accepted along with an attachment to constitutionalism. The Brazilians are happy to be Brazilian, believing implicitly in the prolific potential of their country: 'Our country grows at night when the politicians are asleep.'

Culture

Values

Loquacious	Theatrical
Emotional	Optimistic
Flexible	Future oriented
Hospitable	Group oriented
Avoids unpleasantness	Exaggerates
Exuberant	Impatient
Cheerful	Enjoys being Brazilian
Unpunctual	Compassionate
Breaks rules	Tolerant
Class conscious	Easy racial relations
Loves music, dancing, parties	Imaginative
Grandiose	Unruly
Patriotic	Football crazy

Concepts

Leadership

Brazil is still essentially led by the upper and upper-middle classes. The country has been struggling towards democracy since 1986, before which it was a military dictatorship. Meritocracy is slowly creeping in, but will take some time to be fully accepted. Nepotism continues to be widespread.

Status

Although on the surface Brazil seems to be free from racial intolerance, it is very much a class society. One need only look at the composition of governing bodies. It is still important in Brazil to come from a good family.

Status is slowly beginning to derive from entrepreneurial success and political influence.

Space

Brazilians have a very close distance of comfort (80cm, compared to the British 1.2 metres) and are quite happy working near to each other. They are a tactile, hugging and very extroverted people. Women almost always greet each other with a kiss on each cheek, while men shake hands and give each other a warm pat on the back.

Time

Brazilians actually believe that it's impolite to arrive at someone's house for dinner on time. Business appointments rarely begin as scheduled and often run much longer than anticipated, thus delaying all further appointments.

Cultural factors in communication

Communication pattern and use of language

Loquacious and verbose to the extreme, the Brazilians use gestures and facial expressions to emphasise their point of view. Although appearing over-emotional at times, they only intend for you to understand that what they are saying comes from the heart. The more lengthy their discourse, the more they feel that they will have cemented your loyalty, as a basis on which they can build further transactions and create long-term goodwill.

Listening habits

Owing to the Brazilians' exuberance of expression, their listening habits tend to be somewhat erratic – interrupting their interlocutor with ideas of their own, each individual wanting to make a personal contribution. They aim to form an in-depth impression of the speaker from watching movements, gestures and eye contact, rather than listening intently to what is being said. They have a relatively short attention span.

Behaviour at meetings and negotiations

The Brazilian manager will use the *tu* form to subordinates, but his oratorial delivery makes what he says a *fait accompli*. Brazilian Portuguese, with its many diminutive endings, is highly suitable for expressing emotions and nuances and for making a harsh statement appear less so.

Meetings tend to be erratic, even chaotic, with constant interruption of the agenda under discussion, as participants all come up with their own very creative ideas. The Brazilians like to please and will often tell people what they want to hear, stretching the truth to some extent. In this respect they always claim to have a solution to problems, though in reality this may not be the case. Excessive concern about job security leads to a reluctance to express their own opinions if they fear that these will run counter to those of superiors. Facile, immediate solutions are grabbed at; the result is often a lack of long-term planning.

While demonstrating exuberance and energy at the outset of a new project, Brazilians tend to lack perseverance in the follow-up stage and frequently leave projects unfinished, seemingly without qualms of conscience. Their enthusiasm for initiating exciting schemes is not matched by commitment to results. Americans and others find that constant tracking and monitoring becomes a necessity.

Manners and taboos

The Brazilians tend to be very futuristic in their outlook, tearing down the old and continually building anew, although they are traditional with respect to family and social customs. They accept new acquaintances very readily.

They are generous with their time (often too generous) and they have a tendency to focus on the process rather than the product, which often causes them to lose sight of objectives. They favour interdependence in business and expect to be helped in times of tragedy or failure. Brazilian companies are generally paternalistic and forgiving.

How to empathise with Brazilians

Try not to react suspiciously to the warmth emanating from the Brazilians – they strive to be liked and to please others. If you are stiff and formal, they will not know how to react.

Brazilians excel as 'space invaders' – do not change places if a Brazilian sits down as the fourth person on a three-seater sofa! As they are tactile in the extreme, accept with grace their arm patting and warm embrace. Do not become annoyed at their unpunctuality. Remember, 15 minutes to a half hour is not considered late in Brazil. In this very open and informal society, there is very little the foreigner can do to upset a Brazilian.

Do not hesitate to accept their invitation to social activities – it is a wonderful way to get to know your counterparts and will prove to be a very worthwhile experience for you personally.

Brazilians often experience difficulty in rising above their peers and even talented individuals need frequent encouragement and on-going training to further their careers. They are not great at accepting responsibility – Americans find they constantly need to build up their confidence. One should always show that one has a big heart and that one cares about their personal problems as well as their competence on the job. It is sometimes advisable to show them that one has one's own personal problems and ask them for advice (in a Brazilian context). Show affection for Brazil at all times.

53

CHILE

CHILE IS A CURIOUS SHAPE, BEING either the longest narrow country in the world or the narrowest long one. A glance at the map of South America shows Chile apparently being pushed into the Pacific Ocean by a beefier Argentina, in much the same way that Norway seems to be edged into the North Sea by land-rich Sweden. Both Norway and southern Chile have sunken coastlines to the west, with a succession of fjords making the land look as if it is drowning.

Handicapped by difficult terrain – uninhabitable mountains, deserts and rain-soaked forests – the Chileans have maximised their options by exploiting a variety of land resources and exporting them vigorously in three different directions – Asia, North America and Europe.

The 'Andes barrier' has effectively diminished Chile's interaction with its own continent. Although it takes substantial imports from Argentina,

Brazil and Mexico, its chief export destinations are Japan, the US, the UK, Brazil, South Korea, Germany and Taiwan, in that order. Chile has been referred to as a South American 'Tiger' and although its exports are puny compared with those of the four Asian Tigers, it provides its customers with vital supplies of copper, aluminium, nitrates, lithium, iodine, borax and selenium. It is the world's ninth producer of gold. Chile has also assumed an important position in the export of timber, fresh fruit, fish-meal, farmed salmon (to Japan), several other foodstuffs and agricultural products and is carving out a reputation for the production of high-quality, low-cost wine. The US and the UK are the chief buyers, but Chilean wine is making substantial inroads in the wine markets of Scandinavia, Germany, the Netherlands and even Japan.

Chile's energetic role as a world trader is facilitated to some extent by her reputation for stability, relative to most other Latin American countries. This stability is by no means restricted to recent times. Pedro Valdivia, the Spanish explorer who founded the city of Santiago de Chile in 1541, by clever distribution of land laid the basis for the Chilean oligarchy which, after independence, dominated Chilean history until the twentieth century. By 1850 Chile had become the leading power on the Pacific coast. A large number of Germans immigrated to work the forests and British mercantile pioneers settled in the port of Valparaiso.

Chile's fight for independence from Spain had caused less dislocation than in most Spanish American countries and the land-owning class maintained autocratic rule until a brief civil war in 1891. British capital helped to develop the northern deserts and war with Peru in 1880–81 gave Chile a northward expansion as far as Arica.

An urban class appeared, which pressed for parliamentary government and a centralised education system. Immigration became more selective, many people with specialised skills entered the country and mixed with the aristocratic Spanish élite. The Allende–Pinochet period caused great social unrest, but Chile approached the end of the twentieth century with an open market, democratic rule and the highest credit rating on the continent.

Culture

Values

Visitors to Chile are struck by the 'Europeanness' of the country, matched
on the continent only by the ambience in Buenos Aires. The Spanish
heritage is evident (85 per cent of the people are Catholic) and German
and British connections are strong. The cultural values are mainly
Hispanic. Chileans are extroverts, emotional, human, perceptive, respectful, talkative, personal, dignified and sensitive.

Chileans have many positive features, not the least of which is that they
are the fastest payers in South America. They are well-educated, very loyal
once they are won over and have an intelligently pragmatic view of doing
business. Although they are at first indirect and conceal opinions, they
open up splendidly once friendship has been established. They are eloquent conversationalists and good listeners. Their national pride is ever-
present, but they respect the histories and achievements of other nations,
particularly European ones. Their 'triangular target' for trade – Asia,
Europe and the USA – shows their burgeoning internationalism and feel
for the future. While NAFTA and MERCOSUR are important connections, their wish to maintain strong European ties is significant, as is their
realisation that their geographic position (as that of Australia) offers lucra-
tive opportunities in an Asian-Pacific context.

How to empathise with Chileans

◆ Don't make frequent comparisons with Argentina. The two are quite separate nations defined by one of the world's most formidable natural barriers (the Andes). There has been considerable historical friction between
   Chileans and Argentinians. Chileans are proud of their economy.
◆ As a foreign investor or manager, indicate your concern for the welfare
   of Chile and the Chileans you lead or deal with.
◆ Be compassionate and solicitous in your dealings, especially with those
   less fortunate than you.
◆ Bear in mind Chileans' concern about job security. Be reassuring whenever possible.

- ◆ Remember that Chileans' natural sense of courtesy will often lead them to say the things you want to hear. Truth is somewhat flexible, as in many Latin societies.
- ◆ Benefit from Chileans' rich imagination and vision, but keep in mind their occasional lack of commitment in seeing things through.
- ◆ Share their enthusiasm for literature, music, painting and other artistic pursuits.
- ◆ Like the Argentinians, they see themselves as the most European people on the continent. Benefit from this outlook and willingness to empathise.
- ◆ Show respect for (and enjoy) their fabulous scenery and climate, good food and wine!

Epilogue

ACHIEVING EMPATHY

Changing perspectives in international management strategy

THE POLITICAL CHANGES IN EUROPE AND OTHER PARTS OF THE WORLD IN recent years have been quite startling in their suddenness and dimensions. The rapid *volte face* in what was Czechoslovakia, Romania and the former East Germany, the increasing self-confidence visible in Hungary and Poland, the incredible rapprochement between the USA and Russia, the regaining of independence in the Baltic republics, are all signs of a global transformation in ideological alignments and longstanding alliances.

But these political and military developments are only symptoms of much more deeply rooted changes, over which politicians, governments and international organisations have little or no control. Forces are at work beyond anything we have previously had to deal with. The Industrial Revolution had a tremendous impact on society, but it never quite ran away with us. One invention led to another and the capitalist system organised the finance, labour and production techniques to deal with it. The Information Technology Revolution has left us all floundering. Too much information is available, at too great a speed, from too many sources.

Modern business has faster access to more information than ever before, but by the time it has been sifted and analysed, codified, processed and entered into the system, by the time managers and board members have decided on its impact and implementation, it is often already obsolete.

Furthermore, information management systems are frequently wrong. Information coming from news broadcasts, TV, the press, even news agencies, are more often than not biased or at least flavoured by the source. People at the top of management don't really know where they are going, don't get the information on time, face contradictions such as simultaneous centralisation and decentralisation, teamwork versus initiative, consensus versus speed of decision, etc.

Besides the irreversible changes being brought about by the information explosion and computer dictatorship, other tides which sweep us helplessly along are the incredible advances in medicine, the greenhouse effect and the changes in climate, the unstoppable march of science, the killing off of hundreds of species, the drive for ecological awareness, the collapse of communism and the rising strength of Islam. Add to these factors the reunification and burgeoning power of Germany, the prospect of a Pacific Basin economic club for the twenty-first century, the elimination of most small, middle and even big companies by the multinational giants, a few jokers in the pack like the export powerhouses of Taiwan and Singapore – and it is no wonder that planning a global strategy is beyond the abilities of the great majority of managers and business leaders today.

Moreover, leading management consultants tell us that the bigger the company, the more difficult the internal and external communication, the more cumbersome the decision making, the more chaotic the organisation. Nevertheless, the vaster the conglomerate, the bigger its domestic market, the greater seems its need to expand, export and establish itself abroad. The latter part of the twentieth century has seen takeovers, mergers and acquisitions on a hitherto unimaginable scale and the trend is for even large national companies to merge or become insignificant. Large banks have begun to group themselves in twos and threes. Sanwa and Dai-Ichi Kangyo became the two largest banks in the world through amalgamation.

Ford bought Jaguar, Toyota and Nissan manufacture heavily in Britain, Deutsche Bank has a large stake in Mercedes, IVECO is a merger of the Fiat, Magirus-Deutz and Unic truck companies, AT&T tried to work with Olivetti, even Finland's Kone, Nokia and Huhtumäki have become international conglomerates.

How well are companies prepared for global integration? If the solution is cultural synergy, do we know how to achieve it? What is the route to take?

The interdependence of nations also becomes clearer every day. Leaders are at the centre of an on-going dialogue to achieve mutual security, lessening of tension and confrontation, control of nuclear threat and all-round raising of living standards.

At the business level, global interdependence is emerging fast. The European Union is trying to create a market equal in size to that of the USA. Japan depends on the Middle East for oil and on the USA to buy its products. Russia needs American and Argentinian grain. Countries such as Italy, Britain and Korea, with few natural resources, depend on manufacturing and exports for survival. Small nations such as Finland, Denmark and Singapore develop niche industries with high quality products to assure they maintain the high standard of living they have already achieved. Countries not belonging to one of the large economic blocs hunt desperately around to find one. Geographically isolated countries such as New Zealand and Australia have an ever-increasing problem.

In terms of regional cooperation, there can be no better example than the collaboration and goodwill evident in the Nordic area, where Scandinavian Swedes, Danes, Norwegians and Icelanders enjoy relatively untroubled relations and mutual benefits with Altaic Finns. These peoples often look askance at each other, but there is little doubt that the over-riding factor in arrangements between Scandinavians and Finns is common sense. The rest of Europe would do well to study its merits!

Europeans form a large, fascinating, talented, original family. Unfortunately, like real families, they have their ups and downs, moods, disputes, loves and hates. Yet although impetuous and quarrelsome, this family can be quite brilliant. The calm, disciplined Nordics have demonstrated what regional cohesion can do. British, Dutch and Germans are equally tranquil and organised, neither are they incapable of cooperation. The French have vision, the Italians and Spaniards flair and, once harnessed, great energy. Romania, Poland and the Ukraine have huge agricultural potential. Czechs and Hungarians are knowledgeable, inventive and strikingly capable.

There can be no accurate assessment of the ultimate size, composition or political nature of the European Union. Its realisation in terms of economic, monetary, political, military and cultural integration will, of necessity, be slow, frustrating and painful. One tends to forget that the USA, homogeneous and powerful as it is now, took nearly 150 years to emerge as a unified, purposeful power – and they all speak the same language!

But cohesive or not, Europe is there – and it has several cards to play. First, it is big. European Russia cannot be excluded indefinitely from the Union: this presupposes a market of 750 million people. It is also a sizeable workforce. Europeans are educated: 17 of the world's 23 most literate countries are in Europe. The USA and Japan have the world's two biggest economies, but Europe claims 6 out of the top 10. As far as GDP per head and purchasing power are concerned, European countries have 14 places in the top 20. National debt is very low (6 places in the top 40, 5 of these being ex-communist countries).

The USA and Japan, currently undisputed leaders in production and finance, take Europe very seriously. Both countries have invested heavily in the continent and created strong bases inside the Single Market. London is the home of the world's most sophisticated financial institutions. Rotterdam is the biggest port. German and Swiss machinery and precision instruments are second to none.

However, if we are considering a management model for the twenty-first century, we cannot ignore Japanese systems. The Japanese people do not cast themselves in the role of teachers or mentors, but in an age when our own analysts advocate teamwork before individualism, collaboration and amalgamation before competition, we are seeing a shift from western to eastern culture. It could just be that the Asian model fits the era. The current success of Japan, Korea, Taiwan, Singapore, Hong Kong and China would suggest this. Indonesians, Malaysians and Thais follow in their wake. It is interesting to note that the Japanese (certainly orderly, normative, disciplined people) accept and believe that a disorderly, fast-changing scenario lies ahead of us which will have to be managed.

All is not negative. The world labours under threat of warfare, political dissension, inequality of wealth, uncertainty of the future, lack of morality, complexity of change; but on the plus side we have growing opportunities for social justice, world peace and growth for all. Many new technologies are widely available, easier mobilisation of labour is developing, and some elements of the new generation show moral strength, desire for peace and ecological awareness.

How do we translate good ideas into action? Study of good models shows us that teamwork and people training make an enormous difference, e.g. a pleasant working environment is ubiquitous in Scandinavia. Managers must have multinational skills. They will have to work shoulder to shoulder with many nationalities in the global village of the twenty-first century. They must understand them, speak to them, cooperate with them, handle them, not lose out to them, yet like and praise them. These are our cultural challenges.

The multicultural executive

In this book we have discussed the phenomenon of **cultural myopia** – how ethnocentrism blinds us to the salient features of our own cultural make-up, while making us see other cultures as deviations from the correct. For some powerful societies, confident of their historical success or brilliance (USA, France), it is a short leap from cultural myopia to **cultural imperialism**. At the height of their power, Americans, British, French and Spanish conquerors did not hesitate to set up policies and regulations which were congruent with their own cultural values and not with those of their 'subjects'. Economic imperialism in our present era has hardly lessened this tendency, further complicated by the desire of multinational companies to impose strong (global) corporate cultures.

We have stated earlier that we shall never fully understand the 'others', particularly if the separating factors of language, geography and ideology have been distant. The best we can hope for is to acquire an orientation that enables us to set off in a certain direction to lessen the communication gap between ourselves and our partner. All of us are wrapped up in prejudice – subject to a **natural dynamic of bias**. We cannot proceed to an evaluation or judgement of another without starting with an acute sharpening of our own self-awareness.

A behavioural spectrum

All of us have our place on a complicated spectrum of comportment with dizzying extremes of rudeness and courtesy, violence and gentleness, humility and conceit, and dozens of other behavioural dimensions. We perceive and judge others from the point in the spectrum where we stand rooted. We have a relative, not complete, view. If Swedes look at others through blue-and-yellow spectacles, they will fail to see them or their manners as they really are. They will suspect that all Italians are neurotic poseurs and see the individualistic Americans as lacking in respect for the beloved Swedish consensus. Americans will see Japanese with 'shifty' eyes, while the same Japanese considers Spaniards rude because they constantly 'stare'. The route to self-understanding is to question many of those values which were pumped into you when you were young. Is it always wise for a Finn or a Brit to keep a stiff upper lip? What is wrong with a little Italian feeling? Would not Germans and Japanese – deadly serious at meetings – improve a little if they joked like the Americans? Can't the French, obsessed by logic, feel the power of Japanese intuition or the American hunch? What is special about Spanish honour? Why is silence necessarily golden? If one can't ask a friend (or relation) to do one a business favour, what are friends and relations for?

Once one realises that many of one's cherished values or core beliefs were drummed into us by a biased community which possibly represents only a very small percentage of international opinion, presenting a very limited or blinkered world view, one is more likely to accept the opinions and manners of others as being at least equally valid, if not occasionally superior.

Eliminating one's own barriers

If one is able to see oneself or one's culture from the outside and think more objectively as a consequence, one has a good chance of clearing away certain cultural barriers which would have impeded access to others' thoughts or personalities. Finns must shed their excessive shyness, their bumbling modesty and their distrust of fast talkers. The Japanese must discard their ultra-politeness if the end result is only a fog of incomprehension. The French must rid themselves of their sense of intellectual superiority, and the Germans must realise that their cult of efficiency is not the only one around and may indeed have counter-productive overtones. Americans must occasionally see themselves as an insensitive, dollar-minded pragmatists who erect barriers of misunderstanding, often through well-meant bluntness or excessive informality. As people are shocked when they see themselves on video playing golf or tennis ('God, do I look like that?'), they may see from intercultural training that they are equally gauche or unacceptable in others' eyes.

Empathy

Better self-evaluation and elimination of one's principal cultural idiosyncrasies leads one to the final step towards achieving harmony – that of developing empathy with the other side. **Sympathy** is based on cultural similarities – Swede to Dane, Italian to Spaniard. **Empathy** is based on accepting differences and building on these in a positive manner. The Japanese may come to accept that American directness is, after all, honest. The American may perceive that exaggerated Japanese courtesy is, after all, better than hostility. If the Italian wants to talk 90 per cent of the time with a Finn, who is anyway content to be silent (in Finland silence is fun), then are they not both happy and doing what they do best? Contrasting debating styles can accommodate each other if common goals are clearly seen.

Weapons for empathy are:

- tact
- humour
- sensitivity
- flexibility
- compromise
- politeness
- calm
- warmth
- patience
- preparedness for discussion
- will to clarify objectives
- observation of other side's protocol
- care to avoid irritants
- careful listening
- respect of confidentiality
- inspiration of trust
- above all, constantly trying to see things from the other's (cultural) point of view

This is the profile of the international negotiator. Small side effects, such as eye-contact, posture, personal space and etiquette are all important, but the over-riding factor is the ability to decipher what is basic human nature (which can be trusted by all) and which learned cultural habits will cause variation in human behaviour and therefore must be recognised, accepted and adapted to.

The very act of adaptation, however, is fraught with difficulties. Quiet, introverted Swedes and Finns are reluctant to emerge from their shell of reticence to indulge in an evening's soul-baring with loquacious Italians. They feel that too much unwonted exuberance will lead to loss of identity. Yet it is easier for the introvert to build bridges towards the extrovert than it is the other way round, for the Nordic thought pattern remains opaque to Mediterranean people.

Culture is designed for success and survival – if we are alive, healthy and solvent, we have compelling reasons to believe in our particular formula. Temporary setbacks or, in certain cases, shocking failures, can undermine this confidence. The humiliating defeat of Japan in 1946 led to many Japanese, especially the youth, imitating various aspects of American culture. But certain features of Japanese behaviour could not be subject to adaptation. In Japan, men do not report to women, whatever system of administration the Americans installed.

How much should we try to change others, if we truly believe that our culture is superior? A safe answer is that we should not, thereby escaping the charge of cultural imperialism. But moral conflicts can arise. If we live in a culture where wife beating is the norm, do we advise, accept or adapt?

It is important that we examine closely the nature of conflicts. Besides the clearly moral type mentioned above, other real conflicts arise from deeply rooted philosophical, religious or even political convictions. Thus Islamic beliefs with regard to alcohol, pork and the status of women, or Chinese attitudes to basic inequalities in humans, will continue to clash with what we perceive as more tolerant and humanitarian western attitudes. Such core beliefs are so well buttressed in their respective societies that we are well advised not to persist in challenging them, as changes can only come from within. In fact it is not often that we try.

Another type of clash is pseudo-conflict, that is to say that we feel irritated, bemused or even offended by some aspect of another's behaviour and proceed to condemn it (strongly or mildly) without really attempting to see it in perspective. We see *mañana* mentality, Swiss pedantry and the assumed Asian smile as essentially negative, instead of trying to put these qualities into an understandable framework of cultural behaviour. Pseudo-conflict equates with misunderstanding, or over-fondness for the stereotype.

We cannot exist without stereotyping – it gives us points of reference in determining our behaviour towards strangers. The mind tends to simplify complex feelings and attitudes, including our own. For intercultural understanding we must learn to manage stereotypes, that is, to maximise and appreciate the positive values we perceive, minimise and laugh off (if we can) what we see as conflicting or negative. It is possible to do more accurate stereotyping, e.g. Swedes are often cold and formal, but they conceal, under the diffident exterior, a kind of desperation to prove their warmth and loyalty. Germans often shock with blunt, direct criticism, but in fact they believe they do it in your interest – they are improving your behaviour! We tend towards excessive stereotyping when we are under stress. Stress also reinforces our own cultural characteristics, so a vicious circle develops. Stressful conflict during meetings causes Americans to speak louder, South Americans to gesticulate, Japanese to clam up, Germans to bridle in righteousness and French to restate their position with icy logic. Without stress, Americans are friendly and generous, South Americans affectionate, Japanese courteous, Germans fair and French exuding charm.

Self-criticism, avoidance of irritants and stress, more accurate assessment of the individual, tact, tolerance, adaptation without sacrificing one's integrity, substantial study of our partner's culture, history and language – all these are resources to be drawn on when cultures collide.

We may enrich our own existence by absorbing certain features of other cultures – change them by our own efforts we will not. History has so far allowed cultures that have not been militarily over-run to prosper, survive, languish or atrophy at their own sedate rate of persistence or decline. It remains to be seen if the new forces represented by galloping information technology, rapid globalisation of business and ferociously competing giant countries and economies will result in the devastation of minor or weakened cultures which show inability to adapt to the truly dynamic changes of the twenty-first century.

Bibliography

Axtell, Roger E. ed. (1985) *Do's and Taboos Around the World*, compiled by the Parker Pen Company.

Barzini, Luigi (1964) *The Italians*, London: Hamish Hamilton.

Berry, Michael (1992) *Know Theyself and the Other Fellow Too: Strategies for Effective Cross-Cultural Communication*, Institute for European Studies.

Bradnock, Robert and Roma eds (1995) *India Handbook*, with Sri Lanka, Bhutan and The Maldives, Bath: Trade & Travel Publications.

Condon, John C (1985) *Communicating with the Mexicans*, Yarmouth, ME: Intercultural Press.

Dahl, Øyvind, *Malagasy and Other Time Concepts and Some Consequences for Communication*, Centre for Intercultural Communication.

Fieg, John Paul (1989) *A Common Core: Thais and Americans*, Yarmouth, ME: Intercultural Press.

Fisher, Glen (1980) *International Negotiation: A Cross-Cultural Perspective*, Yarmouth, ME: Intercultural Press.

Furnham, Adrian and Bochner, Stephen (1986) *Culture Shock: Psychological Reactions to Unfamiliar Environments*, Methuen.

Gochenour, Theodore (1990) *Considering Filipinos*, Yarmouth, ME: Intercultural Press.

Hall, Edward T. and Reed Hall, Mildred (1983) *Hidden Differences, Studies in International Communication: How to Communicate with the Germans*, Hamburg: Stern Magazine/Gruner & Jahr.

Hall, Edward T. and Reed Hall, Mildred (1990) *Understanding Cultural Differences: Germans, French and Americans*, Yarmouth, ME: Intercultural Press.

Hampden-Turner, Charles and Trompenaars, Fons (1993) *The Seven Cultures of Capitalism: Value Systems for Creating Wealth in the United States, Britain, Japan, Germany, France, Sweden and The Netherlands*,

New York: Doubleday.

Harris, Philip R and Moran, Robert T (1979) *Managing Cultural Differences: High-Performance Strategies for Today's Global Manager*, Houston: Gulf.

Hendry, Joy (1993) *Wrapping Culture: Politeness, Presentation, and Power in Japan and Other Societies*, Oxford: Clarendon Press.

Hofstede, Geert (1980) *Culture's Consequences: International Differences in Work-Related Values*, Newbury Park, CA: Sage.

Hofstede, Geert (1991) *Cultures and Organizations: Software of the Mind, Intercultural Cooperation and its Importance for Survival*, Maidenhead: McGraw-Hill.

Holden, Nigel J. (1992) *Management, Language and Eurocommunication, 1992 and Beyond*, Institute for European Studies.

Hu, Wenzhong and Grove, Cornelius, L. (1991) *Encountering the Chinese: A Guide for Americans*, Yarmouth, ME: Intercultural Press.

James, Clive (1991) *Brrm! Brrm! or The Man from Japan or Perfume at Anchorage*, London: Pan.

Kawasaki, Ichiro (1969) *Japan Unmasked*, Rutland, Vermont/Tokyo: Charles E. Tuttle.

Kulke, Hermann and Rothermund, Dietmar (1986) *A History of India*, Croom Helm Australia.

Kusy, Frank (1987) *Cadogan Guides – India: Kathmandu Valley–Nepal*, Old Saybrook, CT: Globe Pequot Press.

Lanier, Alison R. (1990) *The Rising Sun on Main Street: Working with the Japanese*, Morrisville, PA: International Information Associates.

Lehtonen, Jaakko (1990) *Kultur, Språk och Kommunikation*, University of Jyväskylä Press.

Lewis, Richard D. (1993) *Finland, Cultural Lone Wolf*, Otava.

Mole, John (1995) *Mind Your Manners: Managing Business Cultures in Europe*, London: Nicholas Brealey.

Morris, Desmond (1985) *Bodywatching, A Field Guide on the Human Species*, London: Jonathan Cape.

Nurmi, Raimo (1986) *A Cross Cultural Note on Australian and Finnish Values*, Deakin University.

Nurmi, Raimo (1989) *Management in Finland*, Turku Commercial High School.

Nydell, Margaret K. (1987) *Understanding Arabs: A Guide for Westerners*, Yarmouth, ME: Intercultural Press.

Peers, Allison E. (1992) *Spain: A Companion to Spanish Studies*, London: Methuen.

Phillips-Martinsson, Jean (1991) *Swedes as Others See Them: Facts, Myths or a Communication Complex?* Lund: Studentlitteratur.

Rearwin, David (1991) *The Asia Business Book*, Yarmouth, ME: Intercultural Press.

Reischauer, Edwin O. (1977) *The Japanese*, Cambridge, MA: Belknap Press.

Richmond, Yale (1992) *From Nyet to Da: Understanding the Russians*, Yarmouth, ME: Intercultural Press.

Sapir, Edward (1966) *Culture, Language and Personality, Selected Essays*, Berkeley and Los Angeles: University of California Press.

Sinclair, Kevin with Wong Po-yee, Iris (1991) *Culture Shock! China*, London: Kuperard.

Stewart, Edward C. and Bennett, Milton J. (1991) *American Cultural Patterns: A Cross-Cultural Perspective*, Yarmouth, ME: Intercultural Press.

Storti, Craig (1989) *The Art of Crossing Cultures*, Yarmouth, ME: Intercultural Press.

Tan, Terry (1992) *Culture Shock! Britain*, London: Kuperard.

Trend, J.B. (1957) *Nations of the Modern World: Portugal*, London: Ernest Benn.

Trompenaars, Fons and Hampden-Turner, Charles (1997) *Riding the Waves of Culture: Understanding Cultural Diversity in Business*, 2nd edn, London: Nicholas Brealey.

Wanning, Esther (1991) *Culture Shock! USA*, London: Kuperard.

Whorf, Benjamin Lee (1956) *Language, Thought and Reality*, Cambridge, MA: Massachusetts Institute of Technology Press.

Glossary

atavistic (atavism)	reappearance in a person of a characteristic which has not been seen for generations
Buddhism	a religion of east and central Asia growing out of the teachings of Buddha, that one must become free of human desires in order to escape from suffering
cadres	an inner group of highly trained and active people in a particular group (company, army, etc.) (French)
Cartesian	relating to René Descartes, French philosopher and mathematician
chauvinism	very great and often unthinking admiration for one's country; proud and unreasonable belief that one's country is better than all others
collective programming	the way a particular group of people or nationalities is trained from a very early age to internalise the behaviour and attitudes of the group
communication gap	lack of understanding of people of other cultures, because of differences in language, cultural attitudes, etc.
compartmentalize projects	concentrate single-mindedly on a project, not allowing it to be influenced by other goals or activities
complete action chains	finish one task completely before commencing another one
complete human transactions	finish all one's business with a particular individual before going on to another task
Confucianism	a Chinese way of thought which teaches that one should be loyal to one's family, friends and rulers, and treat others as one would like to be treated, developed from the ideas of Confucius
context centred	depending on a situation
core beliefs	basic concepts of a national group which have been learned and internalised from an early age

cross-culture	comparison of beliefs, attitudes etc. of different cultural groups of nationalities
cultural display, event	something we do or say which reveals our core beliefs (cultural attitudes) to people of other cultures
cultural imperialism	attempt to impose the tenets of one's culture on others
cultural myopia	inability to see another culture's points of view
'cultural spectacles'	the way our own core beliefs influence how we view other cultures
culture	the customs, beliefs, art and all the other products of human thought made by a particular group of people at a particular time
culture shock	the feeling of shock or of being disorientated which someone has when they experience a different and unfamiliar culture
cyclic time	recurring events
danwei	work unit (Chinese)
data-oriented (culture)	a culture whose people gather information mainly through print and database sources
deviants	people who are different in moral or social standards from what is considered normal
dialogue-oriented (culture)	a culture whose people gather information through direct contact with other people
double truth	two ways of looking at things: the immediate reality and the poetic whole
dusha	the Russian soul (Russian)
école normale supériéure	prestigious tertiary level institute of learning in France specialising in various areas of pedagogy, leading to a career in higher education of research (French)
empathy	the ability to imagine oneself in the position of another person and so to share and understand that person's feelings
extrovert	a person who likes to spend time in activities with other people rather than being quiet and alone
faux pas	social mistake in words or behaviour (French)
feng shui	wind-and-water superstition (Chinese)
force majeure	an event beyond one's control (French)
gaffe	an unintentional social mistake (French)
GDP	gross domestic product
giri	duty (Japanese)
guanxi	the linking of two people in a relationship of mutual dependence (Chinese)
hara kiri	ritual suicide using a sword to cut open one's stomach, formerly practised by Japanese Samurai to avoid dishonour

hautes écoles	tertiary level education in France in specialised areas, such as commerce, engineering etc. (French)
high context (culture)	networking, dialogue-oriented culture
honorific expression	indicating respect for the person being addressed, especially in Oriental languages
horizon (cultural)	one's world view (limited)
human mental programming	the practice of instilling one's beliefs in the young under one's responsibility (or any 'captive' audience)
inscrutable	decribes people whose meaning or way of thinking is not at all clear, mysterious
introvert	concerning oneself with one's own thoughts rather than sharing activities with others
Islam	the Muslim religion started by Mohammed
itadakimasu	literally: I am receiving (Japanese) – similar to *bon appétit*
kaisha	company, firm (Japanese)
karma	the force produced by a person's actions in life which will influence him or her later or in future lives
kibun	saving face (Korean)
lagom	spirit of moderation in all things (Swedish)
language mould	the way our language channels or moulds our thoughts
language of management	how certain management styles are facilitated by the nature of the language of the manager and the group being managed
linear time	a concept of time as a 'line' of sequential events with the past behind us and the future in front
linear-active (culture)	a culture whose people are task-oriented, highly organised planners, preferring to do one thing at a time in the sequence shown in their diary
listening (culture)	a culture whose people listen well, never interrupt and show great deference to others' opinions; they do not precipitate improvident action, allowing ideas to mature
low context (culture)	data-oriented culture, few oral contacts
meritocracy	a social system which gives the highest positions to those with the most ability
messianic	belief that one has an important mission
monochronic (culture)	a culture dominated by precision and propriety, preferring to concentrate on doing one thing at a time
mores	the moral customs of a particular group
'muddling through'	achieving one's goal without proper planning
multi-active (culture)	a culture whose people tend to do many things at once, often in an unplanned order, usually people oriented, extrovert.

networking	the establishing of professional connections with the aim of sharing information, advice or support
notions	the perception by a cultural group of certain basic concepts
on	obligation (Japanese)
Ordnung	order (German)
polychronic	someone who likes to do many things at once, often without precise planning
power distance	a measure of the interpersonal power of influence between superior and subordinate as perceived by the latter, often determined by the national culture
pundonor	honour, dignity (Spanish)
reactive (culture)	a culture whose people rarely initiate action or discussion, preferring first to listen to and establish the other's position, then react to it and formulate their own
ringi-sho	decision making through consensus (Japanese)
saudades	nostalgia, sentimentality (Portuguese)
sisu	perseverance, stamina (Finnish)
skål	cheers! to your health! (Swedish)
space bubble	the personal space which an individual dislikes being encroached on
stereotyping	fixing a set of ideas about what a particular type of person or nationality is like, which is (wrongly) believed to be true in all cases
task orientation	giving instructions or directives to colleagues or subordinates
tatami	straw floor mat, the number of which is often used to denote the size of a room in Japan
tenets	principles, beliefs
USP	unique selling point
values	standards or principles, ideas about the importance of certain qualities, especially those accepted by a particular group
Volkswirtschafts-hochschule	tertiary level education in Germany in the area of economics and commerce (German)
web society	an interdependent society excelling in networking
Weltanschauung	world view (German)
Weltschmerz	'world pain', i.e. depressed state (German)

Index

THE CROSS-CULTURAL ASSESSOR
&
GULLIVER

*Two state-of-the-art multimedia products that are set to
revolutionise cross-cultural training*

The **Cross-Cultural Assessor** is a
unique tool for cross-cultural
analysis. It can be used to create a
personal profile for an individual, or
to assess the 'cultural capital' of an
entire organisation.

◆ PC-based cross-cultural assessment tool using the technology and
design of Promentor Solutions (Finland).
◆ Two hours of lively, fast-paced question/answer tests and question-
naires, followed by auto-generation of a detailed report.
◆ The report analyses many aspects of the candidate's cultural characteristics, including their personal cultural orientation, their attitudes to key business/social issues, their knowledge of cross-cultural facts, their ability to recognise national traits, etc. The report
is also full of useful, practical advice that the candidate can take
away to improve effectiveness when dealing with other nationalities
and self-study material for building knowledge of specific cultures.
◆ Available in single user and networked versions.

For more information, please visit www.crossculture.com/assessor

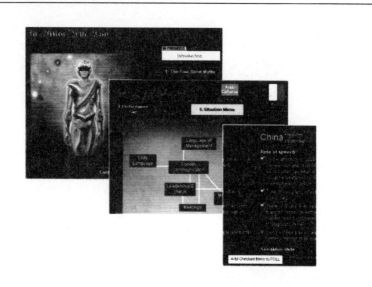

Gulliver, Performing Successfully across Cultures is a revolutionary product based on Electronic Performance Support (EPS) techniques. As well as giving a solid grounding in cross-cultural basics, it also provides tailored 'just-in-time' training for maximum impact and efficiency.

◆ Developed by PricewaterhouseCoopers, Gulliver has two parts: *The Visitor*, a three-hour introduction to the key issues of cross-cultural interaction; and *The Navigator*, a vast knowledge database allowing the user to specify up to 18 business situations across 17 different nationality groups, resulting in instantaneous tailored advice, together with practical examples and exercises.

◆ Gulliver is suitable for a wide variety of users including regular business travellers, consultants with international clients, multicultural teams, joint-venture staff, managers of foreign nationals etc.

◆ Available in single-user and networked versions.

For more information, please visit www.crossculture.com/gulliver

Both Gulliver and The Cross-Cultural Assessor are based on the Richard Lewis Model for cultural analysis. For complete information on all our products and services, please visit www. crossculture.com